O9-ABI-928

REFLECTIONS ON ART

REFLECTIONS ON ART

A SOURCE BOOK OF
WRITINGS BY ARTISTS,
CRITICS, AND PHILOSOPHERS

Edited by SUSANNE K. LANGER

BALTIMORE:
THE JOHNS HOPKINS PRESS

ABIGAIL E. WEEKS MEMORIAL LIBRARY

701.17
L276

© 1958 by The Johns Hopkins Press, Baltimore 18, Md.

Second printing, 1960

Distributed in Great Britain by Oxford University Press, London

Printed in the United States of America by
Vail-Ballou Press, Binghamton, New York

The Library of Congress catalog entry for this book
appears at the end of the text.

This book has been brought to publication with the
assistance of a grant from The Ford Foundation.

Contents

Illustrations, following page 206:

Introduction

THE PURPOSE of this book is to bring together some of the many significant essays on art that have appeared within the last five or six decades, in widely scattered publications, and make them available to readers of English, especially readers who have no great library at their disposal. This is not an anthology intended to give students a survey of trends and schools in aesthetics; it does not offer representative statements of current views. It is a source book to serve independent study on the part of scholars and fairly advanced students in philosophy of art, and those excellent teachers of the arts—of painting and sculpture, music, dance, literature, or whatever else—who do their own thinking about basic principles.

Since the selections are intended for such critical use, they are given in their entirety. The decision to make no cuts entailed several considerations in the choice of essays to be included: they had to be rich enough to justify their entire length, which means that most of them contain more than one important idea. Those that make but one simple statement are very brief. A few that stay close to one idea and yet run to a good many pages carry that idea into great detail, as for instance Dräger's, Reinold's, and Sauvage's papers. They have all been chosen because they make some real contribution to art theory either in the way of a new idea or of clarification in a moot and confused realm. There has been no attempt to balance the several arts against each other. If most of the analytic thinking is found in music, well and good; then there may be more essays on music than on painting or poetry.

This does not necessarily mean that less theoretical work has been done in one art than in another; for a second principle of selection has been *availability* of the piece. Those essays that have been anthologized in generally procurable books have here been omitted. Among these is Edward Bullough's "'Psychical Distance' as a Factor in Art and as an Aesthetic Principle," which was largely reprinted in both editions of Rader's *A Modern Book of Aesthetics* (Henry Holt & Co., 1935, 1952) and in *The Problems of Aesthetics: A Book of Readings* (Rinehart & Co., 1953), by Eliseo Vivas and Murray Krieger, and had, in fact, originally appeared in a journal that is easy of access, the *British Journal of Psychology*, v, 2 (1912). It has been republished *in toto* in a collection of Bullough's essays, *Aesthetics* (Stanford University Press, 1957). For a similar reason I have left out René Wellek's "The Mode of Existence in a Literary Work of Art," which may be found in R. Stallman's *Critiques and Essays in Criticism* (Ronald Press, 1949), and a very valuable article by Roger Sessions, "The Composer and his Message," in Augusto Centeno's collection entitled *The Intent of the Artist* (Princeton University Press, 1941), not to mention Mr. Centeno's own piece from which his volume takes its title. These are only a few examples. A further limitation on my choices was, of course, the unfortunate one of simple ignorance. No one can be versed in the whole recent literature of four or five arts; and furthermore, I was limited to the languages I can read with sufficient ease to have read a dozen papers for every one finally chosen.

In general, these papers deal with the nature of art, and especially the relation of art to actuality; the principles and processes of artistic creation, which involve the relation of the work of art to its materials, and of the artist to the work, to its material, its motif, and its public; the all-important topic of artistic expression and the traffic of art with human sensibility and emotion. Some are "protocol statements," others impersonal, theoretical studies. Some draw upon both experiential and scholarly resources.

Personal experience, in art or anywhere else, must of course be taken at face value; theories, on the other hand, may be critically weighed. I do not agree with everything the authors of these articles say. Thus Mehlis, for instance, seems to me to confuse art and life in his treatment of "aesthetic distance." Yet for anyone interested in that concept it may be valuable to contrast his treatment with Morgan's, and also with Bullough's, to which reference has already been made; for obviously Mehlis opposes "distance" to "intimacy," whereas the other two writers oppose it to something like "participation" or "actualization." Just how these different conceptions are related to each other may well be a key problem in philosophy of art. Sauvage appears to use "form" in the unhappiest way possible when she speaks of one *aspect* of the work of art as its "first form" (meaning something like the scholastics' "first intension" of a word). Her evaluation of English poetic rhythms mystified me at first, for to an English ear the rhythm of "The Raven" seems to jingle rather than to roll in great sonorous waves, and this has, indeed, often been found in contradiction to the somber intent of the piece; but upon reading it as a French person would hear it, without the English syllabic stress that makes it jingle, I was amazed and amused to find it flowing with something like the grandeur of the classical French hexameter. This dependence of poetic style on what is really just national habit of speech and hearing could find no better illustration, and perhaps no other revelation, than in this judgment by a foreign critic. Reinold's complete confidence in the neurological doctrines that suit his purpose, despite their tentative and controversial standing in a fast-growing science, weakens his philosophical position, but fortunately is not as essential to his argument as he apparently believes. More serious is the bizarre character of his last section, because it is due to a confused shift of meaning, from "play" of processes *on* each other ("a play between acoustic stimuli and the entire scope of gestalt experience . . . of the perceiving individual") to "play" of partners *with* each other, and a consequent spurious personification of music that leads to the whimsical absurdity of music playing with its auditor. The conclusion that Baensch asks us to accept with regard to feelings, obviously for lack of the idea of *symbolic presentation*, strikes me as slightly mad.

Yet of course there is a fundamental agreement between these authors and me, or I would have no reason to judge their work as generally sound and important. They are, in fact, all people from whom I have drawn some of my own philosophical ideas. They all either expound or tacitly assume two basic concepts: the concept of expressiveness, as I treated it in *Feeling and Form;* and the concept of "semblance" (Schiller's "*Schein*"), which defines the work of art as a wholly created appearance, the Art Symbol. Their explicit acceptance of these basic concepts, and especially their constant use of them in handling problems of artistic meaning, structure, aesthetic versus nonaesthetic values, distance, talent, technique, and many other subjects, seems to me the surest corroboration·for the philosophy of art I have tried to build on these same fundamental ideas.

A philosophical theory is not called upon to furnish "irrefutable proofs," but concepts that give rise to insight and discovery. One can sometimes prove the consistency of concepts, and inconsistency can always be logically demonstrated; but one cannot prove the excellence of a concept, even if it be logically impeccable, except pragmatically, by operating with it successfully. Concepts give us formulations of fact, ways of putting things; they are coherent or disconnected, fertile in useful derivatives or sterile, enlightening or confusing; but not true or false. Philosophy is not empirical knowledge. Yet to construct the conceptual framework of knowledge—which is philosophical, even when it is made by scientists, artists, historians, jurists, or others who are not professional philosophers—requires some intimacy with the intellectual strains that framework will have to bear. One has to know the difficulties, paradoxes, mysteries of the subject. Therefore I have included some articles in which difficulties are raised, with or without solution. Baensch's paper, for instance, presents such a mystery: a feeling that exists "as a content of the world" while no living being is having it—exists in an insentient object or simply in a place—is certainly a peculiar finding. This was, however, the beginning of a line of thought that seems to me to have reached solution. Compare Baensch's work of 1923 with Garvin's of 1947. Even earlier, in Reid's paper of 1928, the concept of symbolic expressiveness lets the expressive work of art appear as a symbol of sentience and emotion, conveying formulated ideas of feelings instead of "containing" actual feelings without "having" them. The great virtue of Baensch's study is his candor and daring in the face of imminent absurdity. Once a problem is so clearly pointed up as a paradoxical result of accepted premises, it is ripe for solution, often by many thinkers at once. The hardest work has been done; one further idea will solve it.

Other "chestnut problems" of aesthetics become less recalcitrant, too, from the standpoint these authors seem to share. The venerable issue of life and its image can receive surer handling, without any need for evasion or concessions, on the assumption that *everything* in art is created and either serves for expressiveness or weakens the work. The several articles on "distance," especially with respect to the most strikingly mimetic art, that of the stage, take up this matter of *objectification*. The old worry about deluding the playgoer, straining his credulity or begging him at least to "make believe," which haunted Ibsen's generation (and, at intervals, many before), is definitively dead. Bullough's essay of 1912 dealt it the fatal blow. Since then, aestheticians of the theater have developed the concept of dramatization on the same principles as all other essentially artistic processes.

Another major problem made amenable to solution, this time by consistently maintaining the distinction between actuality and semblance, i.e., what goes into the work and what is created (on the perceptual level rather than the level of import), is the old literary problem of "what the poet tells us." Müller and Burroughs (the latter in 1892) have tackled this issue; but the implications of their excellent, little-known papers have scarcely been sighted yet, let alone worked out, with results that might be serious for the current methods of studying and teaching literature.

The chief virtue of a fertile theory is that it allows philosophical inquiry (i.e., conceptual analysis and construction) to go into detail. As an instance, three essays on the relation of actual time to musical time are here presented, each carrying the analysis a little further— sometimes in a philosophical direction (e.g., Marcel), sometimes in a more strictly limited realm. Then, the same notion of time is treated very astutely as a concept relating to art in general (Sauvage), and finally as a problem of just those arts that are usually distinguished from the "temporal" and called "spatial," the plastic arts (Souriau).[1] In a similar vein Bayer extends the notion of *rhythm* to all the arts and finds it a central concept. Souriau, by implication, takes exception to such extensions of the concept of "rhythm," which he considers dangerous to clear thinking (though, oddly, he accepts the "phrasing" of a picture and the "élan" of a building). Which one has the better case is the sort of problem for which this book is to furnish material. The essay by Dräger is hardly to be called philosophical, but is included as an example of the close analytic work that a clarification of concepts involves even within the limited realm of psychology of musical perception. This is the sort of intimate knowledge of *what a concept has to do*

[1] The reader's attention should also be called to a recent article, "The Value of Time in Modern Drama," by Frederick J. Hunter, in *The Journal of Aesthetics and Art Criticism*, xvi, 2 (Dec. 1957), pp. 194–201.

that we need before we can philosophize about music or any other art. For any technical understanding of music, "tone color" is a superficial notion, for it is too vague to determine any ways of creation; in Dräger's analysis it becomes apparent that the various effects loosely so called are not only various, but may each be achieved in several ways. They are all elements of the musical illusion, created effects, distinct from the materials (e.g., loudness, overtones, number of instruments, etc.) out of which they are made.

From the study of artistic creation and expression it is an easy step to that of perception, or artistic intuition; in fact, the relation between them is so close that Croce saw fit to identify expression and intuition. As an example of philosophical reflection based on scientific knowledge and a pure, unconfused artistic interest, dealing with the problem of reception rather than composition, I include Reinold's article on musical hearing. A more general discussion of artistic perception is Steinberg's essay.

Most of these writings bear on more than one problem in the arts. That is why they have not been grouped under general headings. It is too easy for an editor to stress one issue, one virtue, or one point in an article, and for the reader subsequently to miss others that he would have found of particular interest, if his reading had not been narrowed in advance by someone else's analysis. Some of the papers are intimate records of the creative experience and also theoretical statements about art; Flannagan's, for instance, broaches the problem of an artist's control of the material and the material's control over his idea, the interaction of its potentialities and his own; Castelnuovo, in his firsthand report of handling texts for songs, states his demands upon a work of one art that is to be ingested by a work of another art, and implicitly offers us his views on the relations of poetry and music in song. Rohden's piece is essentially about the difference between actuality and art, but it also gives us a good deal of insight into the creative process that takes place on stage. Mehlis, Brelet, Sauvage, Malraux, all treat of the influence of art on life itself, the formulation of actual feeling by its image in art. Yet that is not their central theme.

Because of this many-sidedness of the material here offered, and the many kinds of study I hope it may serve, it were best, perhaps, not to discuss it any further. But a word has yet to be said about the translation of articles from French and German. An editor is often hard put to it to choose between a literal translation and a faithful following of some long German sentence, with strings of modifiers that unroll into as many clauses in English and phrases within phrases rendering the compact, composite German statement. Unfortunately, German scholars today seem to make something of a game out of the involution and concentric packing of ideas, like Chinese boxes, into complex sentences, that the German language permits (a sample from one of our essays may show any reader with a fair reading knowledge of German what the translators had to cope with: "Bestehen vom Bauplan her keine wesentlichen Unklarheiten über die Receptionsorgane und deren Zuleitungen zum Gehirn, die zur Weitergabe der von Uexküll Merkzeichen genannten Sinnesreize angelegt sind, so sind vom Anatomischen, zumal aus der von H. Braus eingeführten „biologischen" Sicht her die auf die noch zu erörternde Leistung der Ordnungszeichen hin im Bauplan vorgebildeten Verbindungen innerhalb des Gehirns schwieriger zu ergründen, aus denen sich das Lokalisationsproblem entwickelt hat"). The French texts, on the other hand, have a wealth of idiom that is capable of several renderings, each with a different sense, and one has to decide in each context with what degree of force the words should be rendered in our less versatile tongue. Add to this the fact that thinkers presenting new ideas often coin new words to distinguish them, which should properly be translated into corresponding English neologisms —something that a translator, more conversant with the languages than with the material, will seldom dare to do—and you have the editor's problem before you. We have tried to render faithfully every subordinate idea, every small modification, in each sentence, without copying a foreign phraseology. But any reader who compares the more difficult texts (notably Bayer, Sauvage, Reinold, and Dräger) with their originals might favor other decisions. In any case, I have to take full responsibility for the translations,[2] though I did not make them.

The illustrations presented another problem. Some of the articles presuppose a fairly wide knowledge of individual works, and of course the number of pictures in a book of this sort is rather stringently limited. So I have chosen one sculptural example to show what Flannagan is talking about; Poussin's *Shepherds in Arcadia*, be-

---

[2] With the exception of Souriau's and Malraux's articles, which were taken from their sources already in translation.

cause it is discussed in more than one essay; Rubens' *Descent from the Cross*, as a really notable example of a key concept that cannot be understood without visible demonstration—the distinction between the representation of time by symbols and the expression of time in forms and virtual motions—noted by Souriau and again by Sauvage. The two drawings placed side by side are intended to illustrate the "personal signature" of the artist's pencil, the individual line that marks a person's work no matter what he depicts, which substantiates Bayer's theory of the "rhythmic constants" in art. The two architectural photographs are a meager visual aid to the last essay in the book, which makes direct reference to so many examples of modern architecture that it really requires a dozen illustrations. Practical problems of securing material have entered somewhat into the choice where only two buildings could be depicted; but the main reasons for showing the Johnson Building were the cultural importance of this American architecture, the synthesis of continuity and stability, horizontal and vertical freedom, space and mass, that it aptly illustrates, and the sheer beauty it imprints on an industrial world. The other picture, Notre Dame de Ronchamp, was of course chosen in view of the author's emphasis on this achievement. Finally, a single example of so-called "modern painting" has to help the unaccustomed reader to judge Steinberg's contention that our most serious and original artists are presenting a new vision of the good old "real world." I hope Gregoropoulos will make Steinberg's point lucid to the thinker with eyes, and Steinberg will illuminate Gregoropoulos' venture for the beholder with notions.

Philosophy always stems from more particular cultural developments, for it is, after all, a process of "philosophizing," and one has to philosophize *about* something. The task demands the tools and invites certain kinds of treatment. Mediaeval philosophy grew out of religious controversies. So-called "modern" philosophy arose from a new ideal of "knowledge" that raised the question of what really could be called "modern" philosophy, and why. The result was that for several generations philosophy became practically synonymous with theory of knowledge. The spectacular rise of natural science channeled it still further into long but narrow reaches, until its whole task seemed to be the critique of scientific concepts. Positivism, physicalism, and in the study of animate nature behaviorism, are the best-known spoils of that excursion. The most profound critique of science, of course, is still going on and rarely produces "isms," but a wealth of philosophical ideas, too difficult for popular statement, that are often ingested in scientific thinking even before they appear in any explicitly philosophical work. The philosophy of science is still in the making. But even in its present rapid career one can see that it will not be only a philosophy of physics; like any organically growing thing, it is interacting with its intellectual environment, to the astonishing transformation of both.

One of the new sources of philosophical thinking is the world-old phenomenon of art. It is a new source because it is just being tapped by modern philosophers.[3] But, like most long-sealed springs, it is strong. Basic philosophical problems that take rise from our reflections on art develop fast and throw new light especially on the somewhat stalemated concepts of psychology and the still wavering, vague, or else prematurely narrow concepts of anthropology. The surest sign of a new life in philosophical thinking may be found in the more difficult and theoretical essays here collected: they refer one to another without polemical intent and seem to belong to the same general advance without any common creed or school. They take issue with each other over special allegations or implications, without simply "refuting" one another, as theorists at the end of an intellectual era generally do. The spirit of philosophical invention, and of what the Germans call "Gedankenexperiment," is still upon them. This often makes the most detailed and analytic studies the best reading.

But philosophical ideas are not a monopoly of professional philosophers; some of these essays are quite nontechnical statements by people who write, and think, in the half-metaphorical language of artists and lay aestheticians. It is a deceptive language, the despair of more logically trained thinkers, and something like an electrified barbed wire to a proper positivist; but if one wants to gather ideas on art from artists, one has to learn this strangely irresponsible studio-language. So I have not balked at the somewhat "purple" style of Gisèle Brelet or the mysticism of Flannagan; as for the undocumented speculations of Malraux and Kraussold, these

---

[3] In the history of philosophy, "modern" means "since the mediaeval period," i.e., including much of the Renaissance, which began at different times in different places and even circles. "Modern" is a somewhat indefinite but useful term.

are the forward thrusts of venturesome explorers. So I offer this heterogeneous collection, impartially, to lovers and custodians and philosophers of the arts, and recommend it to their critical mercies.

As the book finally goes to press, I want to express my thanks to several people who have been helpful to me: first of all Professor René Wellek, for his kind assistance to one hard-pressed translator in coping with the difficulties of the German "impossible" style; then to all the copyright-holders who have let me include articles or pictures in their possession, and especially those who, in generosity, have freely given the desired materials—Dr. François Bucher, Madame Ananda K. Coomaraswamy, Mr. John Gregoropoulos, Mr. and Mrs. Milton Lowenthal, Mr. André Malraux, Mrs. Günther Müller, *The Journal of Aesthetics and Art Criticism*, Max Hesses Publishing Co., the Museum of Modern Art, *Music and Letters, Partisan Review, Perspecta: The Yale Architectural Journal, Philosophy and Phenomenological Research,* and *Revue d'Esthétique.*

The coöperation of the publishers may usually be taken for granted and one's sense of gratitude remain tacit, but in this case I do feel that I owe special thanks to The Johns Hopkins University Press for relieving me of the extensive business correspondence and the great financial outlay involved in making an anthology that usually fall to the lot of its editor, but were in this case most kindly assumed by the publishers. Without this aid, I do not think my source book would have come into existence.

October 1958   S. K. L.

REFLECTIONS ON ART

Beauty as Feeling

VIRGIL C. ALDRICH

> Stranger, when you appeared there on the horizon miles to the east, a speck silhouetted against the dawn, you stepped on my toes and bumped into me. Did you not feel the impact?
>
> Before you appeared this whole expanse was my body, and the light and the colors in it my mind. Then the collision occurred. Now look at me. My body is shrunken to a midget-trunk with four midget-limbs. And my mind is in a skull.
>
> I felt the impact, Stranger. I bid you good-morning—and heartily farewell!
>
> —from an English sportsman's diary.

THE IDEA THAT beauty is a feeling is discredited by those whose aesthetic experience testifies that beauty is objective, since feelings are certainly subjective. Yet one is still disinclined to give it up. The aery radiance of a thing of beauty is very much akin to, if not identical with, the feeling of him whom it enthralls. That is why it is a joy forever. To him it seems as if he consummates his emotional self in the beautiful object. He swathes it with his own feelings, and thereby lends to it a good part of its appeal.

I do not want to deny outright the hypothesis that beauty is feeling but, rather, to supplement it with an account of how, under

3

certain conditions, feeling may become objective and thereby be converted into aesthetic quality. The lack of such an account is the cardinal weakness of current aesthetics. Indeed, aestheticians customarily make a virtue of this failing, on the basis of the belief that no *actual* objectification of feeling ever occurs, only a "seems-so"—which in substance is an admission that aesthetic experience is hallucination. My own experience forces me to look with suspicion on this conclusion, just as it forces me to reject the notion that colors, for example, are only "apparently" at a distance before my eyes.

Now I think it can be shown how colors and sounds occur, not at a metaphorical, but at a literal distance from eyes and ears, *without ceasing to be sensations of the percipient.* And when we understand how one kind of feeling, namely, visual or auditory sensations, can acquire objectivity, we shall be in a better position to suggest how another kind of feeling, namely, emotion, is objectified —or at least to corroborate the belief that objectification of this sort actually occurs even if the details of the process elude us.

So I shall outline very briefly a theory of vision. Its basic principle will explain the objectivity of sound as well, and we shall then have the advantage of understanding the two senses—sight and hearing—which, just because the objectivity they provide for is a condition of that of emotion, figure most prominently in aesthetic experience.

The color of an object is how it feels to the visual touch. When you touch something with a finger, you get a temperature sensation at its tip. Similarly, when you touch something with your organ of sight, you get a color sensation at its tip. Just as you say that a body feels warm to the hand, so you might say that it feels red to what you see with. This induces me to consider colors as the "visual temperatures" of the objects of sight.

But since we do not touch these objects with our physiological or "native" eyes—the contact would obliterate vision—our eyes must not be mistaken for the organ of sight. They are only "native" parts of it. The organ of sight includes something "acquired" also. This, I believe, can be illustrated by the case of a blind man who learns to "see" with a walking-stick. At first, he feels the stick in his hand; eventually, in virtue of a fine process of adjustment to the pavement by means of the stick, he feels *the pavement.* The stick has now become a literal part of himself, where "he" stands for a percipient organism which has functionally assimilated or acquired a non-native member and thereby extended itself to make literal contact with things at a distance from its native body.

Everyone learns to see in an analogous manner. The walking-sticks or "feelers" in vision are streams of light radiation. These must supplement the native optical equipment before any seeing at all can occur. By means of them, the seer eventually becomes an extended body with a distance-reach beyond that of the native organism and actually touches things not in contact with its eyes. It is then that colors, as his own sensory responses, literally qualify the objects confronting his native organism, at the tip of the visual feelers. The functional coalescence of light and nerve currents results in something like an elongated optic nerve the far end of which fuses with the object, tincturing it with color sensations. With not much qualification, this holds true of the hearer as well, air waves taking the place of light, and sound the place of color.

The concept, then, of an expanding or expandable ego or self, incorporating parts of the environment into its own corpus—finally *being* such a body—and thereby extending the range of its immediate experience, will serve as our theory of visual and auditory perception. Perhaps it will shed light on the problem of the objectification of emotions.

The character of one's experience is determined by what one is capable of responding to. Ordinary perceptual experience is responsive to given physical objects or to imaginal representations of them in their absence. Several kinds of animals, including man, are capable of this response. In this attitude, configurated colors and sounds appear as qualities of material things and symbolize either the behavior of the objects themselves or what can be done with them. This is the practical attitude, and can be assumed even toward imaginary things. The field of the practical imagination is occupied by no means only by aesthetic objects but also by material things *in absentia*.

In short, visual and auditory responses *to a physical thing* are colors and sounds which serve to define its nature and its position in space and time, for practical purposes. But what of a response, not to a physical object, but to the configurations of colors and sounds themselves, for their own sake? Let us observe some of the consequences of this new attitude—of which only some human organisms are capable.

In the first place, the sense for the physical location of both object and percipient vanishes at once, due to a swerving of the attention away from the material thing, which latter alone involves a "where" and a "when" in a plexus of space-time relations. Thus, by attending exclusively not to how the physical objects feel (to the visual and auditory touch) but to the "feel" itself, one gets lost in the contemplation of a system of elements which, physically speaking, are nowhere. Such contemplation and such an object are necessary factors in aesthetic experience.

Second, though the sense for the *physical* distance of the object from the native organism of the observer vanishes, what might be called a "psychic distance" is preserved. Or, to say the least, the result is certainly not a subjectification of the system of sensory elements; the constellations of color and sound are not experienced as qualities in and of the native organism of the subject. This, too, is a characteristic of the experience of beauty.

Third, just as we responded to the physical object with feelings (visual and auditory sensations) which literally qualified it, so, when we assume the new attitude under consideration, we respond to these original (sensory) feelings with other (emotional) feelings which may in turn literally qualify them, despite their psychic distance from the subjective pole of awareness. When this secondary qualification occurs, you have assumed the aesthetic attitude and enjoy an aesthetic experience. Who has not noticed the disembodied status of "aesthetic emotions"—disembodied, that is, with reference to the experiencer's own native organism but embodied in the object? In such moments, one's own feelings appear as the aesthetic quality of a thing of beauty. And the belief that such an objectification is "really" impossible is a consequence only of the initially false notion of the "self" or the ego as something cramped within the limits of the native organism. Of course, in a moment of self-consciousness or embarrassment, or during any practical experience, one's emotions are subjectified and experienced as being in and of the native organism, where they frequently become distressing. This was the experience of the sensitive English sportsman whom I quoted at the beginning. Alone on the plain, he had "room" for an aesthetic extension of his emotional self. He became "a brooding presence in the sky," until the stranger on the horizon bumped into him and scared his exposed emotions back into his native body.

There is nothing startlingly novel about the idea that beauty is an "affective" quality of sensory data in the field of consciousness. Indeed, it is currently in vogue, thanks to the numerous supporters of the aesthetic tradition which, following Santayana, has become classical. The novelty—from the point of view of these aestheticians—belongs rather to the idea that the "field of consciousness" may actually include not only the native organism of the subject of experience but other existing bodies as well. On the basis of this notion—rejected by Santayana—I have tried to point in the direction in which plain sense can be made of the hypothesis concerning a real objectification of feeling.

When one makes a purely sensory response to a material existent, he engages in simple perception. But he may respond to it with his emotions as well, in a manner which objectifies them *in the physical object,* via the sense-data. This double qualification of the object is *not* an aesthetic experience. It is being in love with the object. A beloved material thing (generally a living organism), unlike an aesthetic object, is importunate, disturbing, because it is after all a *body,* impelling the native organism of the lover towards it. The emotional substance of the lover becomes so fused with a bodily object of love that it draws his own native organism after it into the place of the beloved. The aesthetic attitude, on the contrary, does not move the native body of the observer because, as we have seen, its object is not a physical thing. It is nowhere, hence physical behavior with reference to it is senseless. One must stop acting to behold beauty. The enjoyment of beauty is a kind of escape from, a going out from, the urgencies of place and time. Probably this factor of escape from existence in the ordinary sense is that familiar but elusive "universal" quality of the experience of beauty—a universality which, by the way, is compatible with the uniqueness of the aesthetic object.

I have argued that no physical object as *physical* is ever an object of aesthetic enjoyment, even though it may be an object of love. But it is possible to "love" non-physical entities, in which case the love-experience is identical with the aesthetic, since disembodiment of emotions is then characteristic of both—a kind of Platonic love. In this sense, one may love even a mathematical system, which would simply convert it into an aesthetic object.

A word about tragic beauty which, in the context of our theory, is quite intelligible: you can objectify a painful feeling or emotion. This does not in itself make the object tragically beautiful, as some versions of the catharsis theory maintain. Simply displacing an unpleasant emotion from a subjective status to a psychic distance does not make it pleasant, or relieve it of its poison. Tragic beauty supervenes upon the object only if, after qualifying the object with an objectified feeling of pain, you respond to the net result with an additional feeling of pleasure which in turn is objectified and thus converted into the beauty of a tragedy. More simply, tragic beauty is a pleasant feeling converted, by objectification, into the aesthetic quality of a previously objectified painful feeling, both feelings being experienced as qualities of the object. Now, a pleasant emotional response to an objectified painful feeling is difficult for most persons, hence the "difficult beauty" of tragedy. The difficulty consists in its requirement of an additional "layer" of aesthetic quality. Simple beauty is a single layer of objectified emotion. Tragic beauty requires at least another layer. The result is the greater "depth" of tragic art, and of the aesthetic experience in which it figures. Such beauty is more than "aesthetic surface." Theoretically, there is no limit to successive objectifications of different feelings into the object without the loss of any one of them, dyeing it in all the hues of a complex aesthetic value.

Ugliness is not an aesthetic value, not even a negative one. There are no negative aesthetic qualities. We call ugly that which resists the influx of our emotions into it, or repels them, or bruises them if they succeed in getting installed therein. The object in the presence of which it is difficult to assume the aesthetic attitude is ugly. And until the aesthetic attitude *is* assumed, there is no aesthetic quality at all.

Many objects, natural and artificial, are ugly in this sense. The aim of the artist is to rearrange contours and qualities with a view to making the world more inviting to our emotions. Some configurations provide more comfortable quarters for our nomadic feelings than others. To beautify anything is to make of it a more congenial resting-place for disembodied emotional selves.

I have said nothing about the physiology of the aesthetic attitude. What happens in the biological organism of the percipient when he shifts from the ordinary sense-perceptual attitude into the aesthetic? Very little is definitely known about this, despite the many physiological and psychological theories of emotion, embodied or disembodied. We only know that some organic states are correlated with aesthetic experiences; such as a subsidence of overt motor-tendencies, drug-produced nervous excitements, etc. I think this physiological information is important, especially for a theory of feelings (sensations and emotions) which argues their actual objectification. But I have been able to do nothing more than suggest a new conception of the conscious self, of which I take the native biological organism to be only a part. It does justice, I believe, to the inescapable sense that conscious experience has— thanks to acquired bodily members—a distance-reach beyond that of the native body, and it is the sort of assumption which encourages rather than cripples further inquiry. In brief, it contains the promise of a more intelligible account of the objectivity of feeling characteristic of aesthetic experience. But it certainly calls for more analysis and systematic exposition than I have been able to give it here.

Art and Feeling

OTTO BAENSCH

IT IS AN OLD CONVICTION that in art the feelings are of great, indeed of essential importance. In the course of intellectual history, this doctrine has been advanced on the basis of a great variety of premises, and has been theoretically followed now in this, now in that fashion. Today it is more widespread than ever, and well known to all of us in the distinctive forms of sensationist, empathist and expressionist aesthetics. In the following meditation, an attempt will be made to give this conviction an objective turn. I hope to prove that art, like science, is a mental activity whereby we bring certain contents of the world into the realm of objectively valid cognition; and that, furthermore, it is the particular office of art to do this with the world's emotional content. According to this view, therefore, the function of art is not to give the percipient any kind of pleasure, however noble, but to acquaint him with something which he has not known before. Art, just like science, aims primarily to be "understood." Whether that understanding which art transmits then pleases the feeling percipient, whether it leaves him indifferent or elicits repugnance, is of no significance to art as pure art. But since that of which it makes us aware is always of an emotive character, it normally calls forth, more or less peremp-

10

torily, a reaction of pleasure or displeasure in the perceiving subject. This explains quite readily how the erroneous opinion has arisen that the percipient's delight and assent are the criteria of art.

But precisely what do we mean when we say that it is the function of art to raise the emotional content of the world to the level of an objectively valid cognition?

We start with a fact of consciousness, that stands in contradiction to theories which, as a rule, we take for granted. According to these theories, feelings exist in the world only as internal conditions of animate beings, while that which is inanimate—for instance, inorganic nature—because it has no soul, has no feelings, either. Nevertheless, we guilelessly speak of the mood of a landscape. We mean, then, that the landscape, because it is without a soul, is naturally also without a mood *per se;* but that the contemplation of it evokes in us a mood, and that we project our own mood, which is caused by the landscape, into the landscape—that we objectify the mood in it. But this is theory! The real, immediate evidence gives us at first no indication of such a process of objectification. That which, according to the theory, is the result of the process of objectification, arises in our consciousness as a fact which is simply there, without indication that it has been created by us. The mood of the landscape appears to us to be objectively given with it as one of its attributes, belonging to it like any other attribute we perceive it to have. And during this perception, we are not at all concerned with the theory that feelings exist only as conditions of animate beings. We never think of regarding the landscape as a sentient being whose outward aspect "expresses" the mood it contains subjectively. The landscape does not express the mood, but *has* it. The mood surrounds, fills and permeates it like the light that illumines it, or the odor it exhales. The mood belongs to our total impression of the landscape, and can only be distinguished as one of its components by a process of abstraction.

To explain more clearly at this point the difference between a feeling that expresses itself and an objective feeling, we will discuss our perception of a sentient being whose inward feelings are aroused; for instance, that of a sad person. The mien and the attitude of a sad person may "express" sadness, so that we seem to perceive directly in the person's appearance the sorrow that in-

wardly possesses him; yet the objective feeling that belongs to a
picture of such a sad person need not itself be sadness. The total
representation of the sad person includes the sadness which is expressed in his exterior, just as much as his figure, the color of his
dress, his environment. It will therefore influence the overall mood
of the total representation. This overall mood may, of course, also
be sorrowful; but it may just as well happen that the total picture
—including the sorrow in his soul, conveyed by his bodily expression—is the reflection of the objective feeling of noble, tragic greatness, or of ludicrousness, or of any other feeling. The feeling which
appears to be expressed in representational painting may be the
same as the objective feeling, which inheres in the work itself, but
this is by no means necessarily the case; so far from it, in fact,
that the two will often stand in a relation of sharp contrast.

There are, then, "objective feelings" given to our consciousness
if it is unprejudiced by theories, feelings that exist quite objectively
and apart from us, without being inward states of an animate being. It must be granted that these objective feelings do not occur
in an independent state by themselves; they are always embedded
and inherent in objects from which they cannot be actually separated, but only distinguished by abstraction: objective feelings are
always dependent parts of objects.

If we ask ourselves in what way they confront us here, we may
designate them most accurately as non-sensory qualities. A perceived object, we all know, presents itself to us as a manifold of
sensory qualities, which are connected in a certain manner by non-
sensory relational forms, and integrated into groups of higher or
lower order. This description, however, is incomplete, inasmuch as
it leaves aside the objective feelings and does justice only to the
purely imagistic content of the object. But how do the objective
feelings fit into the imagistic content? They certainly do not belong
to the form of the object, they are not relations, but belong to the
content. With all the force they might develop, they still lack the
sensory vitality and materiality of sense-impressions, that inner
weightiness which is a part of even the most delicate colors and
the most ephemeral odors. Their relationship to the sensory qualities
is the same as that of imponderable materials to ponderable materials. They share in the non-sensory character of relational forms,
but have something in common with the sensory content, too—
namely the fact that they are temporal qualitative contents, and

even qualitative contents whose variety and richness readily match the prodigality of the sensory field.

If, however, the concrete object contains, besides the sensory qualities, also the non-sensory qualities of objective feelings, then the manner of their inherence is such that the analogy with the status of sensory qualities breaks down. For the latter stand in relation to each other, they are combined, and composed, so as to produce jointly the appearance of the object. Non-sensory qualities, on the other hand, surround and permeate this whole structure in fluid pervasion, and cannot be brought into any explicit correlation with its component elements. They are contained in the sensory qualities as well as in the formal aspects, and despite all their own variety and contrasts, they melt and mingle in a total impression which is hard to analyse. They do not exist for purely sensory perception, nor for relativistic thinking *per se,* but they are inherent in both, and develop their peculiarities only in the total representation of the object, which is a composite of the two. It is well known that Goethe, in his color theories, treated of the "moral-sensory effect" of colors by examining the moods which each color evokes in us. He meant something that presents itself to us factually as the objective emotional character of each color; and he undertook to describe these emotional characters color by color. However instructive this attempt may be for the beginning of an analysis, it is limited in scope because, during the interaction of the colors in the objective representation, their emotional characters mutually determine each other. At the same time they are influenced by the emotional aspects of the relational scheme, and by those which cling to the meaning of the object itself. Thus, in the total impression, as far as it can be analysed at all, the results of the color-by-color analysis seem more or less limited or invalidated. Objective feelings, a chaotic, involved manifold, defy analysis to a large extent; especially as the variability of reality keeps them in a continuous state of change which cannot be arrested for experimental purposes. But here we encounter further conditions that have their source in the way the subjective perception of objective feelings takes place within us.

If we give the non-sensory qualities of objects the name of feelings which exist objectively, then this name indicates that we subsume them under the same generic concept as what we know in our own inner life as subjective feelings. On what, then, is this

common property and relationship based? First, on the similarity
of content, and secondly on the kind of awareness we have of them
both, and on the experienced transition of one into the other. To
clarify this, we shall now discuss the subjective feelings, as far as
the continuance of this investigation requires.

Subjective feelings are also non-sensory qualities. It has been attempted occasionally in psychology to equate them with the so-
called organic perceptions; but however much organic sensations
and feelings—by which we mean every kind of emotion—might
be interwoven in our psychophysical nature, they still remain two
different things. For the feelings *per se* certainly differ from the
sensations of our somatic excitations, as pure conditions of our soul
to which nothing physiological pertains. Like the objective feelings,
the subjective ones also lack the last residue of sensuous presentation. On the other hand, they do belong to the stuff of our consciousness, and are therefore qualitative. In endless variations and
derivations, they flow through our inner life, causing and determining more than anything else its nature and course.

Psychology so far has had little success in its attempts to bring
conceptual order into the manifold of our feelings. This stems from
the fact that these non-sensory qualities are lacking almost completely in distinctness, and in an innate principle of order. Even
in the field of sensory qualities one immediately comes upon very
great differences. Visual and auditory perceptions we can analyse
distinctly, and we can understand them as mixtures and fusions
of simple elements. Furthermore, we are able to range these elements in series of similitudes—such as the color pyramid and tonal
scales. But the possibility of such a classification in regard to tastes
and odors is very slim. In regard to feelings, it disappears almost
completely. Certainly, feelings as experienced qualities are not
vague or indefinite at all, but have a very concrete and particular
character. But to conceptual treatment they are recalcitrant, as
soon as we try to go beyond the crudest general designations; there
is no systematic scheme that is subtle enough in its logical operations to capture and convey their properties. Wundt's well known
grouping into the series pleasure-displeasure, excitement-calm, tension-relaxation, aims at doing something with the feelings similar
to what the color pyramid and the scale do with visual and auditory
sensations. But while the latter provide a satisfactory scheme to
which every given perception' can be readily subordinated, the

former remain a set of general directions for such a scheme, and are of little use in any particular case. Furthermore, the relations themselves do not point toward the inner quality of the feelings, but rather toward the total behavior of the person of whom they are a condition. This is quite obvious in the terms excitement-calm, tension-relaxation; but it also applies largely to pleasure-displeasure. Basically, they serve less to designate differences of qualitative feeling-content, than as collective terms for (respectively) those feelings which we try to retain, and those which we try to get rid of. It is a moot question to what extent we may argue from similarities and differences in the reactions they evoke, to corresponding similarities and differences in the feeling-contents themselves. We are really confronted with a chaotic manifold from which no internal principle of order can be derived. Nothing therefore avails us in life and in scientific thought but to approach them indirectly, correlating them with the describable events, inside or outside ourselves, that contain and thus convey them; in the hope that anyone reminded of such events will thus be led somehow to experience the emotive qualities, too, that we wish to bring to his attention.

In this, the peculiarity of certain feelings comes to our aid. Psychologists differentiate between those feelings which are directed toward an object, being related to it as cause or goal, and those which are not thus connected with any object—between object-directed feelings and feelings without objects. Sorrow at the death of a friend, gaiety inspired by the sight of a spring landscape, the heroic impulse to fight for one's country—these are feelings of the former kind; melancholy or happiness which seizes us without our being able to explain its why or wherefore, a feverish desire for activity that vainly seeks a suitable field of operation, are of the latter kind. Object-directed feelings are naturally much more easily classified, through the objects to which they are related, than are feelings without objects. But, aside from the characteristics of their object relationship, so far as their inner qualitative content is concerned, object-directed feelings lend themselves neither more nor less to description than do feelings without objects. The relation between a feeling and the object to which it is related is a purely synthetic and empirical one, and the concrete nature of one allows no conclusions as to the concrete nature of the other. Assuming that we had somehow obtained direct consciousness of the concrete nature of an object-directed feeling, without knowing anything about the determining object itself, we could make some vague conjectures of its general nature, but without any further sources of knowledge we could not draw any conclusions as to the concrete quality of the object. It is a traditional fallacy in musical aesthetics to conclude that music cannot reproduce object-directed feelings, because it cannot concretely and unambiguously represent the objects themselves. This, however, does not follow. It is quite thinkable that music can represent, for instance, fury over the loss of a penny, with all the accuracy one could wish for, but not be able to convey audibly in this representation that the infuriating object is a lost penny. Furthermore, if music were to reproduce that feeling exactly, according to its internal quality (as we are assuming here), the feeling thus reproduced, without our knowledge of its objective, would not be registered by our mind as "fury." For we can speak of a feeling as "fury" only with evident reference to objects of a certain nature. After a divorce from the object, the internal quality of the feeling (according to the premise) remains the same, but the external aids disappear which would permit us to subsume the feeling under the concept of fury, and we can at most speak of an ill-humored restlessness, or something of that sort. Generally speaking, this means that the object-directed feelings, (aside, perhaps, from certain inherent indications) can only be classified as related to a specific object in conjunction with the consciousness of this determining object itself. But by themselves, by virtue of their internal quality alone, they fall into the same category as the non-objective feelings; and like those, despite their internal concreteness, they essentially defy an individualising description which omits the presentation of external circumstances.

This intangibility of feelings for our cognition has a further cause, beside the lack of internal definiteness and any inherent principle of order, namely the nature of our awareness of them. Only with the greatest difficulty can we hold them in our mind, observe them, and analyse them. And if we succeed to a limited extent, the turning of our inward eye on them often has the disastrous result that they change or even disappear. Our consciousness is turned toward sensory images, representations, abstract thoughts, but not toward the emotions themselves. Although we are aware of them in our immediate experience as momentary conditions of our soul, and although we know that we are excited and filled by them, we have no real consciousness of them as objects. They do not stand in front of our consciousness, but, so to speak, inside it, and they melt and fuse with it, forming an inadequately definable whole. For the purpose of analysis, this unity has first to be torn apart; and this disturbs and changes its character, and often even makes it disappear momentarily. Thus, feelings remain in shadow for our cognition, perhaps most of all at the time when our soul is completely suffused by them. Their fusion with the Self keeps them arrested in the sphere of immediate experience; there they develop their greatest strength. We feel them, but we hardly see them.

What, then, is the status of objective feelings, and in what relation do they stand to the subjective ones? Both are, as we have said, non-sensory qualities, and what we pointed out about the confused manifold of the subjective feelings holds also for objective ones. But the former are fused with the Self, while the latter are fused with an object. Thus one might expect that the difficulties of cognition we have just presented exist for subjective feelings, but not for objective ones. But the difference in this respect is not very great. It is not as if objective feelings were given to consciousness with the objects in which they inhere, as clearly as the presentational and ideational elements of those objects. On the contrary, subjective and objective feelings melt into each other, and in the course of this interchange the objective feelings, too, elude our recognition.

Starting with the subjective feelings, we note that they either arise as objectless feelings from some causes or other within ourselves, or they are definite reactions of our mind to the idea of this or that object, to which they are then directed. Now, subjective feelings have a tendency to color our images of the objects that evoked them, or images that arise in us when they possess us, with their own hues, and this either by direct reflection or by way of complementation. In happy states we will find the whole world delightful, in sad states, dull and dark; when we are annoyed we are likely to see hostile intent in the object of our annoyance, even though we know perfectly well that it does not really bear us any malice; if we are afraid, the thing we fear looms up great and terrible in our sight. Thus from our subjective feelings, objective feelings are born, but never quite reach a state of complete independence. So an observant contemplation of these directly or inversely objectified subjective feelings is no more feasible than in the case of purely subjective ones.

If, conversely, we begin with objective feelings, we find that these have a tendency to radiate into our soul, and this tendency brings our subjective feelings into a well-nigh insoluble entanglement with them, even if we do not give ourselves over to them, but react against their penetration with some affect of rejection. If we give ourselves over to an objective feeling, it can take possession of us completely. A bright landscape puts us into a cheerful mood. In primitive races, passionate music has even been known to incite the listeners to such passion that it issues in action. This devout reception of objective feeling always points toward a state of mind reminiscent of the *unio mystica:* the feeling subject identifies himself with the perceived object, saturates himself with the objective feeling inherent in the object, experiences that feeling as something of his own being. Even if in most cases one remains aware that the objective feeling does not stem from the depths of one's own soul, there are exceptional cases in which this self-saturation may reach such a degree that this awareness is lost. If we fight against the invasion of the objective feeling, then it has already in some measure taken hold of us; and that which is a battle between an external and an internal force, is at the same time a battle between two internal forces, too—but also between two external forces, because our reactive emotions, objectified in their turn, color and change the feeling which inheres in the object. We have here a diffused back-and-forth between Self and non-Self, a unified emotional process which cannot be torn apart.

We become aware of objective feelings only when we feel them ourselves. Subjective and objective feelings are in a process of continuous exchange; and our observing and analysing mind thereby runs into difficulties with objective feelings very similar to those it encountered with subjective feelings: that if we attempt to bring them within the focus of our awareness we disturb them, and this disturbance may even cause their disappearance.

The emotive aspect of the world is therefore shut off from our consciousness in a peculiar semidarkness. Consisting of a chaotic manifold of non-sensory qualities which can hardly be analysed, feelings arise from inside us, and penetrate us from the outside by means of the objects which we perceive or of which we think. Here, subjective and objective feelings touch, interchange, and commingle without presenting themselves completely to the quiet view of our cognition. Thus it happens that an abyss yawns between the unlimited wealth of our experienced subjective and objective feelings, and the few miserable and all too general concepts which we have derived from them. Is there in any other field of knowledge such a gulf between the matter to be conceived, and our conception of it?

To form an idea of the qualitative wealth of feelings, we have to point out the abundance of individually different subjects and their possible conditions, as well as the totality of the world's further contents. We have so far taken our examples of objective feelings from the empirical world of our perception. But not only the objects of our perception are imbued with feelings: all objects we can imagine—fantasies, the fabulous creatures of mythology, religious and metaphysical objects, etc.—contain them as well. They all present to us their peculiar emotive contents, according to their kind. Ideas of value, each of which has a certain emotional character, are of special importance. Thus we speak of the cold light of truth, the harsh stringency of justice, etc. But if each idea of value has its own definite emotive character, this leads us to the notion of objective feelings which are neither psychological nor real at all, because they belong to value-concepts, which have validity but not existence, and are therefore neither psychical nor physical, but nevertheless have a claim to Being. The dialectic of the interlocking of subjective and objective feelings has been presented by Kant, though without use of our terminology, in his idea of the Moral Law. He speaks of a "solemn majesty" of the Moral Law, in face of which one feels "respect," for its "magnificence" of which "one can never see one's fill" (complementary relation of objective and subjective feelings); and then he says that "the soul believes it raises itself to the degree in which it sees the holy law elevated above itself and its frail nature" (subjectification of objective feelings, here favored by the idea of autonomy).

But the ideas of value cast lights and shadows on the reality of life, and these do their part to determine the subjective emotional behavior and the objective emotional character of human beings and of things. The world is permeated by feelings, not only in its natural but above all in its sensuously animated character. The emotional aspect of human culture is especially colored by ideas, so that within it we perceive directly the value categories of human beings and objects as, so to speak, their inherent affective character. Priests, officials, merchants, church, state, economy—these are not only types of persons and institutions with definable traits of composition and conduct, that bear comprehensible relations to the value concepts appropriate to them; but they are at the same time vehicles and spheres of feelings, of a peculiar sort that participates in the emotional character of their respective essential value concepts, either directly or inversely; and they present themselves accordingly to our emotional apperception.

But we have to carry this much further in the direction of the concrete. Each people, each era and each cultural unit within it, and even each individual in its historical peculiarity acts out its own special attitude toward values. From the connection between given natural conditions and the relevant ideas of value there arise, both personally and objectively, individuated figures and images, each of which carries its own emotional character. The citizen of Athens, the Buddhist monk, the Renaissance man, Roman law, the Catholic Church, the Prussian military, the French *salon*, modern industry: one has only to mention the names of such historical phenomena—to say nothing of individuals—and everyone who hears them and knows their meaning will think not only of their context, which can be described in historical objective terms, but will also in each case be moved as by a specific air. This is the emotional atmosphere of these images.

If we look from this point upon the course of history in progress, with its battles and victories, then the fight of individuals and powers for recognition and dominance presents itself, in connection with our considerations, as a battle of various emotional worlds and powers. This makes it possible to hold quite different opinions regarding the effective causes which produce historical decisions. These might consist, both in a material and an intellectual respect, of concrete developments in objective situations (for instance, economic conditions, or the status of intellectual problems), while the psychological and emotionally determined occurrences are unable to exercise any profound influence on these movements. But even matters of fact have their specific emotional characteristics, which change with their changes; and their manifold shifts, working for and against each other, simultaneously appear as changing and conflicting emotional determinations. Under the described conditions these would, of course, be only epiphenomena, only an iridescent aura, a glow spread over history. If, on the contrary, we find their effective force in feelings bursting forth from individuals or whole communities, feelings which compete and struggle for the soul, and try to incarnate themselves in works and institutions; then, of course, the real meaning of the subjective and objective feelings becomes, in this conception, the decisive one. But however one may think about it, history is in any case permeated by feelings which are different at any given times and places, and which change continuously from one individually concrete quality to another.

Next to psychology, it is therefore primarily historiography which has to come to grips with the question of our knowledge of feelings. We saw above how disadvantageous the conditions are for psychology, when it tries to analyse and systematise feelings. The study of history—which has, among other things, to form individual concepts about the emotional character of the historical phenomena, and to make us conscious of the feeling and the emotional atmosphere of the people during the various periods in history—is faced in this respect by perhaps even greater difficulties. For while psychology can start from the living experience of the present, historical research must depend entirely on its sources. The emotional life and aura of the past does, of course, adhere to those sources somehow; and the historian, in reconstructing the past from them, will become conscious of it. But how difficult it is for him to transcend his own subjective emotional limits, and to reach that which we call sympathetic understanding of history! Assuming that he surmounts this difficulty, how is he to reproduce what he understands in words and concepts? Dates, diplomatic negotiations, the progress of military expeditions, the developments of law—in short, the external occurrences and the ways of thought and representation in the past—can be seized upon and expressed. But to grasp and express conceptually what we call the "spirit" of the past, which is in truth mostly its emotional character, is impossible if one does not want to bog down in the crudest generalizations. And this is the point where historical science has to call art to its assistance, the point where science passes into art. What the historian can achieve only inadequately by means of concepts, he can fully achieve by means of art. A historian who wants to portray the spirit of a period will fail, despite the highest intelligence and the most abundant knowledge, if there is not something of the poet in him which enables him, by the manner in which he describes them, to put his representations always into that emotional light, to immerse them in that mood which is appropriate to their emotional character.

But the special question of the function of art in historical research shall not be further discussed here. Our mention of it will serve as a transition to a more detailed development of the statement which we made at the beginning of this essay. Everything which has been discussed so far has served the purpose of preparation.

Beside the subjective feelings which move us, or which become apparent to us as physical expression of the emotions of other animate beings whose inner lives they move, our world is filled with objective feelings which are inherent in objects, which surround and permeate them, without having necessarily to be considered as states of mind residing in the objects. These objective feelings, nonsenuous qualities of the most diverse richness, are in intimate interrelationship with the subjective feelings to which they are qualitatively related. The two influence each other in an analogous or complementary manner, check or further each other. And we perceive objective feelings only by feeling subjectively.

As qualities, all feelings—subjective as well as objective—belong to the apperceptional content of the world; this is true even for the objective feelings which are inherent in ideas that can only be grasped in pure thought. Since they are non-sensuous qualities, our apperception of them, through which we become conscious of them, is also of a non-sensuous sort.

Feelings, like all qualities, are built into the structure of the world as dependent parts or characteristics of objects. They are either states of mind, or properties of things and processes, or unreal ideas.

They escape conceptual scientific knowledge to a large degree: they are indistinct and form a chaotic manifold; they are also hard of access for our attentive contemplation. Conceptually they can therefore be described only in very general and indirect terms. And especially, it is impossible to capture and fix their peculiarities in particular historical concepts. Intuitions without concepts are blind. There is no intuition so blind as the non-sensuous intuition of feelings.

How, then, is it possible to lend them sight? I.e.: how is it possible to effect a synthetic unity in the manifold of these apperceptions, and to endow its formless wealth of qualities with some kind of form? How can we capture, keep, and fix feelings so that their content may be presented to our consciousness with universal validity, without their being known in the strict sense—i.e. by means of concepts? The answer is: we can do it by creating objects wherein the feelings we seek to fix are so definitely embodied that subjects confronted with these objects, and emphatically disposed toward them, cannot but uniformly experience a non-sensuous apperception of the feelings in question. Such objects are called "works of art," and by "art," we designate the activity that produces them.

Since, as we have shown, each and every object somehow contains objective feelings, we must determine more clearly in what respect works of art excel all other objects as repositories of objective feelings. The difference can be given in a few words which, however, need elucidation: the objective feelings inherent in works of art are, so to say, molded in conformity with the works that contain them, and that consequently enforce their pure and always constant apperception in a universally valid way.

The artist, like any other person, becomes conscious of feelings, subjective as well as objective ones, continuously moving back and forth between Self and non-Self in the manner described, as facts of his experience. As an artist, he has to give them shape. But to give shape means first of all to set limits. He must seize and separate from the wealth of his experience complexes which he feels belong intrinsically together. At the same time, he has to carry out a certain process of abstraction and condensation on the infinite manifold of the shapes that were seized and singled out; he has to give them internal limitations, and must divide them into related groups and sub-groups. But because of their peculiar quality and mode of consciousness this task cannot be solved in isolation and by working directly with feelings. The separation, the selective condensation, and the internal grouping of the feeling complex to be shaped can only be accomplished by simultaneously creating and forming the object in which the complex of feelings achieves its existence. In practice, the shaping of the feeling and the shaping of the object into which it will be embedded coincide in one and the same activity.

The separation of the complex of feelings is reflected in the detachment of the object in which it is inherent. The work of art must be an object existing for itself, separated out from the rest of the world of objects. It must exclude all other objects. It must have a frame within which the separated feeling moves about as in a container. This is what has been called the self-sufficiency of the work of art, which was what inspired Schiller's speculations on freedom in pure appearance. Basically, however, it is simply the question of separating the complex of feelings both from the totality of feelings to which it belonged originally, and from the emotional ties with its environment. Very much as a scientific work selects a particular issue from amongst the plethora of problems, defines it and thereby gives it a beginning and an end, the work of art must also be a well-rounded whole. And again, just as a scientific lecture is distinct from conversation and speeches which were held before and after it, the work of art and its inherent feelings must not combine with the objects among which it finds itself, by chance, in time and space, and with their emotional atmosphere. The way the limitation and rounding off in both respects is effected naturally depends on the objective materials which the artist uses in order to endow them with the feeling to be created, and can only be described in relation to them. Besides, it is not even entirely right to say that the work of art stands alone in complete self-sufficiency. To be sure, as an object it is separated from its environment, in which it happens to be (insofar as it does not have to fulfill a function which is in some sense decorative, which would make it a special case.) But as a work of art, it belongs intimately with other works of art of the same master, of the same people, of the same period, etc.; while each work of art reproduces some particular complex of feelings, several of them act in concert in order to fix, in their distinct parts, a larger world of feelings perceived from various points of view. Thus they enter into a relation of mutual clarification and complementation.

But the separateness of the work of art entails not only its being taken out of its community with other objects, but also its dissociation from the accidental strivings of the contemplating subjects. For it is supposed to present to them in an unadulterated manner the feeling complex which is its objective content. What matters, therefore, is that the objective feeling should appear to the subject purely as such, without interference and obfuscation by subjective feeling. The subject, of course, must exclude his subjective feelings during the enjoyment of a work of art, as he would similarly in the case of a theoretical consideration; he must be ready to give himself up to the objective feelings by affective contemplation. On condition of this surrender, however, the work of art should simply reveal its objective emotional content; it should not aim at the excitement of a subjective feeling which arises only as its result, without being inherent in it. This is the difference between poetry and rhetoric: the one contains feeling and transmits it, the other aims to excite feelings; the first wants to be understood through feeling, the latter wants to effect a result.

How does the artist form the non-sensuous qualitative feeling, content feeling, i.e. how does he, in selecting, condense, organize, and connect elements to form a meaningful unity? This task also can be fulfilled only in the creation of the work of art itself. In the form of a work of art, in the organization of its parts into a complex whole, the feeling itself appears to our affective contemplation as something formed.

What, then, is the principle of form for the work of art, and with it for the objective feelings enclosed in the work of art? The answer is: Rhythm. But this is, for the present, only a word, the meaning of which has to be explained.

We all know it from poetics and music theory. In poetry, we understand it as the alternation of stressed and unstressed, long and short syllables, in music as the change in stress and length of the tones, as long as this alternation is not without a plan but observes certain rules. But this explanation is too loose as well as too narrow for a general theory. Too loose, because the difference of stress and length can be reduced to two basic types of stress, the dynamic and the chronological. For the syllables and tones of longer duration are as such also of a greater importance; they stand out more than those of shorter duration, they are heavier, while the others are lighter, just as the dynamically stressed ones are heavier and the dynamically unstressed ones lighter. But if we understand by stressed every kind of weight, and by unstressed every kind of lightness, then the given explanation is too narrow, for there are still other stresses besides the dynamic and the chronological. Thus in music the higher tones, as the lighter, more penetrating ones are [in one sense] heavier than the lower, darker, softer ones—and conversely, [in another sense] the lower, as the broader ones, are heavier than the higher, thinner, and insubstantial

ABIGAIL E. WEEKS MEMORIAL LIBRARY

ones. It depends therefore on the context, whether any single tone emphasizes the quality which makes it heavy, or the one which makes it light. Furthermore, harmonies are also distinctly differentiated between heavier and lighter ones. Those into which the leading tones resolve are heavier, those which contain the leading tones are lighter; from another angle, the basic harmonies of a key are heavier than their secondary harmonies, etc. All these various stresses either work together or against each other, and thereby condition the play of the rhythm in a wider sense. In poetry, the syllables are not only heavy when dynamically or chronologically stressed, but also through their darker or brighter, fuller or more hollow sounds, and finally through the weight of their meanings. Rhythm not only dominates music and poetry, but also, in a wider sense, architecture, sculpture, and painting; the bigger part of a space is heavier than the smaller, one spatial form, whether linear or plane, weightier, more striking, or stronger in character than another; colors, also, are distinguished from various points of view by their greatly varied impressiveness. In addition, there is the greater or lesser weightiness of the objects which are simulated. If, therefore, we want to define rhythm in general, we have to say: rhythm is the alternation between heavy (stressed) and light (unstressed, or less stressed) parts, insofar as it follows certain rules.

But these rules operate by combining heavy and light parts to make rhythmic sensuous unities of lower and higher order in the form of various kinds of alternation of heavy and light stresses. In the construction of such rhythmic sensuous unities, next to each other, in each other, and one above another, the form of the work originates: it is nothing else but its total rhythm. Only inasmuch as a work has form, i.e. rhythm, is it a work of art.

In relation to the total content of a work of art, the form is something abstract, schematic. All its particulars take part in it only because, as heavier or lighter members and groups, they have their meaning in it. Its other characteristics enter into it only by being caught and incorporated in its rhythmic relations. They are *per se* something formed, material. The pure tonal qualities of sounds and harmonies are material; the pure tonal qualities of syllables and words are material; the objective meanings of words and sentences are material. So are the expression-values of colors and forms *per se*, the character of the substances used, the objects reproduced, etc. All of this has its effect and lives in the work of art only insofar as it is carried by its rhythmic groundswell, incorporated in the proportional relations of its rhythmic structure. So the relation of the rhythm of a work of art to the material through which it appears is like that of a category of perception to the sensuous contents it governs, that of the logical form of a treatise to the specific thoughts connected by it. Rhythmics is, in a certain respect, the logic of art.

But how are form and matter of a work of art related to the feeling which is to be incorporated in it, for the sake of which they both exist, since it is by and through them that the feeling is to become objective? We have seen that feelings are qualities, that is of a material even if non-sensuous nature, and that, as an indistinct, chaotic manifold which cannot be dissolved into its elements and cannot be ordered, they escape formulation to a large extent. If form and matter could be distinguished in feelings, it would be very simple to classify the form of the feelings with the rhythm and the matter with the material of the work of art. But a form of feeling does not exist *per se*. And the rhythm is not the form of feeling, but the form of the work of art. As carriers of feeling, form and matter in a work of art are on the same level; objective feelings are inherent in both, and they all mix and mingle to form a complex which cannot be exactly analysed. But in this complex, we feel that the feelings which belong to the rhythm are dominant, as if they were a liquid which dissolves in rhythm and permeates it, thus creating a unity; and since the rhythm is in itself a manifold, and is one with the inherent feeling, the unity achieved is essentially a manifold. What gives the complex of feelings carried by the entire work of art its condensed form and unity? Not the rhythm itself, as form of the feelings; but the feeling which is carried by the rhythm, as a feeling mingling materially and qualitatively with the feelings carried by the matter of the work of art. The feeling inherent in the rhythm is therefore in itself material; but material that acts as an analogue of form in the formless complex of feelings, in a manner which cannot be more accurately described. Thus the complex of feelings remains really meaningless and incomprehensible, whereas the work of art itself is meaningful and understandable.

The assertion that one has "understood" a work of art comprises accordingly a literal and a figurative meaning. The literal meaning is: we understand the work of art if we comprehend it in its

parts and as a whole according to the rules of rhythm that govern it, if we give it the correct rhythmic articulation and combine
its individual parts in the way they belong together rhythmically.
Understanding of the work in this sense is the understanding of
its rhythmical construction, so that it presents itself to our mind
as the rhythmic symbol which it really is. The figurative meaning,
on the contrary, is: we understand the work of art if we affectively
perceive the feeling content that is held and objectified in it. This
understanding is not a real understanding because in this case,
what we grasp does not come to us as something intrinsically
formed, permeated by meaning and dominated by the intellect.
We can arrive at a true emotional understanding of the feeling content of the work of art only through a correct rhythmic-constructive
understanding of the work itself. A correct emotional understanding
is attained through the comprehensible and rightly comprehended
form of the work of art; and what is comprehended, namely the
emotional content of the work, is therefore, if not actually something formed, in the true sense of the word, nevertheless something
comprehended through the form of the rhythm, and therefore
something *quasi* formed. Here too, therefore, we may apply the
word understanding, although in a figurative and extended sense.
It follows from this that the rhythmic constructive understanding
of a work of art is basically possible, without adding to it or including in it any emotional understanding; that, on the contrary,
emotional understanding can only develop by and with an understanding of the form. But it is only in emotional understanding that
the total understanding of a work of art reaches its culmination;
our understanding of the form plays only the role of a servant.
In practice, therefore, the understanding of form and feeling will
always more or less keep step with each other, and the intuitive
dawning of the latter often shows the way to the former.

The pairing of emotional and formal understanding appears
clearly when we try to bring the total understanding of the work
of art to our critical consciousness. Then our direct understanding
of form is replaced by a rhythmic-constructive analysis which,
working by means of theories and proofs, lays bare the form of
the work of art. This analysis may be carried a long way and its
results may be scientifically corroborated to a high degree of probability. It will, moreover, react on the direct understanding of form,
and so will indirectly promote emotional understanding of the work

of art as well. But the analysis itself no longer contains any of that; for it seizes only the scaffolding of the work, only that which is meaningful and comprehensible in it in the strictest sense. The formless, non-sensuous qualities of the emotional complex, which fill out the scaffolding and permeate and animate it, do not exist for rhythmic-constructive analysis, just because it has to abstract from them. A separate critical consciousness of the emotional content of the work of art is, on the other hand, not really attainable. It would mean that the emotional content had to be characterized purely as such; but this can, at best, be done only with the help of some empty generalizations, and is therefore far too inefficient to clarify the affective contemplation of the work. It is possible, however, even if only in a very limited way, to re-present the extrapolated emotional content by artistic means, such as, perhaps, a poetical description. Though this cannot produce critical awareness, its value lies in showing our affective sense a way by which it can uncover the emotional content of the work of art. And since the total understanding of the work culminates in the affective understanding, such poetic descriptions must not be underestimated. As far as they are good and to the point, they alone touch on the essence, while rhythmic-constructive analysis, despite all the triumphs of exactitude which it might enjoy, remains apart from that.

We understand a work of art correctly, then, as soon as we perceive it correctly in the rhythmic-formal sense, and as soon as we feel its true emotional content through this correct formal perception.

But if a work of art is succesful, i.e. if an emotional content has taken form and shape in it, a correct understanding is always basically possible, however hampered it may be by accidental subjective factors. Every successful work of art has general validity; because it can always be understood identically in its rhythmic-constructive terms, this identical understanding also always conveys the same emotional content. This fitness of form to content constitutes its necessity.[1] In fully understanding a work of art, we become aware of its necessity, though we cannot prove it. To obtain such proof, it would be necessary that, after the completed

---

[1] In English writings this characteristic is usually called "inevitability." But the author's word is *Notwendigkeit*, which can only be rendered as "necessity." —Ed.

rhythmic-formal analysis, we would likewise analyse the inherent feeling and then compare the respective results to understand their functional correspondence in detail. But this cannot be done, even if we make some progress in that direction; for in the end, the emotional content evades analysis. Why a work of art with a certain rhythmic-formal nature forces us to become aware of just this specific emotional content and no other, remains obscure. It is the same obscurity which covers the creativity of the artist. We, as beholders, do not know why we perceive just such a content with the form; the artist does not know why he gives the content, which he shapes, just such a form. There is no bridge between the two which could be constructed by the intellect. The "unconscious" factor in artistic creation is nothing but this impossibility of comprehending the necessity which connects the feeling to be captured with the form in which it will be bound. And since this necessity remains incomprehensible even after the completion of the work of art, this unconsciousness never really becomes consciousness, neither in the artist, nor in the beholder.

The value of a work of art, therefore, lies in the degree of necessity that obtains in it. If form and content harmonize completely, then it has universal validity for all contemplating subjects. It is "eternal."

Because of the separateness and the rhythmic-formal nature of the work of art, its content is transmitted to the aesthetically educated consciousness with the highest degree of objective purity and genuineness. The unity of experience, in which we become subjectively conscious of the feelings that the work of art contains in an objectified state, is here entirely determined by the objective aspect, and is distinctly set off from the feelings which move us either as a further effect of the work of art, or by other accidental causes. At the same time, this unity of experience contains everything that is manifested in our contemplation of theoretical matters: consciousness of the necessity with which form and emotional content of the work belong together, consciousness of its aesthetic value. This consciousness is what really and essentially safeguards the unity of experience in us, and does not permit a vague mixture of objective and subjective feelings to arise, that otherwise always enters into our emotional perceptions, even if not always to the same degree. It is what Kant has in mind when he treats of the disinterested satisfaction of aesthetic contemplation; for disinterestedness, we would here substitute the pure object-

dependence of the feeling, for satisfaction the sense of manifestation.

Just as a scientifically inclined person, as a rule, seeks his scientific
data only in restricted fields that accord with his talents, and finds
them only there, so the aesthetically inclined person can, in general,
obtain direct aesthetic manifestations only in a restricted field of
art. And since what is manifested in art is always feeling, he will
be receptive to the aesthetic import primarily where the feelings
objectified in the work correspond to his own way of feeling. There
he brings along the most propitious conditions of receptivity; there,
where his own being is touched to the core, the aesthetic import
will first become apparent to him. Hence such expressions as aesthetic joy, aesthetic pleasure, and aesthetic satisfaction. In themselves, joy, pleasure, and satisfaction are nothing but collective
terms for various kinds of subjective feeling which are internally
quite different from each other (without our being able to explain
the differences between them), and which have externally only
one thing in common, namely: that we seek them, or try to hold
them. The subjective pleasure from a work of art, therefore, which
is tied up with the aesthetic reception of its emotional content
and the consciousness of this import, and promotes these functions,
may be of an entirely different origin and of an entirely different
sort for each different person; what permits us to subsume them all
under one collective term is only the external fact that all people
who experience any of them are attracted by the emotional content of the artistic work. But on such experiences one cannot found
an aesthetic theory. Theory, quite to the contrary, should ignore subjective pleasure and therewith the accidental attitude of the individual subjects. To speak of a "universally valid satisfaction" is
nonsense because the concept presents a *contradictio in adjecto*.

The purely aesthetic contemplator knows how to abstract completely from his personal pleasure. Through the formal-rhythmic
construction of the work of art, he receives the emotional content,
and thus he experiences an enrichment of his emotional knowledge.
This is sufficient for him, *qua* aesthetic contemplator.

The feelings which are formed and fixed in the work of art are
objective, and may be of various kinds according to their origin:
they may originally have figured in actual experience as objective
feelings, or as subjective feelings with or without an object, or as
mixtures of both. Since in the original experience, subjective and

objective feelings are always in a fluid relationship of exchange, and objective feelings therefore hardly occur in unadulterated purity, the objectified feelings in a work of art will carry an element of subjective feeling in them even when they are essentially objective. There are certain landscape painters who have, so to speak, uncovered the objective emotional content of individual landscapes through their pictures: they perceived it to the fullest extent and they were able to give it artistic form; yet these pictures still communicate a subjective coloration in the objective feeling, which we call the personal tone of the artist. No work of art is free of this personal tone. But within these personal limits, the entire world of feelings that is accessible to the artist's experience and cognition is open to him for formation: his own subjective feelings, alien subjective feelings which he is able to seize upon, and objective feelings, as well as all possible mixtures of these. But all feelings enter the work of art as objectified feelings; once formed, they have now become inherent in the work of art; they are therefore objective—in the way we have discussed: namely, by commanding purely objective comprehension through rhythmic form. As soon as they enter the work of art they therefore dissolve the ties with which they occurred in lived experience. The subjective feelings then appear without the subject who had experienced them, the object-conditioned feelings among them without the object which conditioned them. A lyrical poem contains the feeling of a subject in the form of objectified subjective feeling, that no longer involves the subject who had originally experienced it as his own condition; it lives by its own right in the poem, as an objective feeling inherent in it. A religious edifice contains objectively the object-directed feeling of a community towards its God, though it conveys no representation of this God. A pastoral piece of music contains the objective feeling belonging to a landscape, without painting the landscape. Such art forms which use representations of things, descriptions or thoughts as material for their rhythmic constructions naturally gain thereby the capacity to recall the objects to which the feelings they convey originally belonged. Portraits, landscapes, historical novels, divine images, metaphysical poetry, etc., are capable of that. But a painter, for instance, may perhaps use the picture of a real landscape to give form to an objectless subjective feeling; he can use the portrait of a real person to fix the objective feeling of a value idea. A poet can express thoughts not to fix their objective emotional content, but object-determined subjective feelings, etc. The possibilities are unlimited. And the anti-conceptual, peculiar nature of feelings makes it impossible to state in any individual case to which class of feelings the emotional content of a certain work of art should be assigned, no matter how unequivocally the work may convey the feeling inherent in it. Arguments over the emotional character of a work of art originate to a large extent in such difficulties of classification, and not in differences of emotional perception itself.

The difficulty we met in trying to divide feelings into subjective and objective, besets all other attempted classifications, too. Such concepts as for instance naïve, sentimental, classic, romantic, Apollonian, Dionysian, tragic, comic, humorous, sublime, beautiful, etc. are basically nothing but vague collective terms for feelings which we find qualitatively related, though we cannot further demonstrate this relationship by anything in the feelings themselves, and cannot reduce it to distinct characteristics. Aesthetic theories dealing with this problem seek to define such categories by abstracting certain common characteristics from the form and matter of those works of art which express feelings we tend to classify under our various rubrics. Even if this yields some sort of survey, such definitions are always more or less inadequate to any specific case, because we might accept a term as appropriate to the emotional content of a work but not to its physical composition, or, on the contrary, we might accept it as appropriate to the latter, but not to the emotional content. This then gives rise to differences of opinion about the feeling-content of a work, which are born of such theoretical difficulties, and do not necessarily bespeak any real differences of affective perception: this may and mostly will be the same, even while our attempts at conceptual classification differ widely from each other.

The feelings which art captures and objectifies furnish an infinite variety of actual content. The entire wealth of non-sensuous emotional qualities, which is poured forth in the universe and made accessible to human experience in the course of history, and which we have surveyed before, is at its disposal: the moods of landscape that surrounds us, the inner stirrings of our souls and their mutual emotional relations, the affective content of cultural conditions and events, the moral, political or religious ideas that are dominant, strive for dominance or lie defeated, the currently accepted philosophies of life or ideas of value, etc. All this enters into a mutual relationship with the feeling of the several individual artists, as such feeling develops in their personal destinies, and supplies the material which assumes form and substance in their work. This material is, by definition, fluid and transitory, and though the objective emotional content of nature or of a value concept remains in itself unchangeable, its affective perception is never free from individually or historically conditioned colorations, and being thus colored, it, too, becomes transitory. By capturing and fixing this material, art lifts it from the fleeting transitoriness in which it is experienced, and fixes it in images in which any appreciative subject whatever can percieve it, everywhere and always anew. Thus art absorbs the emotional content of the world, as it presents itself to human experience in the course of history, and, relative always to the capacity of the day's performing artists, keeps it universally communicable, and so gives it eternal life. We have no other medium but art that could accomplish this: art alone objectifies that content, clarifies it, and gives it a heightened and permanent realization. Herein lies the purpose and meaning of art.

The work of art that gives eternal form to a feeling thereby accomplishes its task, and thus fulfills its function, no matter what kind of feeling it is that figures in this fulfillment. But feelings, by and large, are closely connected with our value concepts and our evaluating consciousness, as we have shown. And this leads to a second principle of evaluation in art. The aesthetic value of a work of art lies solely in the power with which it forms and fixes a certain emotional content and makes it universally accessible: that is the *conditio sine qua non* of each art work, and the more of this power it possesses, the more perfect it is as a work of art *per se*. But we do not value a work only as a medium that preserves feelings; our evaluation tends rather to aim straight at the emotional content itself. We consider a work of art great and significant, etc., depending on whether we consider the emotional content which it objectifies great and significant. Here it is presupposed that it shall convey the emotional content in an aesthetically perfect manner: a work of art that objectifies an unimportant content perfectly ranks higher as a work of art than one that expresses an important emotional content insufficiently. But if the aesthetic value exists to an equal degree in both cases, the second principle of evaluation becomes predominant. This, however, depends in each case first of all on the personally and temporally conditioned weltanschauung which we ourselves represent. The argument about the value of an art is most frequently not really an argument about its aesthetic value, but about its meaning in the light of some weltanschauung. It is in keeping with the intangibility of the world's emotional aspect which, after all, is ever at issue, that the distinction we have just made is easily formulated *in abstracto*, but very difficult to carry through *in concreto;* which, of course, does not affect its truth. We find indeed that individual subjects tend to disparage and deprecate works of art on purely aesthetic grounds, when actually they resent their emotional contents; on the other hand, they overrate such works of art aesthetically which correspond to the sentiment of their own weltanschauung. To arrive at an objective evaluation is exceedingly difficult here, and as a rule succeeds only when a certain historical perspective is obtained; and even then, not always sufficiently. We accept the appraisals of the past as a given fact and decide now, in accordance with them, which works of art they present as important. But therewithal our own evaluative principles always remain in the background, as we ourselves appraise the appraisals of the past, and accordingly rank the individual artistic periods with relation to each other.

Thus aesthetic criticism has, strictly speaking, only to determine whether a work of art does or does not have aesthetic value: i.e., whether, and to what degree of perfection its rhythmic-formal nature presents and fixes a certain emotional content. In fact, however, it does not usually restrict itself to that, but far exceeds these limits, by subjecting the feelings themselves that appear in the work to an evaluating criticism. But judgments on the value and importance of this emotional content always go beyond the competence of truly aesthetic criticism, however they may hide behind apparently aesthetic discussions. They always presuppose some general outlook on life and the universe, and can be validated only on that basis.

An artist, one who is such by talent and temperament, wants first of all merely to give form and substance to what he has divined of the emotional content of the world; that is the goal of his labor and his life. The works, however, which he thus creates, leave his studio and go out among people, to whom they publish what he felt. What they want now is: to be understood. That means, they want to be rightly comprehended in rhythmic-formal terms, and thus communicate their emotional content correctly. But it means furthermore that they demand recognition for the subjective and objective sense of value inherent in their emotional content; recognition, at least, in the sense of "honoring," but preferably in the sense of agreement, so that the subjects rediscover their own feelings and intuitions articulated in them, or even experience an enlargement and enrichment of their previous emotional world. Using a lofty expression, we then speak of a work of art as being a "revelation" to us. All great art strives to give us such revelations, and demands from us their perception and recognition. The acceptance usually proceeds in the following way: at first the new works of art are "incomprehensible" to us; we see no rhythmic-formal structure in their physical composition, or, making false connections, misconstrue them and read a wrong sense into them. Meanwhile their essence, their emotional content, remains completely closed to us. Then it begins to dawn on us; persons with insight point out to us the true rhythmic-formal relations, or know how to bring the emotional content closer to us by aptly chosen words. At last we see the light, the form becomes clear, the content opens up, the works of art begin to speak to us, and only now are we able to appreciate them aesthetically and to take a philosophical attitude toward them. Everyone who has ever been confronted with a new art form completely foreign to him, and who finally succeeded in penetrating it, has had such an experience. But in these experiences, what we recognize as the true significance of art becomes apparent: that it elevates the emotional content of the world to universally valid consciousness.

Beauty and Significance

LOUIS ARNAUD REID

FEW SUBJECTS IN AESTHETICS have been more discussed of
recent years than the subject of the relation of the "form" and the
"content" of art. Sometimes the terms of the title are these, sometimes
they are different: here it is "expression" *versus* "subject-matter,"
there it is "beauty" *versus* "morals": yesterday it was "art for art's
sake." Within a month of the present paper two distinguished
thinkers, Mr. Roger Fry and Mr. R. G. Collingwood are speaking,[1]
the one on "Representation in Art," the other on "Form and Content" in Art. The title of my own essay might be written more fully,
"The relation of the significance of artistic content to artistic expression, and the contribution of each to beauty."

I propose to begin by writing down a number of statements by
contemporary writers, in order to show clearly the kind of problem
with which we are faced. The writers fall on two sides, one side
being composed, I fear, solely of Mr. I. A. Richards, the valiant
and brilliant author of *The Principles of Literary Criticism*. I will
take him second. The other side is larger. On it is found Mr. A. C.
Bradley, with whom we may begin.

[1] To the British Institute of Philosophical Studies.

37

Speaking of poetry, Mr. Bradley says,[2] "First, this experience is an end in itself, is worth having on its own account, has an intrinsic value. Next, its poetic value is this intrinsic worth alone . . . its nature is to be not a part, nor yet a copy of the real world (as we commonly understand that phrase), but to be a world by itself, independent, complete, autonomous." Now hear Mr. Roger Fry and Mr. Clive Bell. Mr. Fry writes,[3] "Mr. Bell's sharp challenge to the usually accepted view of art as expressing the emotions of life has been of great value. It has led to an attempt to isolate the purely aesthetic feeling from the whole complex of feelings which may and generally do accompany the aesthetic feeling when we regard a work of art." And, again,[4] "I hope to show certain reasons why we should regard our responses to works of art as distinct from our responses to other situations." Mr. Bell writes,[5] "The representative element in a work of art may or may not be harmful; always it is irrelevant. For, to appreciate a work of art we need bring with us nothing from life, no knowledge of its ideas and affairs, no familiarity with its emotions. Art transports us from the world of man's activity to a world of aesthetic exaltation. For a moment we are shut off from human interests." "He who contemplates a work of art, inhabit[s] a world with an intense and peculiar significance of its own; that significance is unrelated to the significance of life. In this world the emotions of life find no place. It is a world with emotions of its own." [6] And he speaks with eloquence [7] of "the austere and thrilling raptures of those who have climbed the cold white peaks of art." [8] Leaving the pure critics and coming to Croce and his followers, one finds a certain difficulty in treating them fairly. On one side of him Croce holds precisely the opposite point of view from that just quoted, for he says [9] that one of the principal reasons which have prevented aesthetic from revealing the real roots of art in human nature "has been its separation from the general spiritual life, the having made of it a sort of special function or aristocratic club." Yet—though for entirely

[2] *Oxford Lectures on Poetry*, p. 5.
[3] *Vision and Design*, Phoenix Library, p. 296.
[4] *Transformations*, Chatto & Windus, p. 2.
[5] *Art*, Phoenix Library, p. 25.
[6] *Ibid.*, pp. 26 and 27.
[7] *Ibid.*, p. 33.
[8] *Ibid.*, pp. 26 and 27.
[9] *Aesthetic*, p. 14, Ainslie's Trans.

different reasons from those of Fry and Bell—he also supports the view that the "content" of art is of no aesthetic importance. "The impossibility of choice of content completes the theorem of the *independence of art,* and is also the only legitimate meaning of the expression: *art for art's sake.* Art is independent both of science and of the useful and the moral." [10] Beauty is "*expression* and nothing more." [11] Mr. Collingwood writes,[12] "Every work of art is a monad. . . . Nothing can go into it or come out of it; whatever is in it must have arisen from the creative act which constitutes it." And Mr. Carritt, a less thoroughgoing supporter of Croce, tells us,[13] "I was myself formerly inclined to the view that beauty was always the expression of . . . an intuition of some value. . . . My reading of Croce has convinced me that the *expression* of *any* feeling is beautiful."

Mr. Richards is all against the aristocratic and esoteric view of art, and urges that its content is a part of and is continuous with life. "When we look at a picture, or read a poem, or listen to music, we are not doing something quite unlike what we were doing on our way to the Gallery or when we dressed in the morning." [14] Again,[15] the gulf between a poem and what is not a poem "is no greater than between the impulses which direct the pen and those which conduct the pipe of a man who is smoking and writing at once." And he speaks [16] of "the myth of a 'transmutation' or 'poetisation' of experience and that other myth of the 'contemplative' or 'aesthetic' attitude." Mr. Richards is, to-day, lonely in his defence of this view. But he is not alone. As he rightly points out,[17] "the 'moral' theory of art (it would be better to call it the 'ordinary values' theory) has the most great minds behind it. Until Whistler came to start the critical movements of the last half-century, few poets, artists or critics had ever doubted that the value of art experiences was to be judged as other values are."

Quotations are seldom quite fair. Those which I have given do seem to me to represent expressions of what are two radically op-

[10] *Ibid.,* p. 52.
[11] *Ibid.,* p. 79.
[12] *Outlines of a Philosophy of Art,* p. 24.
[13] *The Theory of Beauty,* footnote to pp. 28 and 29.
[14] *Principles of Literary Criticism,* p. 16.
[15] *Ibid.,* p. 78.
[16] *Ibid.,* p. 79.
[17] *Ibid.,* p. 71.

posed views about the question of the value or significance of the content of art. But there are, of course, individual differences in the background. I have referred to the difficulty of quoting Croce. Among the critics, Mr. Bell is perhaps the most consistently downright and is therefore the easier to quote. Mr. Bradley is judicial, particularly if his work is taken as a whole, and one of the many charms of Mr. Fry's writing is his willingness to modify or change his views in the light of concrete experience. In view of this, and in view of trends in the remarkable first essay in his "Transformations," I feel that Mr. Fry is ready to be persuaded that the significance of content or subject-matter is more important than he sometimes says. He wrote, for example, in an early essay (1904) on Beardsley's drawings,[18] "The finest qualities of design can never be appropriated to the expression of such perverted and morbid ideals; nobility and geniality of design are attained only by those who, whatever their actual temperament, cherish these qualities in their imagination." Indeed, I believe that if proper accounts of "subject matter" and "significance" and "value" can be given there are grounds at least for an armistice between the opposing armies, if not for permanent peace. In this we must probably except the Crocians, whose aesthetic theory is grounded in a general philosophy of life.

Future agreement seems possible, and even likely, because both sides are so indubitably right in much of what they assert: their mistakes appear to consist chiefly in over-statements. As against Mr. Richards, surely we may urge that the significance and the value of art are to be judged "from within," and not by standards imported bodily from life. Is not the very "finer organization of ordinary experiences"[19] which he admits *not* just the "new and different kind of thing"[20] which he denies? How can he maintain that in a poetic unity values do not become "poetised"? And this without postulating any isolated "aesthetic faculty" on the subjective side. And yet, on the other hand, as against Mr. Bell's point of view, how can we step suddenly out of life and cut ourselves off from it? Surely here are avoidable misunderstandings? Surely the exploration of what Mr. Bradley calls "the underground connection" between art and life will afford some clue to the mystery?

[18] *Ibid.*, p. 236.
[19] *Ibid.*, p. 16.
[20] *Ibid.*, p. 16.

I propose to investigate a problem which has at least an important bearing on a number of these questions. I shall enquire: (1) What the term "subject-matter" may mean, (2) what "evil" content means, (3) what is meant by "significance" and its degrees, and (4) what is meant by "expression" and *its* degrees. (5) Finally, I shall discuss how "significance" and "expression" bear upon Beauty and Ugliness and *their* degrees, with a view to showing especially how significance is intrinsic to beauty.

1. SUBJECT-MATTER

The term "subject-matter" (of a work of art) may mean three distinct things. In the first place, it may mean the external objects or events, or the ideas or feelings, which stimulated the artist to express the particular happenings which moved him, without which the particular work of art would not have been produced. This I propose to call *"primary subject-matter."* The landscape is the primary subject-matter of the picture. Lucy's death was the primary subject-matter of Wordsworth's poem *Lucy*, the idea of Duty the primary subject-matter of his *Ode*. An indeterminate feeling of *joie-de-vivre* or of sadness may be the primary subject-matter of a lyric or a piece of music. By primary subject-matter I mean facts, either external or mental, regarded as independent of all aesthetic interest, which do nevertheless occasion aesthetic feeling and aesthetic expression. The term "primary" here has, of course, no connection with "primary" in the phrase "primary qualities." It is not the bare physical world independent of the conscious organism which is primary subject-matter, but the concrete world of which the artist is ordinarily aware, although he is not at the instant *aesthetically* interested in it. Anything whatever which is going to interest aesthetically an artist, or which, when it is interesting to him, or has interested him, can be thought of as the independent occasion of his aesthetic interest, a thing unqualified by his interest, is primary subject-matter. It is called "subject-matter" because it has a connection with the subsequent work of art. But our interest in it is interest rather in history or in biography than in aesthetic fact. For this reason primary subject-matter is not of central interest in aesthetics, though, as I shall show, it is important to distinguish it just because it is liable to be confused with what is of central importance. Because primary subject-matter is historical or biographical it is not possible to discover it *in* the work of art, though examination of the work may in many cases give us a good idea of what it was. The latter is truer of the more "representative" arts, like painting and sculpture or poetry. If a landscape or a person is "represented" [21] in visual form or by means of words, we suppose that facts in *some* degree similar were what stimulated the artist. In so supposing we leave behind for the time being our aesthetic experience. In less representative arts like music and architecture, on the other hand, the primary subject-matter is often quite impossible to determine—which is to the advantage of our aesthetic souls. All we know is the unique and complete aesthetic fact of the music or the architecture which gives no hint at all of a subject outside itself. Even the artist himself may find it impossible to tell what it was. We need not, however, conclude from this that primary subject-matter was non-existent. We must suppose that the beginning of every aesthetic experience has an extra-aesthetic occasion, whether it be the clear apprehension of a well-defined object or the most elusive of feelings.

Primary subject-matter is called "subject" matter because it does *awaken* aesthetic interest, though it is defined as being unqualified by aesthetic interest. As soon as aesthetic interest is awakened the object of interest loses its aesthetic neutrality and becomes aesthetically qualified. The object so qualified I am going to call secondary subject-matter.

I cannot here consider fully what is meant by "aesthetic" in "aesthetically qualified." Part of what I intend by the term will appear under the heading of "expression." But the most essential characters of the "aesthetic" may be summed up thus: (1) an object to be experienced aesthetically must be a particular apprehended through the senses, either directly, as in perception, or indirectly, through images. Things which cannot be apprehended through perception or through images, *i.e.*, concepts, must be particularized, must be translated into terms which *can* be perceived or imaged. "Duty" for Wordsworth is not the "duty" of the moral philosopher, but becomes the "Stern Daughter of the Voice of God." In apprehending a mathematical demonstration as "beautiful," we perceive or image it as a particular, having symmetry, completeness, expressiveness, internal relevance, and so on. (2) The particular

---

[21] I do not mean "copied": see below, *passim.*

object to be apprehended aesthetically must be (a) contemplated, and (b) contemplated as something which on account of its sensuous and formal nature is itself interesting. It must be regarded as apart from what Clutton Brock used to call "the relation of use" and for a reason quite other than that of interest in practice. (3) The interest other than that of practice for the sake of which the perceived (or imagined) object is regarded is interest in *expressiveness*. The aesthetic percipient is interested in colours and shapes, sounds and tunes and harmonies, because they appear to him to express what cannot literally be contained in their make-up as mere existents. He apprehends them "imaginatively," as the phrase goes, and whilst his attention is focussed upon the interesting qualities and forms of the perceived or imaged object which is contemplated, his mind is aware of affective meanings immediately suggested by the object. The object becomes in some sense *symbolic*, though the symbolism is intrinsic to the object at the aesthetic moment and does not distract his attention beyond it. If this important proviso is kept in mind, we may say that the curving tree stem comes to *mean* what it *is* not: the hollow noise of the drums becomes expressive of eerie fatality. Lucy will become Nature's darling

> "And beauty born of murmuring sound
> Shall pass into her face."

The ways in which this expressiveness works we shall have briefly to consider later.

Subject-matter apprehended aesthetically is "secondary" subject-matter. Sometimes the process stops here, as in the case of the man who is aesthetically sensitive but who is not an artist. Here is "imagination" which does not work itself out or even discover itself fully. With the artist, on the other hand, the apprehension of secondary subject-matter is the first stage of a continuous aesthetic process which ends in the production of a work of art which has a subject-matter intrinsic to it, which I am going to call "tertiary" subject-matter, or, simply, the "content" of the work. The artist, in the first place, apprehends his world excitedly, and in so doing unwittingly qualifies it. If he is a landscape painter he modifies, often unconsciously, that which he sees, as he sees it, so that it comes to satisfy him more, to be more "expressive" of what he feels. What is thus modified in the (imaginative) seeing is secondary subject-matter. But this is not the end. The artist desires more. He desires to make his vision permanent, to enlarge and to enhance it, and to communicate it, it may be, to a possible society. Into his artist's mind instinctively come flooding images of the sensa and forms of the sort appropriate to the medium in which he is accustomed to work. Into the poet's mind come words and phrases and rhythms and rhymes. The painter walks about jerkily; he is painting in imagination (painting, be it noted, which is possible only in the imagination of one who has painted in actuality, who knows the "feel" of his pigments and his canvas). From painting in imagination to painting in the external world is but a step. But it is an important step. For as soon as he begins to manipulate his material, his material begins to manipulate him—though if he is a master he keeps control and allows himself to follow the suggestions of his material only in so far as they conduce to the imaginative enlargement and enrichment of his aesthetic scheme as a whole. Artistic expression is no act of "pure" mind, but a process of progressive discovery through manipulation of a real stuff.[22] And, if this is so, it follows that artistic expression is never complete until it is worked out into a self-fulfilling whole in a material. This whole is the work of art. The *content* of this whole, which cannot be fully experienced until the expression in a material is unified and completed,[23] is "tertiary" subject-matter. Tertiary subject-matter is subject-matter imaginatively experienced *in* the work of art, flesh of its flesh, spirit of its flesh, something which cannot be apprehended apart from the work, though theoretically *distinguishable* from its expressiveness.

So much for the distinction between primary, secondary and tertiary subject-matter of the work of art. The distinction is simple, but, I believe, important. If we do not know precisely what we mean when, *e.g.*, we talk of the relation which the "subject" of a picture or a poem has to the work as a whole or to the artist, we shall arrive nowhere. Examples make it clear that "subject" in ordinary usage may refer to several, or to one or two only, of the meanings. The "subject" of a portrait may mean the sitter, or the sitter-aesthetically-seen before painting, or the content-of-the-work. When we talk of the "subject" in music, we mean normally the

[22] On this *see* Alexander, *"Art and the Material."* Also my *Artistic Experience*, *Mind*, N.S. 138.

[23] *Ibid.*

aesthetic subject, secondary (say, a theme suggested or tentatively stated) or tertiary (the content-aspect of the completed work.) When we say "music has *no* subject-matter" we refer to primary subject-matter. It is clear that the difference between the more "representative" arts, such as painting, and the less "representative" ones, such as music, make it now convenient to use the term "content." Whichever is used, the inseparability of content from expression must be firmly maintained.

These distinctions can, of course, only be stated here, and cannot be proved. Two examples of their possible use, *if* valid, may be stated. The first is that imitationism will become impossible as an aesthetic theory. For in the work of art it is tertiary subject-matter, subject-matter imaginatively transformed and worked out, which appears, and never primary subject-matter. The imitation theory implies either that primary subject-matter can be the content of a work of art, or that tertiary subject-matter duplicates primary, which is impossible by hypothesis. In the second place, if our distinction is valid, tertiary subject-matter is through and through *aesthetic* subject-matter, and it will not be possible to say, as Mr. Fry does,[24] that in a [true?] work of art there are certain purely aesthetic elements on the one hand, and certain non-aesthetic elements on the other hand, or to attempt, with Mr. Bell, to isolate purely aesthetic feelings from non-aesthetic feelings which accompany them. It is true, of course, that aesthetic appreciation may be impure, *and* that works of art are often imperfect and do contain mixtures of the aesthetic and the non-aesthetic. This is true even of great works of art. Mr. Fry takes for an example the case of Raphael's "Transfiguration." [25] He is able to point out conflicts of interests. But the trouble is that such a picture, however great, is anything but a perfect work of art. It does not possess single-minded imaginative completeness. My argument is, not that works of art never, in fact, contain non-aesthetic elements, but that the work of art intrinsically in its nature does not do so, and that Mr. Fry and Mr. Bell are wrong when their formalism leads them to suppose that subject-matter is *intrinsically* non-aesthetic. In fact, it happens frequently enough that good art is spoiled by the introduction bodily of elements from real life, that tertiary and primary subject-matter get mixed up.

[24] *Vision and Design*, p. 295.
[25] *Ibid.*, p. 296.

2. THE EVIL AS CONTENT

Two very interesting questions arise, which must be answered here, as on our answers will depend our final view of beauty and ugliness.

The first question I will simply state and answer dogmatically without attempting to discuss it. It is, Must his (secondary) subject-matter have a *positive* value for the artist, or is it possible that what has for him negative value, what is *for him* evil, hideous, repulsive, can inspire his creation? It seems to me on the whole that the answer is that it cannot. That which appears intrinsically evil to the artist may be for him *primary* subject-matter, it may stimulate, or goad, him into expression. But, as soon as the expressive process has begun at all, the value it expresses will be positive, *e.g.*, the expression of the positive thrills of escape, in addition probably to the expression of a positive ideal of which the evil is the negation. The negation suggests the ideal by very contrast, and this, and not the evil, is the true inspiration.

The second question is intimately connected with this, but is quite distinct and totally different from it. It is, Does the fact that *what* is expressed appears to the *critic* to be *evil*, affect the judgment of the critic about the final *beauty* or *ugliness* of the work? Nothing which appears as evil to the artist, we have suggested, can be his secondary subject-matter. To the artist it must be "good." But the artist may be an evil character, he may be morbid or perverted. And we have to remember that his secondary subject-matter is not primary subject-matter, but is inseparable from his interest and is coloured even in the very act of aesthetic apprehension by the quality of his "good" or "evil" interest which is a function of his character. This qualification by the artist's "good" or "evil" interest in the secondary subject-matter (which can only be known by the critic indirectly) applies, of course, equally to tertiary subject-matter. The artist's imaginative selection and fusion of his medium is at every point determined by his interest. The sensitive critic cannot fail to be affected by this interest-impress (by whatever name he calls it) when he views the final product. The question is, If the interest and feelings creatively embodied in the work (*i.e.,* the content) is felt by the critic to be in any way evil (*e.g.,* morbid or perverted), does this fact in itself affect the judgment of beauty or ugliness? Further, is this "feeling" of the critic a merely subjective affair? Is it just one opinion against another? Or is there some standard of good and evil involved? Can we say A. is right and B. is wrong?

The manner of use of the terms "beautiful" and "ugly" is, of course, partly a matter of personal choice. It seems to me, however, that a critic would not, without artificiality and inaccuracy or without some philosophical axe to grind, use the term "beautiful" to describe the expression of content which he genuinely felt to be evil. Expression of what seemed to him to be the delight (not only in filth or disease or deformity or evil but) in anything, by a morbid and evil mind, might be appreciated as excellent aesthetic *expression,* but he would not regard it as beautiful as a whole. He would, rightly, I think, label it as "ugly," its ugliness depending in this case on its content side.[26]

He would rightly label it ugly because he feels thus about its content. But can we say he is *right* in so *feeling* content to be evil? It is not evil to the artist, or, we said, he could not express it. May not the artist be right? *Is* there a "right" and a "wrong" in such things?

It is tempting to mutter "de gustibus . . ." and to leave it there. But that is hardly satisfactory, for in the first place it is hardly so much matter of taste here as of moral sense. The moral at this point certainly does appear to find its way into the aesthetic whole, and in practice every critic makes *claims,* except at the moment when he uncomfortably feels he ought to disclaim claims as "mere feelings." If there *is* a criterion, then, what is it?

I hope, not indeed to offer a criterion, but to ask, in a discussion on "significance," what is meant by saying that ("good" and "evil") meaning and "degrees" of meaning find any place at all in the concrete work of art. In the meantime, two remarks may be made. One is that it is neither the moral philosopher as interested in general concepts of good and evil nor the practical moralist dealing in precepts and rules who are the proper authorities in such matters. It is the critic, whose discriminating aesthetic intuition

---

[26] *See* below, 5. It is probable that this source of ugliness is much less common than that of failure in expression.

enables him alone to apprehend the meaning which is part and parcel of the individual work. The critic is also a moral being, and his sanity of moral judgment both in theory and practice is certainly no disqualification to him as a critic. And the values of ordinary life must affect aesthetic judgment. But general standards cannot be applied bodily to the individual aesthetic unit. Genuine art goes its own way and insists on being judged primarily, as Bradley says, "from within," through feeling first rather than by reasoning. General reasoning, general valuation, may follow later.

The second remark is merely the repetition of a statement of fact. It is, that the critic *does* judge of good and evil, and that there *is* a definite—though perhaps not definable—point below which content appears on the side of evil. This evil is not, as I have just said, identical with what is definable by external canons as evil. Great literature is packed, not only with "immorality," but with immorality "immorally" dealt with, in the sense that the artist's attitude to his creations would, if generalized, provide a bad maxim for others. In itself, however, no matter how by wider moral standards it be adjudged immoral, his work, which is intrinsic to his attitude, may well be felt to have intrinsic value. Blasphemy, infidelity, licentiousness may be, on a wide general theory, evil. But in themselves they *contain* important positive values, and it is these which being expressed aesthetically are felt by the critic to be good. That which is felt to be evil in a work cannot be, then, evil instrumentally, or evil by external standards. It must be felt to be evil, a reflected evil, of the heart, of the inner man, pervert, abominable in itself, intrinsically repulsive. It is when this is felt that we judge (as I have contended) the aesthetic whole to be *ugly* on account of its content. Whether our feeling of intrinsic repulsion is due to pre-existing moral prejudice is not relevant at the moment. The fact is that we do in practice discover a lower limit beyond which is evil, and, consequently, ugliness.

3. AESTHETIC SIGNIFICANCE OR MEANING, AND DEGREES OF THESE

That the feeling of "significance" yielded by the content of the work has some sort of influence upon the critic's valuation of the work, is implied in our assertions about evil content. On the positive side, I fancy that *e.g.* the significance of the (primary) subject, say in works of a more "representative" kind, would be averred by most critics to have something [27] to do with "greatness." There is no necessary connection, of course, between "great" (primary) subjects and great works of art. But sculptors of the age of Pericles not only chose the great—gods and heroes—as their subjects, but the greatness of their subjects inspired them to see greatly. Again, "Waly, Waly" is, I suppose, no more perfect in its own way than is "Under the greenwood tree" in its way, nor the passage where Samson cries

> "O dark, dark, dark, amid the blaze of noon"

than the last lyric of Comus. The expressiveness of the painting of a flower or an insect's wing may be equally, or more, perfect than the cosmic compositions of Michelangelo the sculptor of the Medici Chapel or Michelangelo the painter of the Sistine. A cathedral and a cottage may be equally "good." In all these things there is, we are supposing, a high quality of expression; and there is significance. But the kind or the quality or the level of significance is in each case different. So also may the feeling of different degrees of value and significance arise from the side of expression in *form*. We may feel that a symphony is "great" and "profound" because it works it-self out in a rich expressive totality. For obverse reasons, a short lyrical piece may appear "small." In both these ways arises the sense of "magnificence" or of "smallness." In the words of Longinus, "Nature . . . from the first implanted in our souls an invincible yearning for all that is great, all that is diviner than ourselves. . . . And that is why nature prompts us to admire not the clearness and usefulness of a little stream, but the Nile, the Danube, the Rhine, and, far beyond all, the Ocean." That from some works we get the feeling, not only of the "clearness and usefulness," but of the beauty, of the little stream, that from others we get the feel-ing of the beauty of the Ocean, and that these feelings may arise either from the side of content or from the side of expressive form, is all that for the moment I am suggesting.

But what do the terms "significance" and "meaning" [28] as used

---

[27] Never everything.

[28] I shall take aesthetic "significance" and "meaning" as identical. The former has, perhaps, a more emotive, and the latter a more logical flavour. It may be that the former is more usually appropriate in aesthetics.

in aesthetics imply? I confess I find this most difficult to answer, and I fear that I cannot offer any but the most inadequate remarks.

Of uses other than the aesthetic use, logical implication and perceptual meaning are important. Logical implication and the degrees with which it is grasped by the mind may be illustrated by geometry and by the difference between the schoolboy's and the mathematician's apprehension of a simple Euclidean proposition. The proposition is an integral part of a system and the system bears upon the proposition. For the schoolboy the proposition has a small degree of implicative meaning, because it is comparatively isolated: for the mathematician it has a much greater degree of implicative meaning, for it is apprehended in relation to the system. Similarly, the "meaning" of what we immediately *perceive,* though not objective in the same sense, and conditioned by the need for practical adaptation rather than by logical validity or by truth, lies in its relation to a wider system. The meaning of single words, such as "dead!" or "found!" or "ice!", used in perceptual propositions, lies in their repercussions, not in a system of abstract thought, but in the system of our practical life.

The meaning of an *aesthetic* datum is similar to logical or perceptual meaning in that the datum "implies" (in a metaphorical sense) what is beyond itself, and is for the apprehending subject immediately qualified by the influence of what lies beyond it. But, as perceptual meaning is different from logical implication, so is aesthetic meaning different from both. The aesthetic meaning of a datum is determined neither by an objective system of propositions, nor by practice, but by the values which happen to be affectively relevant to the aesthetic datum of the moment. In speaking of affective relevance we must be clear—and it is of the utmost importance—that our contention is not that it is *mere* feeling which is enjoyed in aesthetic experience. It is things which are felt, expressive forms which can be apprehended only with some effort. Feeling is but the subjective side of a whole subject-object concrete experience, and there is, in what we have said, no implication either of hedonism or of emotionalism. But aesthetic meaning is determined and controlled subjectively by feeling, and the affective value of aesthetic symbols conditions their aesthetic relevance in any given aesthetic unity. The imaginative selection of the artist is based upon a desire to produce a whole with affective value in which the affective value of every element shall bear upon, shall harmonize with, shall reinforce, shall, in the end, help to constitute the affective value of the whole. Round about an interesting theme as the work is being created come clustering new images, new symbols, chosen intuitively because their affective values contribute to, fuse with and enhance the affective meaning of the whole.

What then is meant by greater or lesser "degrees" of significance? It may be that there is an exact answer to this question which applies to all the arts. If there is, I confess that I myself am at the present time quite unable to formulate it. The fact that some works of art are properly felt to be more affectively significant than others of equal merit of expression seems fairly plain, as I have said. And it seems probable that the degree of this (felt) significance is due in some sense to the degree of intrinsic importance which the values which are assimilated affectively into the aesthetic datum do in fact possess for human beings. The values in the aesthetic whole are "aesthetic" values in the sense that experience of them is inextricably bound up with the experience of expressive forms. But it is human beings who have aesthetic experiences, and it is quite impossible to believe that the general fundamental intrinsic moral values of human life do not (by means of assimilation in the mind of the aesthetic experient) affect the judgment of the aesthetic percipient as to what is profoundly significant and what is not. If assimilation is an essential factor in ordinary perception, how can it possibly be lacking in aesthetic perception? Mr. Richards would certainly seem to be right thus far. (He would appear to be as certainly wrong in his denial of such facts as "poetization.") But what all this means in detail it is extremely difficult to say.

Nevertheless it is important to point out two ways (already referred to), distinguishable but always present together, in which affective significance can qualify any given aesthetic experience. One way I shall call, for want of a better word, "intensive," the other way "extensive." I judge a work of art to have "extensively" great significance if my sense of its significance comes from my enjoyment of the great profusion of values which arises immediately out of its elaborate and perfect working out in *form*. A Bach fugue has great "extensive" significance because its meaning is chiefly derived from its elaborate (but never superfluous or ornate) outspreading of complex form. In "intensive" significance, on the other hand, the effect is that of depth which is obtained rather through meditative enjoyment of *affective* value itself. If extensive significance is apprehended through marked interest in structure and form, intensive significance is apprehended rather through marked interest in the feeling-side of what is apprehended. There is no need to repeat again that *mere* affective value cannot be enjoyed, and that feeling is one side of a concrete experience of a formal object. The argument is only that there is *emphasis* on the affective side, an emphasis which is illustrated by the fact that in "intensive" significance the aesthetic enjoyment of sense-data is frequently prominent. Thus in slow music we dwell on the sounds of single notes and chords, and the pauses give us time to enjoy, reflect upon, and "taste" affective meanings. Contrast significance thus derived with that derived from the last part of Bach's "great" G Minor organ fugue. This emphasis (in "intensive" significance) on interest in sense-data is seen in other arts, in colour interest in painting, in word-sound interest in poetry. Intensive significance is also exemplified in the reflective interest in the "subject" (tertiary) of art, as distinct from its form. The danger of too much interest in form is over-intellectuality and "coldness" which renders aesthetic experience impossible. The danger of the other is that we may be led away from form altogether to irrelevant feeling, to the enjoyment of the non-aesthetic emotions of life. We may even sink to emotionalism and sentimentality. The two aspects (and the dangers of each) correspond roughly, I fancy, to "classicism" and "romanticism" (and their dangers).

Let me repeat that, although we have spoken of "intensive" *and* "extensive" significance, these are but aspects differently proportioned in different cases. In true art-experience you cannot have *mere* intellectual interest in formal pattern like the interest in a jig-saw puzzle. The form must "express" something—affective meaning. And, on the other hand, affective meaning which is tasted and enjoyed and dwelt upon must be apprehended through and in form. It is only a matter of stress, and different works of art (and different acts of appreciation) vary in their stress on tension and extension. If they go beyond a certain limit in either direction they cease to be art. Within this limit, however, we *cannot* say either that the "classic" is superior to the "romantic" or *vice versa*. The following diagram may help to show what I mean:—

Non-aesthetic.	Aesthetic Sphere.		Non-aesthetic.
Emotions, interests, and values of life.	Interest more in the effective side. More "intensive" significance. More "subjective." (Romantic?)	Interest more in formal side. More "extensive" significance. More "objective." (Classic?)	Pure intellectual delight in structure and in solving pattern-problems.
	← ——————— Danger.	——————— → Danger.	

4. EXPRESSION AND DEGREES OF EXPRESSION

I wish now to summarize as shortly as I can what I mean by aesthetic expression, with a view to discussing what is meant by "degrees" of expression.

Setting aside, as irrelevant, metaphorical uses [29] of the term "expression," and setting aside also the merely literal sense, "pressing out" (*e.g.*, I "express" the juice of a lemon), there is one kind of "expression" which is of special interest at the outset of our enquiry. This is the manifestation in bodily behaviour of states of mind. The bodily behaviour of Mr. X "expresses" his state of mind for me when from my apprehension of it I can guess (with great probability) the kind of thing which is happening in his mind. The obvious example of this is the expression of the instinctive emotions. To be *contorted* with fear or to *jump* for joy are "expressions" of mental states.

All expression is not aesthetic expression. These spontaneous bodily manifestations of instinctive emotions can surely be called "expressions" with some justification. There is close biological relation between them and mental states. And yet they are quite distinct in character, *e.g.*, from the aesthetic expression (on the *stage*) of the ridiculous old mayor in de Falla's "Three-Cornered Hat." When then does expression become aesthetic expression? The answer, it seems to me, is that it becomes aesthetic when it is carried out for the sake of its felt intrinsic value. If an expression, which at first was automatic, is repeated for the sake of the sheer joy of expression, at that point it becomes aesthetic. In the first case the

[29] *See, e.g.,* Croce, *Aesthetic,* pp. 95 *sq.*

automatic expression was biologically conditioned. In the second
case its condition is not biological but is a conscious or semi-con-
scious desire for the intrinsic delight of expressing. Further, in this
process of repeating an expression for the joy of it, the content of
the expression, *e.g.*, the anger, becomes transformed. Anger enjoyed
in being acted consciously is not mere instinctive anger, but dramatic (sometimes melodramatic) anger, a very different thing. So
the small boy luxuriates in stamping his very small foot.

Expression in bodily activity is the only *direct* aesthetic expression, because only body *directly* expresses mind. But, of course,
aesthetic objects are not limited to bodily activities, to, *e.g.*, dramatic gesture or dancing. If, however, we speak of objects other
than bodily expressions as "expressive," it is important to realize
that they are only expressive by imputation. There is sometimes,
it is true, a continuity between bodily activity and things external
to the body. The lines of a drawing are, *inter alia,* the continua-
tion of bodily gesture; the flute trembles because the breath of life
is breathed into it. But the great majority of art objects cannot
be accounted for in this way. They are called "expressive" because,
for various reasons, their forms (etc.) directly awaken in our minds
the experience of affective meanings. The objects thus come to have
symbolic value for the percipient. In the actual aesthetic experience the mind (in order to experience the affective meanings)
must concentrate its attention on the object, hardly realizing the
part which its own imagination plays. In reality the object, though
absolutely essential, is only half the story. Its aesthetic expressiveness is non-existent apart from its relation to mind.

There are two main ways in which things external to the body
may be "expressive" (by imputation). One kind of expressiveness
arises by reason of their sensuous and their formal nature, the other
arises through fused association. In any aesthetic whole the affective meanings of the parts suggested through these ways will be
affected by the unity of the whole, as we shall see. It is important
to remember this when discussing the expressiveness of entities
out of relation to a context.

Of expressiveness arising from sensuous and formal characters
I will give only an odd example or two. Sense-data such as colours
and sounds are expressive apart from association: the single "clang"
is expressive even by reason of its simple pitch and its intensity.
Add *timbre* and we get the great variety of the expressiveness or

symbolic value of the "rich," "thin," "hollow," "smooth," "rough," "sharp," "piercing." Notes *speak* to the sensitive listener. Of course, the effect is nothing if not physiological; and as a matter of fact no sensation has more "organic resonance" than sound. But the "speaking" of sound is more than this. The notes of the flute, the oboe, the horn, the harp have affective *meaning* which is in part describable, but never fully translatable because inseparable from actual hearing. Colours again appear to be expressive apart from association, depending on quality, saturation, etc. Probably because the physiological effect of colour is less than that of sound the proportion in colour of direct expressiveness to that of expressiveness through association is less. But in both cases the physiological is (a) an essential part, and (b) only a part, of the whole.

When we come to forms, the same general statements are true. Lines, planes, solid figures in the visual sphere and rhythm and tune and harmony in the auditory sphere express the affective meanings which they do express. Lines are "vigorous," are "emphatic," and circles, ellipses, squares and other more interesting plane figures possess affective meanings. The circle, for example, is said to possess a certain serenity, a peacefulness, being a perfect and self-contained whole. (But, of course, the expressiveness of anything is inexpressible except by the one thing which expresses it.) And when we get into cubic dimensions the possibility of the amount of aesthetic expressiveness increases. The pure appeal of architecture is the appeal of the sheer expressiveness of solid shapes. The masses of the ancient Egyptian monument "express" one (affective) meaning, those of the Greek temple another, of the Gothic cathedral another. And so on. If anyone disputes the facts, he must.

Again, there is expressiveness due to fused association. I cannot pause to give examples; they can readily be found. But let me say one thing of essential importance. The associations must be *fused,* and must not, at the aesthetic moment, be consciously distinguishable from the sense-data or forms which awaken them. Associations must be *intrinsic* to the perceptual datum. It must be contemplation of this which gives rise to the fused associations, so that the mere possession of associations by, *e.g.,* a "memento" does not make it an aesthetic object. The memento points away from itself. Through fused association suggested in a work of art, the values of a very wide range of affective meanings can be brought to bear by a skilful artist upon the present object, making it expressive. Poetry is particularly rich in its use of fused association.

If such, stated in a fashion which has scarcely the dignity of baldness, be the sort of thing which expression is, what is meant by "degrees" of expressiveness? That expressiveness can on our theory have different degrees—a view which is denied by Croce— will become apparent in the discussion of the meaning of degrees.

Mr. Carritt, who disagrees with Croce in admitting degrees of expressiveness,[30] distinguishes [31] three senses in which we might speak of degrees of expression. The first is a difference of "extension" and is admitted by Croce (e.g., the difference between a single word and a novel). The second he calls "degrees of expression" (e.g., Keats' revised draft of Hyperion may be more expressive than the earlier draft). Thirdly comes "depth," which consists in the fusion in a whole of "the most elements which, had they existed independently, would have seemed most recalcitrant to expression." Of the first sense, we may say that "difference of extension" may, but need not, involve greater expressiveness. And difference of extension is certainly not identical with difference of expression. The meaning of these statements, and our attitude to Carritt's second and third senses, will appear in the sequel.

Analysing the problem freshly for ourselves, we may begin by dismissing the sense in which "more expressive" means expressive of more significant (tertiary) subject-matter. This we have already discussed.

Perhaps the most important criterion by which degrees of aesthetic expressiveness are measured is that of the clarity, definiteness and unambiguousness of aesthetic meaning expressed. The simplest instances of these are to be found among sense-data and forms. A patch of an attractive colour taken by itself is more "expressive" in this sense than a patch of an uninteresting one. Some shapes, some rhythms, some melodic and harmonic forms express more definitely and clearly and efficiently and completely than others. When we come to the working artist we find that, by a simple alteration here and there of a sound or a colour or a form, he can make his medium *utter* where before it mumbled vague somethings—or nothings.

This magic of clarification is evident enough, when seen, though

[30] Which he (wrongly, to my mind) identifies with degrees of beauty.
[31] *The Theory of Beauty*, pp. 24 *sqq.*

only the artist can achieve it. And along with increased clarity of expression goes increase of aesthetic meaning. The artist working out a complex whole in material form does not merely clarify. There is *growth* as well. We have seen over and over again that, although they may be considered separately, expression and meaning are most intimately related. This is evident, once more, in the fact of the growth of meaning. Not only, as the process proceeds, does the obscure become clear: the material is continually suggesting new symbolism, new meanings to the excited imagination. These become like new living cells to an organism: they enrich meaning, and they may even entirely transform it. The process is creative. It is not a matter of merely unfolding something which is actually there, it is new production and new discovery by the developing synthetic imagination.

It is the growth of meaning—primarily "extensive" meaning—which conditions the assimilation of individually "recalcitrant" elements. Data which were at first "recalcitrant" come to be seen, as the imagination grows heated, as items which will fit into the scheme of the whole and will enhance it. When imagination is on fire everything that it reaches becomes ductile. The most unlikely, and even impossible, subjects become under the artist's dominance willing members of the whole. It is in this triumphant creation of an aesthetic unity that expression is seen at its highest. The highest degree of expressiveness is attained when the artist has so treated each element in his work that its aesthetic meaning in relation to the whole appears to the competent spectator clear and unambiguous.

The masterly fusion of complicated elements in a whole represents the highest stage of artistic endeavour, and involves the highest degree of expressiveness. But it does not therefore follow that the greater the complexity the higher the degree of expressiveness, or that maximum expressiveness implies any special degree of complexity. Complexity affects degree of explicit extensive significance, as we have seen, but it has no special relation to degree of expressiveness. The shortest, simplest lyric may be perfectly expressive, *i.e.*, may possess the highest degree of expressiveness, of its simple content, if it is unambiguous, unified, complete. Its extensive significance will be less *profound* than a more complex work which is also perfectly expressive (though its *intensive* significance may be much greater). But if in its expressiveness it is perfect, how can we say that it has less than the highest degree of expressiveness? This, I imagine, is in harmony with current usage.

*In*expressiveness means confusion and disharmony of aesthetic meaning within a given whole. But, because a whole (perfect) work of art is perfectly expressive, it must not be assumed that a part of it is necessarily imperfectly expressive. The distinction between perfect expressiveness and imperfect expressiveness is not in essence parallel to the distinction between aesthetic whole and part. The part of a work of art *may* be imperfectly expressive. Or it may not. If you take a picture and cut it into squares, or if you divide a nocturne or a lyric arbitrarily into little bits, the chances are that the expression of the bits will be incomplete. On the other hand, select your parts, and you may get the opposite result. A face in a portrait, a movement in a sonata, one view of a piece of sculpture or of a building, a passage in a poem, all these may be, *taken by themselves*, completely expressive. If we think of them in relation to the larger whole from which they are taken, they may appear incomplete. And if we go on to rejoin them to their contexts they form expressive parts of larger wholes with a "larger" extensive meaning. But subordinancy to an aesthetic whole does not imply intrinsic imperfection.

5. BEAUTY AND UGLINESS, AND THEIR DEGREES

We have now discussed separately the ideas of significance and of expression—two inseparable but distinguishable aspects of one thing—and have found that there are degrees of each. How does this affect the question of the *beauty* and *ugliness* of the aesthetic whole of which they are the aspects? What of degrees of beauty and ugliness?

In the first place, it follows from what we have said that since for us aesthetic significance exists as well as aesthetic expressiveness, and is as fundamental as aesthetic expressiveness, the maximum degree of expression in any given case is not sufficient to constitute the maximum degree of beauty, is not identical with it. Significance must also be taken into account. But neither can significance stand alone. If we do say, as we may, that the profoundest aesthetic significance does *imply* the "greatest" beauty, this is not because significance and beauty are identical any more than expression and beauty are identical, but only because the profoundest aesthetic significance implies complete and perfect expression. Perfect expression, we saw, does not imply the profoundest significance. In speaking of degree of beauty, then, significance and expression are inseparably married: but the marriage is of the old-fashioned kind. For significance is the husband, in the Pauline sense. It is the head of the wife.

Let us now consider, as shortly as we can, some important cases of the problem of the relation of content-value (that judged "evil" as well as that judged "good") to expression. For us the concrete aesthetic object lacks beauty (or is in some sense ugly), not only if there is some failure of expression, but if the content is evil, if it is judged to have negative value. Above this level, beauty is not prevented, but is rendered less significant, by less significant content.

Formally there are the following possibilities:—

Content-value.	Expression.
1. Good.	1. Perfect.
2. Good.	2. Imperfect.
3. Evil.	3. Perfect.
4. Evil.	4. Imperfect.

In the above table "good" means any degree of significance judged [32] by the competent aesthetic percipient to have positive and not negative value. Evil means any degree of significance judged to have intrinsically negative value. Perfect expression has already been described: "imperfect" includes any degree of failure.

The important conclusions are as follows:—(1) The highest beauty will be constituted, as has been said, by the highest degree of aesthetic significance [33] with positive value, perfectly expressed. (2) Anything less than the highest degree of positively valuable significance perfectly expressed will imply a lesser degree of beauty. But, it should be observed, not therefore a degree of *ugliness.* An

[32] Note: only judged, nothing more. The judgment *claims* to be objective. Whether it is truly so or not is, of course, extremely difficult to decide in actual instances, and requires caution and open-mindedness. The principles of how the critic ought to decide I am, fortunately, not concerned with here.

[33] "Intensive" or "extensive." This is implied in what follows unless otherwise stated. Neither, it will be remembered, can be regarded as superior to the other.

aesthetic object is not beautiful or ugly because its significance is not profound. As we saw, the smallest lyric may be perfectly beautiful without being highly significant. (3) *Extensive* significance imperfectly expressed involves not simply a lesser degree of beauty, but a degree—it may, of course, be a small one—of ugliness. (4) If *intensive* significance, even of the most profound kind, is relied upon to move the spectator, to the detriment of perfect expression of significance, or if there is any attempt to substitute intensive significance for expression, if, in a word, intensive significance begins to be derived not from expression in formed sense-data, but from some source external to art, the result, however valuable otherwise, is some degree of disruption of expression, and therefore some degree of ugliness. (5) Any degree of significance judged negatively valuable, however perfectly expressed, involves judgment of the final unit as ugly, and, if we admit degrees of evil, the more evil, the more ugliness will the whole unit possess on account of its content. These are the most important cases.

It is difficult to know what absolute ugliness means, as it is difficult to know what absolute beauty, or absolute anything, means. In terms of our distinctions, content judged absolutely evil, and absolute inexpressiveness, would each be sufficient to condition ugliness. But in practice absolute evil, I suppose, is as meaningless to us as absolute good.

So, too, it is difficult to give meaning to absolute inexpressiveness. When we look at anything aesthetically, however ugly, our imagination has already modified its appearance, for the most part quite subconsciously. Two kinds of situation may, I think, arise: (1) If the scene is one in which we are, otherwise than aesthetically, not interested either positively or negatively (*e.g.*, a haphazard conglomeration of lights, shadows and colours), or if it is one to which our general predisposition is rather favourable (*e.g.*, natural landscape [34] or a house which has been our home), our tendency in aesthetic mood is to idealize what we see and by alteration in imagination to make the inexpressive and unsuggestive expressive and suggestive, so that it appears at least as partially, or in some respects, beautiful. It is at least impossible to say of such a scene, "Nobody can or ever will find any beauty or any expressiveness in it."

2. If, on the other hand, our general predisposition to a scene is unfavourable, as when we see a hideous factory or warehouse or

[34] I do not now discuss whether Nature, if left to herself, is ever ugly.

rows of "artistic" villas screaming and sprawling over the country-side, then we are not inclined to idealize. We feel that wrong has been done. Our attitude in looking at such objects is still aesthetic. We regard them in the light of an idea and imagine what might have been had sensitiveness and good taste ruled. But this time the ideal is set up by way of contrast, which makes sheer stark ugliness stand out. We see the facts as they are; our aesthetic vision implies in this case, not a virtual creation of the object as expressive, but the presence of an ideal of beauty which makes inexpressiveness greater.

These, then, in a summary way, are our conclusions about the relations of significance and expression to beauty and ugliness. If they are valid, it seems to me that we ought to be more careful in our terminology than we sometimes are. It is hardly sufficient to talk simply of "degrees of beauty." When, as critics, we say, "X has a higher degree of beauty than Y," we ought, I think, to state as far as we can (*not* that the content or the expression is "beautiful," but) how much X and Y satisfy in respect of significance, and how much they satisfy in respect of expressiveness. We must not say "more significant *and* more beautiful" as if significance and beauty were separate units to be added, any more than we must say "more expressive *and* more beautiful." We must say "more greatly beautiful because more *significant*," or "more perfectly beautiful because more perfectly *expressive*," measuring by the ideal, which is the profoundest significance embodied perfectly through expression.

The case which I have tried to defend is that significance is not an extra-aesthetic consideration, but that it enters, if properly regarded, into the very tissue of beauty, and constitutes half—and the dominant half—of its nature. I have discussed expression also. That this enters intrinsically into beauty is not much in dispute in contemporary thought. The importance of significance is disputed, very much.

The Paradox of Aesthetic Meaning

LUCIUS GARVIN

THAT WORKS OF ART may possess a meaning is as readily assumed in some quarters as it is vigorously denied in others. There are those who define "art appreciation" as apprehension of the art object's meaning, and in their hands the term "meaning" receives an honorific connotation as referring to that experience the grasping of which is the highest goal of aesthetic aspiration. There are others who look with profoundest suspicion on any attribution of meaning to an art work, on the ground that such attribution does violence to the aesthetic purity and unity of the art experience. In the presence of such sharp divergence of opinion, one is naturally led to suppose that these two groups are employing the term "meaning" in somewhat different senses. It may be instructive to examine, with a view to determining their legitimacy, some of the senses in which meaning has been predicated of works of art.

The question arises whether, in the case of both of the groups just alluded to, the meaning in question is construed as one of a special aesthetic kind. It may be assumed that such is the clear intention of those who consider the "appreciation" of the art work's meaning to be the unique aesthetic achievement. In the case of the second group, since their position can hardly be to deny that non-aesthetic meanings may be found in works of art by those who choose to look for them, it would seem to follow that it is the interpretation of meaning as an aesthetic category to which they take exception.

Non-aesthetic meanings of works of art may be divided roughly into three main kinds. First of all, there are those cases in which by "giving the meaning" of a work of art is meant offering something in the nature of iconographic explanation or symbol interpretation. It will here be taken for granted without further discussion that concern with the understanding of such matters as the symbolic signification of a lion or the religious import of an ecclesiastical gown or a pontifical gesture is extra-aesthetic. The second and third kinds of non-aesthetic meanings of works of art may be termed "historical." The one has to do with the significance of the work of art as related to its author, with its revelation of the psychological forces, biographical incidents, and special motivations that determined the character of the product. The other has to do with the significance of the work of art in its relation to the social and ideological milieu from which it springs and whose currents and characteristics, both manifest and latent, it registers. Again the tracing out of such meanings is the concern rather of the biographer, the moralist, the psychoanalyst, the cultural historian, than of the aesthetic contemplator. It is not, of course, claimed that the classes of meanings just described are mutually exclusive, for they are not determined by a single *fundamentum divisionis*. Nor is it contended that the classification is exhaustive, but only that most of those meaning-references that are patently extra-aesthetic fall under one or another of these three rubrics.

When we turn to the question of the meaning of meaning as *aesthetically* qualifying a work of art, we are brought up sharply by an apparently invincible dilemma. The difficulty is that when we speak of the meaning of anything, reference is implied, on the generally accepted theory of symbolization, to a referent, connotational or denotational, which the thing means. Assuming that it makes semantic nonsense to suppose that anything may mean itself, we are forced to conclude that the meaning of a work of art must lie outside itself. Now this is unobjectionable when the meaning happens to be non-aesthetic. But if it is aesthetic meaning we are dealing with, then, it may be held, we are, by our conclusion, committing aesthetic suicide. For if anything may be said to exist

as common ground in the maelstrom of current aesthetic controversy, it is the doctrine of the self-enclosed character of the art
object. To transgress the boundaries of the work of art is to destroy "aesthetic immediacy." Thus, we are told by MacLeish that
a poem should not mean, but be. If meaning is to be aesthetic, then,
it must perforce remain within the object. But in that case, paradoxically, it ceases to be meaning—or at least meaning meant by
the object.[1]

There is, of course, one alternative here. Abandoning, for the
time being, the attempt to make intelligible the notion of the aesthetic meaning *of* the art object, we may look for aesthetic meaning *within* the art object. One *part* of the object may, for example,
be said to symbolize or mean another part. Such, indeed, is the
doctrine of those who include associative factors along with the
material and formal factors in a painting, and of those who distinguish between the texture (free detail) and structure (logical
thought) of a poem.[2]

Poetry may best serve the purposes of our analysis here, for it
is an art medium which is ordinarily admitted to possess meaning. Except in such rare instances as Dadaism, the words and
phrases of the poem are not taken as completely opaque, but as
bearing some connotation. Most poems, that is to say, have subject matter. But such subject matter or meaning, when treated aesthetically, is not, in strictness, the meaning of the poem in the
sense that it is something external to the poem that the poem symbolizes. It is the very stuff of the poem; not the whole stuff, but
a part which enters into and fuses with the phrases and words
and their assonances and rhythms to constitute the poem as an
aesthetic organism.

It is a curious fact that many theorists, who are by no means
prepared to accept a poetry of pure sound-pattern, nevertheless
resist, by various dogmas and devices, the admission of meaning
into poetry even in this manner. One such dogma is based on the
distinction between the "what" and the "how" of expressed mean-

[1] This difficulty is noted by L. W. Beck in an article on "Judgments of Meaning
in Art," *The Journal of Philosophy*, Vol. XLI (1944), p. 172. His solution is to
make the art object's significance consist of "meaning without the meant" (*ibid.*,
p. 175). I shall discuss this position in a subsequent footnote.

[2] See Walter Abell, *Representation and Form* (Charles Scribner's Sons, 1936);
John Crowe Ransom, *The New Criticism* (New Directions, 1941).

ing, or the "referential" and the "evocative" uses of language, the poet being described as being concerned, in each case, with the latter and not with the former. Now the evocation of feelings, as distinguished from, say, classification or proof, is unquestionably the primary preoccupation of the artistic spirit, but feelings are associated with the "what" as well as (or, better, as fused with) the "how," with meanings *referred to* by the poetic medium. If it be objected that such meanings, even if they be admitted as elements within the art object, are not the aesthetic, but the logical referents of the language symbols, the reply is that they are aesthetic just to the extent that they are treated aesthetically. There is no way of fixing the boundaries of the aesthetic object except in terms of the field of attention staked out by artistic or contemplative perception.[3] Aesthetic objects are not such in virtue of any objective, definitive qualities that they independently display. They are subjectively determined by selective contemplative interest. The aesthetic is where you find it, though doubtless it cannot be found everywhere and the object must be of a sort to invite and not repel contemplation. For this reason, it would be preferable, perhaps, to speak, not of poetry, but of the poetic—meaning a linguistic complex such as tends to invite aesthetic contemplation. Though we may wish, for technical or academic reasons, to retain certain conventional marks as the features *sine quibus non* of poetry, the heart of poetry is not the one that it wears upon its sleeve.

It follows that meanings in the poem will be aesthetic meanings insofar as they are part of the total field of aesthetic regard, that is, insofar as they are attended to, not with a view merely to understanding or using or proving them, but with a view to contemplating them for what they may contribute to the aesthetic import of the whole to which they belong. It is, accordingly, not necessary to protect the aesthetic individuality of such meanings by interpreting them in a special or recondite way. For example: Philip Wheelwright's proposal[4] that we should distinguish logical or literal statements from poetic statements by the fact that the former assert

---

[3] One can never, of course, be quite sure of an artist's intent, but if a painter labels a semi-abstraction "Pink Slipper," it may be supposed that he means to introduce that associative element into the art object; otherwise he can be thought only waggish or perverse.

[4] In an article "On the Semantics of Poetry," *The Kenyon Review*, Vol. II (1940), pp. 263–283.

"heavily" and the latter "lightly," is interesting and suggestive, but the idea of the "fragility" of poetic statements serves less as a description of an inherent property of poetry than as a warning sign admonishing the poet against a treatment of his subject that would frustrate the purely contemplative attitude. It is true that the paraphrastic rendering of a poem will appear, in comparison with its poetic embodiment, artificial and bare. It is also true that the "paraphrastic core" is never more than the core—it is never the whole poem, but is integrated with its mode of expression in the poem in an untranslatable manner. It does not follow, however, that the paraphrastic meaning, because it receives a special treatment in the poem, is not, for that reason, the same sort of entity which might comport truth or falsehood, conviction or doubt, if it ceased to be dealt with aesthetically in its poetic context.

Another proposed limitation on the kind of meanings admissible in a poem takes the form of a requirement that the meanings should be connotative and never denotative. Thus we are told by Sidney Zink that the poetic statement makes no reference to external entities. Its meaning may, it is true, "depend for its nature on prior experience of such external instances," but such reference is "not the function of the statement in the poem." Rather "its poetic reference is to other poetic meanings with which it is aesthetically organized." [5] Meanings do not qualify "an objective referent; they qualify each other." [6] That the rejection of denotative references is not confined to poetry is illustrated by a quotation from Helen Knight, who, after generalizing that "there is no obstacle to cooperation between an experience of abstract meaning and an aesthetic experience," says of the prophetic zeal and energy expressed by Donatello's "Youthful John the Baptist," "if we are to have an experience of meaning which will cooperate with an aesthetic experience, we must not relate the zeal and energy to incidents in John the Baptist's history, nor even definitely to John the Baptist himself; we must simply experience them as we might experience the serenity of a peaceful evening by a deserted sea." [7] Finally, in further illustration of the denial of straightforward denotative reference in art, we may cite L. W. Beck's thesis that aesthetic meaning is connotative because it is not restricted to any *single* denotative

[5] "Poetry and Truth," *The Philosophical Review*, Vol. LIV (1945), p. 144.
[6] "The Poetic Organism," *The Journal of Philosophy*, Vol. XLII (1945), p. 424.
[7] "Aesthetic Experience in Pictorial Art," *The Monist*, Vol. XL (1930), p. 79.

application. Music, for example, is not confined to any one particular narrative pattern, so that when its "structure is organized in
such a way as to make it conform obviously to one particular denoted circumstance, we get program music with a denotative meaning, the interpretation of which leads us away from the medium and
thus reduces the pure aesthesis." [8]

The purpose of these proposed proscriptions upon denotative
meanings is clear and understandable. The internal unity and the
qualitative individuality of the art work, it is felt, must be saved
at all costs. The question is, however, whether the costs are not
too high and are not really unnecessary. Let us reckon further with
these costs.

In the first place, is it true that unless meanings are confined to
the purely connotative, the unity of the art work is dissipated? Is
it impossible for John the Baptist—the historical, actual John the
Baptist—to appear as a denotative meaning-reference in an art
work, painting, or poem? To be sure, he cannot appear as a biological existent in the physical art medium, but it is he, and not
some phantasm or some description connoting him, that is represented by the artist as displaying zeal and energy. A search of documentary sources to determine the accuracy of this ascription or
to determine the historicity of John himself, or even a wondering
if such sources existed, would obviously be a deviation from an
aesthetic employment of the art work. But it is possible to be concerned with an existent without being concerned with its existence. And even in an art work, where the primacy of the qualitative
dimension must inevitably be acknowledged, the substance-quality
dichotomy is scarcely to be discarded. Thus, Dr. Zink's remark, in
connection with the poetic reading of Eleanor Wylie's metaphor
describing water lilies as being "smooth as cream," to the effect
that "the lily qualifies the smoothness virtually to the same degree

---

[8] *Op. cit.*, p. 177. In this article, referred to in an earlier footnote, Dr. Beck
applies his theory of non-denotative or ambiguously denotative meaning to the
entire art object, including both the sensuous and formal and the associative
aspects, and by so doing considers that he has solved the dilemma mentioned in
the fourth paragraph of our discussion. For, he believes, on his theory meaning
has been retained along with aesthetic immediacy. It may be questioned, however, whether ambiguous or indeterminate reference really dispenses with a
referent. Indeterminate reference may be connotative and not denotative, but
to say that a reference is connotative is to say that a connotation is symbolized,
and such a connotation transcends its symbol. Hence, the dilemma remains.

that smoothness qualifies the lily," [9] suggests the puristic extremes
to which the connotational program may be carried. Doubtless
Dr. Zink does not mean that in reading a poem we are entering
a metaphysical jungle where "connotative" shadows are cast, not
by substances, but by other "connotative" shadows. However, even
on a more charitable interpretation, the view under criticism does
appear to involve an unnatural and unnecessary constriction of the
realm of poetic discourse. It is true that when the aesthetic contemplator enters into the region of denotation he is wandering on
dangerous ground and that only the most consummate artist would
dare to guide him there, but it is surely not impossible, under such
guidance, to hew to the straight aesthetic line without slipping into
the quicksands of practical or cognitive concerns. If aesthetic contemplation of particular existents in nature is possible, it should
be possible likewise when these existents are combined with other
elements into an artistic totality.

It is to be noted that images are also particular existents and not
connotative meanings. Are they, then, to be eliminated from poetic
perception? Reader-writer commerce by so subjective an agency
as imagery is notoriously a risky transaction, but the proper pre-
scription is not the elimination of the imagery, but its control
through the leadings of the poetic medium. In the case of music,
imagistic accompaniments are regarded with even greater mistrust,
for example, by Dr. Beck, because they tend to reduce the "pure
aesthesis." But what is necessarily rendered impure, in the case,
say, of program music, is not the aesthesis, which *may* remain un-
contaminated, but the aesthetic object. Such "impurity," however,
is only a matter of complexity of internal organization which, for
the disciplined listener, may serve to enrich rather than impoverish
the musical experience.

Let us turn now from discussing meaning *within* the art object
to essaying a solution to the problem broached earlier, that of finding an aesthetic meaning for the art object as a whole that will not
lead us away from that object. The answer is one that may appear
to take liberties with the term "meaning," but it need not be thought
to do so if meaning is understood as symbolic reference in its broadest sense. The solution proposed is as follows: What an art work
means, aesthetically, is simply the feeling-response obtained from

[9] "Poetry and Truth," *op. cit.*, p. 141.

it in aesthetic contemplation. In what way may this position be regarded as effectually resolving the paradoxical element in the notion of aesthetic meaning? Two explanations, either of which, perhaps, is sound, are possible.

The first one calls attention to the point that the emotion obtained, though *actually* outside the object contemplated (namely, in the contemplator), is *phenomenologically* within the object, being perceived as one of its qualities. This view, espoused by Santayana [10] and Ducasse, [11] may be said to permit the transcendence of the object by its meaning, required in symbolic reference, at the same time that it suggests the immanence of the meaning within the perceptual field, required in genuine aesthesis. The other explanation holds whether or not the emotion is considered to be describable as a quality of the object. It simply notes that within the total field of aesthetic awareness there are two discriminable elements, (1) that which is attended to (the object), and (2) that which (1) evokes or symbolizes (the emotion). The latter element transcends the former, so that the requirements of the meaning-relation are met, yet, since each element is internal to the aesthetic consciousness (if in different ways), there is no loss of immediacy.

It will not be possible here to elaborate on the emotionalist aesthetic implied by each of these explanations, except to say a few things about it as it pertains to the problem of aesthetic meaning. Perhaps the chief objection that will be raised against our solution of that problem is that when the spectator or critic of a work of art seeks for its "meaning," he is after something more logical and less ineffable than an emotion. Otherwise the judgment of works of art becomes impressionistic criticism of the most inarticulate sort.

It is, of course, true that "objective" criticism, insofar as it is aesthetic and not historical or technical, must be in terms of those characters and qualities of the art object that are publicly identifiable and expressible. For just this reason, however, it may perhaps be said that such criticism must be indirect and quasi-impressionistic. Direct aesthetic criticism is essentially subjective and is pointed at the emotional nuances evoked by the qualities of the

[10] *The Sense of Beauty*, p. 49.

[11] "The Esthetic Object," *The Journal of Philosophy*, Vol. xxxv (1938), p. 324.

object. But when criticism becomes "objective," it must address itself to the qualities which are the objective correlates of the emotions.

In any event, aesthetic experience, before the critical attitude has been superimposed upon it, is more than attention to the features of the thing experienced. It is more than just inspection, disinterested and neutral. The quite generally accepted identification of aesthetic contemplation with "immediate experience," with simple, undifferentiated, unplotting apprehension, is misleading. The aesthetic attitude is passive and receptive, of course, but it is, to use Gotshalk's phrase, more than "stupid staring." [12] It is staring which is emotionally oriented, inviting the object to present, not just itself, but its charm or its repulsiveness, its warmth or its coldness, its special import for the sensibilities. It is not enough to say, as does John Crowe Ransom, that we need merely attend to the object and "let the feelings take care of themselves," since it is "their business to 'respond.'" [13] It is possible to enlist and encourage that response, not, of course, as to its nature, which must be left to the promptings of the object (it is here that the passive character of contemplation is manifest), but as to its incidence and its purity. It is possible, in other words, to look deliberately at the object as the potential symbol or bearer of emotional awareness as yet unrevealed. To approach the art object in this manner is, in a most significant sense, to seek its aesthetic meaning.

[12] "Beauty and Value," *The Journal of Philosophy*, Vol. xxxii (1935), p. 607.
[13] "Criticism as Pure Speculation," *The Intent of the Critic* (Princeton University Press, 1941), p. 96 f. D. A. Stauffer, Ed.

On the Problem of Artistic Form

PAUL STERN

THERE ARE TWO prevalent opinions, apparently quite opposite, on the nature of art: according to the one, the ultimate function of art is to express convincingly some process or condition of the inner life; according to the other, its function is to create images which, by clarity and harmony of form, fulfill the need for vividly comprehensible appearance, which is rarely satisfied by reality. Actually, neither clear representation of external form, nor the expression of an inner life or experience, however achieved, is in itself sufficient to create art; rather, each depends on the other. In the living work of art the two concepts can be separated only by means of an abstractive process, and hence neither one by itself can be judged aesthetically. Form and content are unequivocally coordinated, and any change in one necessarily entails a change in the other. Critical judgment will, indeed, always be restricted to pointing out individual traits of the inward content or the external appearance of a work. Thus one or the other still seems to determine the evaluation of the whole. But even though in criticism we can extract and fix only single elements, in direct artistic judgment we do not lose their interrelation, nor forget the whole from which we separate them.—The Dionysian and the Apollonian elements,

as deified basic forces of human existence, lead to art only con-
jointly: the deepest fulness of life must be made apprehensible to
sense, and, at the same time the clearly apprehensible must sensibly
express the truest vitality, if real art is to come into being.

II

For the layman who wants to be artistically elevated, edified or
delighted, the inner vital feeling expressed in art is the most important aspect. Some movements in art can, in fact, be characterized by their intrinsic directedness toward the world, or the nature
of the vital feeling conveyed by them, even if their aesthetic credo
places more emphasis on the formal aspects of their products. The
general public, insofar as it follows art movements, almost always
goes by the content. Unbridled passion, severe and unapproach-
able greatness, and expectation trembling with tender restraint,
will ever find not so much true admirers as partisans, who are
artistically moved only where they find a reflection of what they
themselves are keyed to at the moment.

Even the creative artist often has difficulties in freeing himself
from this orientation towards a "movement," a one-sidedness that
probably goes hand in hand with the intensity of his inner development, mainly under the spell of technical experiences and preferences, from which he finally advances to firm aesthetic demands.
Assuming or accepting without reflection the inner experiences
which are part of artistic creation, as creator he aims at clarity and
intrinsic balance in his work. The obstacles he encounters in his
work force him to seek solutions. If he is a thinker, he will try
to deduce and formulate his problems and solutions in the light
of more general ideas: the content that struggles for expression
takes second place beside the means through which it is to find
expression, the audible or visible elements of the external world
in the treatment and deployment of which his artistic drive manifests itself. His aesthetic philosophy is thereby delineated. Every
truly great artist, everyone who as a result of his attitude toward
art in the narrower sense has not lost sight of the more extensive
profusion of human potentialities, among which the pathos of
dominating thought must not be wanting, has sensed these aspects
of his mission: To ascertain what is accessible to his formative in-

fluence; to encompass its aims in *one* glance; to capture the ever recurring, ever paramount features of successful renderings, recognize their dependence on the laws, and to establish them by clear thought. This pathos, however, is easily lost, especially by the artistic individual. Such a lack he may even proudly call "instinctiveness." But "instinct," as it is defined in such a context, is a very positive assuredness of inner decision in judgment, attitude, and action which shows up precisely in his thinking—for thinking is, in the final analysis, an action as much as is artistic creation; only where instinct is weak does thought remain without support. True thinking relies on instinct and must be able to rely on it. Whoever fears he will alienate himself from his instinct by thought indicates that either his thinking or his instinct or both are inadequate.

III

Yet, the attitude toward the technique of his art in the widest sense which characterizes the artistically creative and thinking individual causes him easily to underestimate the internal content in his evaluation and critique of the work of art; he is in a measure content with a good piece of work when inner conventionality or even lifelessness of the work should demand rejection. The principles that govern his work, the rules he has imposed on himself, easily become the criteria for judging the artistic achievement as such. This may appear justified where an offence against reasonable rules indubitably is to be measured against the result to be judged. But one thing cannot remain hidden on closer inspection: that the observance of a formal principle, a rule, can never *per se* guarantee an artistic result. It may be a necessary condition for artistic success, but it is not a sufficient one. Not *that* a rule is followed, but *how* it is followed, makes a work of art.

The reason for this is that theory can treat only one by one, or perhaps in pairs, the elements of an art, that is to say the "dynamic factors" with which it operates, and which function in its works (as in painting the tone, color, line, plane, space, volume). But artistic workmanship can combine these factors at will and vary their importance. Each of them has its specific effect and its own laws, can be moved to the foreground or can recede and yield its importance. And finally, each one of them will contribute more or

less to each work of art and must therefore be organically attuned
to the whole. In this process every one of these dynamic factors
is more or less important to each of the others, each serves to accentuate or clarify one of the others or the whole. Yet none is merely
subservient, each one always has its own say, its own value in the
structure of the work. The mere line of an artist, measured by élan
or quiescence, pressure or delicacy, can in itself unfold a profusion of values—shading, arabesque, perspective, shape, or movement. Color and shading accentuate partitions of the plane, and
simultaneously give compelling direction to shadow and light, and
consequently also to the three-dimensional image; this in turn reveals to the mind's eye more or less distinctly a set-up characterized
by lightness or heaviness, by rest or motion.

IV

The practical aesthetics a creative artist can thus develop would
finally lead to a systematic comprehension of all the "dynamic
factors" of each art. But therewithal, the emerging image will always be characterized only from the outside, and relative to the
stages of an increasing insight. Yet it is essential for the aesthetic
view that all external elements are felt directly as an embodiment
of something internal, as expressions of a certain condition of inner
life as a state or as an action, in rest or in motion. After all, tables
and chairs, too, have their own kind of livingness for the artist's
eye. But whether this intrinsic life be embodied concretely—(by
being represented in natural existence or happening)—or abstractly
—(as in a graphic arabesque or a decorative, colorful ornament)—
it must always be the pervasive keynote in the treatment and combination of the given external factors and stages. Whoever wants
to judge the beauty or uglines of an image must, therefore, start
from the external impression, but constantly try to deepen his perception to such a point that what he perceives appears as the vehicle
of a certain kind of inner vitality.

A plastic form, viewed from an external and technical standpoint,
may be ever so richly "apparent," ever so well executed in color
and line,—but if it lacks that precise attunement of all "dynamic
factors" to the keynote which only feeling can furnish and hold,
then the whole artistic effort is in vain. This attunement to a single

keynote is the really essential element in the domain of the several dynamic factors themselves. Where it is wanting, the impression of a unified whole cannot be achieved and the parts lack direct and convincing relation to one another. No externally devised methods to circumvent this basic failure will ever be able to mark the extent of available artistic possibilities, let alone exhaust them. The crucial point is always the relevance of all the factors and their sub-factors to the one inner vital feeling. This is what determines the judgment of every true art critic, spontaneously and instinctively. Nothing but the application of this principle to the totality of possible "dynamic factors" can give the old, vague demand for harmony in a work of art a really useful meaning. Here and only here, furthermore, lies the otherwise wholly elusive criterion of an organic or teleological element in a work of art, of the "unity in variety" by which people formerly sought to evaluate it, or of the perfection of "form," which nowadays they like to stress in seeking to determine artistic values.

v

It is only when all the factors of an image, all their individual effects, are completely attuned to the one intrinsic vital feeling that is expressed in the whole—when, so to speak, the clarity of the image coincides with the clarity of the inner content—that a truly artistic "form" is achieved. Hence the vividly expresed form of this or that image must not be regarded as the essence of artistic form as such: even though, on the other hand, clear apparency must be acknowledged as a prerequisite for artistic effectiveness. The emergence of the "image" is the most essential intermediate station on the way to a deepening perception which finally leads to comprehension of the vital content.

Still less should one confuse artistic form with some sort of pattern, although we must remember that there is often great artistic wisdom contained in conventional schemata, which are even, in some measure, really essential to comprehension of art. But any such pattern is generally more or less adapted to certain fundamentals of inner life and involved with the practices of definite schools or movements, and may easily be felt as a shackle when new inner values struggle for expression.

Even the divergence in dominant talents among artists will necessarily modify the traditional forms. Individual artists differ in talents mainly by virtue of the dexterity with which each exploits and combines what we have called dynamic factors (tone, color, line, plane, figure, deep space, etc.). In so doing they loosen, from the outside as it were, the fundamental tradition and prepare the way for variations of the basic feeling to be expressed. There is endless argument, especially among artists, as to whether these variations of vital feeling expressed in art do not merely stem from advances in technique (for instance, the derivation of the Gothic from the technique of the pointed arch.) This represents a serious misapprehension of the insoluble interconnection between the internal and the external in all forms of art. It is also a clear confirmation of the peculiarly one-sided attitude mentioned above, especially on the part of artists towards the external conditions of their work. Actually, new possibilities in the technique are refined and carried into a personal style only when they coincide with a vital feeling struggling to be expressed. If such coincidence is lacking, the result is, at best, an attempt at stylization.

Thus it is, after all, the sense of life which determines the manner of expression in art and is responsible for the evaluation and application of newly discovered technical possibilities. It is also the criterion for the choice and emphasis of the dynamic factors in the various styles: the delicacy of the early Renaissance leads to a preference for two-dimensional effects, for the "planar," as I should like to call it, and to the all but bodiless grace of profile, the almost arabesque use of all linear elements in the plane of the picture, such as Botticelli has shown us. On the other hand, the more pompous and self-conscious mood of the Baroque concentrates on the struggle for dominance embodied in the volumes and the reaches of its space, thus stressing the three-dimensional aspect of perception, the "spatial." It is almost needless to point out that a study of the combinations and emphases of dynamic factors could be of highest importance for a systematic characterization of historical styles in general, and indeed for an outlook upon new stylistic possibilities. The latest Parisian movements and their techniques might well be considered from this point of view.[1]

[1] The article was written in February, 1911.

VI

Finally, artistic feeling in the narrower sense, by which we realize the harmony between the dynamic factors in a work and its basic spiritual tone, must not be confused with general vital feeling. The former always constitutes the highest tribunal for all decisions regarding artistic creation and criticism. The intellect can never anticipate such intuition, it cannot calculate its loss, nor replace it with its own accomplishments, for artistic decisions are always made with reference to the given fundamental and validated by it, and would needs turn out differently for another fundamental. When Kant speaks of art as a play of the emotional forces, he indicates with one word the position of artistic intuition beyond the realm of the intellect. The intellect takes part in the play of emotional powers but cannot supply them from its own resources. Beside the intellect, the evaluating and responsive soul with all its wealth of inner tensions and solutions must come into its own, if the art image is to result from the play. The significance of the intellect for the artistic tradition stands firm: recognition of what is empirically proved, derivation from it of underlying laws, and the utilization of the acquired insight. To clarify all this in philosophic terms should not be denied to the intellect, but rather imposed on it by virtue of its function. But intellect alone does not suffice either for artistic creation or for artistic evaluation. Both take place through the agency of artistic feeling. Only through such feeling can we grasp that peculiar "harmony between the internal and external" which becomes apparent in works of great art and which, if we may say it once more, rests in the complete harmony of all dynamic factors that play a role in perception, with the inner vitality which finds its expression in the total image.

Thus the artistic image, according to its nature, *also* meets the demands for "clarity," to which the creative artist has always and justifiably ascribed so much importance. However, this demand has been intensified in our reflections on the subject, for it no longer applies only to the *external* form of the image, as we believe to have shown, but it also takes into account the content of the second idea expressed at the start, according to which art should express convincingly a condition or occurrence of *inner* life. In art it is not only a question of clear perceptibility of something external and the perfect preparation for it, but of creating for the mind's eye a fragment of existence clearly comprehensible to the innermost recesses of its life.

It is in some respects not only an external but at the same time an inner clairvoyance which we, as artistically creative individuals, try to immortalize, and as recipients, try to gain for the purpose of participating with the entire force of our own vital feeling in the completely comprehended image. The indispensable total clarity of the art image combined with the internal harmony of all its factors and the equivalent fundamental of vital feeling is the essence of "artistic form."

The Aesthetic Problem of Distance

GEORG MEHLIS

IT MAY BE INSTRUCTIVE and edifying to organize a wide field of human cultural activity and the wealth of its results in a one-sided but clear-cut way according to a certain single concept, throw the spotlight on it *in abstracto,* and then pretend that all understanding can be derived simply from that concept. But in so doing we must needs go wrong from the outset, since even the greatest conceptual system imaginable is inadequate to master even a small fragment of life. Yet there is a certain advantage in this one-sidedness, because aspects of life and culture, when illuminated from a certain point of view, achieve a more solid outline in their relation to one another and are thus rendered accessible to comparison and analogy. Only with these reservations, and realizing entirely the narrowness and limitations of the chosen angle of evaluation, do we make the assertion that in art, in artistic life, and in religion (which latter we mean to include in our considerations by way of comparison) nothing is so important as the law of distance. We boldly claim that in these areas detachment means everything and that the appreciation of beauty, the aesthetic joy of life, and religious reverence are dependent on distance.

Though science and the moral will may strive to grasp their

79

objects directly, and the strong and mighty impulse of these intellectual disciplines may aim at breaking down all barriers that
separate subject from object, yet those other human interests, by
virtue of their peculiar nature, must embrace the law of distance.

But here we have to counter, first of all, the possibility of a dual
misunderstanding, i.e. first, that distance is synonymous with contrast and tension—we mean something entirely different from the
"principle of contrast"—and secondly, that our concept of distance
is connected with the obvious spatial relationships involved, for
instance, in the artistic contemplation and evaluation of a painting that requires the right place and the right distance from the
observer in order to be beautiful and impressive.

Distance is not the equivalent of contrast. Contrast is, we might
say, more of an internal quality of the object, a structural law of
its composition. Each work of art is based on the original contrast
between form and content, which is mastered and brought to rest
by the artist. The aesthetic problem of removal, on the other hand,
lies in the aesthetic behavior and its object, hence in the subject-
object relation of the aesthetic reality.

Distance is not the equivalent of contrast. If we judge the artistic
value of an aesthetic creation by the measure of unity and contrast,
we must realize that the victory over contrast is part of the essence
of the work of art, part of the structural law of its internal nature.
Whereas in the moral realm, even apart from the attitude of the
subject's moral, cognitive consciousness, the tension must never
be completely removed, since the idea of the incomplete and fragmentary is necessary for its existence, aesthetic evaluation requires
the complete mastery of all tension. Unity by transcendence of
contrast, closure and isolation, freedom in appearance, "self-enjoyment," these are categories of art which quite frequently are stressed
and which, with their infinite store of meanings, are partially understood. But distance is an entirely different matter, one that must
not be cancelled out; a state in which the work of art should rest
and remain forever. And when we now speak of the work of art,
we mean not only the artistic creation, but also the artistic creation
of life, the beautifully formed human being contemplated from the
aesthetic point of view. We do not conceive of distance as mere
removal in a spatial sense, nor think of it in absolute terms. We
mean not only a spatial but a relative distance. By distance we mean
temporal remoteness, too, whatever has been shifted into the per-

spective of memory by a certain lapse of time. Neither do we want to say: the farther removed the more beautiful, but we only want to bring out the aesthetic importance of a certain aloofness which exists for the beholder of art as well as for its creator. Finally, we do not even consider the concept of distance in its literal, merely sensory meaning, but in a certain metaphorical sense. This is best understood if we explain the concept of removal, as we perceive it, in terms of its opposite, namely that of intimacy. In so doing we can quite generally say that intimacy is inimical to beauty and that it must necessarily destroy the aesthetic phenomenon.

This statement may at first appear paradoxical, and the objection will immediately be raised that a close familiarity with art media and acquaintance with the technique of the artist, a rich knowledge of material, significance, and aesthetic meaning, should serve rather to heighten artistic impression. Does not the true art connoisseur and the artist himself enjoy [the object of] aesthetic perception and creation much more strongly and intensively than the layman who is an alien to art? Isn't it essential to understand things in order to care for them tenderly and to enjoy the fulness of their beauty?

Here we have to stress two considerations. The statement that intimate familiarity with beautiful objects enhances one's appreciation and enjoyment of beauty has such an air of obviousness and assumption, that for this very reason we are inclined to doubt its validity; furthermore, familiarity is by no means synonymous with our concept of intimacy. To be sure, it is generally true that familiarity with the artistic object and art media enhances one's aesthetic impression. But even this fact is subject to certain limitations. It happens very often that an artist loses the right relation to his work. During the days of creation he lived in intimate community with the creatures of his imagination; time and again they have passed through his world of experience, and time and again he has observed their form and gestures, expression and motion, voice and behavior. Time and again he has tried to explain to himself the peculiar import of their characters and wills. And now, they are completed and exhibited in the objective context of the work of art, freed from their creator's world of experience. But he no longer recognizes them, or can no longer appreciate them, because they have become too familiar to him, they have lived too long with him in the closest communion.

Then a stranger has to come, look at them, and elicit from them their mute secret without violating their self-containedness and their separateness in strict observance of distance. For this is the sin against a work of art and against beauty in general: that we destroy the circle of austere separateness which it has established to preserve its peculiar nature. There is a tremendous violation involved when a work of art and its images, or even the beautiful images of life, are drawn into an individual's existence, subordinated to the narrow sphere of his experiential world, and removed from their own proper sphere with the arrogant assertion that they come into their true rights at the place where he keeps them. To take such an approach is to destroy beauty and make it incomprehensible. Never attempt to make the images of great art the companions of your daily life; do not permit their mute splendor to pervade your everyday dreams. Rather, keep them apart from the dust and trivialities of daily life and linger with them only in the rare moments of elevated joy of living. Do not touch them with the kind of egoism and painful jealousy that only wants exclusive possession of beauty. Restrain that destructive covetousness! Display works of art freely and splendidly so that they may claim the admiration to which they are entitled!

For the art historian, too, this familiarity breeds difficulties in the analysis and criticism of an art object. A refined connoisseur may on occasion do great injustice to a work of art. He has lost the strong, original relation to its form because he has lived with it too long. Now it can no longer reveal to him the precious joy and youth which is part of its essence. Now he has heaped dark ashes on these free and luminous creations. And yet he did not lack perception of them, nor a fine and tender relationship with them. He is, after all, the highly attuned and well disposed lover of beautiful and precious objects. His position in relation to the work of art is also especially difficult because a peculiar paradox obtains in the history of art: it is that the science of what is forever past and gone, that great science which incorporates an essentially tragic element, is concerned with that which can never grow old and die: the free creations of imagination that have eternal life and eternal youth. Art must necessarily harbor hostility towards history even greater than its aversion towards philosophy. Art inclines to be eternally young and mysterious, while history tends to make art old, and philosophy, to make it conceivable.

But we have already stressed that familiarity is never synonymous with intimacy. Only the latter entails that neglect of distance which the idea of beauty forbids. We can, indeed, conceive of an intimacy of friendship that is filled with high values. We appreciate such a living relationship, but it is based on a different sort of value, which either lies in the idea of friendship itself, or has a moral origin. We want to be rightly understood: intimacy does not necessarily destroy the values of life and therewithal friendship itself, but only the aesthetic aspects of human relations and friendship. Intimacy has a great retinue of charms and joys. It does much to strengthen and elevate our existence. It is not inimical to life, only to beauty. But since it is inimical to beauty, and since beauty means so much in our lives, intimacy always runs the danger of a painful loss.

There are numerous examples to show that beauty is destroyed by non-observance of distance. What young heart has not, at some time, been elated and made happy by the works of our great, idealistic poet?[1] Then, later, we lost our relation to them, in the detailed features of our former love. And was not this alienation primarily caused by a neglect of the aesthetic precept of distance? If only someone had guided us with more care and understanding to this beautiful visionary world, or it had but been left to us, pure and untouched, as we first understood and accepted it! If only they had not resolved the forms so carefully, handing back to us time and again fragments and details, us, who so longed for the beautiful whole and the living sense of unity! These analysts of art works are like the botanist who dismembers flowers. Both destroy beauty. But the latter's conscious intention is not to serve beauty, but to establish characteristics in the organic structure which serve for its classification within a certain system. A priest of another deity, he thereby dissolves beauty. It is different with the analysts. They claim to act in the spirit of beauty, but they do not understand its spirit and cannot find it. Always concerned only with the external form, they play their tiresome game, and without tenderness and aesthetic consideration they reach with clumsy and avid hands for the naked body of beauty.

What is true of beauty in art is no less true of beauty in life, and we believe that it takes the close juxtaposition of these two objectives, and of the questions relating to them, to show how generally

[1] The reference is to Schiller.—Ed.

our aesthetic principle holds in the whole realm of beauty. A great humorist and practical philosopher of the Romantic Movement applied the rule of remoteness to the closest relations and most personal values in life, by saying that friends, lovers, and partners in marriage should have everything in common, except the bedroom. Everything else should they share: their beautiful thoughts, that meet in sympathetic chords, reverberating each in other with quiet understanding. They should share life's sustenance, and even the body be no longer an exclusive possession. They may meet in the highest ecstasy and enjoy one another completely, but only for a short while should the ultimate be seen and enjoyed. The loving embrace must be followed by the silent and patient separation, so that the creative imagination may quickly and quietly repair the image of innate beauty that the seering breath of passion touched, moved, and disrupted. And therefore they must not share their place of repose, but love should approach the beloved in perfect strength and full armor. The weapons of beauty should adorn them both, and they should always be strong in giving and receiving. The lover should always be new for his beloved, the friend for his friend, beautiful emotion and excitement should give their desires ever fresh nourishment. The exuberance of youth must never be satisfied with "abject coupled complacency."

This limitation and restriction of amatory intercourse is demanded by the aesthetic rule of distance. In the long run the petty incidentals of physical presence menace the beauty of the visionary image that I have created of the human being I love. Insofar as beauty is of decisive significance in my love relationship—since, according to my understanding and interpretation, it is only thus that the primitive forms of sensuality acquire a content of infinite meaning— the destruction and the obfuscation of the image created by the desire for beauty will cause the strength of love itself to wane and gradually disappear. For a short period, to be sure, the love object may be given to the lover, to touch and blissfully embrace, without any danger to the beauty of the love relationship. After all, the full sense of love includes a demand for the development of sensual desire. Even in a love formed on the basis of aesthetic values sensual desire must be accorded its due. It cannot be a question of mere beholding, of the kind of disinterested pleasure with which we meet dead works of art, and those living works of art that are and remain created forms for my artistic enthusiasm; for in the love relationship, a coming together and a fusion, with heavenly moments of passing intoxication, is of the essence; but the observance of the law of distance will reveal itself in the courage of leave-taking in the consciously willed separation from the object of my love.

Certainly, love is destined to die insofar as it is interwoven with the temporal fate of the senses. It has its moment of fulfillment in the most beautiful surrender and the attained understanding of the lovers, and then must necessarily wane in consequence of sickness, age, misunderstanding, and death. Nevertheless, the law of distance is able to counter certain dangers that threaten this beautiful relationship, and protect it from tiring and cooling off. For this, too, a certain keeping of distance, a concealment of emotional qualities from the object of love is required. The great value relations in life, love and friendship, should never be quite clear and transparent as we live them. We spread over them the beautiful veil of illusion, and they should always hold a last residue of insolubility for us. In certain ways, lovers should remain a lasting enigma to one another. They should always offer each other something new to guess and interpret. Then the feeling of dull indifference and lack of interest which threatens the strength and beauty of love with a premature end may never overtake them. This enigmatic and insoluble element that obtains in every strong human relationship and is rooted in the depths of individuality, has its counterpart in the realm of art; it corresponds to the intrinsic form of the aesthetic idea, which gives to the work of art its significant unity and eternal character and which defies every attempt at conceptual solution.

Inimical to the aesthetic norm is that intrusive and obtrusive kind of gesture which seeks to interfere in another realm from the vantage ground of a limited, personal ambient—without justification and without any deeper meaning, merely for the sake of correcting, merely because the distortion and changing of the other is a flattering and pleasing show of power. This is a violation of aesthetic standards. There are few people who know how to carry over the aesthetic respect that we owe a work of art, to the relation of friendship, so that they render the loved one that tender consideration of all feelings and emotions, that acknowledgement of his peculiar value and the pleasure in his individuality, which is incumbent on an understanding friend.

It is characteristic of unartistic natures to emphasize the details too much and enter too much into minutiae. The knowledge of detail all too often disturbs artistic pleasure in the whole. Therefore the artistically educated layman has perhaps many advantages over the perfect connoisseur, because unimportant and ugly details might escape him and thus not detract from his enjoyment of beauty. How painful is an uneven verse or even more a false note to the connoisseur! How sad its effect, since it destroys the illusion of the work of art. The absolute connoisseur cannot arrive at an unadulterated pleasure of poetry, because the defective metrics of a verse evoke his displeasure, uneasy anticipation, and presentiment of disappointment and disenchantment, as he scans the lines of the frivolous poet.

How often have we heard the words: This is good and beautiful, we cannot deny it our appreciation, but we also cannot live with it: not with this human being, this landscape, this work of art. No, we *should* not live with it, in the sense of making it the companion of our everyday associations. We cannot listen every day to Beethoven's symphonies, we cannot appreciate beautiful people daily and hourly, we cannot always look down from the heights of Camadoli on the blue Gulf of Naples. Beauty should enter into our lives only rarely, but when it does we have to be prepared to receive it hospitably. We must accord it that quiet reticence and isolation which compels the religious consciousness to let the curtain fall in front of the holy of holies. Nothing is more inimical to beauty than that harem life of enjoyment, where beautiful figures cannot be numerous enough and are sacrificed to personal whim and caprice by being always on hand for a quick fulfillment of desires.

In trying to solve the problem of distance especially with regard to its aesthetic significance, we must needs connect it with the ideas of recollection and anticipation, for the beauty-creating force of recollection and anticipation is obviously related to the idea of distance.

The mysterious depths of memory have never yet been explored and penetrated by anyone. It is simply a fact that we can store our experience of the beautiful, that it is within our power to recall the images of the past in their fullness of life, that we can admit them to the sphere of our conscious mind and, enjoying them anew, we can understand them ever more deeply and more beautifully. Each epoch of experience takes its place in a specific context which we may seek and in which we may remain, disregarding everything else we have experienced and ignoring the existence and conditions of our environment. These worlds of experience and memory are our permanent possession. They are the only paradise from which we cannot be expelled. They have the advantage of assured property for which we no longer need to fight. They have a quality of completion that is denied to the present. They are imbued with the entire magic of the miraculous, because they possess a reality which we do not understand. They are the great miracle of the spirit, for they are past and yet can be ever present, they are and yet they are not. In them rests the wealth and entire force of our individuality. They elevate us above merely momentary existence. In them rests the possibility of forgetting old age and transfiguring death. And in the course of history the mnemonic gift of the individual expands into the memory of mankind.

The experiential constructions of memory are made by a force that creates beauty. The remembered images of the past are beautified by the peculiar process of retention. Our soul forgets whatever insufficiency and discomfort it suffered during its actual enjoyments, and adorns the entire treasure of experience with glowing colors. Everything difficult and sad recedes, only the beautiful memory of joy, bright and shining, is retained. Here, too, is the law of distance which for the sake of beauty demands remoteness.

Something similar holds true for expectation, the realm of hope and longing. As memory beautifies the past, that no longer exists, with a thousand illusions, and dissolves and banishes everything ugly and uncomfortable, so fond expectation causes the future, not yet in existence, to blossom into a beauty never to be realized. The pleasure of the present may be greater than the enjoyment of the past and the future; but the appearance of the unreal, of that which was or is to come, is more beautiful, because here the obstructive and weakening elements of embodiment have been eliminated by the transfiguring work of the imagination, or have been replaced and enhanced by felicitous allusions and connections. Thus beauty gains by the distance of expectation, just as it gains by the distance of the past.

We can, perhaps, love only what is known and familiar to us. But the object of aesthetic pleasure may equally well be the distant and unknown. If, then, love itself has an aesthetic character, the feeling of love must also be controlled by the law of distance. Those who love only the beautiful, whose affections are destroyed by ugliness and bad taste, should be ever reminded of the law of distance; for profane proximity destroys the bliss of pure aloofness, as ugly frequency and intimacy annihilate the enjoyment of the rare and unknown.

But it is not only the enjoyment of beauty that is subject to the law of distance, so that without observance of this law we cannot fully enjoy the art products of life or of imagination. There is a further condition that relates rather to the genesis, the creation or birth, of the work of art. The work must be enjoyed in accordance with the process of its creation. The birth of a work of art, however, is governed by the law of distance.

Let us first consider the work of art in the narrower sense of aesthetic reality, for instance a masterpiece of plastic art. Its material and direct meaning are taken from nature or from life. What makes it a work of beauty for aesthetic contemplation is the artistic handling which lends shape and significance to the mere material. But in order to find the aesthetically important element in the living reality the artist must remove himself from it. As long as he lives as an animate being with other animate beings he cannot elevate himself above their life. Therefore the creative will of the artist entails a certain renunciation of settled comfort, and precludes the familiar enjoyment of many aspects of life. He can participate in them only fleetingly, as a transient. To portray life, he must remove himself from it. He remains in the closeness and intimacy of personal relationships only so long as he does not exercise his divine profession. But the profession of the artist is not a profession in the ordinary sense. It is rather a calling which seizes the entire human being and takes possession of him.

Something similar holds true for the origination of the living work of art, the creation of nature and life. If mere nature is to become aesthetically significant then it must appear to the understanding eye as an image, divorced from its material aspects. In order that a human being may appear simply beautiful, I have to subject him to a separation which removes him from the incidentals of his surroundings and embodiment. To perceive his contour and understand his style I must furthermore renounce my personal relationship to him, and sacrifice the love and desire due him to the artistic articulation of his particular essence. Thereby he is necessarily removed into that distance which accords with the contemplative appreciation of his appearance. The desire for possession and enjoyment will be silenced in the face of the quiet and assured beauty of the perfect image.

The significance of the law of distance becomes apparent, furthermore, in religious life, which seems to point to a certain kinship between the aesthetic and the religious feeling. In religion, too, the disregard and destruction of distance may be fateful. This is taught by the profound myth of the fall of man, in which human and divine love are drawn into the conflict of aesthetic-religious and theoretical norms. They had found each other pure and were allowed to enjoy each other in the nude, they were amiable and beautiful one to the other, beautiful and amiable also in the eye of the great Master who had created them, as long as they obeyed the law of distance and shunned the tree of knowledge. Innocence means being removed from all reflection. It is the gentle virginity and immediacy of life, the quiet, self-contained existence. And this aesthetically relevant life has its religious significance, too, because whatever reposes in itself is, after all, perfect. Because it is endowed with the magic of the mysterious and veiled, it constitutes the source of all religious yearning.

But the drive for knowledge is the enemy of beauty and of the quiet secret, and thus it breaks the divinely erected barrier letting loose man's greed for the unknown and mysterious. It destroys the sweet mystery, and the hard and barren knowledge now gazes with its terribly grim everyday face upon the unveiled world. Because the eager drive for knowledge strove to approach the deity too closely it destroyed innocence and, in so doing, the beauty and sanctity of nature, blundering into a conflict with it and its creator. Ejected and exiled, it lost itself in lonesome remoteness from God.

For religious life the law of distance also holds true. To be far from God means to be close to God. This means that the divine must remain protected from uncalled-for haste and importunate zeal. Also, we cannot feel and understand the divine if we limit it with the finiteness of conception. This precisely was the sin of that yearning Wisdom of which we are told in the religious philosophy of the Gnostics. It became infatuated with the original cause and the abyss of the world, only to be hurled into the void in punishment for its sinful love. We must never possess the object of our religious longing. It must never become our property, even as the beautiful must forever remain separated from us.

There are forms of religious life intended to overcome the distance between God and the soul. They harbor the danger of leading to a dissolution of the religious relationship. Mysticism requires that the soul be accepted and absorbed by the force of divine love, as the dewdrop by the sun. It makes everything divine. Magic, on the other hand, is inspired by a mad individualism to control the divine Being and usurp His power. In this way it consumes with burning passion the attributes of the divine. Its boundless cupidity reduces everything to soul and finiteness and concrete form.

Only where the divine stands undefined in quiet distance from the desire of the soul, and this distance is maintained, the religious relationship is removed from all danger and misinterpretation. Then it is preserved to the soul in luminous beauty as a blissful other world.

Thus the effectiveness of religious life, too, requires the maintenance of the law of distance; and is threatened as soon as the set limits are not observed. Here we have an important point of contact between the aesthetic and the religious realms. But while the risk of overcoming the distance has been taken by religious genius, and will necessarily be taken time and again—sometimes with glimpses into a higher religious life—the beautiful in artistic form and image is so very much determined by the aesthetic law of remoteness that the lover, protagonist, and creator of beauty can only be conceived as a preserver and keeper of its solitude and chastity.

The Nature of Dramatic Illusion

CHARLES MORGAN

WHOEVER TRACES THE rather meagre history of dramatic criticism from Greek times to our own will observe that it has taken two principal forms—the analytic and the impressionistic. The analyst's purpose has been to lay down rules and establish universal standards óf judgment; the impressionist's, to set up no god but his own taste, and to write a history of the voyage of his soul among masterpieces. The value of his criticism has thus depended upon the value of his soul—always an uncertain factor; and though writing of this school, when practised by men of quality, has yielded great treasures, the liberty, the artist's privilege necessary to impressionistic criticism has been shamefully abused, and is nowadays too often made an excuse for arrogant and disorderly variations on the pronoun "I". There is, in modern criticism, a real danger of anarchy if its erratic movements cannot by some means be related and stabilized. With every development of dramatic technique and every departure from classical structure, the need increases of a new discussion which, observing the changes of definition since Dryden and the vast accumulation of material since Lessing, shall establish for the stage not indeed a formal rule but an aesthetic discipline, elastic, reasoned, and acceptable to it in modern circumstances.

91

It is my purpose, then, to discover the principle from which such a discipline might arise. This principle I call the principle of illusion.

Before attempting a more precise and technical definition of illusion, I will strive to give a general impression of it and to show that the idea is a necessary foundation of criticism.

There has been in recent years a tendency among serious critics to revolt against what they call the literary criticism of plays. Drama, they say, is a composite art, and to criticize it as though it were the work of the dramatist alone is unreasonable and unjust. With this statement of their case we may all agree, but they have gone much further. Wishing to depose the dramatist from an exaggerated pre-eminence, they have attempted to establish another monarch in his place; and they differ in their choice of a successor. Mr. Gordon Craig's emphasis is all on the designer of scenery and costume; Mr. Ashley Dukes, though a dramatist himself, writes unblushingly of the producer as the artist-in-chief; and they have powerful supporters, for the appearance in Europe of stage artists of genius—men of the quality of Stanislavsky, Reinhardt and Craig himself—has drawn eager and worshipping eyes to the producer's share in the theatrical collaboration. This kind of enthusiasm, though we may not share it, is useful if we examine its psychological origins. What is the genuine need underlying this modern critical revolt against the dramatist? What is the genuine need which prompted the Americans to invent—as I am now inventing—a new critical term? I call mine "illusion" and struggle to define it; the Americans call theirs "theatre". Unfortunately the true meaning of the American word "theatre" has been blunted by common usage. When they say now that a play is "good theatre" or "bad theatre", they mean that it has punch or is tediously lacking in it—in brief that it is, or is not, vigorously theatrical; and they are able to declare that, though a piece has no genuine critical value, it is, for all that, good theatre. But what lay at the root of this American word was, I am sure, a desire to find a critical term which should express the unity of a stage representation, the same spiritual unity which made the productionists revolt against the dramatist's pre-eminence.

This unity, this essence of the drama, which I call illusion, is not the same with the Aristotelian unities of action, time and place, though in plays that accept the Aristotelian form they are included in it. It is, perhaps, best thought of as being to the drama what the soul is to the mind, and those who deny, or say that they cannot perceive, a distinction between soul and mind and will not therefore concede the real existence of the soul, will certainly refuse to recognize the real existence of illusion.

I will not press the comparison, which is intended to be illustrative and no more. What I am certain of is that every playgoer has been made aware now and then of the existence in the theatre of a supreme unity, a mysterious power, a transcendent and urgent illusion, which, so to speak, floats above the stage action and above the spectator, not merely delighting and instructing him, as Dryden says, or purging his Aristotelian emotions, but endowing him with a vision, a sense of translation and ecstasy, alien to his common knowledge of himself. The hope of this illusion is the excitement, and the experience of it the highest reward, of playgoing. Strangely enough we become conscious of its approach, as though there were a sound of wings in the air—before the play begins. The curtain is still down, the house-lights are still up, but we are in a theatre and, if experience has not embittered us, are dreaming that this evening or another evening the beat of wings will grow louder in our silences, the supreme illusion will stoop down and gather us, the hosts will speak. Again and again we are disappointed. The curtain rises and the play is found to be an ugly bag of tricks; instead of the authentic currency of experience we are given a trickle of counterfeit coin, rubbed for generations between the fingers of plagiarists. But now and then a persistent playgoer's hope, or a part of it, is fulfilled. The order of his experience is always the same— a shock, and after the shock an inward stillness, and from that stillness an influence emerging, which transmutes him. Transmutes *him* —not his opinions. This great impact is neither a persuasion of the intellect nor a beguiling of the senses. It does not spring from the talent of the dramatist alone, or of the actor alone, or of the musician alone, or from an aggregate of their talents. It is not the work of any one artist-in-chief whose name is written on an earthly programme. It is the enveloping movement of the whole drama upon the soul of man. We surrender and are changed. "The outward sense is gone, the inward essence feels," until, betrayed by some flaw in the work of art or failure in ourselves, we begin to perceive again, not the drama, but its parts.

"When the ear begins to hear, and the eye begins to see;
When the pulse begins to throb—the brain to think again—
The soul to feel the flesh, and the flesh to feel the chain—"

—then illusion is broken. We return to our little prisons and through
the bars are the critical spectators of a play.

I do not wish to suggest that a play which fails to produce illusion
of this intensity ought to be condemned, for I have just written of
that rare extreme which creates ecstasy in the audience—a veritable
rebirth, a carrying out of the senses which seem to bound our
humanity. What I wish to establish is that, though the intensity
of our experience of it may greatly vary, there is something, some
power, some influence, some underlying unity, latent in the drama
which has never yet been given its due place in criticism. You may
think of it in what terms you will—as a synthesis of the arts of the
theatre, as a hypostasis proceeding from their perfect unity, or you
may say that it has no concrete existence but is at best a philosophical idea, a critical fiction. Well, beauty itself has no concrete existence and is, perhaps, a critical fiction, but it is one of the neces-
sities of thought. And I suggest that as a wise man bases his criticism of life, not upon judgment of its parts, but upon apprehension
of its unity, so judgment of the drama is to be founded on its illusion
and not on its form or on the emotion it creates.

That is a general impression of what I mean by illusion. Let me
now consider it more closely and indicate one of its distinguish-
ing qualities.

It is a common error to praise a play because, as the lady in the
stall behind me never tires of saying, it is "exactly like life". This
is an error for two reasons: first, that if a play were exactly like life
it would be a bad play; second, that no play has ever been or ever
can be exactly like life, and the lady is a liar. What she means, of
course, is that the play does not outrage the naturalistic convention
which she accepts. She will look at a photograph of her own son,
whom she ought to know, and exclaim that it is exactly like him—
whereas what she means is that the photograph represents him
to her in an accepted convention of black and white. If she had
lived in ancient Egypt and had been given by the gods the same
son and the same photograph but different pictorial conventions,
it is very possible that she would not have recognized her offspring,
and would have greatly preferred something more rectilinear. But
fascinating though the subject of varying convention may be, I
must not now pursue it. The lady's first error is more relevant to
my general argument.

Aristotle said at the opening of the 'Poetics' that "Epic and tragic composition, also comedy, the writing of dithyrambs and most branches of flute- and harp-playing are all, if looked at as a whole, imitations." Against this my own statement that "if a play were exactly like life it would be a bad play" may look a little small. The lady in the stall behind me would, if she were familiar with the 'Poetics', quote Aristotle with gusto. But Aristotle is one of those men of genius whose sentences, if taken out of their context, can be made to mean anything. To read a little farther into the 'Poetics' —to observe indeed that Aristotle includes dithyrambs and flute- and harp-playing in his group of imitations—is to realize that he was by no means a photographic naturalist of the same aesthetic school with the lady in the stalls.

It is true that art is rooted in imitation, and that, when it is cut off from that root and becomes decoration only or didacticism only, it dries up and withers. It is rooted in imitation—but in imitation of what? Do not let us say of ordinary life, for the phrase, though Aristotle himself uses it, has no precise meaning. Mr. Baldwin is said to be a representative Englishman; his life is presumably the ordinary life of an English ex-Prime Minister; but I do not see him as you see him, nor do we see him as Shelley would have seen him. How, then, is art to imitate him? It cannot. It can imitate my view of him or yours or Shelley's, but in each of these imitations there will be more of Shelley or you or me than of the hypothetical ordinariness of Mr. Baldwin. All that art can do in the way of imitation of a given natural subject is, first, to negative a spectator's own preconceptions of that subject so that he lies open to imaginative acceptance of a different view, the artist's view, of it, and secondly, to impregnate him with this fresh, this alien understanding. Illusion is the impregnating force—in masterpieces permanently fruitful, in lesser works of art existent but without endurance, and from machine-made plays, however well made, absent. How often we say of a play that it was "a good story" or "an admirable entertainment"; that it was "cleverly constructed," or that its "characters were natural and alive"; and, having thus praised it, add with a vague sense of disappointment, "but there was nothing in it." What is the critical equivalent of that evasive phrase? The formalists have no answer; the impressionists have none. Does not the phrase mean that the play had no impregnating power? Though it had a thousand other virtues it was without illusion.

The lady of whom I have spoken believes that, in the photograph of her son, she has seen her own impression of him. Evidently she has done nothing of the kind. She has been persuaded to forget her view of him and to accept the camera's as her own. When she goes to a play, which seems to her exactly like life, she has been persuaded to abandon her own view of life and to accept the dramatist's. It is true that, when the dramatist is of her own imaginative and intellectual kin, the exchange is not revolutionary, but, when he is a man of genius and has power to persuade her to take his view of "A Doll's House" or to see with his eyes the lamp thrown at wife and mother by Strindberg's Father, the results are prodigious. That lamp of Strindberg's still hurtles through the domestic air, and by Nora a million feminine squirrels were converted into tigresses whose cubs still embarrass us.

And why? Not because the lady in the stalls had ever before thought of herself as resembling the lady of Strindberg's lamp; not because, if she was a squirrel, she had ever perceived, until Ibsen pointed it out to her, the limitations of her comfortable cage; not because these great plays were like life as she had formerly understood it; but because her own preconceptions were stilled and afterwards impregnated. What stirred her, what influenced her, was not delusion, which is of herself, but illusion—that divine essence above the battle—which is of the drama. Wordsworth of all men helps to make this point clear. He is expressing his dislike of chatter:

> "I am not One who much or oft delight
> To season my fireside with personal talk
> Of Friends who live within an easy walk."

He is not attracted by—

> " . . . ladies bright,
> Sons, mothers, maidens withering on the stalk. . . ."

Better than these, he says, does—

> " . . . silence long,
> Long, barren silence, square with my desire;
> To sit without emotion, hope or aim,
> In the loved presence of my cottage fire,
> And listen to the flapping of the flame,
> Or kettle whispering its faint undersong."

The remarkable word in this passage is "barren". The later stanzas show that he means not barren absolutely, but a silence barren of trivial and personal thoughts which might be a bar to a more profound impregnation.

> "Dreams, books are each a world; and books we know
> Are a substantial world, both pure and good.
> Round these, with tendrils strong as flesh and blood,
> Our pastime and our happiness will grow.
> There find I personal themes, a plenteous store,
> Matter wherein right voluble I am. . . . ."

What he is speaking of here is the impregnating power of artistic illusion working upon a mind naturally silent, naturally meditative. In the theatre there is no natural meditation, no flapping flame and, unhappily, no kettle. Dramatic art has, therefore, a double function—first to still the preoccupied mind, to empty it of triviality, to make it receptive and meditative; then to impregnate it. Illusion is the impregnating power. It is that spiritual force in dramatic art which impregnates the silences of the spectator, enabling him to imagine, to perceive, even to become, what he could not of himself become or perceive or imagine.

Inquiry, now, into the nature and origin of this impregnating force will expose the root of the theory. Illusion, as I conceive it, is form in suspense. The phrase is obscure and must be explained.

Analytical critics have all supposed that form is valuable in itself. They have based their judgments on a study of form, first establishing by general argument what they consider a perfect form for tragedy or comedy, then asking us to match particular plays with it. It is not surprising that they so often weary themselves in crying "This is not a play" when they encounter dramatic expression that does not correspond with their ideal form. Their confusion, and it is a confusion that has run through the ages, springs from their failure to perceive one plain truth—that in a play form is not valuable *in itself;* only the suspense of form has value. In a play, form is not and cannot be valuable in itself, because until the play is over form does not exist.

Form is *in itself* valuable only in those works of art into which the time-factor does not enter, and which, therefore, come to us whole. Painting, sculpture and architecture come to us whole; they are directly formal arts. An epic poem does not come to us whole, but a short lyric or a particular line therein may almost be said to do this, so slight, by comparison with an epic, is the time-factor involved. A play's performance occupies two or three hours. Until the end its form is latent in it. It follows that during the performance we are not influenced by the form itself, the completed thing, but by our anticipations of completion. We are, so to speak, waiting for the suspended rhyme or harmony, and this formal suspense has the greater power if we know beforehand, as the Greeks did, what the formal release is to be.

This suspense of form, by which is meant the incompleteness of a known completion, is to be clearly distinguished from common suspense—suspense of plot—the ignorance of what will happen, and I would insist upon this distinction with all possible emphasis, for suspense of plot is a structural accident, and suspense of form is, as I understand it, essential to the dramatic art itself. The desire to know what will happen, when it exists at all, is a quality of the audience's delusion; it springs from their temporary belief that they are witnessing, not art, but life; it is the product of deluded curiosity, and is often strongest in the weakest minds. It is obviously stronger in a housemaid watching a play by Mr. Edgar Wallace than in a cultivated spectator of the Aeschylean 'Prometheus', and it would become progressively less strong even in the housemaid as by repeated visits to the theatre the designs of Mr. Wallace were made more familiar to her. I do not wish to speak contemptuously of suspense of plot, for it often contributes to the pleasure of play-going and reading; it has this value—that it keeps our eyes on stage or book. It may draw attention to a work of art and has been used by great artists for that purpose, but it is not essential to the art itself. Suspense of form, on the contrary, is one of those things without which drama is not.

It may be objected that without form there can be no suspense of form, and that to this extent a formal critic is justified. My argument is that he is wrong in insisting that particular dramatic forms are valuable in themselves. What rhyme is begun matters less than that the rhyme be completed; what harmony is used matters less than that it be resolved; what form is chosen, though it is true that some forms are more beautiful than others, matters less than that while the drama moves *a* form is being fulfilled.

Dramatic illusion, then, is the suspense of dramatic form, and is to be thought of as men think of divinity—an essence in which they may or may not partake, a power which may or may not visit them.

The task of applying this theory of illusion to particular plays
must be left to the twentieth-century Lessing, who writes the book
to which this paper is a foreword. Having defined the idea, I must
be content to give a few indications of its practical value, and of
the effect that its acceptance might produce on criticism.

Its value rests in its universality. Not long ago Mr. Granville
Barker, speaking on "The Coming of Ibsen", quoted the damning
judgment of many critics of the 'eighties on plays now acknowledged to be masterpieces. They were very disturbing to a man who,
within little more than an hour after each performance, writes his
opinion on nearly two hundred plays a year. It is alarming to think
that Mr. Granville Barker, whose youth is perpetual, will rise up
in 1980 and make hay with a file of *The Times* newspaper fifty
years old. Even the closest study of the theory of illusion will not
make any man infallible, but I do believe that it will protect critics
from many of the errors into which our predecessors so easily fell.
The adverse judgments of Ibsen, which now seem to us most unreasonable, prove upon examination to have been inspired by the
old prejudice about form. Ibsen, intent upon introducing new subjects to the stage, was creating new shapes to contain them, and
the rigid formalists, clinging to prescribed form, condemned him.
For the same reason Strindberg has been denied the recognition
due to him, though the time will certainly come when it will be
perceived that, in such work as 'To Damascus' and 'The Dream
Play', he prepared the way for what is best in the modernist movements. He was an Expressionist long before Expressionism, as a
cult, was heard of, and did with genius what hundreds of charlatans
are now attempting to do without it. Ibsen has partly broken through
the formalists; Strindberg has not; and both are considered freaks
because they do not bow down to that spirit which still presides
powerfully over the English theatre—the spirit of Sardou. The
reason is that English playgoers and critics are still bound, consciously or subconsciously, to the idea that suspense means suspense
of plot, and that form in drama, as in the plastic arts, is a static
thing and valuable in itself. A critic who understands the theory
of illusion would never fall into the error of saying that Ibsen, because he did not strive for suspense of plot, was ignorant of the
theatre, or that Strindberg, because he created new forms and
rhythms, was not writing a play. Instead of making these rash errors
the critic would say to himself, "Here is something with which I

am unfamiliar. Here is a man struggling for a new form. I cannot judge his work as I would judge sculpture or architecture in which there is no time element. While the play is in progress I must yield myself to this moving, developing, organic thing, the suspense of form, and must realize that only when the complete form is known will the suspense of it have full effect on me".

If the critics of the 'eighties had said that to themselves when they took up their pens, Mr. Granville Barker would have been robbed of his powder and shot. The theory of illusion is universal, because it enables criticism to keep its balance amid the shock of new forms.

It is universal, too, because it establishes a standard of judgment which may, with intelligence, be applied to plays of all kinds—to tragedy, to comedy, and even to farce. The illusion of tragedy is the highest of all; the illusion of comedy differs from it in intensity but not in kind. The illusion of farce is, I admit, a cripple who has lost a leg. It is barren; it impregnates no silences. But a farce, if it be good in its own kind, has a unity, an "essence above the battle", and it certainly has suspense of form. Indeed, there is hardly to be found a more illuminating distinction between suspense of form and suspense of plot, or between illusion and delusion, than may be perceived in a good farce. Who cares in a farce what will happen? Who believes that anything is happening? We are not deluded by the fantastic narrative nor made curious by it. Our pleasure, if we are pleased, arises from the farce's skill in binding us by its own peculiar symmetry, and from its power to create an illusion, which is never delusion, of a world good-humouredly insane.

The theory of illusion has a third and very important claim to universality—namely, that it may be applied, as no other critical theory can, to plays that do not depend on a conflict of individual character, and thus supplies a link between very ancient and very modern drama. Nearly all criticism has presumed that such a conflict is an essential part of the drama. I am persuaded that it is not, and that if critics remain wedded to this idea of individual struggle and bound to the forms appropriate to it, they will blunder in their judgment of the drama of the future as critics in the past blundered in their judgment of Ibsen and Strindberg. This was deeply impressed upon me when I went to Delphi to see in the ancient theatre performances of Aeschylus—the 'Prometheus' and 'The Suppliants'.

What I wrote then returns to me with increasing force whenever
I contemplate the problem of illusion:

"It has often been pointed out as remarkable by commentators
on 'The Suppliants' that Aeschylus, having decided to use the
actor and having latent in him that prodigious power to thrust
forward the history of the drama of which his extant pieces are
evidence, should here have employed the actor so little. Only in
the sharp dialogue between the Argive King and Herald, it has
been said, is there contest of individuals and a complete, though
momentary, emancipation of the dramatic from the narrative or
ritualistic form. The reason commonly given for this, and indeed
the only reason deducible from an unacted text, is that Aeschylus
was as yet half-blind to his own discovery; that he held the actor
in his hands as a child holds a strange toy, knowing not how to
use him. This explanation, this misunderstanding of Aeschylus,
lies, I believe, at the root of the charges of obscurity and primi-
tiveness that have been brought against the play. In performance
at Delphi it is neither primitive nor obscure. When once the
chorus is felt as a living presence with collective individuality
and character, the play appears, not as a primitive struggling
towards a new drama, but as a fully developed product of an
older tradition. In departures from this tradition Aeschylus was
certainly experimenting, but the impression given by the performance is that the experiments were being made as much in
reluctance as in eagerness. Whenever the actor shows his head
above the choral unity we feel instantly that, though the tension
(or suspense of plot) is increased, an extraordinary composure,
a deep and passionate perfection of design, is being dissipated.
What was this composed perfection that our drama is without
and that Aeschylus, for all the promise of a different form, was
reluctant to sacrifice? May it not have consisted in this—that
the collective formalism of fifty Danaïds may more serenely express the universal truths of the spirit than the particularized
portrait of one woman? Is it not possible that the pre-Aeschylean
drama held already a key that gave it freedom from the bonds
of naturalism (and of individual character)—a key for which
modern dramatists from Strindberg to Lenormand have been desperately seeking? The Chorus, we know, had other and less aesthetically conscious origins, but by the time of Aeschylus it had

probably become a highly conscious aesthetic instrument used not merely ritualistically and lyrically, but as a synthesis of humanity that our particularized and personal stage has lost." [1]

A synthesis, I would add, towards which our stage is now moving. Perhaps the most significant evidence of this movement—this link between modernism and the pre-Aeschylean theatre—has been, in London, Mr. O'Casey's attempt in 'The Silver Tassie' to rediscover the Chorus, and to reintroduce the compression of verse into drama with a contemporary setting. This play was rejected by the Abbey Theatre and Mr. W. B. Yeats; it was condemned by many critics in the same tones of misunderstanding and intolerance with which Ibsen was condemned; fifty years hence Mr. Granville Barker will have them all on his list. And it is not at all surprising that, in an age which still bases its judgment on Aristotelian forms or on Dryden's definition of a play, criticism should be at fault, for neither Aristotle nor Dryden leaves room for the pre-Aeschylean and Twentieth-century synthesis. Our criticism is rooted in Dryden's idea of a "just and lively representation of human nature . . . for the delight and instruction of mankind"—an idea that denies Strindberg and the pre-Aeschylean chorus, and will, unless it is revised, deny much more in the days to come. The theory of illusion, if received as a basis of criticism, would make unnecessary these fatal denials. While maintaining, in the idea of form in suspense, much that is good in the old critical disciplines, and so preserving criticism from the impressionistic anarchy that threatens it, it would, in the complementary idea of illusion as an impregnating force, restore to criticism a spiritual liberty and boldness that it has lost.

[1] *The Times*, May 12th, 1930.

Music and Silence

GISÈLE BRELET

MUSIC AND SOUND cannot be pure surface show, inert data imposing themselves upon us from the outside: their whole being is in their action, since they live only by their perpetual rebirth. Hence they exist only by virtue of their unceasing victory over that silence which they embrace in order always to conquer anew their fragile and immaterial being, and to oblige the listener to participate in the inner act by which they are defined.

Sound is an event: by its coming it breaks an original silence, and it ends in a final silence. And music, like sound, projects its form upon a background of silence which it always presupposes. Music is born, develops, and realizes itself within silence: upon silence it traces out its moving arabesques, which give a form to silence, and yet do not abolish it. A musical work, like all sonority, unfolds between two silences: the silence of its birth and the silence of its completion. In this temporal life where music perpetually is born, dies and is born again, silence is ever its faithful companion . . .

IF MUSIC, which is a *becoming*, is to live, it must be incarnate in ordinary time; but it is not to be confused with such time. The

103

musical work, which has a certain duration, is not compelled to occupy a given moment of time. And, transcending that actual time from which it takes its flight, in time music escapes from time; for the nature of music is to be forever contemporaneous with those very moments during which performance makes it actual.

Now silence—which marks the boundaries of a work of music, and never ceases to envelop it during its unfolding—protects music from all the exterior noises which are the events of the ordinary world, and prevents the web of music from being confused with the web of a world which must remain alien to it. Within the zone of silence in which music comes to life, it creates for itself an autonomous becoming, the independent construction of its own forms, beyond that actual becoming which it must nevertheless encounter upon each of its successive reincarnations.

If silence bears and supports music, it is in order to remove it from the external world, by creating round it an atmosphere of calm collectedness in which it can flower. For in this calm, those who listen no longer hear anything but the voice of their inwardness, that inwardness for which alone music lives, far from the world of matter and space which noises symbolize.

In that original silence from which the musical work emerges, the soul broods over itself—and only in itself, in its inner essence, will the true substance of sounds be revealed to it. A musical work supposes the silence which precedes it: it cannot be born until it has effaced the exterior world and space in order that the hearer, turning in upon himself, may find in himself that active and pure duration which music will fill with life. That silence into which music is born is not pure nothingness: in it dwell an attentiveness and an expectation. Therefore the original silence must be respected—both by the performer and by the listener—for in it music, isolating itself from all that it is not, confronts us with the pure possibility of itself. Too often the Westerner neglects to prepare himself to hear, whereas the Hindus and the Tibetans have long considered "the birth of sound" as a religious mystery into which the soul may not enter unworthily . . . But the birth of sound only exists for those who, respectful of that original silence from which music arises, feel the hidden springs of inwardness rise in them. Music, like sonority, is real only for those who have been able to desire it and to wait for it. A good silence, *heard* by the performer who is about to play, brings him an intense confirmation: already he is one with his audience, in proportion as they, with him, are discovering the inner principle from which is born, and through which will live, the sonorous form.

SILENCE, which isolates music from the ordinary world, just as it prepares the soul by liberating it from alien impressions, reappears in the music itself: it always exists in music, actually or implicitly, whether sounds disappear before silence, or whether silence is obliterated by them. Whatever may be the continuity of musical form, it always returns to that fundamental silence from which, seemingly, it has delivered us only to make us better aware of its virtues . . .

Music reflects in its form the very essence of time. Now time, both creative and destructive, the force of our life and also its invincible limit, is composed of being and non-being, of actual realities and of possibilities which will never be realized; and music, to be its faithful image, associates sonorities—symbols of the realized and the actual—with silence, symbol of indeterminate and obscure virtualities, of the infinite potencies of becoming. If the musical work falls back now and again into silence, to be reborn from it, those silences are not scattered bits of nothingness in the duration of the music, shattering its being and breaking its continuity; rather they are of one substance with the music; for the reality of sounds emanates precisely from the powers of silence.

Silence is thus the symbol of possibility—and of freedom; furnisher of possibilities. Musical time, like our inner continuity, is not a logical structure; and that original silence into which music is continually dissolving, expresses the freedom of the musical form, which, like consciousness itself, exists only by virtue of continual creation. One might say that silence is the very substance of music, since in it the individual sounds dissolve into the possibility of all sounds. In this way the sonorous form would be the determination of an original silence in which sleep all the virtualities of sonority. But that form would lose its meaning without the continual escape of the particular sound from the infinity of its possibilities. For in them is born expectation, which is attentiveness to musical form, and participation in the act that will engender it. If sound seems to surge forth from silence, it is because it cannot in fact be born except from the movement by which, in silence, activity was already orienting itself towards the making of sound.

Silence, which interrupts the sonorous form without breaking it, is the instant made manifest, and, because it is bound to the instant, that unreal division between the past and the future, silence is inseparable from unrest, from anxiety. In silence, a being is identified with its pure freedom, with that pure possibility of itself which it discovers when it retires within itself. Not only for sonority, but for the mind as well, silence is an oscillation between nothingness and being. Upon what paths will the mind be launched by the sonorous form, and shall it ever experience the fulfillment of that form, as yet in search of itself? The drama of the sonorous form becomes the image of the inmost drama of the mind. In silence, beyond sounds and music, the mind questions itself. But such interrogation is not alien to music . . .

If in the musical form each sound, each phrase, has a halo of silence, it is because its essence is to be perpetually nascent and renascent. Like the mind, sound never stops dying and being born again, for it consists in movement from possibility to enactment; and melody, like our own lives, is nourished by those deaths and rebirths.

MUSICAL FORM builds itself by the very power of silence. First of all, it cannot exist except when, in the indistinct tonal space, pre-eminent points emerge, harmonically defined, leaving them a silent space. The melodic curve lives by the intimate union between what it affirms and what it leaves out. But there are two kinds of silence: that which must remain empty, and that which must be filled. The virtual silent space upon which melody traces its form must remain a thing understood: as Riemann has shown, it is from the primitive spatial continuity which melody implies and presupposes that it draws the indivisibility and the unity of its movement. But in the silences which separate the various melodies, the various phrases of a work, tonal space is interrupted: for it must no longer tie together, but separate. This brings about an empty silence no longer subtended by a virtual tonal space—in order that the melody which is dying away may come to an end and close in upon itself.

Silence possesses, then, a power of determination: what we shall call its *formal* power. It is silence that distinguishes and individualizes sounds and phrases and delimits the period of time in which they are enclosed: its action builds an ordered becoming. And punctuation, like rhythm, expresses this necessary "breathing" of the musical phrase in silences which define its contours.

In pure continuity, melody must vanish. Just as, to describe its arabesque, it needs the distinction of privileged points in tonal space, so it must also have the distinction of fixed instants of time —instants subject to the law of rhythm. Melody demands the rhythmic organization of becoming. Bergson is wrong when he invokes melody to strengthen his analyses of pure duration. Melody is as much distinction and order as continuity and fusion. But it would be pure fusion, if silence did not introduce into it determinations that allow its form to be born. From silence emerges the temporal order of music—that is to say, music itself.

Becoming and movement, too, arise from silence. Absolute continuity would be confusion—and it would be immobility. There is movement only when there is transition through distinct and original moments in time, and melody only moves because it is unfolding through distinct sonorities which make its motion *measurable*.

Silence, which distinguishes the different elements of melody, builds this authentic continuity, not the indistinct Bergsonian continuity in which musical notes dissolve, but an intelligible continuity, logically articulated in becoming. Far from causing the musical form to crumble, silence constantly folds it back upon itself and upon its action. If melody goes on by constant renewal, it can only do so by finding again, beyond the break, the vital force of its beginning.

In its objective aspect, silence effects distinctions; in its subjective aspect, silence is less a breaking off than a joining together. And the alliance of sounds and silences, instead of being a succession of absences and presences, merely expresses the indissoluble union, in real and heard music, between the sounds given to the mind, and the act by which the mind gives them to itself. The various sound-elements and phrases of musical discourse, despite the zone of silence which surrounds them and allows them to be distinguished from one another, are nevertheless joined in a unity; the silence which separates them objectively, unites them subjectively, for it is the occasion of their spiritual synthesis. In any silence, indeed, an echo of the past meets an inkling of the future:

a memory and an expectation. In it the pure powers of the·mind become visible, without which the musical form could not be constructed.

It is evident, when one thinks about it carefully, that musical form, this moving synthesis of memory and expectation, lives as much by silence as by sound. For it becomes reality by the union of past and future—the silence of what is no more and the silence of what is to come. It could even be said that a virtual and silent sonority surpasses the real and sensible in importance . . .

THE TEMPORAL CURVE of melody, like that of the whole musical work, is never given to us: we make it for ourselves. Musical time transcends the moments of actual tone experience and takes shape in a silent and spiritual *now*, where form can hold sway.

In heard music, all sounds, all harmonies—so their sensory reality ordains—return into nothingness one after the other; but it is the nature of musical form to take them from their ephemeral existence by ranging them in a curve which stretches beyond them— and gives them their meaning. Melody and musical form only exist when the heard sounds, in their emotional transience, gather together in a synthesis which can make them live again spiritually. For the sounds which have vanished live again in their form, in the mind which thinks that form. Thus music, in its temporal web, reconciles the two contradictory poles of being: its emotivity and its constructive activity; time experienced and time contemplated in music are one, and from that union are born its forms. For experienced duration can be fixed only beyond itself, beyond the sensory reality of the sounds, in a contemplated form which indivisibly surmounts it and is its realization.

Musical form, which in the world of sense can never give us anymore of itself than swiftly disappearing sounds, is created only within ourselves. For the development of music requires an act, occurring at each sound and yet superior to them all, which at once gives them their individuality and serries them in a single becoming. Always incomplete in its sensuous reality, music becomes complete beyond sound—in a silence filled only by our act . . .

Melody and the musical work exist only in the simultaneity of a form, in a "successive present," since their becoming is at the heart of their indivisible presence. Yet it would be contradictory that this simultaneous form be realized in perception itself, for sensuous sound can only be one with form if they are situated on two different levels, simultaneous form transcending the pure succession of heard and evanescent sounds. In pure succession the various sounds cancel each other out: the presence of one expresses and must express the absence of all the others; if they were all given to us at once, they could only contradict each other, and no form whatever would emerge from their meeting. They can only harmonize, therefore, by renouncing their sensuous existence—and participating in a single form which makes all of them actual at once in a silent synthesis . . .

IN THAT INITIAL SILENCE from which the musical work is born, it already announces its future, that future of its own self, which is as yet only pure possibility, and which it will change into reality. When it begins, it unfolds both through heard sounds, and into a silent future which it never ceases to project before itself, a future which will not cease to be until, by coming to an end, the musical work brings about its own self-conquest. The performer, starting with the first sounds of the work which he is playing, must first "create the atmosphere," attune us at the outset to a work as yet unknown to us, by even then invoking its future being. The work which is being born must awaken in us desire for its completion, for the tracing out of its temporal curve. Yet that future which it engenders and which we people with potential sonorities must be *determined* by it, and yet not *predetermined*, so as to magnetize our expectation, and not annihilate it by depriving us of that element of the unforeseen which is nonetheless something we *expect*.

The silent and unreal future gives meaning to the present: a few sounds, a few chords, are enough to create in us a whole system of expectations which the work will have to meet. And in these expectations one can distinguish a whole hierarchy modelled upon the musical form and its various articulations. On the one hand there is a generalized expectation which seizes the work in its totality ahead of time, as it were, and which is oriented towards its fulfillment and end. Within the limits of this general expectation are created others more particular: that of the immediate harmony, of the completion of this bit of a phrase, of this phrase

. . . Thus the whole work is integrated into a hierarchy of expectations which it creates in order to satisfy.

There is no possession without attention and expectation. The performer is already capturing his audience in that initial silence when we sense that he is turning himself and us toward the future work; but that silence only makes us attentive in proportion as it arouses expectation. The ear really hears only what it secretly wishes. It is the silent desire for the tonic which confers all the brilliance to its audible, tonal presence. We know that there is, in composition as well as execution, a technique of postponement which, perpetually causing expectation to be reborn and to grow, by the very refusal to satisfy it, permits us to come to the realization of a full and intense possession. Expectation is a mental preparation.

The listening state of awareness is always straining toward an *absence,* toward the moment when that absence will become presence. This tonic—which the work seems to delight in withholding from us, while yet implying its potential presence—does not this tonic, by its absence, give the musical measure its movement? The musical work feeds on our expectation: even though it has an objective foundation, it achieves fulfillment subjectively. Thus we come to understand that its objective form and the real and sensuous sounds maintain in themselves, and yet far from themselves, a silent expectation which alone gives them their entire reality.

MUSICAL TIME requires an equal fullness in all its different moments, thereby confirming its unity and continuity. But this is an entirely spiritual plenitude. From a tenuous form, almost empty of substance, a crowded and lively passage may flare out; and conversely, musical time may remain empty despite a multitude of sonorous events filling it. We might even assert that material density sometimes forms an obstacle to its truest plenitude. Thought must always be victorious over that sonorous matter whose sensible richness it creates; and through that matter there must always be visible, as by transparency, the ordering activity of the mind. The musical form can embrace silences without thereby being destroyed or having its coherence threatened; it is enough that music impart a meaning to them: then they are no longer gaps or empty spaces scattered through it, for the very continuity of its movement animates and sustains them.

The silent instant can be as full as the sonorous instant, if it is integrated into the form: it is empty only materially, and if sound be absent, thought dwells in it.

But next to these peopled silences, there exist empty silences, no longer dominated by the musical form—and by that very fact intensely expressive. Empty silence gives us an acute and moving awareness of our subjective duration, and of how much it depends upon ourselves: in it revives that anguish from which the musical form delivered us, and into which it plunges us again, abandoning us to that moment when being is given up to its potentialities . . . We no longer rush toward the future along with the musical work; we rediscover our loneliness. The expressive silence exiles us from musical time.

It is rhythm which makes manifest the existence of silences which insert themselves—and us—into the tonal form. In rhythmical configuration, the "silences" which replace absent sounds are silences of *tonal* duration, but not of *musical* duration. For they have the same value as the sounds which they replace, and whose negative equivalents they are. These silences are therefore full—full of musical duration because they are prescribed in a rhythm which gives them their formal and objective meaning.

In rhythmical form, silence plays an essential role, carving out its contours and allowing the rhythmical figures to be constituted by the distinction and synthesis of their units. What demonstrates clearly that silence cannot be empty or void, that it can even be a pre-eminent and important element in tonal form, is that there are silences in rhythm which are strong moments—accents: these accents are therefore purely in the mind. But if they are in us, and not in the form, they have no meaning, except by remaining subject, in us, to that very form . . .

Yet there is an empty silence, no longer part of the rhythm, unforeseen by the rhythm. It disorganizes the form, and thereby causes a burst of expressiveness. These are silences of "suspension," since they hold up the course of the musical form; momentary stops in objective musical time, which permit the free flowering of subjective duration. These stops have no special notation of duration, but a simple notation of *indication:* the hold; and even this hold is more often lacking than not. Here musical duration, to exist, must lose itself in our duration, as its need of performance shows; and the hold merely testifies to the presence in music of irrational periods of time, dependent on the performer's wish, and infinitely better manifested by silences than by sounds—being freed as they are from tonal form, and thereby necessarily bound up with our subjectivity. These irrational silences, which give its living quality to music in performance, are in a sense continuous; but, being an expression of the subjectivity of the interpreter, they must be left to his free initiative; and so they escape notation entirely. The musical form must breathe to live; but it only breathes beyond itself, in the subjectivity which receives it and lends it vitality . . .

Just as there are full and empty silences, there are *musical* expectations and *psychological* expectations. Musical expectation always comes back to the objective tonal form by submitting to its requirements. And that silence which is integrated with the form receives its plenitude precisely by the expectation which musical time animates and fills. However, along with that full and creative expectation which loses itself in the very movement of the tonal form, there is a psychological expectation in which time, empty of musical matter, is no longer lived as movement forward, but as an obstacle breaking the forward movement of musical time. Silences and expectations are expressive or formal: they involve us in the form or separate us from it. In classical form expectation is always oriented toward possession; in the romantic form expectation, cultivated for its own sake, remains, and is destined to remain, unsatisfied: then appear those silences which break the form in order to deceive our expectation and to prolong it by refusing it satisfaction. Those silences which escape from form are expressive in proportion as they are able to cause, far from the discipline of musical time, a free and imaginitive unfolding of psychological duration . . . If full silence is animated by the momentum of objective form, empty silence is subjective: it is in us, and no longer in the music itself.

In addition to absolute silences, there are relative silences; in Beethoven and Wagner certain tonal events are only there to announce others to come, so that their meaning is extrinsic to themselves instead of being immanent; thus they cannot, according to the expression of Pierre Souvtchinsky, "adequately fill" musical time, which consequently finds fulfillment only in our subjective duration.

Within the silence—absolute or relative—of tonal duration and of musical time, emerge subjective duration and expression; sensibility, abandoned by rhythms, oscillating according to its whim, is given over to its own movements—and disorders: regrets and desires are born which are out of tune with the musical form. Here, consequently, expression is (as so often) a breaking of the form, a manifestation of the "human, all too human," as it throws off the yoke of formal constraint . . .

WE MADE A DISTINCTION between silence which is integrated into form and silence which escapes from it—or even destroys it. And yet perhaps we ought not to establish an absolute opposition between these two kinds of silence, since any silence has only a subjective reality. As experiments have shown, even when silence enters into a rhythm as an integral part of it, silent duration is appreciated with less precision than tonal duration—so that, in some measure, the dissolving activity of subjective duration is always manifested in it. It appears that the rhythmic precision of a performance suffers by rhythms in which silences predominate; and that silence is not integrated into the total rhythmic figure except when sound predominates, compensating for its lack of precision.

There is, however, also a silence which is *supposed* to escape from the rhythm, a subjective and irrational silence which has value in and for itself, and maintains the autonomy of its existence. This irrational silence is introduced by the punctuation which is placed outside of the rhythmic figures, in order to deploy them by determining and delimiting them. The silence of punctuation, because it is exterior and superior to the rhythmic figures, has a merely irrational and subjective duration; but precisely because it refuses to be integrated into the form, it can construct it—and fulfill it, beyond its actual passage in time, in our own minds.

Silence, then, can escape from form not only to destroy it, but also to construct it. In silence the two contrary aspects of our subjectivity find expression: its weaknesses and powers, its passivity or its action.

Although it is not integrated into rhythm, the silence of punctuation is not a pure nothingness; it is true to say rather that it is the fullest and most important moment of musical becoming: the very moment when it is made real. It is in the silence of punctuation that the passage of one rhythmic figure or phrase to another is accomplished, while the totality of that figure or phrase is virtually recapitulated in it. Generally speaking, the musical form must sometimes yield to becoming in order to construct itself, and must sometimes resist—in order that we may construct it. Silence interrupts time, that form may emerge. For the form which, as we know, lies beyond the audible duration embodying it, is only complete in the mind. So it is in silence that the mind, withdrawing into itself, actualizes and possesses form. The musical form, which transcended sounds, and gradually constructed itself beyond their sensible presence, gathers itself together and achieves fulfillment in a silence now definitively separated from them.

The melody, while drawing toward its end, moves back toward its beginning,[1] for it only exists at the moment when the two commingle. Thus the cessation of the audible melody is the advent of the melodic form. The musical work—and the various phrases of which it is made up—achieve fulfillment only when, curving round toward their beginning, they come full circle on themselves and manifest their transcendance over that ordinary time into whose keeping, for a few moments, they entrusted their form.

Musical time is a union of movement and rest. But if movement gives it life, it is born and finds fulfillment in silence and rest. And if the end of the melody is mingled with its beginning, that is because, having emerged from the mind, it must return to its place of origin. The silences of punctuation allow the musical form not only to define itself objectively, but also to penetrate our inwardness. In breathing, the musical form recovers its vital inward force —which is none other than our own.

The tonal form, as aforesaid, is continuous creation, and this explains why it never abolishes that original silence from which it was born. Activity, in order to construct musical becoming, must perpetually begin again, turn again to the past to embrace it— and to go beyond it. Melody is an alliance between the continuous and the discontinuous; but the discontinuous is taken up again, at once a possession and a new beginning, capture of the past and creation of the future. In silence, we feel that musical becoming is not something given, nor any *thing*, but that it is, like our own inner duration, creation and freedom. Sound and melody only exist by virtue of the act by which we recreate them, by virtue of

[1] Tonality gives proof of this necessity by requiring that the musical work begin and end on the tonic.

that "inner singing" with which we welcome them, to our inmost being. They are the incarnation of a gesture and an act; through these
they are born and fulfilled. And silences, far from threatening the
continuity of the musical form, are a return to the act out of which
it is born—not only in time, but outside of time, in the intemporality
of its form.

Silence, which is a privation of sensuous sounds, appeals by that
very fact to an inner activity, which overrides it and so wins back
what had been given up to it. Thus silence exists only to change its
vacuity into plenitude . . .

At the moment when the musical phrase is complete, the mind
is free to make, or not to make, a synthesis of it—to grant or to refuse it existence. For it is the province of the mind alone to construct form, and thereby to rescue from oblivion the sounds which
were its material support. Silence is the sanctuary of the mind—
and of the freedom of the mind.

The musical work, melody and rhythmic figure, are framed between two periods of rest, two silences. The musical work is a
series and a hierarchy of curves which envelop one another. But
these curves and their union are never given to us: the mind must
give them to itself—give itself to itself—by the act of memory
which reunites the sounds scattered through time into an indivisible form. There is therefore a silence which is full and musically
occupied, although purely subjective. This silence is assuagement
and possession, for it prolongs in a spiritual form a previous tonal
enjoyment.

Both the composer and the performer must reserve, within
the musical duration, silences which allow the mind to appropriate,
to conquer freely, what was originally imposed upon it. But silence,
realm of the mind's freedom, can give occasion for its triumph or
its error. There is a *good use* for silences, and music must in some
manner hold us to it. If there are too many silences, they destroy
the musical form by causing a predominance of subjectivity, which,
given free rein, disengages itself from the discipline of musical
form. Modern music tends to repudiate the irrational silence placed
outside of the form, and in its objectivism only permits itself those
almost material silences which, integrated with the form and compelling the mind as much as would the very tones they replace,
forbid the listener any movement towards liberty. But too full,

too compact a musical duration dissipates the mind by dissolving it in sonorous matter, by alienating it from itself, and by preventing it from concentrating upon its own inner essence.

Silence, the absence of sensuous sounds, is a presence of the mind and of form. In the silence of material music is born that silent music of the mind which is always immanent in audible music. The plenitude of musical time requires empty spaces of time and silence which shall actualize in its purity that inner duration which is the hidden essence of musical duration.

A great sparsity of tonal events occupying a musical duration may actually give it a fullness which it has not when it is too crowded. Their very rarity is the price of their being more fully possessed; and the silences, giving rise to the mental act, intensify their sensible presence.

Musical time is meant to be occupied by the active presence of the soul. The accomplished performer "takes his time," for he understands that music lives not only by sounds, but also by silences which cause the very soul of the performer or the listener to be steeped in music. The mediocre performer, however, hustles the notes instead of linking them together flexibly and freely: for he fears the breathing spaces and silences which break the continuity of the form when one does not know how to give them their spiritual content. Silence must never interrupt musical duration, which must always animate and permeate it. If there are performers whose silences are but nothingness and absence, there are others who know how to be present in them, and, animating them with musical duration, make the silent instants as living and full as the audible ones. Is not beautiful phrasing precisely the art of silence, the art that links it to sounds in an intelligible continuity? If the perfect performer holds his audience as much by the power of silences as by that of sounds, it is because in them also musical duration makes us feel its law . . .

Thus we see the ambiguous nature of silence—by turns destructive and constructive, capable of annihilating form or fulfilling it. But this ambiguity is the mark of its subjective essence and of the appeal it makes to our freedom. In it the musical form accepts its dependence upon us; and whereas, in sound, form forces its requirements upon us, in the silences it behooves us, of our own free will, to remain faithful to it. In silence, the mind can will musical duration or deny it.

Now we see why performer and composer alike fear silences: they always oscillate between two extreme values—nothingness or plenitude. By turns expressive or formal, they set up the form, or set themselves against it.

In rapid passage, silence tends to lose its expressive power—to be stripped of all save its formal power. For rapidity adapts our subjective duration to the time of the work and does away with any strained relation between the two. It delivers subjectivity from its own wildness and disorder, bringing it entirely under the rule of form, drawing it into the momentum of form, making it one with the essential act out of which musical time is created.

In slowness, silence acquires its full expressive power, but in slowness also we are more particularly menaced by its destructive power, that possibility of annihilation which resides in it. Slowness, by opening a gulf between subjective duration and the time of the work, invites subjectivity to a certain self-indulgence: slowness permits our subjectivity to listen to itself, and to live withdrawn from the objective form, along the edge, as it were, of its constraints. Nevertheless, the composer and the performer must know how to create in slowness long silences filled with musical duration . . .

Even in the irrational silences of punctuation, which seem to escape from musical duration, the latter must not be interrupted: an elastic continuity connects the various phrases across the silences, across their breaks; connects and unites them into the total and indivisible form of the work. And the "dynamic calm" of a performance stems from these resting-points of punctuation, which do not break the continuity of the musical form, so long as that continuity, always reigning over the soul of the performer, reigns likewise over those very silences during which its sensory reality ceases to be.

The irrational silence of punctuation exercises, and must exercise, a formal function: far from being an abandonment of form, it must express possession of it. In such silence, form must be fulfilled.

In romantic form, silence is destructive and not creative: being the expression of the pure becoming of awareness and of its infinite aspirations, it ends upon an unsatisfied desire, and not a possession. And that final silence in which it ceases to be heard does not turn it back to its beginning: for in it dwells no completed becoming, closed in upon itself. Romantic form remains deliberately open: that is why it readily rejects cadence and that fulfillment of form which cadence expresses. Romantic silence, far from defending musical duration against subjective duration and ordinary time, allows it constantly to communicate with them, and to end incomplete, by becoming lost in their incompletion. Silence is what makes musical form close in continually upon itself, what gives it completion. Fulfillment is only realized in cessation. The very word "completion" bears witness to the intimate bond which unites fulfillment and cessation, since it designates both one and the other, indivisibly. Romantic form, however, rejects that silence which is completion; and that is why it never presents itself to us in a synthesis of its parts, but dissolves into that "infinite melody" which will not be the prisoner of any synthesis.

By contrast, the formal silence of classical music, although its essence is subjective, completes the form, both objectively and subjectively. If silence is an escape in the direction of future possibilities, it is also a taking into custody of the past. Just as in it the future takes shape, so does the past become spiritualized. One may well say with Mozart that the silences in music are more important than the sounds, since it is in these silences, filled by the mind and its action, that the musical form is achieved. Silence is the spiritual echo of music, the dwelling-place of its final reality and its flowering.

When music relapses momentarily or definitively into silence, that silence is not nothingness or privation, but possession and fulfillment. When real sonority fades away, then is born the remembered sonority of thought. Silence gives the act of memory the means to construct form. By withdrawing us from audible and material music, silence compels us to possess it in truth, which is to say, in the mind. The sensuous sounds must vanish—for the spiritual act which alone is capable of possessing them to take place, by identifying them with that inner and silent music which is the origin and end of what we hear.

The silence of expectation had already alerted the activity of the mind. But the most perfect spiritual plenitude does not belong to the silence of expectation, which implies an oscillation between possibilities and irresolution, but to the silence of possession in which the mind, wedded to form, assimilates its perfection.

When the melody and the musical work comes to an end, they

do not immediately return to nothingness, but, closed in upon themselves, they are then present to our thought in their entirety, and their becoming takes place in an indivisible present. The work dies in silence but also is realized in it: and the silence of its completion is filled with its spiritual essence.

MUSIC CANNOT EXPRESS FEELINGS in their precise nuances, but its forms, because they are temporal, and express the very forms of our inner duration, arouse in us "pure" emotions which are related only to themselves, and cannot put a distance between us and them. One comes to understand why silence admits of two aspects, expressive and formal, which are indivisibly bound up together: in determining duration, silence determines our subjectivity itself, at the same time with the form of music; and formal silence possesses an affective quality, a pure expression which has no other content than that form which it engenders in our duration. From silence emerge, therefore, a wide range of "temporal" emotions bound to pure time, which transcend music without being extrinsic to it. An imaginary drama—the symbol of our inward drama—underlies musical form.

There is an anguished silence, born from an interruption and a breaking off, in which one's being, rudely torn from the fullness of the senses and the joyous rhythm of form, finds itself abandoned and given over to its potentialities. It rediscovers then those empty moments, that pain which is the awareness of a time no longer animated by activity, the pain from which music sets us free. Calmer emotions too are born in silence: there is the moving and self-communing silence of birth and emerging into being; all genesis is deeply emotional, for it makes us participate in that activity which is the root and source of being. In silence the emotion of expectation is also created—expectation, which is filled with the richness of potentialities, submissive to our imagination—anxious expectation, directed towards an unforeseeable future, to be feared—or hoped for? When we listen to a musical work, we accompany it with our desires and our hopes, and without them its form would be deprived of reality and meaning. There is, finally, the emotion of pure becoming, of that progressive falling of sonority into silence, which gives us an acute awareness of the flight of time and the essential sadness of our temporal life.

Particularly expressive is that moment when tone and the musical phrase, dying away, are insensibly transformed into their own memory and, dying to sensible life, are reborn in the mind which harbors them. But this silence, however expressive it may be, is no longer anguished: for the act of the mind which fills it is victorious over its nothingness and wrests from death what had just been swallowed up in silence. There are therefore serene silences, in which the calm of possession is reflected, in which activity, freed from the constraint of heard sounds, rejoices in itself and its free powers: such is the silence in which the work, completed and fulfilled, offers itself in its entirety to the contemplating mind.

And so there are silences of divers affective qualities, but which can all be classified under one of the two headings we have established at the beginning: expressive silence and formal silence. To sum up, we might say that expressive silence insists upon the anguished, troubled aspect of pure subjectivity, whereas formal silence makes manifest its active and creative powers. Expressive silence and formal silence embody the two contrary values between which affectivity oscillates, its values of darkness and light, its disquietude and its assuagement. Silence can be the pain of annihilation and breaking off, or the joy of affirmation and fulfillment: nothingness or plenitude. Yet in the musical work that peaceful silence which is affirmation and fulfillment must be finally victorious, must save musical becoming from mere becoming and enclose the work in its definitive form. Towards this peaceful silence the musical work constantly tends, as though it were only truly born when it contracts into an indivisible present which encloses musical time in itself. The repose of silence, a symbol of the suspension of time, confers eternity upon the musical form and, depriving it of its sensible existence, makes it one with its essence.

Be it possession or expectation, and endowed with whatever affective quality, silence must invoke what goes beyond it, the transcending act of the mind. It is filled by the mind, for it is the mind's own presence to itself.

Privation is spiritual possession. "Love is the son of poverty," said Plato; likewise one might say that music is the daughter of silence.

The spiritual act only awakens in the absence of its object, and from that initial deprivation is born its movement towards its object. Often the sensible presence of things and beings prevents the mind from possessing them, for, by imposing their presence on the mind, they divert it from acting. Everyone knows with what intensity an object or being materially absent can be present in our imagination. It is the very nature of the mind to make of absence the instrument of presence.

It is in their absence that objects and beings realize in us their spiritual essence, and it is in that absence of itself which is silence that music achieves fulfillment. That is why sounds must fade away and die for the musical work to be born.

Time in the Plastic Arts

ÉTIENNE SOURIAU

I

Nothing is more dangerous for the exact and delicate understanding of the plastic arts (design, painting, sculpture, architecture, and minor arts) than the rather banal description, "arts of space," in contrast to the phonetic and cinematic arts (music, poetry, the dance, and to this group we must now add the cinema), characterized as "arts of time."

This contrast, subscribed to by a great number of aestheticians from Hegel to Max Dessoir, has its historic origin in the philosophy of Kant, particularly in the contrast he makes between the external senses, to which the form of space would be inherent, and the internal sense whose form would be time. The desire to bring music and poetry into the realm of the internal sense (in order to see there "the soul speaking directly to the soul") has often led to a real misunderstanding of the extent and the cosmic reach of the plastic arts, stripped of their temporal dimensions, and of their content according to that dimension. This is what I would like to demonstrate in this article.

Every work of art creates its own universe. And whoever speaks of a universe speaks of a whole built upon a space-time net-work. This is as true of painting or architecture, of ceramics or of landscaping, as of music, poetry, or the cinema. I shall not consider here these last-mentioned arts (or the frequent misunderstanding of the role of space in poetry or in music).[1] I shall consider only the problem of plastic time.

II

Naturally, the ill-founded contrast between the arts of space and the arts of time has some foundation in sense. There are obviously notable differences in the manner in which time is used in one group and in the other. But what exactly are those differences?

One may say: the difference is self-evident: a musical, poetic, choreographic, or cinematic work is unfolded *in successive moments,* while a pictorial, sculptural, or architectural work is seen *in its entirety in a single instant.*

But this last point is *clearly false.* In the case of painting, which uses space in only two dimensions, no doubt a single glance which catches a view of the whole is possible, and it is even of great importance for aesthetic appreciation. But it is not sufficient. Can one appreciate the full beauty of a painting without a period of contemplation wherein successive reactions take place? Baudelaire went so far as to say that the period of contemplation and the prolongation of its effects in the memory constitute a sufficient criterion of artistic value. Hence his formula: "Art is the mnemonics of the beautiful." Without going that far, we see at least that in all the arts there is a "time of contemplation" filled with successive psychic facts, more or less prolonged, and of which the aesthetic content is important.

But when we consider the works of art which use space in three dimensions, the facts are still more topical. A statue presents aspects of itself which are aesthetically quite different, depending on the point of view from which one regards it. The sculptor himself must have foreseen these different aspects, and combined them in a specific

[1] The very original works of G. Bachelard: *Water and Dreams* (1941), *Air and Dreams* (1943) constitute a direct study of poetic space (although the author does not assign them quite this significance). A study of musical space is yet to be done.

relation wherein the block of marble or bronze is only the instrument and the material means. Is it necessary to say then that the spectator can only see these different aspects one after the other and in a certain order? His movement around the statue brings to view, as it were, melodically, the various profiles, the different projections, shadow, and light; thus the most complete appreciation of the aesthetic complexity of the work is gained only by the moving spectator.

It is the same for a cathedral as for a monument. It is only by a dangerous abstraction, favored by certain habits of teaching or of technical thought, against which we must react (consideration of diagrams, of plans, and of working-drawings) that one can conceive of a work of art as a totality seen in a single flash. In so far as it is offered to the sight, to the aesthetic appreciation, to the emotion or to the contemplation, the cathedral is successive: it delivers itself little by little in different spectacles which are never simultaneous. The cathedral of Chartres, seen from afar rising above the plain of Beauce, or from near by when one is in the cathedral court; seen from a straight-front view or obliquely, or from the side; seen finally from the interior, according to whether one has just entered by the west door or whether through a series of changing perspectives one slowly approaches the choir;—presents with each aspect an artistic quantity which is absolutely different, and no one of them is seen simultaneously with any other.

No doubt, the *physical frame* inclosing these successive aspects remains materially unchanging. No matter. The disc on which a musical composition is recorded also remains materially unchanging. The disc however is but an instrument for the orderly presentation of the work which itself is the structural law of the latter, and which governs the musical *execution*. One must see in the same way the movement of the spectator around the statue or the architectural monument as a plastic or view-absorbing execution, which unfolds in order the various aspects which are held within the physical frame, and which are the aesthetic reason for that frame as it was planned.

Are there profound and basic differences between this "plastic execution" and a musical performance? In a musical, theatrical or choreographic work, the order of successive presentation is set, constant, precisely measured and determined. In painting, sculpture, or architecture, this order is not determined: the spectator is free to stand where he likes, to move at will and in any direction he pleases, or to remain in one place for a long time while only his eyes move. The order in which he views the object and the speed with which he shifts from one point to another are up to him.

So it is. But let us exaggerate neither restraint nor liberty. The reader of a poem is free to slow down or hurry his reading, to linger in meditation or to come back several times to a loved passage. On the other hand, the lover of cathedrals is held to an extremely set order which obliges him to regard in continuity and through a regular and sometimes irreversible succession, the various aspects through which an harmonious impression is established. He will proceed to the perspectives of the nave only after the main portal has been presented to him, like an opening chord; he will see the windows of the transept appear only as a kind of surprise of sudden modulation after the procession in regular harmony of the perspectives of the nave, modified at each step throughout its length. And who will dare to say that this ordered succession is unimportant, or that it has not been artistically foreseen by the genius of the architect?

There exists one art in which this *melodic order* of view by means of a *set progression* is structurally fundamental: that is the art of landscaping, an art too often neglected in its importance by aestheticians, but on whose aesthetics Francis Bacon, Rousseau, Kant, and Poe have all commented. There a path is not merely an ornamental line draw upon the ground (or on the plan). It is likewise the law of the way through the garden which conditions the successive and ordered appearance of the view, sometimes gradually changed, sometimes revealed as a surprise. A park or a garden, which is well planned (that is, conceived by a true artist such as Le Nôtre, Kent, Ligorio or Forestier) is a collection of stylized scenes, appearing to the promenader according to a melodic succession which is foreseeable and artistically arranged.

If we understand this, we note immediately that even in painting there is something analogous. The movement of the eye, in a picture, is doubtless not forced or determined, but it can be directed, by virtue of a kind of gentle and firm influence without which the composition of a picture would be unintelligible. Auguste Rodin, who applied in sculpture very conscious conceptions (inspired by Rude) of the evocation of movement by a temporal displacement of the different parts of the work according to the phases of the action, insisted with reason that the same fact exists in painting. In his *Conversations*, assembled by P. Gsell, he studies from this point of view the composition of the *Embarkation for Cytherea*, by Watteau, in an authoritative manner; we shall say why presently. We know, on the other hand, that certain surrealists have attempted to extend this principle even further. (The "lithochronism" of Domingues is one of the best examples.) But here a difficulty arises, from the fact that they have presented the result of thought activity anterior to the work, without concerning themselves (on principle) with establishing in the work any means leading to a dynamism of analogous thought in the mind of the beholder. It is one of the points where theory in the hands of the surrealists has wronged artistic practice.[2]

III

These last facts bring us an important step forward. There is no longer a question of a simple *psychological* time of contemplation, but of an artistic time inherent in the texture itself of a picture or a statue, in their composition, in their aesthetic arrangement. Methodologically the distinction is basic, and we come here (notably with Rodin's remark) to what we must call the *intrinsic time* of the work of art.

The significance of these words (valid for any of the arts) is particularly clear and striking when we deal with the representational arts, as in the normal case with painting and sculpture (and also for literature, the theater, etc.). Any work of art of this type establishes, as we were saying just now, a universe. Let us call it "the universe of the work," and let us give these words a meaning entirely analogous to what the logicians since De Morgan call the "universe of discourse."[3]

A novelist, or more precisely, a novel, presents a coherent grouping of people and things, systematically connected in place and in action. It is this universe which I accept and consider for a while as real, by hypothesis, during the whole time that the reading of the novel lasts (and even a little beyond). The content of the universe of the work is all that exists in space and in time according to this hypothesis. Now the space and time which make up the

[2] The best documentation on these facts is to be found in the *History of Surrealism* by Nadeau.

[3] Cf. Lewis, *A Survey of Symbolic Logic*, Ch. III.

framework of this universe must be considered as intrinsic to the representative content of the work, and entirely distinct from the space and time occupied by the physical form of the work, or by the reading of it, or meditation about it. For example, the time of a novel, (that is to say the order in which its events are supposed to follow each other) is completely different from: (1) the order in which the narration is unfolded, and (2) from the time it takes to read it. The narrator may, for artistic reasons, now follow steadily the thread of the adventure, and now come back to give explanations on earlier happenings that have brought about the situation. The order of narration is then utterly distinct from the intrinsic order of the succession of events in the imagined universe.[4]

In the theater, where there is much less liberty in the narration, the time of the work and the time of the performance follow generally the same order.[5] And yet the distinction between the two times is important. Particularly is their tempo or rate of speed constantly different. Time in the work always passes more rapidly than the time taken in the performance. (I speak, of course, of time during the stage action; it is quite a different thing for the time of the intermission.) [6]

Their extension is not always the same. Time in the work outruns at both ends time during the performance: before the situa-

[4] Is it necessary to say that this analytical distinction is not only theoretical on the part of the aesthetician but that it is inherent in the practice of art? The decision, on the part of the author, to keep the reader in ignorance of the background of the situation, then to disclose it to him suddenly and purposely by an explicit return to the past, perhaps little by little by imperceptible touches, or even to leave it quite unexplained, constitutes a deliberate method of composition basically inherent in the art of the novelist; and generally directly conditioned by his most personal and fundamental conception of the art. Nothing is more curious than to study and to contrast from this point of view Balzac, Dostoyevsky, and Conrad.

[5] At least it has been so for a long time, and has made for a strong contrast between the time of a novel and the time of a drama. In the last twenty years, time in the theater has acquired greater flexibility; and notably there is no longer any hesitation in making use of the return to the past. But this is certainly due to an influence of the motion picture on the theater. The movies have almost from the beginning made use of the "novel time" rather than "theater time."

[6] We must note that this relation is quantitatively measurable: I can affirm that on the French stage at present it is at a minimum of 3/2 for speaking time (three minutes of time in the play represented by two minutes of performance); and it goes much higher for silent scenes—waits, prolonged silences, etc., where fifteen or twenty seconds are easily estimated to represent two or three minutes and more in the play. But we can note also that it seems to have diminished

tion that we find when the curtain rises, the characters are supposed to have lived, to have had experiences which have brought them to that situation which the "exposition" must permit us to imagine. At the end, when the curtain falls, we are also often allowed to see in perspective, more or less clearly, the future of these people who are taking leave of us. We guess that Leandre will marry Isabelle, that Oronte will be consoled, that Colombine will have other adventures, etc., etc. We have been shown only a few selected and fragmentary moments of time in the designated universe, but it is understood that this time, continuing, extends far beyond these moments, and can be reconstructed in our mind on a much broader plane, exactly as the space that is show on the stage is but a piece cut from the imagined universe, and extends in all directions in a way which also can be reconstructed by the mind—and in which the imagined topography is almost as exacting as real topography.

All that has just been said concerning the novel or the theater can be said about a statue or a picture, and is of extreme importance in aesthetic analysis. A picture such as the *Mona Lisa* designates in space the universe of the work on a vast scale. To speak roughly, at least two kilometers in depth are suggested by the perspective of the landscape. What there is to the right and left of the space visibly represented has as much aesthetic importance as what is actually represented. This is true of what lies outside the picture before one—before the implicit spectator, the phenomenological "I" of the witness, implied by the aesthetic structure of the work;

steadily since the beginning of the seventeenth century. I have in my hands an unusual and careful study by Anne Souriau of *Space-Time in Corneille* which gives precise estimates on this subject. Besides the rule on unity of time in this period gives us precise measures (notably for the *Cid*, where the agogic excess was noted and criticised from the beginning, although the point was contested by Corneille). The theatrical sensibilities of a play-goer of the seventeenth century accepted very readily a relation of four to one. But one can show that in the plays of Dumas fils (on the French stage in the second half of the nineteenth century) the relation can be estimated at a minimum of two to one. It can go higher. (I speak of course for time in speaking.) In *L'Ami des Femmes* (1864) a monologue which cannot take more than ninety seconds at the most in real time is supposed to last (watch in hand) five minutes. It is, of course, a "gag." But considering the technical mastery of Dumas in the art of the theater, as demanded in that period, there is no doubt that he gives us there a consciously precise document on the relation of the two times, in his estimation in the theater at that date. The figures which I give here, rest, of course, on a much more detailed documentation.

better still, the person at whom Mona Lisa is looking, as if at no one. In sculpture where the content of the surrounding space is always implicit, the aesthetic importance of the entire space of the work is still greater. The *Victory of Samothrace* is surrounded by the sea, by the wind, by the waves cut rhythmically by the course of the ship. And the genius of the sculptor is that he has given to his block of marble, to his statue, the power of arousing *necessarily, immediately, powerfully* all that surrounds it by means of which the absolute success is evident, but which cannot be judiciously analyzed without taking account of the relation of the block with the implicit environment that it suggests, and which gives so much breadth to the created universe.

Is it necessary to say that a certain length of time and a certain rhythm in that period are likewise characteristic of that universe? The entire body of Niké has just straightened itself; her chest swells, filled with the breath which will make her trumpet sound as the ship advances. And one of the aesthetic secrets of this masterpiece is this choice of a prerogative moment that is still capable of keeping its relation with a long unfolding of continuous action, so that the psychological time of contemplation is enclosed within the time of the work and participates in it without effort and almost without limit. Study from this point of view the endless attempts of sculpture (or painting) to express movement, and you will see that the painful impression given by horses rearing, dancers or runners stopped at the wrong moment makes it impossible to have the time of contemplation (which is prolonged by immobilizing the body represented) coincide for more than a second with the time of the work, which demands that the body momentarily suspended in the air drop immediately to the ground. Compare then the *Dance* of Carpeaux (at the Opera in Paris) with the *Dance* of Bourdelle (at the theater of the Champs-Elysées): the obvious artistic superiority of Bourdelle lies in a better choice of the prerogative moment represented. If in itself this moment is not lasting, it is such at least that it must be periodically rediscovered by the effect of a rhythm imposed both on the time of the universe of the work and the time of contemplation, and that is the key of their agreement.[7]

In painting, notably, the time of the work may attain dimensions

[7] The importance of this choice of the moment in a given situation is well known. It has been subjected to a searching analysis using a precise example in

equal to and at times greater in breadth than theatrical time itself.

If I look at the *Shepherds in Arcadia* of N. Poussin, I am obliged to be aware of an immense stretch of time. One may even wonder if it is not excessive. In any case, it is obligatory: no artistic comprehension of the work is possible if one does not take account of the temporal basis implied by the ages of the various persons, the presence of the tomb recalling those who lived formerly in the same place, and in the future, that inevitable death (*et in Arcadia ego*) whose shadow falls upon love and present happiness, saddens and adds greater meaning to the tender gesture of the young woman and the expression on the face of her lover. This rhythm of life and death, in the past, the present, and the future, this return in thought to the past, with a corresponding movement toward the future are all part of the fundamental aesthetic structure of the work. And the vastness of this double movement (one of the most outstanding in art) gives to the time of this painting certain artistic traits that are essential to it.

IV

There is then no doubt about this importance of time in the plastic arts, about its double presence as time of contemplation and intrinsic time of the work and about the existence of an interplay of harmonies and disharmonies between the one and the other of these two times.[8]

I should like now to bring some order to the aesthetic study of

an excellent study, the principle of which we approve completely, by Lucien Rudrauf (*The Annunciation, Study of a plastic theme and its variations, etc.*). See especially the list of the seven distinct moments possible in the theme of the Annunciation, in spite of its extreme simplicity of action. These moments are very different in their aesthetic and sentimental values.

[8] If one wished to be absolutely complete, one would have to consider still two other times: (a) the time of the conception and execution of the work. But the latter is of no aesthetic importance except as it is evoked by the finished work, and plays a part in its artistic effect. I shall note further on the dangers of confusion in this respect (particularly in connection with an article, cited below and very interesting by Marcelle Wahl). (b) The time of the material permanence of the finished work. For example, the fact that an architectural structure is visibly ancient, and bears the marks of the action of time has a certain aesthetic

these facts by undertaking a brief comparison of time in music with time in painting. Time in music has been the subject of many studies from Plato and St. Augustine to Bergson and many others. It might be worth while to make use of this extensive and precise knowledge to uncover the facts, analogous and contrary but less· exact and less well known, that play a role in the plastic arts.

The three chief classifications of aesthetic facts relative to musical time concern (a) its dimensional extent (b) its structure, notably in the form of rhythm, (c) its agogic (tempo or speed) variations. Let us study the same facts in the plastic art, principally in painting (but let us not neglect sculpture and architecture when these have a bearing on the subject).

V

A musical work occupies and organizes a time which varies from one or two minutes to two or three hours (the works of the lyrical theater are the longest, and may extend far beyond this limit if one considers a group such as the Wagnerian Tetralogy, the performance of which requires several days). This period of time always has an exact beginning and a precise end, characterized musically. For example, in classical music, there are strict rules governing the moment the voices begin, and when they stop on the cadences. And, between the beginning and the end, certain rules, equally precise,—the use of "broken cadences," "interrupted," etc.—serve to mark the continuity of the temporal development in spite of the partial and temporary stops.

With rare and accidental exceptions, outside of properly artistic conditions, (time tables of the opening of expositions or museums; ritual presentations of works of religious art during ceremonies, etc.) it is not the same in the plastic arts: the time of concrete presence (time of contemplation) is not defined. The contemplation is never very long: who remains more than a few minutes in pure aesthetic contemplation before a painting? All the phenomena of contemplation take place during a period of from thirty seconds

effect. But one can always go back in thought to the time when the work was new ("when the cathedrals were white"). It is for these reasons that we shall not linger here in these two points of view.

to ten minutes. A longer time would begin to be abnormal, and would suppose causes and consequences outside the purely aesthetic attitude (for example, facts relative to religious mysticism, or the iconographic study of the work, etc.). In this time, impressions are produced of which some are solely relative to the subjective attitude of the spectator (a shock of surprise or a slow captivation of the mind, attention or distraction, revery, or a participation in a dynamism, etc., etc.). But one can say that there is always more or less rapidly, more or less lastingly, a more or less central moment of coincidence and of harmony between this time of contemplation and the time itself of the work, at least when the aesthetic effect is profound.

As for this intrinsic time of the plastic work, one can say that its organization, in general, is *stellar* and *diffluent*. The time of the work radiates, so to speak, around the prerogative moment represented. The latter makes a structural center from which the mind moves backward to the past and forward to the future in a more and more vague fashion until the moment when the image fades gradually into space.

Let us consider the *Presentation of the Virgin in the Temple* by Tintoretto. The group composition dictates the movement by means that are topographical, morphological, and dynamic. That is, a spiral staircase between the shadowed wall of the temple and the cloudy but clear [9] sky. Mary is half-way up the stair, walking slowly toward the group of priests about to welcome her. A slow and gentle rhythm of movement is suggested by the detail of the wide tread of the stairs, no doubt to emphasize the smallness of the young girl alone among groups of people. One feels that she has just climbed the three steps that separate her from St. Anne. One accompanies her in thought to the threshold. Any longer prolongation or more complete regression would be in contradiction to the evident theme of which the pictured moment is the stellar center. But the influence of contemplation along this course is easy and sure if one does not prolong the time of the work, and if one leaves both ends of the action undefined. [10] There is a delicate charm in continuous time with misty edges.

[9] "Cloudy but clear"—cloudy but *bright?*—Ed.

[10] A kind of aesthetic accident that is rather curious may occur in this connection. It may happen that a work of art incites its spectator (or reader) to a revery, a kind of imaginary romance lived subjectively where the work of art is for-

Let us compare *Heliodorus Driven from the Temple* by Raphael: here we receive a shock in quick and dramatic time, but it is difficult to prolong (certain people and animals represented in the act of running or jumping are caught in mid-air and must fall back to the ground). A fact characteristic of most of the great compositions of Raphael is this: the time of a certain part of the picture (here the right side, the dramatic one) is not homogeneous with the time of the other part (here, the left): on the left side many of the people are caught in indifferent and conventional attitudes which belong unhappily to this "time in the studio", if I may say so, where Raphael is responsible for some of the worst faults of academicism. This is the great defect in his *Placing of Jesus in the Tomb*. There, time is neither fused nor suspended, it is clumsily arrested in positions that are obviously studio poses taken without any fusion with an action which might prepare them and prolong them, and which, moreover, are contradictory if one should attempt to prolong them. This is, in general, a fault of Raphael as soon as he tries to get away from those prerogative moments which may be prolonged in repose or in cyclic rhythm and in which on the contrary he excels.[11]

One could in painting, use the terms "poetic" and "dramatic" for these two kinds of time on condition that we understand that it has nothing to do with the emotional atmosphere of the work, but only with the structure. One can call "poetic" a time when the pictured moment links and blends with the previous and subsequent moments capable of prolonging contemplation a long time, without differentiation between that prolongation and the intrinsic time

gotten, since it was but the inspiration and the pretext. No doubt this inductive power is linked very closely to certain aesthetic qualities of the work. It may even have been expressly desired by the artist. But if it goes too far, and produces effects which separate from the work, it comes in conflict with the true contemplation, and may become aesthetically abnormal. The man who likes music for the mental images it helps him form does not really like the music. On this same subject there are curious facts in the history of religious art. In general the mystics ask that the image lead to thoughts which are detached from the work itself and cause it to be quickly forgotten. And in this their attitude is clearly different from the purely aesthetic attitude.

[11] As for temporal dualism in Raphaelesque composition, consider the *Transfiguration*: the time of all the upper part is a time of slow and cyclic rhythm; the time of the lower part is one of dramatic shock encumbered in several places by those unlikely poses of which we have spoken: where it is impossible to blend with a before and an after.

of the work; and "dramatic" a time so closely connected to the
prerogative moment that it cannot be linked to what follows or
to what precedes without evoking images in striking contrast with
the spectacle of the prerogative moment. As an example: *The Blow
of the Lance* by Rubens. The close relation of the time of the work
with the pictured moment is the structural key to its dramatic
character along with a thousand other plastic factors unnecessary
to analyze here. Compare [it] with the *Descent from the Cross*, also
by Rubens, in the museum of Antwerp.[12] However dramatic the
theme and the plastic whole may be, the linking in fusion, the
gradual sliding down of the body, the agogic slowing of the action
almost to immobility, create this contrast between the dramatic
character of the action and the poetic structure of the time, which
is one of the profound reasons for the strange character (almost
voluptuous in one detail) of this work that has caused so much
literary comment, because of its double moral perspective in profound contrast.[13]

I cite here facts which have as much to do with rhythm and
tempo as with dimensional restriction or openness, and with the
narrow or wide stellar structure of the time. I can separate only

[12] There is no *Descent from the Cross* by Rubens. in the Antwerp museum,
but two in the cathedral. From internal evidence—the "poetic time" of the
descending motion, and its contrast with the dramatic tension of the subject—
the reference seems to be to the version I have used in illustration of this passage.—Ed.

[13] One may present these two moods of plastic time in another aspect. They
correspond to what L. Rudrauf properly notes, in the work cited above, concerning the contrast between the "transitory moment" and the "indefinite period,"
for the expression of which he has recourse to the distinction the philologists
make between the *perfect* and *imperfect* (temporal aspects of the verb). Consequently, he distinguishes a "present perfect" (or perpetual and unchangeable),
and a "present imperfect" (or transitory moment). "In fact," he adds, "painting
and sculpture know these two moods also." (He should say: these two "aspects"
to maintain the grammatical analogy; cf. Vendryes, *The Language*, 1921, p.
117.) The remark is as precisely correct as it is important. To give a striking
example, compare, on the Tombs of the Medicis, the temporal aspect of the
Night, which sleeps and of the *Dawn*, which awakens. No doubt, Michelangelo's
Dawn awakens eternally, one may say so, and one could contemplate that awakening perpetually. But that eternal instant remains transitory in its essence, so that
there is contrast between the eternal and the transitory, between the contemplation, and the time of the work. While with the *Night* there is harmony no matter
how long contemplation may be.

abstractly, in order to analyze them better, these various factors which are always systematically combined in a work of art.

One last fact is worth noting here: the prompt closing of the time of the work with a definitive ending can be no more than a seeming end, contradicted by a reopening, and the effect is more powerful. If a painter depicts a horse galloping toward a wall which is only a yard away, I know that a brutal shock is going to put an end presently to this incident. But when Rembrandt shows me *The Angel Leaving Tobias*, if my first impression is that the angel rising with beating wings is going to crash into the vaulted ceiling of the room, obviously the intention of the painter is that I imagine that it is no obstacle to the angel, so that the moment, which is, at first impression, dramatic, is reopened by a kind of spiritualization of the angel, a flight toward the heavens, and disappearance, thus prolonging poetically the initial dramatic effect, and contributing greatly to the impression made by the work.

VI

I shall insist less on the facts relating to the *organization* of the period of time, particularly to rhythm, because they have been more often noted and studied by aestheticians in connection with the plastic arts.[14] What must be said is that these facts have sometimes been exaggerated by giving the word rhythm a too extensive and too vague meaning. There is no rhythm (if one gives this word a precise meaning but as general as possible) unless there is an organization of a continuous succession through the cyclic repetition of the same basic scheme (which is of course susceptible of various concrete forms). There can then be purely spatial rhythms. The history of decorative art gives us many examples. The cyclic repetition of the same motif, or of analogous motifs of the same dimension, is constantly met in decoration, especially with the primitives. One sees it also in architecture (a colonnade is the simplest type among the *functional* elements in architecture, but in a general way architectural *decoration* is rhythmic, be it in vertical or in horizontal direction). On the other hand, in sculpture which is not included in an architectural synthesis, and in isolated

[14] For example, by W. Drost, Pinder, v. Schmarsow, Marcelle Wahl, etc., etc.

pictures, such spatial rhythms are rare; because forms of symmetry, balanced groupings, and more or less geometric schemes of composition are not sufficient to create a spatial rhythm, in the strict sense of the word.

Finally, if we speak of temporal rhythm (and that is what interests us here) we must be even more strict. Certainly the successive themes of visual perception can be organized rhythmically in time, as the experiments of Koffka have proved forty years ago. But are these facts constant or significant in the contemplation of plastic works, or in the intrinsic time of these works? One must be very reserved in saying so. No doubt when contemplation becomes revery, and produces phenomena that bring it close to hypnosis, one sees a rhythmic plan established. But most often, normal conditions of contemplation prevent such an occurrence. Thus the fact that the attention of the spectator moves from one part of the picture to another at will works against the formation of a rhythm in the true sense of the word. Finally when the time of the work is clearly rhythmic (for example by the depiction of a rhythmic action: dancing, walking, the movement of waves, or reflections on the water, the fluttering of leaves, etc.) we must note that art in general tends, by the choice of a prerogative moment, to suggest a kind of mental equivalent to rhythm, by the permanence of this prerogative moment, rather than to demand that the mind actually travel the complete rhythmic cycle. If for example one studies psychologically the contemplation of a work such as the *Dance* by Bourdelle (one of the most powerful plastic portrayals of rhythm that exist), one will see that there is produced with regularity as a kind of *thesis* or accented time, a coincidence of the subjective rhythm and the objective time; while with the *arsis* the representation becomes mentally vague, when a kind of discrepancy should occur between the mental image (which would show another moment of the action) and the visual image. If from time to time a rhythmic plan is thus suggested, most often one's thought tends to take a kind of "pleasure in repose" in a participation with the element of stability, which is a function of rhythm, and on which the artist has based his work in the choice of the pictured moment.

There are other facts of the organization of time to which the idea of rhythm is wrongly imputed, but which are none the less very important: for example, this group movement, the general "arabesque" of a picture; that the spectator at one time contemplates in desultory fashion, at another grasps intuitively as a whole. It is a powerful influence in the organized plan of contemplation as well as in the over-all understanding of the composition, its expressive value, and its style. It is often expressed by technical details, for example by the sense of touch. Marcelle Wahl, among others, has shown in her book on *Movement in Painting*, its importance in the composition and aesthetic characterization of works such as the *Creation of Man* by Michelangelo, *Venus and Music* by Titian, *The Death of Sardanapalus* by Delacroix. This author is mistaken, in my opinion, to speak of rhythm in this connection, not only because the term is not scientifically exact, but because it leads to phrases such as "rhythms of creation and emotion," which seem to me mythical notions.[15] But once this error in terminology is corrected, there is no doubt that the quest, in the form of characteristic arabesques, of a kind of ordered movement of the dynamism of the work through space and time corresponds to something positive and important.[16]

The profound nature of this concept will be better understood, and the positive study of it more successful, if we think of such an organization, in its temporal aspect and scope, as corresponding exactly to what is called in music the *phrasing;* distinguished both from the melody (which is based on the differences of pitch) and from the rhythm (based on the repetition of an *arsis-thesis* system). Like rhythm it is based on facts of intensity (nuances) even while its form is extended over a dimension analogous to that of melody.

Whoever distinctly grasps these ideas, will feel the importance of what we must call the *phrasing* of a picture; and for example, the stylistic importance of the differences observable between the slow, full, majestic *phrasing* of a Veronese (that of Tintoretto is more suave with equal plenitude), the rugged phrasing of Cara-

[15] M. Rudrauf (quoted above) is also wrong to speak of rhythm for facts which belong both to phrasing and tempo. But except for this faulty term, the facts which he observes and notes in regard to the dynamic organization of the picture in its relation with the time of the action are very carefully and thoroughly studied.

[16] Notably in the Case of Eugène Delacroix such aims are entirely normal. Certain precise indications in his memoirs show that he was consciously preoccupied with artistic factors of this kind. It is what he called the "torsion" of the picture.

vaggio, powerful in its boldness, brutal, even a bit melodramatic; the essentially polyphonic and architectonic phrasing of N. Poussin; or again the pathetic and tormented phrasing of Delacroix. It is entirely reasonable to note a likeness with these characteristics in the music of Palestrina, Monteverdi, Bach, or Berlioz.[17]

VII

Plastic tempo is very closely allied to all the preceding facts. But it is distinguished from them in principle. In music, the tempo is the *qualitative* [18] impression of slowness or of speed expressed by indications such as: *adagio, andante, presto,* etc.; and of which the slightest variations often have a great expressive value. It is understood that in painting and in sculpture, it is impossible by objective means to account for an impression of slow time, very slow, to the point of immobility almost (as depicted in works such as the *St. Jerome in his Cell* by Dürer, or the *Song of Love* by Burne-Jones, or *Mourning* by Saint-Gaudens); or an impression of moderately rapid, truly agitated or fantastically violent movement, as demonstrated in these three stages by the *Spring* of Botticelli, the *Rape of the Daughters of Leucippus,* by Rubens, and the *Horse Frightened by the Storm* by Delacroix. But one must not forget that it is the same in music where no count of the number of notes

[17] We are not dealing in vague analogies. For example, on the subject of the close relationship in style (and in aesthetic doctrine) between Caravaggio and Monteverdi, one may read an excellent and thorough article by René Jullian (*Pro Arte,* January 1946). And perhaps this historian of art, who is also a learned aesthetician, has not made use of all the elements which not only permit of a comparison but make it necessary. Thus, one of the characteristics of the *phrasing* of Monteverdi (the unprepared attack with certain dissonances) is easily comparable with certain characteristics of the rather brutal dynamism of the compositions of Caravaggio (the attack by grouping people in a luminous ray of light producing violent contrasts of shadow and light, and modelling detail only at the other extremity of his trajectory: see for example his *Death of the Virgin*). Naturally, Caravaggio never thought of imitating Monteverdi, or vice versa. But the normal evolution of art has inspired both of them not to fear the boldness, the formal violence of successive dynamism that their predecessors would not have dared.

[18] Cf. Hugo Riemann; or Liszt, preface to the *Dante-Symphony;* or Lionel Landry, *Musical Sensibility,* 2nd ed., p. 35.

per second can suffice to indicate the temporal rapidity which comes from causes which are aesthetically much more subtle.[19]

Thus, a slow *tempo* or a sprightly one, sliding gradually to a limit which has almost an eternal quality or animating the universe of the work with speed toward a future opened up or soon closed, is among the essential characteristics of a picture, a statue, and, up to a point, of an architectural work. No doubt, in this last case, (architecture), since there is no *depicted action*, the nature of this "tempo of the monument" is more difficult to grasp. But it is easy to understand that the physical or psychic *work* of a monument can imply a very clearly characterized rate of speed. The *tempo* of the Greek temple, of the Romanesque church, of the Gothic cathedral in the primitive style, the middle period, and then the flamboyant, is obviously more and more rapid. One could comment upon this along spiritualistic lines taking account of many elements, among which the character of the decoration has a great symptomatic value. But in the realm of pure technique it is also easy to find positive criteria. The examination of the forms of bell-towers from the eleventh to the sixteenth century (for example, a group like Brantome, Morienval, Senlis, and Notre Dame de L'Épine in France) will suffice to illustrate the facts. Forms which are at first square and squat, then much less heavy and more perforated, with more absolute elevation in height, and a basis of support less broad with a greater vertical elevation, make a dynamism from low to high which is more and more rapid in its tempo. It is connected with the idea of "élan", which, however subjective it may appear, can be studied morphologically in profound and exact fashion. Thus it is impossible to separate it from the idea of the rapidity of an essential movement, which has become spiritual, going in the opposite direction from the forces of gravity and decay.

These last facts of course suggest the idea of a symbolic rela-

---

[19] A passage in demi-semiquavers of an *adagio* pours out more notes per second than a *presto* in white and black notes. [In English, more usually, "half-notes" and "quarter-notes."—Ed.] Even the length of each measure is not a sufficient criterion of the agogic (rate of speed), although certainly it is a most frequent and most normal proceeding to shorten the measure to give an impression of acceleration. But there are also purely harmonic means (for example the "retard" and the "anticipation") and polyphonic ones. In the "stretto" of a fugue, the "entrance" of the voices at brief intervals to time gives the characteristic impression of haste.

tionship between the concretely structural facts positively presented
in the "cosmos" created by the work, and a transcendental content
which would prolong and surpass it. But I do not wish to enter
upon these considerations, which belong properly to philosophy
and metaphysics. What we have already seen is sufficient to permit
certain useful conclusions. Here they are.

VIII

1. The positive analysis of a work of plastic art cannot be sufficient unless it takes account of those time factors of which we have
just spoken, as well as of the facts reducible to spatial considerations. The more scientific one wishes to make aesthetics, the more
one must consider these factors. The universe created by a plastic
work always involves a time of which the principal characteristics—
dimension, "aspect" (in the philological sense), rhythm, tempo etc.—
must be considered in a complete analysis, and often have an importance essential to the study of the art of which the particular work
is an example.

2. These facts would be of great significance also (although we
have not insisted on this point of view) for the psychological, philosophical, and even scientific study of time. Because one would
have but an insufficient and imperfect conception of the way in which
man thinks of time, if one did not take account of the documentation
which aesthetics furnishes on this subject. In that immense and
fundamental activity of the human race, the realm of the arts, man
exercises the power to master time, to fashion and form it, to vary
it qualitatively, and to generate it by means of which the greatest
plastic masterpieces form the most authentic evidence.

3. In so far as there is a difference, in regard to time, between the
plastic arts and others, the advantage is on the side of the plastic
arts. I do not hesitate, in fact, to say that time is *more important*
aesthetically, and more worthy of study, in painting, sculpture,
or architecture than in music, the dance, or the cinema. Here more
delicate and more profound perspectives are opened up. Why?

Because, in the arts which are obviously temporal, time is the
palpable stuff of which the works are fashioned. The symphony,
the film, and the ballet are spread out, laid down, on a bed of
time; the time spent by the auditor or spectator is practically pre-

determined. His psychological experience must pass through a mill, as it were, where the work is measured out to him moment by moment according to the creator's will. The composer and the dramatist are the masters and tyrants of a direct and obvious time. If they make good use of it, let us applaud, of course. But their task is quite simple in this regard.

But the painter, the architect, and the sculptor are masters, by a more subtle magic, of an immaterial time which they establish when they create a universe whose temporal dimension can extend or contract in a moving and curious way. Now a brief and fragile moment is brought to life brilliantly, perfectly; again the extent of the universe can reach to the equivalent of eternity. On this temporal frame is modeled a content that can be as rich in rhythm, in impetus, in variation of speed or slowness (and hence in human or transcendental significance) as all musical or literary temporality. But this time is never suggested except by means that are indirect, oblique, and subtle. However fragile, delicate, unsubstantial may be these means of suggesting time, they are the key to the greatest success in these arts. Plastic time is an essential time, of which the particular characteristics in each work form the most moving evidence of the power of the artist, in creating a masterpiece, to flash before our eyes a world to which he invites us, and where we may live.

Bergsonism and Music

GABRIEL MARCEL

THERE IS NOTHING, in a sense, more contrary to the spirit
of Bergson's philosophy than raising a question such as that which
constitutes the subject of this study; and this is true for several
perfectly valid reasons.

In the first place—and with all due respect to Thibaudet—there
is probably no idea less Bergsonian than that of Bergsonism. In
fact the inherent tragedy of that most difficult and powerful thought
is its inability, because of its very premises, to ever become converted into a system, or in other words, to complete itself without
negating itself at the same time. Why, in so far as it is itself a higher
mode of life and spirit, would it, also, not bear the stamp of the
unforeseeable or of perpetual creation, and thus be condemned—
or consecrated—to remaining forever open, far indeed from ever
being "closed up" or rounded off into the vault of a church? Consequently, there would be little point in taking a body of propositions
called Bergsonism and trying to draw from it any particular corol-
lary applying to music.

Furthermore, the idea of a theory of music, even of the very
possibility of such a theory, would seem to have little chance of
finding its content in Bergson's philosophy, which has always been

as greatly concerned as that of Aristotle or Comte with maintaining the absolute specificity of the various spiritual domains, or modes of experience, and which always looked with discomfort and distrust upon any attempt to *rationalize* those modes and replace them with abstract equivalents. It is wholly consistent with everything we know about Bergson to admit that for him, were a philosophy of music possible, it could only be at the end of a long investigation of somewhat the same nature as that to which he had formerly subjected biology, after experimental psychology. In other words, it would be a serious mistake to believe that Bergson's writings up to the present day [1] could themselves justify to his mind any particular statement on the nature of musical inspiration or the special world it reveals to us. Still it is indeed necessary to realize that such an investigation could not consist in the simple conscientious collating of facts and information bearing either on the psychology of the musician or on his technique. It should be totally imbued with the vital breath that gives life not only to Bergson's books, but to his thought, considered both in its aesthetic and personal unity. This, after all, means that the investigation could be made only by him; and *he will not make it.* He is called upon by other undertakings that he feels are more important and that will doubtless take up the years he might still devote to philosophical speculation. True, Bergson has often liked to maintain that he has brought no more than a partial contribution to a great collective work which others after him would continue. It seems he would say that the time has come for the philosopher to cease making over-ambitious syntheses and be satisfied with limited results that will gradually organize themselves—and in a way unforseeable by the very ones who will have brought them about. Were this really the case, we would have the right to hope that one of Bergson's successors will someday bring us the philosophy of music which the author of *Matière et Mémoire* has not provided, but which would continue his psychology. Unfortunately it is to be feared that this optimistic and social view of speculative endeavor is in great part illusory; and besides, it is perhaps in contradiction with the doctrine of philosophical intuition set forth by Bergson, particularly at the Congress of Bologna. No one can have any confidence in Bergson's *disciples*, he himself probably less than anyone else. When they are not just annotators, they will be

[1] 1925—Ed.

virtuosos playing dangerous variations on themes whose solidity and precise power of development they are surely in no way capable of evaluating.

All these preliminary comments may seem beside the point. Yet I believe them indispensable for strictly limiting the importance of the reflections that follow.

Actually it is extremely difficult for a reader of Bergson not to assume—and wrongly—that a certain philosophy of music is contained in the theory of concrete duration. And perhaps under those conditions, we have the right—without entertaining any illusions as to the ultimate value of this study—to undertake an elucidation of that philosophy itself; and to see to what extent it is in agreement with direct experience.

IT WOULD SEEM DIFFICULT at first to believe that it was only by chance that Bergson so readily used a tune as an image in order to communicate what he meant by pure duration. Let us reread, in particular, the well-known page of *l'Essai* [2] (p. 100): "Pure duration is the form which the succession of our conscious states assumes when our ego lets itself live, when it refrains from separating its present state from its former states. For this purpose it need not be entirely absorbed in the passing sensation or idea; for then, on the contrary, it would no longer endure. Nor need it forget its former states: it is enough that, in recalling these states, it does not set them alongside its actual state as one point alongside another, but forms both the past and the present states into an organic whole, as happens when we recall the notes of a tune, *melting, so to speak, into one another*. Might it not be said that, even if these notes succeed one another, yet we *perceive* them in one another, and that their totality may be compared to a living being whose parts, although distinct, permeate one another just because they are so closely connected? The proof is that, if we interrupt the rhythm by dwelling longer than is right on one note of the tune, it is not its exaggerated length, as length, which will warn us of our mistake, but the qualitative change thereby caused in the whole of the musical phrase."

Obviously, in reading a page such as the one I just quoted and

[2] *Time and Free Will*, transl. by F. L. Pogson (London, 1910). Page references in the text have been changed to fit the standard English translations from which the quoted passages are taken.—Ed.

which is far from being an isolated case in Bergson's works, one is tempted to wonder whether a certain well thought out experience of music would not, in a way, be at the origin of the doctrine, *underlying* it, so to speak. Here again, however, one must be extremely careful: has not Bergson resorted to this musical comparison simply in order to avoid any ambiguity, and after all, could he not just as well have used as an example a *spoken* phrase, in which the words and the silences that separate them also organize themselves so as to form an indivisible whole? I myself am thoroughly convinced that this is true. Concrete duration is not essentially musical. At the most—and using a language of which Bergson would, and should, disapprove—one could say that melodic continuity provides us with an example, an illustration of pure continuity that the philosopher must apprehend *in itself,* in both its universal and concrete reality.

Yet this general observation does not prevent us from wondering to what extent the theory of duration, as it is set forth in *l'Essai,* for example, contributes to the elucidation of the nature of what I should like to call the phenomenon of music. Moreover a preliminary distinction must be made here. It does not seem as if *l'Essai* could provide us with any direct explanation of *elementary musical values.* It does not explain how it happens that sound takes on an irreducible emotional coördinate; and the following sentence in the first chapter of the book (*Op. cit.,* p. 44) gives us no help whatever in clarifying the difficulty: "How," asks Bergson, "will the expressive or rather suggestive power of music be explained, if not by admitting that we repeat to ourselves the sounds heard, so as to carry ourselves back into the psychic state out of which they emerged, an original state, which nothing will express, but which something may suggest, viz., the very motion and attitude which the sound imparts to our body." I would not dream of contesting the truth of that statement; but it is perhaps dangerous to assume, as Bergson here seems to do, that, strictly speaking, sound emanates from a psychic state, that it is possible for us to go back to by means of a kind of rebounding shock.

On the other hand, *l'Essai* is appreciably more instructive when it comes to the musical idea, or in other words, the tune in itself. Let us leave aside the somewhat unsuitable words I felt it necessary to italicize in a previous quotation. An analysis, such as the one Bergson outlined, unquestionably brings out—or at least helps to define—the altogether special type of unity which a tune has: a unity both undivided and fluid, the unity of a progression, not a thing. Yet perhaps, although I don't dare state it positively, the complex reality of musical experience in some way goes beyond Bergson's description of it. Here I should like briefly to bring out one point. Exactly what happens when I *follow* the development of a tune? Is it quite enough to say that the notes of a tune interpenetrate and organize themselves? Bergson speaks of (*Op. cit.* pp. 103, 104) "the successive notes of a tune by which we allow ourselves to be lulled and soothed;" and this helps to understand how he imagines—or more precisely, how he refuses to imagine—musical becoming. All things considered, it would seem as if listening to a tune was, for him, a way of dreaming it, what a German would call "hineinträumen," a kind of almost boundless releasing of life, a pure inner flow. And that way of living the tune, becoming the tune, is doubtless in complete opposition, according to him, to the act by which it would be represented as a line, that is, spatialized. But I am not certain that the absolute opposition between the "lived" tune and the represented tune is not too intransigent. To follow a musical phrase is not only to go imperceptibly from note to note; it is also to dominate that passage, at least to a degree, and Bergson certainly admits it. But is not that act of domination— which is in no way a mode of conception or intellection—one by which what is, in fact, flowing becomes consciousness of that flowing, and, in some ways at least, the representation, the figuration—but non-spatial—of the becoming? When we speak of the beauty of a melodic line, the aesthetic qualification does not apply to the inner progression, but to a certain figure which is, I repeat, non-spatial, or at least whose extended world can only provide us with symbolizations that we feel are inadequate. This would assuredly require long clarification; and I fully realize how the idea of a non-spatial figure might offend the mind. But in order to account for the musical experience, are we not obliged to introduce a notion of this kind? As I go from note to note, a certain whole takes shape, a form builds up which can certainly not be reduced to a succession of organic states, any more than an object is to be confused with the perceptible changes that its presence causes in the subject. It is in the nature of this form to exist, perhaps, only in duration, but also to transcend, in a way, the purely temporal mode according to which it appears. From this point of view, it is relatively easy to perceive what is generally meant by musical comprehension. Is it not in fact identical with the act by which the form builds up? Then, not to understand would be precisely to remain at the stage at which the states follow one another, or even interpenetrate, but without submitting to a *real musical being*. Unless of course it is agreed that incomprehension stems from the fact that the successive sounds do not even organize themselves, but on the contrary, remain discontinuous; it would then be no more than a total failure of memory of a consciousness incapable of going beyond the purely instantaneous. Right or wrong, I tend to believe that such is the interpretation that Bergson would be inclined to give of a phenomenon as universal as it is ill-defined. Yet does this take into account what experience shows us? I should think it doubtful. All of us have gone through those moments of inner illumination in which the phrase we were following, but without recognizing its internal necessity, suddenly appeared as consistent with its mysterious essence. But that act of apperception, whose equivalent could no doubt be found in the religious or mystic domain, is in no way reduced to the sympathy which makes it possible for me to become one with the phrase, to live it. I would willingly say that this is not a *surrender*, but on the contrary, a kind of *mastery*. Do we thus return to what Bergson calls intuition? Possibly, but actually nothing is less certain. Does not intuition, by its very nature, grasp what is in the making, the creative becoming as it springs forth? Now, is not the revelation in question rather the discovery of an order that had probably not been abstractly *conceived*, but of which it would be equally impossible to say that, strictly speaking, it was *given?* Everything happens as if we had been suddenly united to the musician's will, as if that will, having become ours, found its sole satisfaction in the idea. Just as philosophical solutions, far indeed from having an intrinsic significance, remain relative to a certain way of conceiving problems, so musical order here is a *consummation*. It is accepted by us at once only on condition that it shall *in some way satisfy an expectation*.

Music that I do not understand is, literally, music which corresponds to nothing within me. And is it not obvious that we are now reaching a territory where Bergson's thought stands ready to welcome us? It seems to me that the musician is asking me to place myself on a certain spiritual plane, where I should have the possibility of *meeting him*. "The hearer," Bergson wrote in connection

with attentive recognition, "places himself at once in the midst of
the corresponding ideas, and then develops them into acoustic
memories which go out to overlie the crude sounds perceived, while
fitting themselves into the motor diagram." (*Matter and Memory*,[3]
p. 145). I believe that this applies here with a minimum of trans-
position. A person who does not grasp a musical development is
in a position similar to one before whom a foreign tongue is spoken.
The conditions make it impossible for him to break down and then
reorganize the indistinct whole that is given him all at once. Only
of course in this instance, it would not, strictly speaking, be memories corresponding to sounds, which would overlie them. Yet we
must remember that for Bergson, a memory is by no means that
enfeebled reproduction of perception to which associationist psychology claims to have reduced it. The author of *Matter and
Memory* never stops cautioning us against any such interpretation,
which to his mind implies the most profound ignorance of spiritual
life. Memory and perception are entirely heterogeneous with respect to each other; and I wonder whether it would be a distortion
of Bergson's thought to maintain that pure memory, that is, completely removed from the actualizing influence of the body, is by
its very nature elusive. I do not believe that we could ever form an
image of pure memory. We can only imagine it as a limit placed
beyond, or more precisely, on this side of the representable. Consequently, I should not think it absurd to claim that the musician
appeals to our *memories*, which alone can make it possible for us
to—I will not say actually *understand* him,—but *hear* him. And
it can be shown that any true musical creation consists first of all
in conjuring up in us *a certain past*. This would not seem to me any
less obvious as applied to Mozart than as to Schumann, to Wagner
than to Debussy. And perhaps we would not be entirely taken in
by a metaphor in saying that the musician of genius is like a prism,
through which the anonymous and neutral (optically neutral) Past
that makes up the inner depths of each one of us, becomes decom-
posed, specific, and colored by personal nuances. A temporal prism.
I by no means shut my eyes to the not only paradoxical but almost
sophistic aspect inevitably assumed by such a way of conceiving
musical originality. But this stems precisely from the fact that we
are, for the most part, still very far from having assimilated the
most original elements of Bergson's doctrine. When I speak of the

[3] Translated by Nancy M. Paul and W. Scott Palmer, London, 1911.—Ed.

decomposition of the past, it is indeed difficult not to believe that I mean subdividing it into *historical sections*. Mozart would transport me to Vienna in the 18th century; Monteverde to Mantua a century and a half or two centuries earlier, etc. Moreover that sort of evocation would be achieved by means of a play of association of ideas which are diversified *ad infinitum*. But actually there is no question here of any such thing. In this instance, the past is not any particular section of a historical becoming, more or less explicitly assimilated to a movement in space, such as a film sequence. It is rather the inner depths of oneself, inexplicable with respect to what the present not only arranges, but—again and most particularly—qualifies. These multiple pasts are really sentimental perspectives according to which life can be relived, not as a series of events, but to the extent that it is an indivisible unity which can only be apprehended as such through art—art, or perhaps love.

It stands to reason that this analysis is much less suitable to some types of music than to others. Stravinsky, far indeed from resembling such conjurers of the dead as Debussy or Fauré, for example, seems, on the contrary, in some ways to make every effort at isolating us from our pasts and bringing us into an *intensified* present or, if I may say so, a cosmic present, in which personality is annihilated.

Despite deceptive appearances, it is by no means the same, in my opinion, for Wagner, who extends our memory into a theogony and reëstablishes a continuity between personal duration and the duration of the universe. It could be shown, I believe, that Stravinsky's art, because of the way in which he abolishes any distinction between the superficial and the profound within pure dynamism, is an absolute opposition to a philosophy according to which Being can be grasped at degrees of intensity or, more precisely, of interiority, hierarchically arranged, by means of the endeavor, itself graduated, of a consciousness at work on itself. Stravinsky's world is foreign to consciousness, and I, myself, am strongly tempted to believe that it is *on this side* of it. Moreover it is solely for this reason that one can join M. de Schloezer in referring to Stravinsky's music as "objective music."

These indications, appropriately exploited, would perhaps make it possible to elucidate in some degree what we mean by a profound musical idea.

The profound idea would appear, I believe, to have a dual character: on the one hand, it seems to come *from afar;* on the other hand, it corresponds to the slackening off of an effort, or to what I should like to call a *slackening off from above*. I am convinced that if we succeed in analyzing these two aspects of the profound idea, we will succeed in attaining fundamental truths. First of all, it is exceedingly remarkable—and I am beginning with the second point—that voluntary concentration is by no means enough to give us the feeling of this new dimension we call depth. Works such as D'Indy's string quartets, in which that concentration is carried to an extreme, are most significant in this respect. There, when the release occurs, it is always in the direction of the development, that is, the mechanism. In the case of the greatest musicians—and I am thinking of the Beethoven of the late quartets as well as the Fauré of the quintets—it might be said, on the contrary, that this release occurs in an opposite direction and by avenues that are ordinarily closed to the artist. Corresponding to this release is certainly the fact that the most profound idea is at the same time one which would seem the most *natural* to me: only here again, one must pay particular heed. For the word natural can have two contrary meanings: were I to hear a work today written by one of Debussy's more able disciples, for example, everything would seem *natural* to me, in that everything would fall at once into certain prepared frameworks. Not only would that music in no way upset my habits, but it would even spontaneously adapt to them because it is itself the result of imitation. But a short while ago, I used the word natural in quite the opposite sense. There is *non-surprise* the moment that there is *non-resistance*. But that *non-resistance* can perfectly well not have been caused by the existence of habitual forms in which the given elements have been cast. It can result from the presence within me of a void (but not yet felt as such), an active absence, and a kind of appeal made by the void itself. Such is often the case in love, and I believe that the same is true in the greatest art. Moreover we have come back to the experience of satisfied expectation which is at the heart of aesthetic intellection. In this sense, the profound idea is one which hits me just where I am still vulnerable, where the hardening acquired under the influence of repetition, that is to say, the mechanization of myself, still contains gaps. In a word: it builds me; it is *formative*.

And now, what is that distance covered within me by the idea? Here we come back to what I said a short while ago about the function of the past in music. But I think it is necessary to add that the past from which the idea would seem to spring is fundamentally an *unutilized* past; and at this point, one of Proust's remarks might be used, if not to complete Bergson's thought, at least to illustrate it in a most valuable way: "At whatever moment we estimate it," said Proust (*Cities of the Plain*,[4] II, p. 114), "the total value of our spiritual nature is more or less fictitious, notwithstanding the long inventory of its treasures . . ." And the profound idea has the miraculous power of putting an end to precisely that *unavailability* of ourselves. It reëstablishes between me and myself communications that I believed to have been destroyed. Current psychology enlightens us on this point: I receive a letter which I open with a feeling of vague and almost impersonal curiosity; but that letter brings me a serious piece of news that affects me. Everything happens as if the letter were forcing my ego *to come out,* as if it were driving it out. Emotion is actually the discovery of the fact that "this concerns me after all." In short, it brings me back to the consciousness of my own existence. I believe that what happens here is of a quite similar nature: the profound idea is that which brings about a sudden *remembrance of myself,* but does not—at least in principle—imply any represenation of a past event, whatever it may be. It leads me at once to a plane on which *I am with myself;* and were there a possibility of establishing a foundation for a musical mysticism, indeed it seems to me that this would be it. But one can see immediately the extent to which a philosophy of pure quality such as Bergson's contributes to the intelligibility of that progress in interiority; while, on the contrary, a metaphysics of the concept would be unable to provide even the possibility of that advancement towards a spiritual marriage.

I am fully aware of both the deficiency and the obscurity of the indications I have tried to set forth. In fact only special studies devoted to the musical inspiration of the great creators would be capable of clarifying them, each of the creators being considered as the bearer of a message—without intellectual content, but one which continually renews the soul that deciphers it and reconciles that soul with itself.

[4] Translated by C. K. Scott Moncrieff. New York: Random House, 1927.—Ed.

Music and Duration

BASIL DE SELINCOURT

IN DAYS BEFORE THE DOORS of the purgatory of criticism
had closed behind me, in the fond days of youth when I still nourished dreams of entering the heaven of art, it was music which
beckoned to me most imperiously, and the heavenliest attribute of
music to my budding perception was its lastingness: *himmlische
Länge!* How early, alas! I became familiar with that comment
dropped on the enchanted air at the close of some favourite composition: "a little too long, isn't it?": a comment that would precipitate all magic from the element and leave a company conscious of
the stiffness of human muscles and human faces and wondering
whether it was not time for tea. Ruskin's dictum, that Bach had an
incorrigible faculty for running on, decided me, I recollect, that
there must be one reservation even in a boy's worship for Ruskin.
The greatest musician to my mind was he who gained Paradise and
stayed there; and the greatest of instruments the organ, partly because of the fascination of its mechanism and power, but also for
its celestial faculty of sustainment.

What are the relations in music between length and meaning,
duration and effect? The question is not so simple as it once appeared to me, but I have never completely abandoned my old in-

152

stinct. Music is one of the forms of duration; it suspends ordinary time, and offers itself as an ideal substitute and equivalent. Nothing is more metaphorical or more forced in music than a suggestion that time is passing while we listen to it, that the development of the themes follows the action in time of some person or persons embodied in them, or that we ourselves change as we listen. The clash and confusion are the same as when in a picture we see one saint performing three miracles, two in the foreground and one in the middle distance. For the space of which the painter makes use is a translated space, within which all objects are at rest, and though flies may walk about on his canvas, their steps do not measure the distance from one tone to another. These tones lie side by side, but their meaning for the mind is lost if the eye passes over them spatially; they speak and they exist as one harmonious impression. The time of music is similarly an ideal time, and if we are less directly aware of this, if composers themselves are less aware of it, the reason is that our life and consciousness are more closely conditioned by time than by space. We look at a picture and in the same glance see real objects surrounding it and the room in which it hangs. The ideal and the real spatial relations declare their different natures in the simplicity of the contrast which we perceive between them. Music, on the other hand, demands the absorption of the whole of our time-consciousness; our own continuity must be lost in that of the sound to which we listen. The conception is difficult because of its inclusiveness. Our very life is measured by rhythm: by our breathing, by our heart-beats. These are all irrelevant, their meaning is in abeyance, so long as time is music.

It is sometimes suggested that music, in thus reducing the passage of time to an irrelevance, gives an analogy or foretaste of the experience of eternity. Philosophers tell us that the spiritual life is "out of time" and some seem to attach a meaning to such words. We know that the beginning and the end of a musical composition are ideally contemporaneous in this sense, that each, to be understood, requires a mind either anticipating or retaining the other. But in that sense the act of understanding would require contemporaneity in everything. If we are "out of time" in listening to music, our state is best explained by the simple consideration that it is as difficult to be in two times at once as in two places. Music uses time as an element of expression; duration is its essence. The begin-

ning and the end of a musical composition are only one if the music
has possessed itself of the interval between them and wholly filled
it.

For this reason, there is no more crucial test of a composition than
the test of length. The piece that seems long is the piece that has
failed to suspend our consciousness of real time. The meaning of the
sounds has died away from us, and we have remembered that the
hands of the clock are going round. It is not always the fault of
the music; nor when the music is at fault, is the blame necessarily
the composer's. There are players in whose hands the opening
movement of Beethoven's Waldstein Sonata seems long while they
are still thrumming the first subject, there are others from whom
Schubert's Sonata in Bb falls like a dream of unearthly rapture,
which nothing can disturb; we wake as from any other dream spell
to find that we have slept a minute or an hour. The question of
length is obviously conditioned by a great many different factors,
most of which are foreign to this essay. Tastes and temperaments
differ in hearers as well as in performers; different kinds of composition have also the times and seasons and the moods appropriate
to them. For a proper judgment we must assume all these to have
been favourably assorted. Then there are many conditions of musical
form which predetermine the length of a movement. Music is, in
one of its main branches, an art of accompaniment; the genesis of
most of its patterns, historically considered, has been external to itself; the song, the dance, the ceremonies of religion have been the
evocation and have provided models. Even when the conception of
instrumental music as an artistic medium had been finally defined
and purified, the conventions of contrapuntal writing still imposed
accidental formalities. Indeed, if the foundation of a movement is
an adagio theme for fugal treatment by eight voices, the pattern,
however concisely treated, cannot unwind itself in a short space of
time. Even Ruskin's reference to Bach had this amount of justice
that a fair proportion of the works of that greatest of composers
may be classed as exercises in counterpoint and considered as the
unremitting, methodical, victorious expansion of a thought which
the first thematic statement held in germ; so that the interest has
been more in completeness and perfection of expression than in the
substance of the thought itself. Briefly, a certain kind of musical
exercise, and certain occasional adaptations presuppose the filling
of a measure or the unravelling of a skein. And then there is pro-

gramme music, already covertly alluded to. Here music is in chains
to a system of metaphor, the treatment is but semi-musical, and the
question of length, though a burning question, is extraneous. All
music is ultimately conditioned by the physical capacity of the
hearer, and representative music, just because it looks outside the
art, because it has no intrinsically determined end, is too often conditioned by nothing else. The greatest of representative composers
have been inclined to ignore the limits of human endurance. It is in
the nature of music to flow on; and by the time it has told its own
story and the composer's too, both have as a rule completely over-
reached themselves.

What part then shall we assign to duration in the development
and expression of the pure musical idea? Has not duration in music
a qualitative as well as a quantitative value? Here two thoughts seem
to converge. The first is that the foundation of musical expression
is repetition. That which the writer most scrupulously avoids, the
musician most diligently seeks. Repetition begins with the bar, and
continues in the melody and in every phrase or item into which we
can resolve it. The growth of a musical composition may be compared to that of a flowering plant, with its multitude of leaves and
blossoms and intertwining stems and branches: where not only the
leaves repeat each other, but the leaves repeat the flowers, and the
very stems and branches are like un-unfolded leaves. It is true that
the flower alone, the single spray, contains in itself the whole beauty
of the plant that bears it; but in the form of suggestion, of implication. To the pattern of the flower there corresponds a further pattern developed in the placing and grouping of the flowers along the
branches, and the branches themselves divide and stand out in
balancing proportions, under the controlling vital impulse. For the
true expression of that impulse, the whole plant is needed; its repetitions are not redundancies; they are means by which the fullness
and soaring intensity of its life are exhibited. They amplify and
exalt its beauty, by relating it in a hundred different ways to the
elements of power and freedom out of which it sprang. Musical
expression follows the same law. The comparison of music to
architecture, which is a commonplace, has been based on a recognition of the significance and satisfaction to the ear of balancing
periods of sound, of a symmetrical structure. And yet the comparison
is in one respect unfortunate because architecture is so much more
than music an art of use, its forms and their meaning being indeed

determined by the ends which they are designed to serve and its beauty involving a reconciliation between two competing standards: whereas in pure music the meaning and the beauty are indistinguishable, and its greater like its lesser repetitions have no other aim than the development and creation of that meaning and that beauty. Repeatability is thus in music an element of the beautiful.

Hardly then have we spoken of the conventions involved in contrapuntal writing before we are brought to recognise that they rest on a perception of what is most vital and persistent in the influences that determine pure musical form. The danger of the style was that it offered a framework more likely to be filled with notes than with music; yet the mere fact that he knows the frame is there and that it will be filled provides the hearer with a strong basis of musical pleasure. A part of the delight we feel in the opening of a great fugue by Bach or at the first statement of the subject in one of his pianoforte concertos lies in the immediate conviction it gives us of having embarked on a voyage, of having taken seats in a non-stop train, which, whatever the character of the scenery it passes through, will carry us smoothly and take us far before it brings us to a platform again. This sense of security, this faith in distances ahead, is not easily separable from musical enjoyment. Milton, whose only experience was of the kind of music we are discussing, harps on the beauty of its persistency:—

> Untwisting all the chains that tie
> The hidden soul of harmony

and

> In linked sweetness long drawn out

The value of repetition in music belongs of course to the peculiar inwardness of the art. A musical composition must be content to be itself. The reference and relations into which analysis resolves its life-current need point to no object, no event; they take the form of the creative impulse which is their unity and they repeat one another because iteration is the only outward sign of identity which is available to them. Repetition is also a basis of form because, as we have seen, it balances retrospect by peopling anticipation. The simplest form of melody is that of a phrase handled twice over in such a way that the voice is led first to a point of temporary repose and then by the same path to a point of final repose, and the sense of finality is often enhanced by a repetition of the first, the inconclusive strain, giving the added influence of a suspension, a postponement to the return home. In the sonata form we see a translation of this simple scheme into the language of gods and heroes. It provides a formula for the development of expression through a series of anticipated recurrences, such recurrences affecting not merely constitutive turns of phrase but flowers of melody, with their leaves and the branch on which they grow. The demand of the form is thus for themes the meaning of which increases as they recur; repetition has become extensive instead of intensive; and the danger of a convention asserts itself in a new aspect. The repeated first section, twice leading us to our point of temporary repose, gives us a characteristic joy, when, as we break away into the free fantasia, we say "Two of that to *one* of this"; yet one formula of repetition is as idle as another, and the significance of this one tends to vary in inverse ratio to the length of the "repeat." The beauty and balance of many movements depends on the restatement of a long opening; but repeats are often indicated or arranged because it is the custom, not because they are in the music, and as a device for the development of musical expression the formal repeat is obviously primitive. There is no virtue in hearing the same sounds twice over; the virtue is in the perception that they are at once the same and not the same; and a point is easily reached in the sonata at which, waiting too long for this perception, we feel the transition when it comes inadequate. Perhaps it was the architectural parallel which sustained this error. The conditions of architecture favour formal symmetry; but the masses in a composition of music move in obedience to subtler laws. There are two eyes in the face, but though they are alike they are not identical, and the hair rises differently on either side of the brow above them.

We have said that there is no virtue in hearing the same sounds twice over; but is it not the critic's nemesis that, in the very pursuit of the truth it is his mission to evoke, he is so often led to deny what he most wishes to affirm? Music being the art of repetitions, it was impossible to avoid remarking that a mere identity has as little value here as elsewhere; or, may we say, almost as little? for there is a reservation. There are themes the joy of which is only given as we hear them over and over again. The pleasure of the rondo, in its simplest forms, is just the pleasure of being brought back by a succession of detours to the same flowing melody, and any modification of the melody when it recurs would, in many instances, destroy the value of its recurrence. A close analysis of our pleasure in these exact recurrences will reveal here too an element of foresight as well as of retrospect. The repetition of a melody without change is a signal to us that it is not being repeated for the last time; with our present delight there mingles therefore a secure hope of bliss still in reserve for us; and thus we taste again the pleasure of continuity, the restfulness of yielding ourselves to the flow of sound and knowing that it will not fail. In the rondo of Beethoven's E minor Sonata, this pleasure in mere recurrence unites with another source of satisfaction. For here we repose not only in the sense of the recurrences but also in the unending amplitude of the theme itself; and perhaps we remark this quality the more because it is consciously developed by the composer. It may be, even, that where we remark it less, its effect is more perfectly assured.

And so we pass from the thought of repetition, with its more or less mechanical associations, to one which lies nearer the essential, that of continuousness. For there are themes, there are movements, of which the flowing, brooding, piercing, or exalting accent conveys its spell, achieves its translation for us by its very persistency. We have taken a work of Beethoven's to exemplify what we mean, and we could mention many others of the same composer which have the same continuing inward charm. The third movement of the D minor Sonata is one. Nevertheless the quality we wish to define is more conspicuous in the music of Brahms, of Schubert, of César Franck, than in that of Beethoven. The weights in the scales of the vast genius of Beethoven incline on the side of the dramatic and intellectual; contrast is his element rather than continuity, and we can even think of him as of a man who used rather than was used by music, a man who might, at will, have been a philosopher and who was, in fact, a tragic poet. A certain aspect of musical expression has, through the immense sway of his influence, tended to obtain a prominence above its due. For, in spite of the limitless dramatic possibilities which are included in the musical medium, music is in essence a contemplative rather than a dramatic art, and contrast is, in strictness, of no value in music except so far as by means of it the contrasted elements become each more perfectly themselves. Because of Beethoven, we incline to think of musical ideas more in relation to their course, and though the complete musical perception includes all these things, the being and element

of true music is surely just its course, its onward flow. I have sometimes compared the clear and sparkling tones of his Septet with
the indecisive and overweighted movements of the Octet which, at
about the same time of life, Schubert modelled upon it, and my
judgment has always gone in favor of the relatively formless work.
Handling, presentment, design have a higher significance in music
than in any other art, but even in music the distinction between
form and substance does not disappear and the ultimate standard
is in the substance still. A great failure is better than a moderate
success; an imperfectly presented idea may mean more than a perfectly presented one. Not that there is the least concession to be
made to incompleteness for its own sake, still less that there is any
virtue in cloying exuberance and redundancy; but that, as in poetry
the test is not what verse is most musical but what thought is fittest
for music, so in music itself design is second, inspiration first. The
artist's final achievement is to recognise his inspiration and to
master it; and the profounder the inspiration, the more it tends to
lead him on.

In the works of Bach we have an example at once of unfathom-
able inspiration and consummate technique. He is, for all time, the
typical musician. His very name means music. Music, the river of
life, flows from him in a broad flood, deep, swift, clear. A buoyancy
and energy that everywhere press forward to perfect plenitude of
expression characterise the whole of his work; whatever the theme,
he has the musician's natural joy in the complete unfolding of it.
His prevailing note is that of joyous activity, but splendour and
majesty in attainment and the effort and anguish of the travail of
creation are equally his, and, beyond both, an intimate and pen-
etrative brooding vision from which beauty rises, as if a well
brimmed over. The Fugue in G♯ Minor, with its theme of tranquil
reverie, its sustained melodiousness, its ecstasies of harmonic research, is an example of this ultimate, inclusive, most musical vein.
Words are futile to convey an impression of the associations in which
such music moves and has its being; the greatest poets occasionally
find through words some suggestion of the realities of which we are
here immediately assured. But how many times has the Fugue in
G♯ Minor been performed to audiences who did not find it long?

Many more considerations might be urged, but to insist would
prejudice our theme. Continuance in music is an element of beauty;
there is a qualitative as well as a quantitative significance in musical

duration; the loveliest themes are dwelling themes, themes that ask to be dwelt on, themes the loveliness of which renders itself up as the composer dwells upon them. Where significance grows as the phrase repeats itself, where the theme passes from phrase to phrase with ever amplifying associations, we are breathing the atmosphere of music in its purest form. For by its gift of unencumbered beauty, music has, above all the other arts, the power to lift and translate us and to assure us of heaven.

> Là est le bien que tout esprit désire,
> Là le repos où tout le monde aspire,
> Là est l'amour, là le plaisir encore.
> Là, o mon âme, au plus haut ciel guidée,
> Tu y pourras reconnaître l'idée
> De la beauté qu'en ce monde j'adore.[1]

By its detachment from earthly surroundings, while it creates a thousand problems for the composer whose temperament involves him in representation and gives scope for the elaboration of maze upon maze of astounding or exquisite but always more or less irrelevant intricacies, music is the strength and release of all whose gift is the true heavenly commerce. And this commerce holds us, it is as much a communion as an expression. Music is a form of action; a composition, we have lately been reminded, is an influence which exists only as it is brought to life in each performance. It is not strange, then, that the higher the beatitude it attains to, the longer it inclines to rest in it; for constancy is one of the marks that distinguish the real from the illusory and is the very foundation of knowledge in a world of change; and we can understand why the musician's hardest task is to learn that rapture itself obeys the law of measure and at its appointed time must cease.

---

[1] There is the Good that is the mind's desire,
There the repose to which all men aspire,
And there is love, and joy forevermore.
There, O my Soul, to highest Heaven conducted,
Thou shalt behold the Essence unobstructed
Of Beauty, that on earth I did adore.
                                                        —Ed.

Notes on the Superposition of
Temporal Modes in the Works of Art

MICHELINE SAUVAGE

IT IS UNDENIABLE that a work of art is temporal, that there is a temporality in any and all works of art, however valuable and firmly-grounded the distinction between the plastic and the musical arts may otherwise be. Anything is temporal which is in time, or involves time, or is a prey to time. Such is clearly the case with a sonata, a novel, a poem, a motion-picture, or a theatrical production; such is likewise the case with a canvas, a monument or a bas-relief. All these are quite evidently entities concerned with time.

And yet such a formulation is excessively vague: as vague as the words *temporal* and *temporality* themselves. Let us therefore try to define more precisely the time parameter in a work of art. As we do so, we see the single and undifferentiated notion of temporality break up into a plurality of discrete levels.

The most obvious of these levels, because it is the most general of them, is surely what Étienne Souriau calls "the temporal insertion of a work of art." The word *temporal* is in this case both clear and in conformity with present usage. The work is in time, subject to time, with all that this involves in the way of *history*, of change and of adventures, for the physical work itself as well as for its "message" (if I may be allowed the use of this detestably facile

word). Da Vinci's colors "dull" as they grow old. *The Cid,* after a
period of artistic senescence, has recently been given new life and
popularity by the production of Jean Vilar.

There is no need to labor this point. Undoubtedly it is a form of
temporality, this obligation on the part of all art products to undergo
the effects of time; but it is a form so common, and shared with so
many other things, that there is no reason to single them out in
particular as examples of it—except of course for purposes of a
learned monograph.

Much richer in possibilities is the second level of artistic temporality: the fact that the work of art uses time as one of its working
elements. Here too the word *temporality* has its ordinary usage: a
sonata, a novel, a poem, a motion-picture, a play, as much as a
mythical hero, are temporal because they *require time.* The time of
each of these divers forms can be studied, the duration, that is,
with which they achieve their structure, the rhythm by which they
develop. Each of them constructs in actual time its own special
artistic time, musical, dramatic or narrative. These times can be
compared. Musical time can be compared with dramatic, the time
of a novel with "ordinary" time (it would be rash to call it "real").
Within each form there are multifarious works that articulate still
further the time in question, and open a field of finer detail to our
investigation. In the case of a musical work, this holds in a nearly
literal sense (*tempo,* of course, comes immediately to mind), and
in an exceptionally obvious, perceptual way, being audible, even
if not entirely accessible, to those least versed in the art. But even
if we set aside this perceptual advantage, the temporal structure
of André Malraux's *La Condition Humaine* is no less monumentally
and manifestly contrary to that of *Madame Bovary,*[1] or the melancholy slow pace of Tristan to the bounding rhythm that Don Juan,
the man of "a thousand and three," imposes on all the works engendered by the myth, than is the time of Beethoven's 21st sonata to that of, say, any of Bach's *Brandenburg Concertos,* to
pick a random example from the first association that comes to
mind.

This temporality (T2, if we may so call it) may be less evident

[1] By the temporal structure of a novel I mean its primary form, not that of its
secondary form, which here should be that of the "story" recounted. The latter
will be discussed below. The expressions *primary form, secondary form* are used
in the sense of *La correspondance des arts,* pp. 86 ff.

in the "spatial" arts, which do not use time directly and seem even
to involve an extra-aesthetic intention of negating time. Here duration "leaves form unchanged, and takes no part in it, since it is not
of its essence." [2] But a canvas, a monument or a bas-relief do nonetheless demand time, the time needed by the work to be revealed
to the spectator, as he has to look again and again, to await different
hours of the day, to walk round the object, to draw closer to it or
move farther away from it, etc. [3] Certainly, "the vision of the whole
is . . . obtained only by successively looking at different parts of
the object . . . But the eye is not content with a single perusal, so
he repeats it until he establishes a determinate dynamic which he
fixes as a vision of the whole;" [4] we are, then, dealing in some way
with a provisional temporality, since "at the moment when one becomes aware of the completion of the whole, the conscious mind
loses the temporal movement which had been stimulated by the
incomplete vision of the work." [5] Only, that provisional temporality
that goes with contemplation must always begin anew; it can never
be acquired once and for all. It may be that the spatial arts have
not (according to an elegant formula) an "atemporal time," [6] but
their time, however different it may otherwise be from that of the
temporal arts, is in this respect of one kind with it. It is on the same
level as that time which we discussed in the preceding paragraph,
level T2.

T2 belongs to the primary form of artistic works, T1 to both primary and secondary. A third level belongs entirely to the secondary
form, to the representative aim. Let us say provisionally that T3
consists of the temporal significations implied by the thing represented; or again, to use a current term, that it is *time evoked*. Depending on the point of view one wishes to adopt, it may or may not
appear the most interesting. No matter. What is of moment now,
is that it is the most tricky. Since it leads to ambiguity and confusion, it requires a careful approach, with concrete examples.

[2] Gisèle Brelet, *Le temps musical*, v. 1, p. 4.
[3] It is a fact of experience that one can suddenly realize that one has largely
failed in the contemplation of a work by not giving it its due measure of time,
its due measure of approach in time. At the moment I am thinking of the astounding documentary film, all in ingenious plays of lighting, by Maurice Cloche, on
sacred sculpture in France: revelations . . .
[4] Gisèle Brelet, *op. cit.* p. 9.
[5] *Ibid.*
[6] *Ibid.*, p. 4.

HERE IS A PICTURE by Eekman: "Off the Gallows" [*Le Dépendu*]. T1 is its date, 1943, and includes everything that an appropriate enquiry (I happen to know very little about it) would tell me of the work, of its fate after it was painted, of the important dates of its life as a picture. Let us go on.

About T2, one could write a great deal. The plastic organization of the canvas imposes a compelling *order* on the discovery and exploration of it. Thus the man, by the place he occupies in the vertical dimension of the picture (which, dealing with secondary form, presents him in the foreground, walking in solitude toward the spectator and the world outside of the canvas), and by the composition as a whole, is *first* to solicit our attention, *before* the tree which he partly obscures; and the tree *next* reveals the silhouettes of the burial procession (the people who, in terms of representation, carry the dead man to his resting-place in the ground). Moreover, certain elements of this form have a plastic prerogative which inseparably involves a temporal prerogative: our attention is *first* oriented to the neck and legs. In contrast to this, the bent leg, the cleared barrier and the objects occupying the lower right corner impose by their "constellation" (to borrow a Gestaltist term) a *simultaneity* of perception, etc.[7]

And T3? Have we here time "evoked"?

Of course. Here is a man walking—what a flexion in his left leg! In the dimension of narrative, the essential quality is precisely the large movement of striding over a barrier, the step that leads to freedom. Behind him another man is busy with the gallows-tree— cheated: this rope that must be removed, this vestige that must be done away with, juxtapose in the picture the previous instant and the present instant, constituting a perfectly adequate allusion to the immediate past. As for the burial procession, on which the unhanged man is turning his back, it too is an allusion to the temporal, to the temporal *par excellence:* death. Furthermore (we must insist on this), here is a complete, though elliptical, tale of an event, the death of the deceased. We can, if we wish, assign it a limited time span (the usual delay between death and the graveyard . . .)

---

[7] To say nothing of the long temporal career which investigation of the picture on the secondary level calls forth, with all the attendant analyses, suppositions, evocations, fancies, all of which come about successively and gradually (I cannot look at it today without having in mind the Lazarus theme, but that association was not an immediate one . . .).

and a proximate future (in a few moments they are going to bury him).[8] All this smacks a bit of mystification; but it is useful for our investigation of time. I forgot that the anecdote in the scene is not without any indication of the season: see how bare the trees are.

In short, this story involves time. The existence of this time, the kind filmologists have termed *diegetic*,[9] enters the representation as a sort of *temporal* sign, as one speaks of a local sign for sensation. It is a *temporal* sign, still in the ordinary sense of the word: although diegetic time is quite distinct from other modes of time in the work, this signature lets the thing represented declare its allegiance to the temporal order. In this case the representation is essentially non-successive; the picture is there all at once; and yet there is a before and after in the world it conjures up for us; time passes in it, since we see the marks and the effects of time.

Is there anything more? A temporality T4? Not that I see.

But now I pick up another album, and I happen ("The book falls open at the oft-read page") upon a familiar reproduction of a painting by Poussin: the *Shepherds in Arcadia*. Straightway and with no difficulty I find the three preceding levels. Indeed, one cannot but be struck by the importance of T3, by the dilatation an exceptional tract of time puts into the painting. "One may even wonder if it is not excessive. In any case, it is obligatory: no artistic comprehension of the work is possible if one does not take account of the temporal basis implied by the ages of the various persons, the presence of the tomb recalling those who lived formerly in the same place, and in the future, that inevitable death . . ."[10] But here, is there really nothing else? These vaguely melancholy dreams that rise up every time one looks at the painting (it makes no difference that from a strictly aesthetic viewpoint this is an adulteration of the pure metal), or again, precisely that extraordinary importance of diegetic time, this sort of insistence by the artist which unmistakably goes beyond the pure temporal description of an episode, however elab-

[8] Cf. on this sort of temporal radiation of the work, Étienne Souriau, *Time in the Plastic Arts*, this volume, pp. 122–41; see p. 132: "As for this intrinsic time of the plastic work, one can say that its organization, in general, is *stellar* and *diffluent*. The time of the work radiates, so to speak, around the prerogative moment represented. The latter makes a structural center from which the mind moves backward to the past and forward to the future in a more and more vague fashion until the moment when the image fades gradually into space."

[9] Cf. *Revue de filmologie*, v. 7, nos. 7–8, p. 233.

[10] Souriau, *op. cit.*, p. 130.

orately developed this may be—all these lead us to look above T3, above the tomb, above the dead man in the tomb, above the shadows cast by the lateness of the day, above the prolonged perspective of future and past which opens at the heart of this so-called Arcadian instant: to look for more time. Why "this rhythm of life and death, in the past, the present, and the future, this return in thought to the past, with a corresponding movement to the future . . ." if it is not meant to induce in the spectator a meditation on "that inevitable death (*et in Arcadia ego*) whose shadow falls upon love and present happiness, saddens and adds greater meaning to the tender gesture of the young woman and the expression of the face of her lover." [11] *Et in Arcadia ego:* death is in Arcadia too . . . Have we not here a *time intention,* or somehow an *exhibited* as opposed to an *implied* time (time *evoked* now begins to appear ambiguous)? Or, perhaps even better, a *time represented* over and above the time of what *is represented?* In short, a time of level T4?

The question, however, is elusive and complex. It would be difficult to elucidate it entirely in the case of a pictorial work. A poem will serve better to clarify it.

Let us choose Edgar Allan Poe's *The Raven.* Let us skip over T1 (the literary history of the poem) and T2 (its phonetic and metrical structure). What shall we say of T3? It is, as before, the temporal sign which influences the universe of the poem, a temporal implication of what is represented: "Once upon a midnight dreary" and "Ah, distinctly I remember it was in the bleak December," etc. But here I have no hesitation: one cannot fail to see, beyond this temporal sign—and, frankly, of greater interest—a still further time: time invoked, described, symbolized, feared, hated, whatever you will, in this poem which is sustained by a manifest time intention from beginning to end. This is so evident that even apart from its beauty and artistic perfection it remains a valuable document for the psychologist. In it one can find the signs of a fair number of behavior patterns relative to time: imagination of time, feelings about time, etc. The first in particular here merits an exhaustive study, which could not fail to be fruitful. The malign symbolism of the whole genus *Corvus,* and of the raven especially, attested since Antiquity by the Western mind, easily and naturally assumes the function of representing time—as is shown for example by the myth

[11] *Ibid.*

of the quarrel between Athena and the raven over the bird's prophetic powers. Here, the old European mythic source is tapped and explicitly brought to bear, to make of *The Raven* an image of maleficent time.

Have we here a distinct level? Are we truly justified in assigning a T4?

To be sure, the aspect of time we have set forth above has not escaped analysis. Only it has not been distinguished from the preceding aspect, and hence temporal implications are currently confused with time represented in a single indivisible level T3. Thus we find: "A literary work in prose twice contains its represented time: [12] time implied in the ideas of the work and time realized in its structure," [13] whereas poetry combines an experiential, essentially musical, time and a time "bound up with the content of the words." [14]

Now it is clear that this time "implied in the ideas" or "bound up with the content of the words" is twofold. In fact there is no reciprocity between time of what is represented and time represented; and while it is more than doubtful that a figurative work could be found in which T3 is totally lacking, the same is clearly not the case with T4. In a poem like Coleridge's *The Rime of the Ancient Mariner*, T4 is missing but T3 is always made extremely precise, as for example in the first stanza of the second part:

> The sun now rose upon the right;
> Out of the sea rose he,
> Still hid in mist, and on the left
> Went down into the sea.

Moreover, they are independent, at least in principle: [15] thus in Poe's poem, the fact that the raven is made into an image of time seems not *necessarily* connected with the midnight hour and "bleak December" (T3), any more than the time intention revealed in *et in Arcadia ego* is connected with the anecdote depicted in the

[12] Furthermore, reservations need to be made concerning the equivocal use here of the expression *time represented,* since time "realized in the structure" of the literary work (T2) is dependent on *time of the representation.*

[13] Gisèle Brelet, *op. cit.,* p. 21.

[14] *Ibid.,* p. 16.

[15] I say: at least in principle, since the question (of some importance) needs to be raised of a pragmatic relationship in any work between T3 and T4, just as between T2 and T4. Cf. *infra.*

Shepherds in Arcadia, since we can imagine an entirely different pictorial interpretation of the same moral idea.

As a matter of fact, the confusion frequently goes further, so that T2 is not distinguished from a T3 which is itself not distinguished from T4. The result can be a serious inaccuracy in the investigation of artistic time and of the reciprocal conditioning of temporal modes. So the following: "The time of a plastic work is purely subjective, in us rather than in the work; the work does no more than evoke it and invoke it, for it is powerless to acquire time in its own right and to inscribe it in the objectivity of its form." [16] The "subjective" time (an unfortunate epithet) of the plastic work is T2; as for T3, it is just what is most clearly inscribed in the objective form, and upon this T4 can superpose a different sort of time again, but one which is no less objective.

Let us concentrate on the determination of T4. This is, in fact, sufficiently important to raise a problem of vocabulary.

IN SPEAKING OF T3 as time *evoked* we were certainly using an equivocal term. To assign a kind of temporality to the thing represented is certainly to "evoke" time. But in a different sense we also evoke time when by some means or other we give it a direct, sensible, and somehow personal presence in the work—that is, an image.

Shall we say that T4 is a fourth level of *temporality* in the work? That would be dangerous, because it would make almost inevitable the very confusion we are pointing out.

T1, T2, T3 are unquestionably levels of *temporality* for a work of art, since they indicate that the work, considered under its primary or secondary aspect, is *in* time, is *temporal*. But if, in dealing with T4, I use the word *temporal* of a work of art in which I discern a time intention, if here too I speak of temporality, it is clear that I am using the word in an entirely different way, because I now no

---

[16] Gisèle Brelet, *op. cit.,* p. 10. Cf. also p. 7: "A painting, regardless of the painter's own desire, cannot signify time without ambiguity, for time is alien to the very materials of the painting and to what is most especially pictorial: color." But if I may clarify the matter with a simple example, the several hundreds of students aged seven to fifteen whom I have asked (for reasons that have nothing to do with the present problem) to represent time by a watercolor or crayon composition, all had to express T4 despite the deficit of T2, and without necessarily seeking the aid of T3 (in fact this recourse is a frequent one, but that is something else again).

longer have in mind that the work is *in* time, but rather that it bears *on* time.

Someone may point out that "sense A" of the word *temporal* in Lalande's *Vocabulaire:* "that which is in time, which concerns time," juxtaposes the two usages purely and simply.[17] But the ambiguity of the word becomes only too evident in the confusions which it authorizes or engenders. In psychology, if you want your interlocutor to know what you are talking about, it is not enough to speak of "temporal behavior," or of psychology of time. Psychology of time is the investigation of temporality in mental phenomena; that is, of time as a factor in temporal phases of behavior, or behavior *in* time (all behavior is in time, but time plays a more or a less decisive role in some cases than in others). Psychology of time may also be a different study, namely a study of acts which, besides being in time, deal *with* time,[18] and which are also called "temporal." Janet among others pointed out several years ago the necessary distinction between these two points of view, which are as separate as is the perception of time from the time of perception; but he did not bring up the problem of the word. In aesthetics, one falls into the same ambiguity in speaking of time in a work of art. Where it is possible to write: "Music arouses . . . a whole variety of temporal feelings . . . feelings of its form as temporal," [19] a statement in which the reader is aware that he is slipping from one sense to another, but feels an intellectual discomfort nonetheless; or again: "spatial arts could not live in consciousness if they did not evoke its temporal life," [20] in which the ambiguity is hopeless: where such equivocation is possible, the need for a term that would allow and guarantee the distinction is palpable.[21]

[17] The word has no entry in H. Piéron's *Vocabulaire de la Psychologie* (Presses Universitaires de France, 1951). Lalande's *Vocabulaire* is therefore the sole authority to which one can properly refer.

[18] A few examples to clarify matters: the verbal expression of time, its psychological or mythological representation, feelings about time, handling of time, etc.

[19] Gisèle Brelet, *op. cit.*, p. 14.

[20] *Ibid.*, p. 7.

[21] In an essay devoted to the myth of Don Juan (Le cas don Juan, Ed. du Seuil, 1953), I spoke myself of the myth as temporal, studied its temporality, and so forth: the ambiguity is a flagrant one, for the myth can require time without bringing time into question, and the latter point was what I had in mind: I dealt with it in this manner only to avoid having recourse to a technical vocabulary ill-suited to the tone of the essay.

Let us return to the superposition of modes of time in the work. T1, T2, T3 unquestionably designate three discrete levels. And yet their plurality, for all its reality and importance, does not eliminate a certain unity of *aspect* (in the grammatical sense). Affiliation with the temporal order, in whatever way it is manifested (for the work of art, by its primary or secondary form, or both at once), is always temporality. T4, on the contrary, is not the work in time, but time in the work. Since we call what is in time *temporal*, let us call what bears on time *chronian* [in French: *chronien*].[22] T1, T2, T3 designate the temporalities of a work, T4 (if this analysis is correct), its *chronism*. Chronism is never without some kind of temporality. But the converse is not true.

A painting like the *Shepherds in Arcadia*, a poem like *The Raven*, a motion-picture like Cocteau's *Orpheus*, a mythical hero like Don Juan, present all four levels; superposed one on another within them are all three temporalities and chronism. Such works have the greatest possible richness of time.

THE SUPERPOSITION of modes of time T2, T3, and T4 (we omit T1 here for obvious reasons) in a work of art has an inner reason in each case: it is unlikely that their combination could be made casually or by chance—which, of course, is not the same as

---

[22] I must admit I find the adjective displeasing. *Chronism* is fine, but *chronian*, especially in the indispensable use with a privative, is graceless. I first thought of *chronal* [in French: *chronal*], which is infinitely more satisfying to the ear. But difficulties arose. 1. "Chronal" has already been used by Leclère and Michel Souriau, in their *Introduction au symbolisme mathématique* (*Rev. ph.*, 1938, 1, p. 366), in a sense different from ours; 2. etymological purists find little support for its bastard derivation—a Latin suffix joined to a Greek root. To be sure, it is not hard to find cases in French of births equally illegitimate which have nonetheless been recognized by usage and the Academy: what, for example, of *chronicité*, which takes a word doubly Greek and makes it into a noun formed on the model of substantives in *-tas, -tatis*? And wouldn't it, besides, be pedantic to take exception to that *electrodermal* reaction [réaction électrodermal] which in France is now (M. Bloch) replacing the psycho-galvanic reaction? But anyway, I refrained from using *chronal*, lest I incur, like Molière's Martine, the reproach of having offended grammar all my life, or rather of having offended linguistics. How unfortunate that chronic [chronique] has already been monopolized! It is all the more unfortunate in that its present usage is incorrect, in defiance of etymology itself (for whose sake I hope I will be forgiven the length of this note). χρονικός, *chronic*, in fact means "concerning time" and χρόνιος, or *chronian*, means "long-lasting," and is used of "chronic" illnesses, for example by Hippocrates.

to say that it must always be conscious and deliberate. This opens a singularly rich perspective on the work. We shall confine ourselves to a few fragmentary observations on its nature, in order not to draw these notes out to excessive length.

It is evident that any chronism has a choice of means, and that these means are in no way interchangeable, nor is their choice indifferent. Let us first illustrate this by psychological considerations. Psychology has determined, for example, that imagination of time is organized round a limited number of thematic images, and that it is possible to determine statistically an order of preference for these images (thus in Europe visions of water are most common). This order of preference varies in accordance with the affective attitude by which the imaginative process is oriented: in Europe images of earth are more often bound up than those of water with a time pessimism, and this is an association deeply rooted in the subsoil of our mental life.

It is the same for the chronism of a work of art. A fixed chronian intention restricts the artist's free choice of the possible temporalities of a work. The case that comes immediately to mind is the combination T3-T4. A tomb and a nearby tree to suggest turning shadows, and sundials (*sicut umbrae dies nostri*) amid innocent shepherd youth, were exactly what was needed for that melancholy sense of our mortality which permeates the *Shepherds in Arcadia:* by being just a bit too obvious, this combination of T3 and T4 has the effect of somewhat overlaying the plastic elements of the picture with the literary. And who could fail to choose, for that maleficent time of which the raven is the image and emissary, the midnight hour and bleak December, the darkness of night and of the sinister winter solstice, in preference to any other time of day and season? This is still perfectly simple and obvious.

In a general way, what I make bold to call the *chronian temperament* of an artist predisposes him to the use of a certain characteristic temporal machinery in the universe of his works. Everyone will have noticed how Shakespearian heroes are always running out of time: you will recall

> Come Desdemona, I have but an hour
> Of love, of worldly matter and direction,
> To spend with thee [23]

[23] *Othello*, 1.3.298–300.

and

> Had I but time, as this fell sergeant, Death,
> Is strict in his arrest, O, I could tell you—
> But let it be; Horatio, I am dead.[24]

This may turn out to be of more interest to the psychologist than to the aesthetician, insofar as the relation is evident or even commonplace. More subtle is the use of the technical invention of slow motion in order to recover a time whose essence (and whose evil) is to be irreversible, as we find it in *Orpheus*. More subtle again is the frenetic and, if so I may call it, supermultiplied rhythm which the myth imposes on the destiny of Don Juan, the hero who has chosen time against eternity. Here are subjects worthy of aesthetic analysis.

But the most interesting, as well as the most difficult, investigations are certainly to be found in connection with the relationship T2-T4. To be convinced of this, you have only to recall that extraordinary moment in Mozart's *Don Giovanni* when the rhythm of the chords, heard simultaneously with the voice of the Statue that calls the sinner to the choice of repentance or death,[25] articulates in its time another time (the hero's own), which is shrinking and running out. Such passages cause us to doubt momentarily "the incompatibility of pace which always prevents music and dramatic action from keeping step with each other."[26] In any case, they show the necessity of determining on each occasion how the primary temporal structure of the work corresponds to its chronism. Can one imagine, in *The Raven*, a rapid pace instead of those majestic, enveloping, ineluctable waves?

> Ah, distinctly I remember it was in the bleak December,
> And each separate dying ember wrought its ghost upon the floor.
>
> .   .   .   .
>
> In there stepped a stately raven of the saintly days of yore.
>
> .   .   .   .
>
> Perched upon a bust of Pallas just above my chamber door—
> Perched and sat, and nothing more.

[24] *Hamlet*, 5.2.334–6.

[25] Act 2, scene 15.

[26] Roland-Manuel, *Rythme cinématographique et rythme musical*, quoted by Gisèle Brelet, *op. cit.*, p. 20.

To do so would be a failure to understand that the time envisaged by the poem is not "irreparable" [27] time (*fugit irreparabile tempus*), the object of a light melancholy which is satisfied by a rope-dancer's rhythm, but *irremediable* time, the object of anguish. The sonorous and metrical movement of this poem is to be explained in the same fashion as the "ominous" immobility of the bird on level T3:

> And the raven, never flitting, still is sitting, still is sitting
> On the pallid bust of Pallas just above my chamber door;
> And his eyes have all the seeming of a demon's that is dreaming,
> And the lamp-light o'er her streaming throws his shadow on the floor;
> And my soul from out that shadow that lies floating on the floor
> Shall be lifted—nevermore!

It is simply, I think, that this structural temporality is amenable to a finer instrumentation.

For this reason, the relationship T2-T4 is capable of a depth and diversity to which T3-T4 can attain only with difficulty. In the absence of a good T2-T4 relationship, T3-T4 borders on the facile, on a loose and superficial conception of what must really be experienced in the vertical dimension of the soul and the work. Chronism can sometimes do without T3 (a simple arabesque can directly induce a feeling of time) and suffer no loss, but hardly without T2; unless T2 and T3 are one, each being, on its own level, the exact duplication of the other: Shakespearian drama offers many outstanding illustrations. The exploration of this vast domain rightly belongs to the professionals in aesthetics.

[27] In English, "irretrievable;" the French word *irreparable* has the same double meaning as the Latin.—Ed.

The Concept of "Tonal Body"

HANS HEINZ DRÄGER

WHEN JAQUES HANDSCHIN, in his book entitled *The Character of Tone* (*Der Toncharakter;* Zürich, 1948), distinguished between "central" and "peripheral" tonal properties, he furnished a key concept to the psychology of tone and music.[1] His central properties are pitch and "tonal character" (by the latter he means "the systemic being of the tone," "its essentially musical being"), and his peripheral properties, duration, intensity, and timbre.

This distinction implies an evaluation in the spirit of the old *"musica,"* hence a perfectly justifiable groundwork for occidental musical conception. It should be noted, however, that musically central and musically peripheral do not necessarily mean primary and secondary in respect to the technique of composition. When Schönberg, in the third of his *Five Orchestral Pieces,* opus 16, introduces a constant chord with ever-changing instrumentation, the musically peripheral property of timbre has become primary as a means of expression. Something analogous is found in Alban Berg's "Wozzek," where all the instruments, entering successively in a crescendo, sustain the same tone.

[1] By "tone" we always mean, as does Handschin, the musical tone, including the vibration devoid of overtones.

174

Handschin's distinction between central and peripheral tonal properties is preceded by a consideration whether "it be legitimate to differentiate the tone from its properties, since it does not have the same relationship to them that an object customarily has to its properties; the paired concepts, object—properties, should not be applied to tone, since a tone is not just another object; it should itself be regarded only as an attribute (more or less equal to a property) of an object, which latter is still to be found." Handschin (justifiably) dismisses this consideration, but grants that a tone is "neither tangible nor visible but fundamentally a process."

I should like to say that a tone is both an object and a process, not only because the perceived process traces back to an object (which is also the case in seeing), but also because in hearing, it is the process transmitted from the [originating] object, that we perceive as an object (which is not the case in seeing). Accordingly, a tone is a hypostatically perceived process.

At any rate, this is the sense of the words which Handschin applies to his properties (with the exception of pitch); the sensory qualifications refer very little to hearing (except loud-soft, perhaps shrill), but mostly to the sense of touch (in this connection they refer either to form: round-pointed, compressed, or to surface properties: hard-soft, smooth-rough), and furthermore, to sight (bright-dark, dull-brilliant) and the temperature sense (warm-cold). They may also refer to internal structure (full-hollow, dense-loose) and to weight (heavy-light).

For all these characteristics the concept [1a] of "tone-color" is usually employed. This expression is perhaps the most infelicitous of all those used for tonal characteristics, since the impression of really colored tones in the sense of yellow, blue, etc. is always and quite justifiably considered vague or at best very subjective. In regard to this concept I should like to draw the following distinctions:

a) *The Sonal Character* appears when, with varying frequencies, the material, format, and playing of the instrument remain constant, as it might appear on an ideally constructed piano. The objection that low-frequency piano tones would be perceived as round, but high-frequency ones as pointed (which, after all, would indicate a change in the character of the sound) does not hold. If we conceive the piano tone in the image of a sphere, tones of

---

[1a] Here the author is obviously taking exception to a *term*, not a concept; but he writes "der *Begriff* 'Klangfarbe,'" so we can only write "concept."—Ed.

both high and low frequency must be regarded as spheres. Then the high frequency tones might appear pointed because of their smallness, but not because they have changed their form. The head of a common pin, when pressed against the human hand, also gives the impression of a point when compared to a bowling ball, although both of them have spherical form.

b) *The specific quality of the sound,* when substance or volume or touch is different, in which case even identical frequencies produce different sound impressions.

The second concept, also borrowed from optics, and closely connected with "tonal color," but not directly applicable to the instrument, is "brightness." Here I should like to differentiate:

a) *A general brightness* in the case of tones of different frequency but with the same sonal character; high-frequency piano tones are brighter than low-frequency tones. (In the Old Russian church melodies three of the various levels are called "dark," "bright," and "triple bright.")

b) *A specific brightness* as the specific quality of sound possessed by different tones even in the case of identical frequency; the tone a' sounds darker on the piano than on the zither.[2]

The above-listed terms include in their application some characteristics to which Handschin denies the status of properties. He prefers to call these "phantoms": extensiveness, weight, and density. "Extensiveness, weight, and density: here I cannot see any perceptible properties. These are aspects under which pitch (not, of course, the tonal character) may appear to us, or perhaps rather *feelings* which we connect with pitch; at any rate, elements which we ascribe to pitch rather than derive from it."[3] In contrast to this he states a few lines below: "still, it must be emphasized that pitch, after all, does not have any real designation, since the word 'pitch' itself is only a transferred designation. The real fact of the matter is that when tones with increasingly rapid vibrations follow one another we get the impression of climbing—somewhat resembling the way the Greeks used the expression 'heavy' for a low tone and 'pointed' or 'sharp' for a high tone."

From this we may conclude that all the aspects of tone, as the words above express them, have the same fundamental validity,

[2] In this connection see also G. Albersheim: *Zur Psychologie der Ton- und Klangeigenschaften,* 1939; Handschin, *op. cit.,* index.

[3] *Op. cit.,* p. 248.

though perhaps not in exactly equal measure, and may be accepted on a par.

Our inquiry here will be limited to the aspects: volume, density, and weight, i.e. those which G. Albersheim calls the "material characteristics of tone."[4] It will be shown that these characteristics, which offer the best justification for W. Köhler's concept of "tonal body," have structural significance in music.

VOLUME

"The bigger the stream the lower the tone," Beethoven wrote under a sketch for his *Pastoral Symphony*. There is probably no other aspect of frequency as elementary as this one; a tone has a *frequency-volume*. "Small children spontaneously speak of small things in a high tone, of large things in a low register. The meaning of a phonetically identical word may change, as it does for instance in the Sudanese languages, by means of 'high-tone' or 'low-tone,' in the same sense (of small-large)."[5] We do not intend to espouse a false "physicalism," but cannot overlook the connection between low-frequency tones and large instruments, or between low-frequency tones and great wave lengths and air volumes, or finally between the excitation of the long nerve fibers of the basilar membrane by low-frequency tones, and the impression of a corresponding tonal volume on the other. The antonyms high-low express the facts of the case no more plastically than small-large, for when passing the threshold of perception tones do not create the impression of "subliminally high" and "subliminally low," but always seem to remain "in the ear;" indeed, their impression changes into a feeling of pain, which of course indicates the most intensive contact. The tone of highest frequency becomes so small that it penetrates painfully into the receiving organ, while that of lowest frequency becomes so large that it causes pain because of its oppressive fullness. As feelings of pain, both impressions are necessarily primitive, and have their analogues in the physical realm.

The objection will be made that the different duration of tones with identical frequency upsets this co-ordination of frequency

[4] *Op. cit.*, pp. 104 ff.

[5] E. M. v. Hornbostel: "Psychologie der Gehörserscheinungen," *Hdb. d. normalen u. pathologischen Physiologie*, 1926, p. 708.

and volume. The reply is: Tones of different frequency (but the same degree of loudness) possess, like their definite given magnitude, also a definite fading period. Thus, as different masses of a substance, when subjected to equivalent impulses (relative to their mass), differ in reverberation-time; so a long piano string reverberates longer than a short one. This fading-out time is identical with what William Stern called the "psychical present." It is not an absolute value, but it is the time value that is relevant to the temporally evolving musical form, and therefore the relevant value in the creation of musical time. In the construction of an instrument (we here refer, of course, only to instruments with a fading tone) the time value ascribed to a definite frequency is, indeed, greatly modified. In the case of the piano, for instance, the reverberation time of the high-frequency tones is "artificially" extended, since in composition high and low frequency tones must meet the same demands. Various epochs, moreover, develop different ideals in this regard, so that no single, valid relation between frequency and natural fading period can be postulated. But the tone of very briefly or very long reverberating instruments is nevertheless perceived as temporally abnormal, as that of the xylophone, or of its precise opposite in this respect, the vibraphone.

Now, sustained tones require, beyond their natural time value, a certain necessary "breadth of consciousness," i.e. the addition of a spiritual-temporal attention, as contrasted to the physical (purely sensory) perception of the tonal body. The relatively swift exhaustion we experience in listening to organ music may be traced to the fact that the organ tone (despite all variation achieved through registration), unrelieved by vibrato or dynamic modulation, demands this breadth of consciousness, i.e. temporal-spiritual vigilance, uninterruptedly and in unchanging intensity.

It is obvious that various tonal volumes imply various degrees of mobility (in the sense of different rates of succession) in tones of different frequency, just as a small insect needs many little wingbeats to cover a given distance, while a large bird manages with but a few. "The great sounds," writes von Hornbostel,[6] "are stout, viscid, hard to move." A. Schering characterizes the principle of thoroughbass as an "architectonic structural principle," [7] according to which "the basso continuo, the organically (!) undulating middle voices,

[6] *Op. cit.*, p. 708.
[7] "Über den Begriff des Monumentalen in der Musik," *Jahrbuch Peters*, 1934.

and discant tones, passionately moving, and even dissolving in quite phantastic diminuendos . . . show a statically conditioned tripartition." The expressions "architectonic" and "static," oriented toward the corporeal, take on their full meaning only with reference to tonal volume.

On the other hand, the impression of ponderousness or agility in a melody cannot be traced to the frequency alone. This aspect is determined rather by the spacing of the tones and the rate of their inception. Even a high-frequency passage appears ponderous, if there is too large an interval between the individual tones. It is then somewhat like the toddling of a child—the effect is clumsy even if the movements are rapid. A natural ponderousness is peculiar to low frequency tones, partly because of the long inception period of their vibrations, due to the amount of material involved, and also because of the greater latency period of their development in the ear.[8] This natural effect can be supported by corresponding instrumentation: Wagner's Mime motif would lose considerably, if it were, say, intoned by an organ instead of by low, bowed tones with a long inceptive vibration period. On the other hand, the impression of ponderousness due to a long inception period can be counteracted, as on the baroque organ, where, according to E. Thienhaus,[9] to each of the 32-foot pipes a 4-foot pipe was added, so that in relation to its air volume the 32-foot pipe produced its sound very quickly. Even the intentionally prolonged accompanying noise of the attack, in the middle and high-frequency pipes of the baroque organs, contributes (besides its "tone announcing" function in clarifying the polyphonic composition) to the equalization of inertia between low and high frequency tones. The corporeal impression of a greater or lesser inertia can also be attained by interpretative means. Thus, for example, in the answering string-quartet style the inceptive vibration period is shortened as much as possible in the attack on low tones. Conversely, on the piano, with its less differentiated inceptive reaction of high and low frequency tones, the latency period is simulated by means of agogics.

Aside from frequency, the tone volume is also dependent on loudness. A tone of given frequency has, when played louder, a greater

[8] On this subject see A. Wellek, "Der Raum in der Musik," *Archiv für die gesamte Psychologie,* 1934.

[9] "Orgelbaufragen im Lichte akustischer Forschung," *Archiv für Musikforschung* IV, 1939.

volume, and vice versa; it has a *loudness volume*. This coincides with the everday experience that approaching sound waves become louder, receding ones softer. To the human perceiver, coming nearer generally means becoming larger (for physical objects) or becoming louder (for sound). In the case of tone, the two impressions fuse, since a tone is both an object and a process.

The correlation: increasing loudness = increasing volume, is primarily conditioned by the equation: summation of tones = air quantities (of the same frequency and amplitude). In order to reach a definite volume in this way requires a greater number of high-frequency tones than tones of low-frequency. This fact is illustrated in the string section of a symphony orchestra. The number of instruments decreases from the violins to the contrabasses because their specific volume increases in the same order (even though it does not increase in exactly the same proportion, since basically musical factors play a part here). Increasing loudness = increasing size is, secondly, effected by enlargement of the amplitude of a tone (dimension of its quasi-sound-force).

Tones of different frequency can thus be made the same size. In the first instance the volume of a low-frequency tone is balanced by a larger number of high-frequency tones; in the second instance the long wavelength of a low frequency is compensated by the greater amplitude of a high frequency. The latter way of obviating frequency differences is probably determined theoretically by the threshold of feeling in the case of high-frequency tones and by the threshold of hearing in the case of low-frequency tones. In practice, however, the capabilities of instrument and player usually set limits to it long before these threshold values are reached. For this reason even the loudest high-frequency tones may not achieve the same impression of size as soft ones of low frequency. The greatest equalization is possible in the middle register, while at the extremes the difference in size becomes increasingly apparent.[10] By the aggregation of high-frequency tones, volume equality with low-frequency tones is theoretically possible up to the limits drawn by the thresholds of hearing and feeling. However, since the increase in loudness is slight even when the number of instruments is multiplied, this possibility is practically never presented.

To be sure, two tones of the same loudness still differ when the one is played by a solo violin, the other by a violin ensemble. In the

[10] On this subject see Handschin, *op. cit.*, p. 249.

concert hall this results simply from the greater spread of the group. With a loudspeaker transmission, however, the spatial difference is eliminated, and yet the sound difference remains. The difference does not consist in a greater fullness (in the sense of a greater volume) of the sound produced by the ensemble, but in its plurality (which, after all, tells us something about the numerical fullness but nothing about the fullness in respect to volume). The reason for the difference in sound is that the individual violinists (even if we assume a never-present sound identity in the instruments) execute bow change and vibrato neither simultaneously nor in the same manner. The attribution of the sound difference to the fullness of the ensemble effect, which is greater numerically but not in respect to volume, and which I at first opposed with scepticism, becomes convincing by a comparison with the organ. In the organ sound the plurality is considerably less apparent, in the case of a combination of stops very similar in sound. The reason is that the individual tones show very similar compensation processes and are intrinsically quite structureless. For a perfectly fair comparison we should, strictly speaking, assume stops of identical sound. But even without this really justified premise the difference from the string ensemble cannot be missed. The impression of plurality in the sound of the winds of an orchestra, which by contrast with the string sound appear much less structured, is considerably less. It is more difficult to tell whether two or three flutes (in unison and in tune, of course) are playing than whether two or three violins play together.

DENSITY

The density of a tone is first of all determined by the average speed of the vibrating particles, the so-called vibration rate, which increases with the frequency. In terms of our previously developed concepts this would be its *frequency-density*. In this connection von Hornbostel writes: [11] "The large sounds are non-dense, loose, confused . . . the small sounds, on the other hand, dense, tight, compact, concentrated . . ." G. Albersheim describes them in the same way.[12] From a physical viewpoint this is correct. But it is not valid for the curve of the threshold of hearing, since with diminish-

[11] *Op. cit.*, p. 708.
[12] *Op. cit.*, pp. 105 ff.

ing frequency increasingly larger sound forces are necessary to make them audible. We must, therefore, first differentiate between a physical and an auditory density, as we did, analogously, between sound force and loudness. The auditory density (which is the only one of interest here and henceforth simply called "density") remains approximately constant up to a vibration number of about 2,500 (in the musical sound force areas). Only in the higher frequencies, i.e. from about c' up, does it change in accord with v. Hornbostel's rule, without satisfying its claim to exclusiveness. Presumably v. Hornbostel bases his conclusions on investigations in this frequency range.

The relation between physical and auditory density shifts once more in keeping with v. Hornbostel's rule, approximately between the vibration rates of 250 and 1,000. This shift, however, occurs only with loudness of about 80 decibels and up, which can just about be attained by a large orchestra but is an exception in ordinary musical performance. Perhaps judgments of auditory density involve some feeling for the density of the human body in comparison to a given sound density (comparison of pinhead and bowling ball).

While the density of a tone is dependent on sound rate, it is also determined by amplitude. Thus a tone of a given frequency obtains, by means of dynamic intensification, a different density, its *loudness-density*. Hence, even if v. Hornbostel's definition applied, it would at least be one-sided. According to him, high-frequency tones would, certainly, be relatively denser, but not only they would be dense: for loud low-frequency tones would be so, too. The existence of a loudness-density suggests the possibility of equalizing the greater frequency-density of a high-frequency tone with the greater loudness-density of a low-frequency tone, thus bringing both to the same "general" density. Between the approximate vibration rates of 2,500–8,000, this equalization is, indeed, actually possible. For practical purposes, however, the narrowness and boundary location of this frequency range deprive it of musical significance. It is not comparable to the importance of the equalization of frequency volume and loudness volume.

The two principles of dynamic control—now by aggregation of tones, and now by increase of amplitude, i.e. intensification of tone —show quite different effects in regard to density: In aggregation the density remains constant with changes of amplitude; in intensification the density varies with the amplitude. The difference between sliding and impulse dynamics is thus given additional clarification by taking density into consideration.

In the third place, a tone also has density as a specific property of sound, dependent on its gar.ut of overtones; i.e. it has a *timbre-density*.[13] A clarinet tone has less of a timbre-density than an equally loud oboe tone. Only by means of the correspondingly greater loudness of the clarinet tone do both become equally dense. The smaller timbre-density of the clarinet tone is compensated for by the greater loudness-density.

We can observe a special "play with density" when string players play in positions instead of crossing the strings in passing to the higher frequency tones. Because of the radically changed relation of thickness and length, the string assumes a more compact form and the tone a new timbre character, a greater timbre-density. Out of these considerations for timbre, musicians in the baroque period avoided the playing of positions for its own sake. The opposite attitude in classical and romantic music is known from innumerable instances. But to what degree an excessive difference in density is obviated even in a romantic melody in order to preserve its architectonics, is shown by measures 28–68 of the andantino in Schumann's piano concerto. Here the change in intensity desired within the parts of the melody is attained by playing in positions on the cellos (measures 30, 34, 39, 54, 58, 63) and the violins (measures 65, 66), while the "middle" density necessary for the coherence of the melody is achieved through the separation of the cellos from the violins (measures 41, 64). Among the possibilities of varying this "play with density" only one may be briefly indicated: When in the case of transition into a higher range the timbre-density is increased by means of a decrescendo, the loudness-density is decreased.

WEIGHT

Musicians and psychologists consistently call low-frequency tones heavy, high-frequency tones light. This definition makes it clear once more that the current assumption, which is that the density of a tone increases proportionately with its frequency, is not tenable. Otherwise a high-frequency tone would have a smaller volume and

[13] Thus also G. Albersheim, *op. cit.*, p. 200.

a larger "general" density than a low-frequency tone of the same loudness and the same timbre-density. But both would have the same weight (for, if we use expressions such as volume, density, and weight at all, we must also grant that weight is determined by volume and density). That would mean, furthermore, that all tones of the same loudness and the same timbre-density make the impression of being equally heavy.

With the confirmation that the (auditory) density (in the musically relevant ranges of frequency and sound-force) remains approximately constant, we now find that the tonal weight is also directly determined by frequency: A low-frequency tone is heavy; a high-frequency tone light. This constitutes its *frequency-weight*.

With increasing loudness the volume grows, and with that also the weight of a tone. This is its *loudness-weight:* In the case of intensification-dynamics, the tonal weight increases with the loudness-volume and the loudness-density by means of the magnification of amplitude; in aggregation-dynamics, the tonal weight increases only by means of increasing volume. An enrichment of the gamut of overtones causes it to increase also by means of increasing timbre-density. This *timbre-weight* in its dependence on the timbre-density can, of course, also be different, in tones of equal loudness and equal frequency. The equalization of weight in tones of different frequency is therefore possible, by means of increasing the volume only (aggregation dynamics), or volume plus density (intensification dynamics), or the density only (timbre-density). Naturally, all three possibilities can also be combined.

THE ANALYSIS of tonal-body characteristics resulted in the following concepts: Frequency and loudness volume; frequency, loudness, and timbre density; frequency, loudness, and timbre weight. With the help of these concepts it is possible to define more exactly some features of the sensory tone-process, which up to now have been too vaguely designated, e.g. "tonal intensity" or "heavy movement." In addition they enable us to complement Handschin's concept of the "musical-central" characteristics by description of three types of musical composition:

1. *Musically pure composition.* Its criteria are: identical tone character (and with that also the same tone quality) in all parts; the same inceptive period for all tones; restriction to the smallest possible frequency range, in order to let volume, density, and weight

of the tones—given the same loudness—disclose the least possible difference, so that the change in frequency as such, and with it the tone character, become as nearly sole operators as possible; equally fast movement in all parts.

2. *Musically-architectonically determined composition.* Its criteria are: Identical tone character (and with that also the same tone quality) in all parts; the same loudness of all tones; utilization of the total auditory range; hence, furthermore: different tonal volumes (perhaps with different inceptive period); different tonal weights, but equal tonal density; with increasing frequency, increasingly rapid tone sequence.

3. *Musically free composition.* It is free in all respects. The degree and the frequency with which it diverges from musically pure composition determine the "musical slope," which is oriented by the central musical conception.

The Essence of Rhythm

RAYMOND BAYER

THE AESTHETIC OBJECT does not confront us like other objects in the world. When I am dull or inattentive, I am no longer aware of it; when eager or curious, I savor it anew. This feature alone should suffice to make us recognize the singularity of its nature. In both cases, however, my eyes are seeing the object. It remains there, whether it is apparent to me or not. There is something like a fatigue phenomenon in the perception of Beauty, a factor in aesthetic contemplation which has always been described as subjective. It either restores the spectacle to its proper domain or rejects it. If we confine ourselves to that radical experience, the reality of the aesthetic object, *qua aesthetic*, will be compromised. The subjectivity of Beauty becomes irreducible.

That is not all. Something essential to the work shows itself in a further trait. Again the aesthetic object shows a peculiar nature. If, as we have just seen, it depends upon the Self whether that object is to be revealed or obscured, then in turn it depends upon the object, whether the Self shall be captivated or shall withdraw. In this sense, the more precise a technique is, the more it *exists:* that is, if it seizes consciousness as in a very close net, and will not let it escape without an inner *transformation.* Consider any work of

186

art whose magic is patent: our soul, steeped in it, does not pass through unchanged; one might even say that therein lies the authentic nobility, the criterion of the aesthetic object. Thus, if I judge it in terms of my appreciation, the object at first glance appears variable to me, a function of my Self; but if, on the other hand, I regard it in terms of its execution, the Self submits to the commanding work. Psychologism seeks to reabsorb all into mind, formalism tends to spatialize the aesthetic datum. You may go to the heart of psychologism, scrutinize the depths of formalism: neither one doctrine nor the other accounts for the aesthetic phenomenon. Holding strictly to the facts—this is our first realization—*the aesthetic object must be envisaged as a strange composite of Self and Thing, a compound that appears initially and by its very nature inseparable.*

We are told, not without real insight, that here the mind is involved in the forms. These forms could not exist divorced from us. Yet the prerogatives of the aesthetic object are inviolate. The mind is fundamental to the geometrician's forms, too. In the science of geometry as conceived by a Spinoza, which consists in deduction according to cause and adequate understanding of generated figures, mind certainly underlies the figures: and still more so, no doubt, when it derives their formula by the processes of analytic geometry. Yet, thought and the world, like learned men unaware of each other, seem to sit down each at one end of the table and to carry out independently their calculations relative to these forms, wherein they will eventually meet. Beneath these figures, this perfect sphere engendered by a half-circle, one feels that mind is present; but nevertheless, in a certain sense, it withdraws from them. What, then, causes mind not only to underlie aesthetic forms, *but to dwell in them?*

For art is validated only by that captivation; that is the issue preliminary to any formalism. We are thrown back both to the notion of a thing which may vanish or may take on the brightness of a meteor before the unstable Self, and to the notion of a Self imprisoned by the object, held by it as a hostage. The problem which confronts us is evidently the following: What is the specific characteristic, to be isolated in the work, which causes it to be *ipso facto* aesthetic; the element whose presence summons the object to the world of the Beautiful or whose absence refuses it entry? In other words, when the object and the Self meet, what is it that *changes* in the Self, but *persists* in the object? At bottom we are looking for the characteristic reality of that semblance which is art.

For this, one must not fail to note from the outset a third feature in the aesthetic object. This will advance us one step toward the knowledge of its nature. To this phenomenon *sui generis,* we are going to give the provisional name *reversibility of affect.* The aesthetic object has the characteristic that human emotion is not lost from it: the work of art possesses the unique property of being at the same time product and source. Let us look within ourselves the better to realize this fact; there is a double movement throughout the work of art of fixed and restored emotion. Take another product of creative activity, some inert, machine-made object: through this nothing is carried over from the artisan to us. There is a break between the creation and its creature; one might say that the movement, once broken off, is no longer either received or transmitted. Take, on the other hand, the Judge of the Sistine Chapel, that God who separates the Chosen from the Damned. Here you would not speak of a bit of flotsam left on the beach, from which life has departed without any record of the wave which carried it there. Everything, on the contrary, bespeaks the flow of genius: The Verdict, and the eddying confusion beneath, the whole Last Judgment restores to us the initial emotional experience which was its creative cause. It is like a strange but real exchange between the painter and you through the object thus crystallized, but changed. At this stage nothing of him is lost; you still participate today in the grandeur of the act. For the artist knew how to objectify: what the wall gives us is his passionate will, and that very power of willing is reconstituted in the prisms of our minds. Thus the laboring "poet" has found in his work not only his impetuous master, but also his interpreter. How can such a miracle—I mean the resurrection of feeling —be possible? Now master, now servant, the artist reveals to us his states, the receiving and the returning. *Something is preserved which explains the value of art and our captivation.*

We are now going to shift our point of view. An examination of our judgment confirms our analysis of the object. The peculiar phenomenon in judgments of taste is that they are distinguished by a mechanism with two triggers. Consider an authentic judgment of reality. From subject to predicate the attribution is not in the least indirect: the relationship stands without any intermediary. Here, however, the mechanism operates on three terms: there is the object, there is the *resonance* which its impression leaves in me, and, finally, there is my judgment. The element of affect comes like a screen between the image of the thing and the judgment of the Self. This feature suffices to give the aesthetic judgment its physiognomy. For among these three terms that we have posited, the relation changes. The immediacy of the judgment departs, in fact, from the object: it falls back, instead, on the resonance, a secondary cause. It is the emotion remaining in me that my verdict of the thing expresses. No doubt, this verdict is still of the object: there is even reason to believe that, quite obscurely, it proceeds from it with the same necessity. But in this indirect judgment, made up of actual feeling and resonance, I no longer proceed by implication or exclusion: I mean to say, by a play of concepts; we know it has even been maintained—and not unreasonably—that the intervention of a concept would suffice to invalidate my verdict as a judgment of taste. It is, in truth, still knowledge that takes shape in the work of art. But who does not see that a judgment of reality would leave no other trace in our minds than a conceptual knowledge? Here, on the other hand, we are confronted with something quite different, with knowledge, no doubt, but of an *excitable* kind—something which seems essentially analogous to an inclination, gratified or frustrated. Such a galvanization must have its cause. This truth which I do not *assert* by my judgment, but to which I commit myself invites us to meditate on the error of an analysis which would lead to a premature reduction of the aesthetic object. But through this vibrant and magical phenomenon of *commitment*, which remains the master-trait of the new judgment, we can also understand more fully how the representation of the object can sometimes suddenly fail to be aesthetic in face of the dullness of the Self; why, nevertheless, the Self is not free but a plaything in the imperious ban of the work; and finally, under what condition either of inexpressiveness or emotional reversibility the object remains unimportant or else is lifted into the world of the Beautiful. Here we find summed up, in one psychical trait, all the characteristics of the work of art. *What we have described is certainly a judgment under a spell.*

I I

So by a sustained methodical examination of the various notions relating to the domain of the Beautiful we can make a special abstraction from the phenomena, and find an element fit to throw sudden light on our question. The aesthetician is put in possession of a law.

Phenomena of the aesthetic order are all characterized, on every level, by a certain constancy: and this constancy is revealed to us by the study of rhythms. Aesthetics can, indeed, be a purely historical study: in that case its work is simply the definition of an epoch or a Golden Age. It is confined to examining and describing the revolutions of taste. These are the conceptions of the first level. Next it has to deal with a second set of ideas, which also belong to its proper domain, and require a *categorical* study: determining the modalities of the Beautiful, specifying it, so to speak, as sublime, as baroque, as graceful or as humorous. Finally, aesthetics can undertake to resolve the problem of *essence* and go on to the description of aesthetic "types," namely special kinds of objects in which one may delightedly see a purified representation, and, as it were, a symbol of Beauty. Now, whether we be dealing with the description of an aesthetic period, or the scope of a category, or the determination of essences, we always end, in fact, by recognizing on each level a special kind of constant, *always the same:* and the more expert the eye of the aesthetician becomes, the more convincing will be this perception.

To back up the idea with an example: whoever undertakes to describe the panorama of taste at the beginning of the eighteenth century in terms other than a subjective impressionism, will notice the gradual emergence, over and above the diversity of forms and arts in process of rearranging their canon, of strange outlines of a new general form and what amounts to a peculiar kind of constancy. This type of constancy is imparted to these arts and to these forms by revolutions in their structure and balance: a balance and structure blessed with a typical change of *rhythms.* A painting by Watteau, a minuet by Campra, the scenes of the Opéra-ballet, the accents of the "Déjeuners dans un parc," or the "Réunions de comédiens," likewise the lively dance at the Opéra, the work of a Camargue or subsequently of a Vestris, have, when we delve deeper into the precise, minute, scientific observation of these works, a number of secret correspondences which are obviously the fruit of a law whose piecemeal discovery continually fortifies our original induction.

We suspected some coherence: our taste prepared us for it. But, examined now as if *from the outside,* the rhythms assure us by their scansion, their vigor, their distribution of accents, as well as by a certain curve of meters and tempi in the ordered pace of the aesthetic object, that the table of invariants and devices does indeed stem in every detail from something like a predetermined economy, whose appearance everything confirms and nothing contradicts. This table of invariants, thus seen in the light of a true revolution in taste, is the rhythmic form of a *time*.

Let us assume a second phase of the inquiry: namely, that hereby it were possible to track down not just the outline of Golden Ages, but, so to speak, a physiognomics of categories. The aesthetician might now see a variety of images arising: thus the beetling mountain, the raging sea, the cosmic infinity of worlds, sustained by a latent rhythmic measure (relatively clear by virtue of its austere evidence)—all these might engender, for instance, the idea of the sublime. With such an hypothesis he might be led to describe this second level of aesthetic phenomena also in terms of abstract rhythmics, and by the same procedure, establish some kind of constancy. Here, too, the coherence of the concept would rest on some invariant. And this is precisely what we learn from scrupulous analysis of the facts. Thus grace, which some tend to identify with pure caprice, lets all its rhythms proceed in two climates, so to speak.[1] The nature of the object has little significance here. Petrovitch has written a little book which treats of mechanisms common to different phenomena: there are common rhythms underlying the disparity of the major arts. The dynamic rhythm of grace is effected by speed in effort, languor in repose; tonal rhythm is marked by a transient excitement and a surrender; pictorial rhythm is built up on sporadic tension together with nonchalant relaxation, so that these pulses of alternate storm and calm are based on a balanced dispersal of the stress, whatever graceful object we may be considering. It even happens that, in working with this idea, one may reach a more abstract invariance, which would hint at the existence of an archetype of rhythms: a patient inventory of the denumerable riches in the realm of the Graceful reshapes it into images of a rare coherence for the mind. Its realm exhibits a system—as your eyes finally discover—of an invariable mode of being of the psychic Self: I mean all the distinct gestures and appropriate rhythms of *alacrity*. Thus

[1] The author's phrase, "la grâce . . . voit tous ses rythmes passer pour ainsi dire par deux climats," is hard to render: the idea is that they always combine two principles of tempo.—Ed.

on the basis of an idea, an inner equilibrium is figured forth. It is the rhythmic form of one *type* of the Beautiful.

Let us go further. In an investigation one presently finds a fantastic epitome of these aesthetic ideas about predominant "types." Earthly objects would thus be elevated by assignment to some chosen sphere of beauty: cosmic infinity is a representation of the sublime; the swallow, or water, or the rose have always been the *symbols* of grace. The pursuit of such a demonstration of essences is thrilling and peremptory. Each of these earthly objects, or rather, each of these concrete symbols of a formal beauty, is in harmony with the rhythmic presentations of art. You think you apprehend the swallows, but you really apprehend only a point describing curves, an ardent cry followed by a long silence, and that bipartite body made of shadow and light. You think you are describing a swan, but in depicting it you are only rehearsing the aesthetic principle of continuity. The reason for this is that these objects tend to resolve themselves, insofar as they remain symbols, into a series of abstract but perceptible rhythms, as if each one were a certain definite value for a new kind of equation for which a formula, were it only exquisite enough, could be verified. The reality of the facts, despite the special guise that the idea assumes in becoming concrete, leads us to their discovery. Correspondences may well become obfuscated; but what underlies the aesthetic "types," and leaves its definite and precise imprint, is the rhythmic image of an earthly *object*.

It would seem, then, that we are dealing with a *perceptible* quality in the object. If the discovered basis of the aesthetic constants can be thus deduced and recognized within this conceptual system, where more and more exact discoveries and well-directed investigations would constantly bring us back to a rhythmic scheme in works of art, the aesthetic object would lose its random character. Art would be dominated by a precise law. That is to say, we are no longer in a causal desert wherever the realm of the Beautiful extends, nor in a universe where genius breaks the law. On the contrary, the perceptible universe and its determinism regain possession of us when face to face with a work of art; the analysis of the world is thereby broadened. To isolate a constant in terms of which all ideas may be defined and which applies to all the phenomena is no small consequence of the establishment of rhythmic forms. In every case, an individual form underlies each work, and is the carrier of the rhythm. It is this rhythmic image which, in the course of changing our critical thought, comes confusedly between us and it, as the impact of the object precedes but prepares the the judgment. But this law of art, which is a fact, and to which every aesthetician has to assent in the course of his aesthetic research, this constant of a new kind, now permits us to catch a glimpse of other perspectives.

III

Rhythm is thus the essence of art. It is the law of the Beautiful, and here we find the specific abstraction that we were looking for. The recognition of this truth, perhaps, enables us to resolve the problem of the alternatives with which aesthetic theory has always confronted us.

In the first place, rhythm has the contradictory privileges of being both *perceptible* and *inward*. It undoubtedly participates in duration, as this is incorporated in the movements of consciousness, but it can also be perceived as a scansion of space. Rhythms are images of reality that take their place in space and audible time. The plane of rhythm is therefore at the true intersection of the interior domain and the realm of things. We have here, so to speak, a stage prior to the object and to the Self: you *see* the rhythmics of art falling into visible systems, forms and structures in the universe; you *feel* it in the inner world, maintaining cadences and discipline. Were one to doubt its nature, it would not be difficult to make an experiment on oneself. Examine directly how rhythm makes itself felt: you have only to immerse yourself in the perceptual realm. Suppose you go into a museum and look at a show of drawings. Even before you come close, the name of a master is on your lips. A characteristic property inherent in his pencil strokes causes you to recognize the special quality of this artist among all others; it has given to his creation an indefinable kinship and profound physiognomy. Here, spread out before your eyes, is a way of proceeding, of stopping, of scanning; an image of energy or relaxation, the imprint of a caressing or destroying hand which is his alone. And, moreover, this perception is all you need; in it you have the whole of his rhythm. Now let us consider in what way rhythm, too, is in the nature of an experience. When we are leaving a concert, our mind holds the imprint of it. The perception of some characteristic rhythms that have reached the listener haunt and disturb him: they carry over to him, establish themselves and persist in his mind. Whatever doubts we may have about the mechanism of this phenomenon, the psychic persistence will force itself upon our consciousness and, spontaneously, involuntarily, we recover the melody. It pursues us while we walk along the street. We are subject to its stubborn persistence. For several more days the rhythmic wave created in us will go on; our soul, like a thing possessed, taking its bearings and, as one might say, the impetus from memory, will continue to project these rhythmic fragments into the world of sense, tending after its own fashion to reconstitute the whole of the tonal entity. An essentially two-way, synthetic character thus allows us, perhaps, to explain how rhythm can be an image of the world, and at the same time a trait of the Self.

There are two worlds of art: the realm of *design* and the realm of *experience,* universes whose reciprocal action is as inexplicable as it is certain. But these heterogeneous realms could doubtless be reconciled, as by a transactive force, if art were in essence that undifferentiated rhythmic whole, that nebulous entity which envelops both the object and the Self: we should have found, so to speak, the logically prior reality that can either fall back into [physical] regularity or open out into psychical tempi, from which the aesthetic object and the artistically conscious subject might be found to differentiate, and finally to confront each other as distinct entities in the world of the Beautiful. The rhythms which further establish these two concepts, and, I might say, mold them in reference to one another, seem to derive that office from a state wherein the object and the Self, otherwise empty abstrations, shed light on each other. Both take shape there, each separately, and become solid and real: in this double condensation, the object, by virtue of its formal perfection, wins its full reality and its resistance as an object to the Self; the Self, rich in discipline, regaining its own psychic economy, finally lays hold upon itself. Judging by simple observation, the power of rhythms seems to build up simultaneously, by one and the same activity, the perfect, indestructible, and contrasting effigies of the Self and the object: that is to say, the masterwork of both. These measures and this recurrence which are the substance of rhythm, are certainly what effects the transition from one of these worlds to the other, wherein each element is preserved, even while carried over, in the master-fact, expression: derived from the mind and held in the symbol. Otherwise one cannot understand why, in the meditations of philosophers, the Beautiful has always appeared as a realm that straddles a common boundary: yet the more perfectly formed the work of art, the more, paradoxically, it is felt. The primary contradiction of art, namely that it shapes and unites two worlds, may now be resolved. The two worlds make contact in this phenomenon that is at once perceptible and internal, fixed in space yet pervading the Self. *The plane of rhythms is the place of intersection of object and subject.* This plane, moreover, represents something further: the contradiction between mathematicism and hedonism is expressed by it, too, and is also factitious. Let us look more closely at the pleasure of the Beautiful: it is a triple star. No doubt, sensuous pleasure is never absent; it even constitutes a kind of primary source of joy, with its retinue of gratified inclinations and exquisite sensations; besides, no one can abstain from the heady excitement of sounds and colors, the vocal magic of words. But here we have a pleasure at once coarse and refined, which cannot be an end in itself. The pleasure of the senses is still something made up of our own disposition, with its desires and prejudices, even with the injustice of its tastes: and that is not a specific pleasure. To the vulgar mind that is, indeed, the pleasure of the Beautiful. We recognize a second pleasure, the delight of the intelligence, where the mind takes hold of the technical aspects of the work in order to analyse them. The aesthetic object is like an ordered spectacle, the rules of which must first be felt, then investigated. This is an austere pleasure, and the fruit of knowledge. The construction of the work reveals itself to the discerning eye, we enter into contact with the object, we see it rise up before us with the beauty of a performance: but this pleasure, born only of knowledge, leaves a savor which the most sophisticated tend to take for the height of critical taste, quite as much as for a first degree of desecration. Knowing the norms, discovering perfection, is perhaps the second star in the pleasure of the Beautiful. Still, this is not the pleasure we are seeking. It is, after all, merely the pleasure of the *technician*. There is another pleasure, a very superior one, one which is in any case quite distinct; and this pleasure cannot do without the two others—it involves them and draws upon them. This last is an autonomous pleasure, and it takes some attention to recognize it, despite its autonomy. Pure aesthetic joy consists precisely in that rhythmic equilibrium which the Self attains when it is face to face with the work of art. All the ins and outs of a form which, though captured, is still seeking itself, are ready to imprint themselves on our soul, in scanning the activated and fluid substance. Rapture now comes to me, but in a closed form: I receive the rhythms along with the image of the object. It is like an indirect dynamics. Thus there is, in the high discipline of feeling, a pleasure which subsumes those of the sensuous and technical points of view and is colored by them, but is itself specific. It is surprising, to say the least, that this has never been given its systematic place among the pleasures of the Beautiful; that in the first place it has not been described, and secondly, that no account has ever been taken of the aristocracy to which it has given rise. This pleasure, consisting of the specific taste for rhythm, is the true pleasure of the *artist "nature."* Here, too, mathematics is seen at once to recover its rights. Charles Henry once determined the dynamogenic points by which the work of art, reduced to formulae, must necessarily please: of course, this is taking too simple a view of the intimate structure of the Self. But, in the obscure depths of the subject, Leibnitzianism maintains its profound truth of a numerical, though unconscious perfection. Numbers which we cannot know subtend the rhythms, and the rhythms are bases of pleasure. *The plane of rhythmics, with its measure of feeling, is the locus of intersection of mathematicism and hedonism.*

The nature of rhythms forces us, finally, to take a stand on a third option. The moods of the Self, if there be such, should be strictly distinguished from pure aesthetic feeling. It is the weakness of psychologism to confuse them. Not all rhythms penetrate the subject on the same level. That is the point. Let us pause for a moment to consider the mechanism of this rhythmic imposition the object makes upon the Self. In this phenomenon alone there are hierarchical degrees, and a sort of intiation into art. Our moods are, no doubt, fundamentally involved. This means that the construction of the aesthetic work cannot be undertaken without entailing in its progress the remains of some concrete affectivity reflected in mental states. The first rhythm of the work as we encounter it is no more than the precipitate of these states, transferred to the canvas. Our rhythms, which are engendered by it, at first only mimic it. Let us suppose that you are contemplating a masterpiece like the Mona Lisa. The first wave of psychic rhythm comes to you from that ambiguous expression, that direct translation of a complex personality. The aesthetic theme thus visibly manifested was only too easy for art critics to point out, and has been exploited all too much. It is therefore just—and inevitable—that today a reaction of public opinion should deny its value. The controversy, however, cannot make us forget the psychological truth of it, the fact which such an aesthetic judgment was meant to interpret: moods play before the mind and imprint upon it, through their rhythms, their own dynamics. We shall call this state of rhythmic imposition, in which the world of actual feeling is directly represented in the work, the *mimetic stage*. In pure aesthetics the validity of this stage has been contested: in other words, the play of moods is only a substructure. There is a second level in the hierarchy of imposition. We are still invaded by rhythms, but in a more abstract manner: this is on another plane. For the beholder of the *Gioconda* there are cadences in her countenance which haunt him, and which can no longer be accounted for by a mood. To that formalism of feeling we should have to refer the rhythm and play of those crossed and languid hands, the slight turning of the torso in the chair, and of the head on the torso: such a configuration of gesture has, in its turn, rhythmical intension. On this second level, where the rhythms of the object work on us, we discover a phenomenon of vibrant abstraction: the cadences now retain only the bare outline of the act and the pure image of feeling to throw their light into our consciousness. We shall call this second plane of imposition or penetration of rhythm the *symbolic stage*. Here we have, already, what seems almost a contraction of the work; it folds back upon itself, so to speak, and no longer delivers to the subject the whole of its substance. It is a rhythmic composition of the action, of which the pattern alone reaches us. Art, however, does not stop even there. The aesthetic object is rich in contractions of a second order, and there the rhythms define themselves in their purity: here, at last, we reach the third and last level of imposition, the technical stage. But now the whole psychological content has been detached from the work, leaving only an imprint and a form. The clarity of the rhythm rules out the moods and becomes aesthetic and beautiful in the measure in which the feeling no longer has any name. The self and the object, harmonizing on a single plane of equilibrium, reserve their independence in every other way. This is like an algebraic generalization, or rather, like an aesthetic abstraction which is carried out in the perception

of the object. The *Gioconda*, to return to our example, offers us at
the depth of this third level, like an unknown and unique language,
its magical play of whatever is revealed and expressed, the bare
cadence of its contours, the contrast of the whole figure with its
background which the grace of their apportionment divides. Here
is art itself, now a self-sufficient system, that formulates or expresses: it imparts a rhythm to us by virtue of, and just to the extent of,
its *strangeness*. On this level the rhythmic signature, in lone sub-
sistence above the concrete, reaches the height of art, and at the
same time attains the abstract perfection of its calligraphy. This
is the stage which we shall call *cryptogrammatic*. But precisely because the pure aesthetic sentiment, born from the distribution of
rhythms, moves back and forth, reserving and spending itself, as
it were, to evolve variable levels of strangeness and isolation; and
because so pure a feeling disengages itself by degrees from moods
(far from being coextensive with them) and moves easily from the
concreteness of the psychic Self to a somewhat more abstract rhythmic order, and from this second rhythmics to the supreme and final
abstraction; precisely because of this we leave self-expressive feeling
behind us, and rise even to where no symbol is adequate any more,
so the symbol in its turn changes into the pure convention of a
sign. But, equally, art keeps its profound character by virtue of these
successive withdrawals. I mean the character of being synonymous
with the *adjusted*. For the precise interplay of the three phases is
art itself. The highest achievement of art, one clearly feels, is to
effect mysteriously a backtracking from level to level, whereby at
each depth of imposition of rhythms the Self and the object become
more free and recover their individuality, until at last they no longer
communicate except at this single point where there is total communication, the extreme point of an entirely rhythmical, supreme
duration. Aesthetics would thus preserve only the *discipline* of feeling. But thereby we could understand just how the value of a work
of art acquires its exact measure and preciosity from the sureness
of those retractions and ellipses. To sum up, it would seem that pure
aesthetic feeling by nature breaks away from the play of moods and
from the psychic Self, as experience shows us and as the evidence
of our inner consciousness demands; they are, in fact, going in opposite directions, the one being enhanced while the other is in abeyance. We must see, then, a superior order in the aesthetic domain,
apart from the mind in a certain sense, and apart from the forms;

an order in which forms and mind are integrated. Psychologism, that confines itself to the vibration of moods, is futile; an unconscious heterogeneity of formulae, scrupulously retaining nothing that comes from life, would be worthless. Between the work of art and the subject a correspondence of balances is maintained, reaching perfection precisely along their ridge of highest abstraction: like a realm comprising the common boundary of forms and mind. This discipline of rhythms is still a feeling, but it is only the *form* of feeling. For the rest, in art, it leaves behind the level of moods where it began. Yet, however high it may soar, and from whatever alien sphere its rhythm returns to us, it cannot—and now we can see why—but keep the mark of its origin and remain, distilled though it may be, an image of life: *the order of rhythms is the order in which psychologism and formalism are reconciled.*

I V

Here are the consequences. They concern the nature of the aesthetic object, the structure of the contemplating Self, and the essence of Beauty.

Let us take up again the preceding example of a composition by Watteau and an opera by Campra. The nature of the aesthetic object will perhaps become apparent. Of course, painting and music, the world of sight and the realm of hearing, are not of the same nature. Each of these two senses is invested with its own perfection. Nor does any relationship emerge, but instead there is evidence of two heterogeneous universes. Here are two worlds, each self-contained: two constructed, coherent, autonomous worlds. They are truly the realms of two *special* senses, with their specific ranges and the control of their incommensurable instruments. The issue now becomes clearer. For that constancy of rhythmic forms, which constitutes the undercurrent of artistic works, is found at the core of all the arts. It dominates their closed universes. It extends even to our contemplation of objects in the world, and to the aesthetics of Nature. This rhythm in things is like a sensuous quality, an authentic quality which is, however, channelled through all the senses. We must conclude that rhythm comes to us from certain objects in the external world, just as we perceive movement, shape, or number. The sameness of rhythms, that law of constancy which governs all phenomena of the Beautiful, has indeed that effect. The aesthetic object is always built on some particular order of sense; every art selects one, every art thus brings its own homogeneous world of sense to its private kind of perfection. Yet, if a rhythm embodied in these is the characteristic of *art,* then, according to whether the rhythm vanishes or is reborn in the depths of the psychic Self, I for my part shall have my desertness or my rapture; but the aesthetic object, in which pathos is reversible, conserves in either case (for this would be its nature) ever perceptible, the miraculously recovered emotion with its caesurae and its accents. This differentiates it from realities that have no fascination: here is where the beautiful object, in relation to the mere object, receives its definition. The creator endowed it with a rhythm: *and rhythm is that further, common, perceptual element which brings an object into the world of art.*

The same law might lead us, in the second place, to a new study of the contemplating subject. One might get at the subject *from the outside.* If a work of art is a sensuous form given to rhythms, if it is a rhythm cast in a form, then the Self is subjected by the object to what we might call an indirect dynamics: the aesthetic emotion of the Self under the spell of the work, is certainly a product of discipline. This emotion, being rhythm, is vibrant but fixed. The object gives to the subject its own rhythmics, setting a measure for him, placing the accents. The Self, as though molded by the world of sense, here frees itself and suspends its flux for one instant detached from itself, held by a strange, unknown, yet perceptible architectonics, its balance matching that of the work feature for feature. But at this point I return from the sensible world to my own Self. If, then, I can delve into that universe which every beautiful object is, a perfect world of rhythmic impositions, and if by hypothesis I could carry out the investigation of it in every detail, I should be able to know the mind itself with all its rhythms, having grasped the rhythms from *without the mind.* In the work which we are examining, everything is written correctly: the laws of the inward world are revealed in the analyzed actuality of works of art. All that pertains to the Self is set forth in the object and shaped for the mind: the image of its emotions that confronts it in the work, is a true replica of its own rapture. Here is the soul's equilibrium, reproduced as a perceptible and external quality. Thus every work puts its stamp on us, but at the same time keeps it for eternity, preserved for the inquirer's eye: here we should have the possibility of an objective psychodynamics. From such close study of the work, anyone who has eyes to see can fairly draw profound and permanent insights into his innermost Self; for while art holds the order and structure of the enthralled mind in its power, *what each and every aesthetic object imposes upon us, in appropriate rhythms, is a unique and singular formula for the flow of our energy.*

On such an hypothesis, finally, the Beautiful is the intuition and presentation of a balance sheet. The Self measures itself against the resistance of the world, and measures itself symbolically against the resistance of art. Every work gives us the schematized and disengaged memory of a volition: each work of art would convey the resultant of forces acting between symbolic systems. Before its judges, it would bear witness to their moves. Success, with its steady equilibrium, is thus the last word of aesthetics, as action is the first word of art. The aesthetic world preserves a human harmony. Its special feature is that it resembles a picture of a man projected into the perspective of rhythm. The essence of the Beautiful is, in a way, superior to the sensible and to the intelligible: in any case, it eludes them both. The *active* life of the Self, on the contrary, is met and complemented by the product of art, as gymnastics is by physical care. Aesthetic contemplation holds the echo of a creation. It is a matter of exact work: an activity both free and constrained. Beyond understanding and imagination, the hard contact with reality is taken up in the object, rhythmically modelled into shapes, and by symbols: a contact which we experience in reliving the fixed rhythm of the object. But as we discover its imprint, the aesthetic savor which lies in going over images in this way is no longer of the same order as pleasure or pain. Here is our third conclusion about delight or disappointment: *The delight in the Beautiful is of the nature of a triumph.*

If, then, it is true—as everything would seem to indicate—that the constancy of rhythmic images is indeed that invariance which underlies every conception of an order of the Beautiful, or, better, which is at the heart of all aesthetic ideas on every level, the problem of analysis of rhythm is the [aesthetic] problem itself. No other is more urgent. Its dominating form imposes itself on art: it ushers in the entire cycle of aesthetic problems concerning the confrontation of the human subject with the work of art.

Morphological Poetics

GÜNTHER MÜLLER

APPROACH AND SURVEY

The creative drive as the basic force of all literature and the involvement of this drive with the ways of life of periods and peoples demand a corresponding adjustment of our critical approach to literature. Normative poetics has become impossible through the realization that historical peculiarities have an autonomous existence and that artistic production is unpredictable. It would be absurd to derive certain formal rules from the works of a great poet, be it Homer or Sophocles, and set them up as a measure for the poetry of other nations and periods. It would be absurd for the reason that poetic fulfillment is not attained through the observance of abstracted norms but through the vital realization of an inner law.

This does not mean that a systematic and appraising comparison is impossible. To make it possible, however, it is necessary to penetrate to the deeper layers of poetic creation. A single work can never be a pattern applicable to all. But each truly poetic product can make its contribution to the field where the formative, creative forces are dominant. It is only from these forces and from their fundamental structural laws that general rules can be derived. Such

202

"rules" will above all sharpen the eye for the nature and structure of poetic reality. The new poetics, for which the literary profession in Europe is preparing itself in the most widespread localities, while tackling innumerable problems, will have to be established in this frame of simple structural laws.

I. THE TWO BASIC PRINCIPLES

Two obvious, given facts may serve for our guidance. Because they are so simple, because they go almost without saying, they have been easily ignored. Yet, precisely at the foundations of a discipline the simplest facts are of special importance because they lie close to the origins of its problems. The two conditions relevant to morphological poetics are:

1. Poetry is a *linguistically conveyed* reality.
2. The force by which the linguistically conveyed reality of poetry is produced is a *natural* force.

The first condition, all by itself, encompasses everything relating to the involvement of poetry in the history of nations. With the second we pass beyond the antithesis "rationalism—irrationalism" to the creative causes, which neither permit nor require any justification. Moreover, the two basic conditions are obviously intimately connected, for the poetic-creative natural force does after all manifest itself in the genesis of the linguistic structure.

Now, it is the function of morphological poetics to elucidate the laws that obtain here. Such a poetics never gets into the position of playing off one masterpiece against another of a different kind, nor of having to make the formulas derived from one work applicable to works of another nature. It can do justice to the great writers by their own laws, and no systematic pressure forces us to brand Shakespeare, Racine, and Schiller as "wrong" by comparison with Sophocles, or to find Pindar, Horace, and Petrarch "wrong" by the standards of Goethe. In this poetics it is not a question of a derived, conceptional right or wrong, but of an insight into the play of vital forces and their mutually conditioning interactions. Such insight into the universal formative laws and their variations then makes possible a comparative evaluation of the various kinds of expressive forms. This procedure is similar to that followed in botany, where the beech is not interpreted as a pine gone wrong, but where the special virtues and limitations of both are comprehended and placed in relation to various human evaluations.

At first glance it would seem as though the making of such a poetics would entail the overthrow not only of all our previous efforts in that discipline, but also of the critical study of literature in general. Where in this frame of reference is a place to be found for the historical orientations, from the history of ideas to sociology, for the psychological trends and those of source criticism, to mention but a few? Would not the study of literature in the frame of such a poetics be reduced to the investigation of style, to linguistic philosophy and a kind of "biology?" A closer look will easily show that here it is a question rather of a firmer basis and a more unified relation of all existing approaches to a work in literary study. The realization that *poesis*,[1] as an original expression of human natural forces, constitutes the truest subject of critical study, is a realization that will be strengthened as we move in the various methodological directions. But none of them will be dispensable if a new, progressive poetics is to be brought to the highest possible perfection. Only in this respect does a limitation exist: poetics is not a discipline concerned with writing in general, but a discipline expressly concerned with *poetic*[2] writing. As such it needs to consider non-poetic writing, even though it may otherwise be of the greatest importance, only from a defining point of view. But the very differentiation between poetic and non-poetic writing will be furthered by a morphological poetics. In this process, moreover, there is bound to be a clarification, too, of many basic concepts used in literature, which are deemed self-evident, but actually have a variety of meanings, such as "nature," "naturalness," "beauty," "idea."

II. DEVELOPMENT OF THE
BASIC PRINCIPLES

The two phrases "Poetry, a linguistic reality" and "Poetry, a natural reality" express simple observations. In order to make them produc-

---

[1] This word, borrowed from Greek, has very nearly the same sense as the German *Dichtung*, which means all fictional composition, not only poetry in the strict sense (*Gedicht*).—Ed.

[2] Here, again, *dichterisch* is used, referring to *Dichtung*, and not *poetisch*, "poetical" in the narrow and more familiar sense.—Ed.

tive in the search for poetic, formative laws, they should now be developed to a certain extent. They need not be validated, for anyone can make the observations that lead to them. More precisely, one cannot concern oneself with poetry at all without repeatedly encountering these facts.

The fact that *poesis* is linguistically conveyed and is in this sense *a linguistic reality* does not oblige the student of poetics to become involved with the philosophy of language and its various systems. For him the chief consideration is that speaking does not create objects and movements, but merely denotes them. "The wrath of Peleus' son, O Muse, resound" (Dryden) does not make Achilles physically present here and now, but by that line he is presented in another way; a way which has made him apparent through the centuries. Similarly, any word spoken serves to present us with the thing it means. We may describe this kind of presence as the reality of verbal and propositional meanings. In this sense we can say: Literature consists of language structures and the resultant meaning structures.

Two things are to be noted here especially. Language does not merely form immaterial and incorporeal meanings but a "tonal body" of varying sensuous power. It forms this tonal body by means of an articulated succession of bright and dark, low and high, broad and narrow tones and noises, and the articulated succession produces rhythm. But the meanings do not exist without connection side by side with this rhythmically moving tonal body, but are created by it, never quite leaving it, much as a plant is produced from the soil. And just as the meanings transmit to the tonal parts a characteristic tonality, so the meaning receives a certain tinge from the language tone and language rhythm. When Goethe begins one of his divan poems with "The Sun, the Helios of the Greeks," he does not merely make a mythological allusion but above all endows the tonal body with an enrichment which gives the meaning of "sun" a noticeable strengthening of light and color. Naturally, this holds not only for the single word but just as much—indeed, even more —for the sentence and the combination of sentences, in which, after all, the language, its tone, and its rhythm really are developed. Now, it so happens that a much greater rôle is played by the tonal body of the language in poetry than non-poetic works. This indicates a peculiarity of the poetic language form, namely an appeal to the senses and an imagery which are stronger and more significant in poetry than in non-poetic writing.

The second point to be noted here is the following: If we ask for the identifiable substance which gives a piece of literature real existence, we find a sequence of sentence structures and a continuity of "meaning structures" conveyed by the sentences. But these expressions are perhaps open to misinterpretation. They may be taken to mean that in literature only a logical relation of subjects and predicates should be recognized, which obviously would be wrong. "Structure" does not necessarily mean a rational single system of relationships. And in literature it is obviously a fact that the subordinate parts of a sentence and of a complex of sentences may also come together in non-logical relationships. These relationships, just like the tonal body of the language, make for a special kind of perceptibility, or for a presentation not so much of concepts as of appearances, "phenomena."

This leads to a further consideration. The sequence of sentences, which proceeds, as it were, in a one-dimensional line, does not produce a parallel line of meanings, but creates a polydimensional structure, which hovers like a kind of sphere over the run of sentences. The meaning of a statement made late in a series of sentences may have a strengthening, incisive, or destructive effect on a meaning expressed much earlier, as, for instance, Gretchen's "Neige, neige, Du Ohnegleiche" ["Incline, incline, Thou peerless One"] in the closing scene of *Faust*. This also occurs, of course, in non-poetic writing, as one can see even at the other extreme, the style of mathematical proofs. But in this instance we may also readily see the difference, for there it is logical validity that is to be achieved, just as at the end of a factual report it is factual truth. In the case of the poetic structure of meanings, on the other hand, the sequence of sentences and the immensely rich and varied fabric of meanings are all in the service of a self-contained appearance, a dynamic picture or image, which makes the forces of life visible to the mind's eye.

There is another point that may be noted to make the difference between poetic and non-poetic writing plainer. In the linguistic structure, a conceptual structure is concomitantly made. Now, non-poetic language is such that the meanings point directly to objects and actions, here and now. Whoever wishes to buy flowers or challenge an opponent, whoever gives a report of an event or drafts an itinerary, forms sentence and meaning structures. But he does not form them for the sake of the structures, but by means of these

Mrs. Milton Lowenthal Collection

1. JOHN FLANNAGAN, Jonah and the Whale

Louvre

2. POUSSIN, Shepherds in Arcadia

Antwerp Cathedral

3. RUBENS, Descent from the Cross

Louvre

4. REMBRANDT, Lion

Meta and Paul J. Sachs Collection, Fogg Museum of Art

5. DELACROIX, Arab on Horseback Being Attacked by a Lion

C. S. Johnson & Sons, Inc.

6 . F . L . WRIGHT , Johnson's Wax Administration and
Research Center

7. LE CORBUSIER, Ronchamp Church

8. JOHN GREGOROPOULOS, Wall Painting, Athens

structures he enters into the denoted world, reaches out for things, and causes events to occur among things. In poetry, on the other hand, there is no reaching out from the meanings into the world of things. Poetry does not exist in the here and now, but, rooted in the here and now by its language, it grows into timelessness and ubiquity, which for the present we only designate as the characteristically poetic sphere of existence. "O'er all the hill-tops / Is quiet now" (Goethe-Longfellow)—it is senseless to inquire to what time and place this applies. Odysseus lands never and always in the country of the Phaeacians. King Lear, Don Quixote, Des Grieux, Werther, Bovary, Copperfield never and always travel their respective roads. Even where historical destinies have been turned into poetic form, as in Shakespeare's historical dramas or Schiller's classic tragedies, poetic reality has divorced itself from the historical "now and at no other time" and acquired the poetic "never and ever." It could be said that the poetic language comes to rest in the structure of meanings, if it were not precisely there that it employed its whole power, which normally transcendant power for the creation of a perceptible presentness and a perfect, life-giving field of forces.

In this context one can better understand what every reader of poetry occasionally senses, and what proves, upon closer inspection, to be a cardinal fact: namely, that what matters in true poetry is not the asserted propositions, their correctness, validity, and importance, but something else. This other element is created by means of the asserted propositions, as the characters of a drama are created by the lines they speak. The interaction of the characters thus developed creates the "world" of the drama. In the same way, the separate statements in an epic or lyrical poem also create images whose interplay permits the "world" of the poem to emerge. This world is what matters in poetry. Yet although this world has its being in complexes of meaning, it does not consist of conceptual structures nor a theoretical system, but rather, of the timeless and placeless harmony of many dynamically charged meanings. Certainly it is not irrelevant to the virtual world in the realm of poetic placelessness and timelessness, by what propositions it is created. It makes a difference whether a play closes with a comment on the gods who have heaped every misfortune upon a human being (*Antigone*), or with a compassionate cry: "What she must have suffered!" (*Rose Bernd*). This determines a feature in the physiognomy of the work. But the individual sentence, the individual meaning possesses poetic life only in the fabric of the *whole* and cannot be lifted from that whole without destruction of its veins. And, above all, a conceptual statement, no matter how profound in its content, is unable to render what poetry as a totality sets forth.

Poetry exhibits with extraordinary force the universally valid principle that a word does not derive its full sense from its formal definition but from the single, particular context in which it is spoken. Furthermore, and of far greater import: poetry does not deliver its message by conceptual statements directed to the intellect, but by language-formed images for our contemplation. By this process poetry makes the unutterable things of this world expressible. What a sunrise, a devoted glance or a gesture of rejection tells us, cannot be captured by the most detailed rational description. Poetry, on the other hand, is able to a certain degree to express what otherwise is ineffable in the world. Not by saying it with statements but by making it apparent through a mysterious interaction of meanings conveyed by the sentences. The process which creates such an interaction we call "forming." And the perceptible appearance with which poetry speaks to us is indeed form; not form as a casual outline, but as the "existential complex of an actual being" (Goethe), whose play of forces manifests itself even in the outline.

That the poet and the beholder are both indispensable for the realization of this play of forces hardly needs special remark, but it does need special investigation. The literary situation is such, however, that it is better to approach the question of the poetic process and the poetic effect only after the question of form has been clarified. Otherwise it is too easily distorted by considerations of art psychology and cultural pedagogical tradition. On the other hand, an elucidation of the poetic laws of form may also throw some new light on the questions of poetic creation and its effects.

The poetic form, which has been considered from the standpoint of linguistic reality, is brought into an illuminating connection by application of our second basic principle: *Poetry as a reality of nature.*

We customarily designate as "nature" the inorganic world as well as plant and animal life. In juxtaposition with this we place the world of the intellect or of culture. In this classification poetry necessarily comes under culture and thus stands in a certain opposition to nature. But another and wider concept of nature also exists, pointing back to the concept of *physis* in early Greek science. From this point of view nature includes both the vegetative and the intellectual products. After all, both thinking and artistic creation are produced by living organisms with the aid of their organs. This has, indeed, occasionally been ignored, because certain conditions of life placed special emphasis precisely on the difference between physical and intellectual development. Indubitably a difference exists, but it does not go so deep as to justify, let alone necessitate, our viewing cultural creations out of connection with organic development and interpreting the concept of nature in such a way that it excludes intellectual effects and creations. On the contrary, many important findings demand that the concept of nature be broad enough to encompass culture as a characteristic product and mission of human nature.

In modern times it was especially Goethe who entertained such a concept of nature. His statement in the sixteenth book of *Dichtung und Wahrheit* (*Poetry and Truth*) is of greatest importance to poetics: "I had arrived at the point of considering my innate poetic talent as a phenomenon of nature." This dictum may aptly lead to a search for the laws of poetic art from the realm of historical accident to that of ubiquitous basic forces. It will also serve to clarify the product of *poetic* formative force in relation to all other formative forces of nature. But herewith the poetic form also moves into a closer connection with the forms of organic nature, and it becomes justifiable to search for analogies of their respective formative laws.

For this, too, Goethe has given us indications. Here I would especially quote the following significant maxim: "Art is a second nature; also mysterious, but more comprehensible, since it originates from the intellect." And for the investigation of forms in organic nature Goethe worked out the main lines of his natural philosophy. He himself calls his natural science "morphology" and points out how closely it is connected with the impulses toward art and imitation. It justifies an attempt to look upon poetry quite seriously as a reality of nature. In so doing we shall inquire to what extent poetic form may be conceived in correspondence to the forms of organic nature.

III. TYPE

If we examine an arbitrary series of poems from the viewpoint of form, a correspondence with the forms of organic nature comes to the fore in an important relation, and our previous observations and considerations so far attain sharper outlines. Every poem—or, to speak more cautiously, every poem of the European cultural sphere— like every plant and every animal, constitutes a certain *unity*, a small world with a cycle that has its center within the form itself.

Normative poetics, too, established the law of unity. Our reflections, starting from the linguistic reality, also revealed a unity, namely the appearance of every poem as a unity of integrated meanings conveyed by the language. If now we also find unities in the productions of organic nature, we may attempt by virtue of this parallel to determine more closely what constitutes poetic unity.

Obviously it is not equivalent to a unity of the purely intellectual kind, although this, too, may play a rôle. (While in large areas of lyric poetry thought does not predominate at all, there are large areas in drama where action is based precisely on the duality of antithetic patterns of thought, on an irreconcilable conflict of "ideas." A good part of the power of epic poetry springs from the wealth and the interplay of diverse units of motivating thoughts.) But in both poetic and organic creations the unity of form is achieved through the collaboration of many elements and forces. They are attuned to each other from the start, without being, for all that, univocally fixed for the whole duration. On the contrary, a change in *one* force causes each of the others to change. This shifting interplay is part of the vital progress of a work; in its unity and totality it is at the same time the form. Goethe summarizes this unity of natural organisms in the proposition that in an organic body all the parts tend to produce an effect on the individual part, and each individual part, in turn, exerts its influence on all the rest. This can be directly applied to the unity of poetic form.

In the case of organic bodies the various organs and their functions are mutually dependent. The heart and the lungs cannot operate without each other, nor can they function without the glands. Each part influences the activity of all the others, and in this intimate relationship of all, the unity forms and maintains itself while constantly changing. Such a coöperation is also demonstrated by the poetic form and its unity.

We touched on some of this above in connection with our reflections on the linguistic reality. The organization and integration of this reality may now have become more lucid. The sound and rhythm of the language are not independent of one another, nor are they independent of the meanings of the words and sentences with their sounding, rhythmically moving sequence. Of this we have already spoken. Only in a unique, specific sequence do the meanings attain their full, radiant life, so intertwined they can hardly be extricated. In the course of all this billowing interflow the determinant outlines and the more subtle transitions emerge. Here are images and movements, physical processes and emotional transports, thoughts, ideas, and moods, that arise as meanings out of the sequence of sentences and shape themselves into the timeless and placeless virtual forms, so that in the whole course of the poem this apparition of form does not merely "run off" like a length of film, but grows.

How very important this form is has already been shown. What remains to be shown is how, in the creation of form, every part is affected by all the others, and each in turn exerts its influence on all. In poetry we might consider as "parts" the individual ideas, images, etc., and also the larger relationships created by them. The little worm in Klopstock's hymn *Frühlingsfeier* ("Spring Festival"), is such a part, but so is the barricade fighting in Hugo's *Les Misérables*. In the application of morphological poetics this would have to be analyzed in greater detail. For a résumé of the basic features we have mainly to note that the unity of poetic form, as in the case of the unity of organic creations, is not intellectual or rational, but is the unity of structural parts and forces.

This is the nature of poetry, the way in which the formative power of nature manifests itself in the sphere of poetic reality. In contrast to that, the conception and interpretation of nature is primarily a matter of weltanschauung and cosmology. These explicitly or implicitly affect the processes of particularization within the general nature of poetry, which make it incumbent on morphological poetics to pursue such manifestations as "naturalistic," "realistic," and "idealistic" poetry.

Here, too, the interplay among all the parts is to be observed, and we shall see how an idealistic, realistic, or naturalistic conception of reality influences images, ideas, and rhythms, as well as their conjunctions, and is influenced by all these elements. On the other hand, it is a *qui pro quo* when in the name of poetry some literary subspecies, such as idealism or what not, is demanded and all others rejected. Certain periods, certain groups of people are captivated and satisfied by idealistic, others by naturalistic poetry. In this process the struggles of cosmological theories may be carried on. But in reality these struggles have nothing to do with the question of whether or not a work is *poetry*. And this is, indeed, not a conclusion drawn from our "definition" of poetry (which is really no definition at all but a description of a situation, of a basic phenomenon, if you will), but it is the distillate from our hoard of real poems. If a poet or a critic programmatically advocates classical or romantic or even naturalistic writing as the only true poetry or literature, how does that change the poetic ranking of the *Divine Comedy,* the *Comédie Humaine,* the classical tragedies, *Faust, Der grüne Heinrich, Manfred,* or the *Rougon-Macquart* series? It is as though we were to demand the exclusive cultivation of rye or barley or wheat, which may, of course, sometimes make good sense for certain practical purposes. Such labels as "Realism" and "Naturalism" are no measures of value but special characterizations for the comprehensive formative law of unity; and as such they are, as aforesaid, a subject for morphological poetics.

But for the critical differentiation of poetry from non-poetic linguistic works, we have to strike out in another direction. Where a weltanschauung and metaphysical or moral theories are rhetorically expounded or speculatively developed, we are not dealing with poetry or literature, no matter how clear and profound the theory or how fascinating the argumentation. But when they contribute to the creation of a unified form, then we have poetry, if in the linguistic development a unified, intrinsically animated form comes into being.

In this sense a fiery, clever, purposeful speech, such as that of Mark Antony in Shakespeare's *Julius Caesar,* may indeed contribute very significantly to the development of the character in question. But *Werther* or *Faust* is not great literature because Werther's or Faust's philosophy of life might be theoretically correct, but because in these works a human encounter with the world finds formulated expression. And the same holds for all cognitive elements in literature, not only the philosophical and moralistic; it holds, for instance, for everything that serves the exposition of the context. These elements are "parts," and they act as members or forces; they can be separated and observed in their historical co-ordination or for their educational value. From experience we know that they influence critical opinion to a great degree and are oftentimes the basis for the acceptance or rejection of a literary work. This draws the literary scholar's attention forcibly to the problems of poetic effect. But in answer to the essential question as to what constitutes poetry as such it has little to offer. On the contrary, it is striking that compositions quite without theory, such as many folksongs and fairy tales, may possess incomparably stronger poetic reality than those with intellectual claims. For example, Tiedge's *Urania* and Gutzkow's *Wally* are poetically insignificant despite their wealth of ideas, as is F. Schlegel's *Lucinde,* while Stifter's *Bunte Steine,* despite its want of theoretical thoughts, belongs to genuine literature. And what importance does Fénelon's *Télémaque* or Haller's *Vom Ursprung des Übels* have as literature beside a sonnet by Ronsard, or Goethe's idea-less *König von Thule?* (If an epic example is desired instead of the lyrical, we might mention the idea-less *Iliad.*)

We cannot enter into further discussion of how vaguely the word "idea" is often used in the study of literature. Suffice it to say that it sometimes refers to the leading thought of a world interpretation, or to moral demands, or again to principles of evaluation. The demand for "ideas" in literature points for the most part to a wish for "the moral of the story," that is, to have the practical application presented.

This wish, confronting a work brought forth by a creative natural force and made into a unified reality of form by means of stylistic expression, is not essentially different from a question regarding the practical usefulness of a cow or a rose (which can indeed be made useful, as can poems. But their coming into being and their existence proclaim immeasurably more about the laws and forces of life than does their specific usefulness).

In quite another sense, however, we may speak very significantly about "idea" in poetry as well as in the case of living organisms. For the form of a poetic work is its idea, in the sense of "eidos," of existence comprehensible through reflective contemplation. Idea as eidos is brought into being concretely, non-theoretically, and formatively by *every* true poetic work. We just touched upon the manner in which the so-called "ideas" may also contribute to the development of the form. But the eidos of a poem, its intangibly manifest form, this and nothing else is the message that a poem as such conveys, and that no other kind of "teaching" can achieve or replace. The poetic form is the sole form in which vast and important secrets of nature are disclosed and brought to light, but not directly and explicitly in concepts and propositions.

Hence: Poetry is a reality of form, created by means of stylistic expression involving an interplay of meanings; this is the core of morphological poetics. It is at the same time the determination of poetry as a *type,* and "type" is again used in the sense of Goethe's morphology (in which it is especially developed in the osteological outline). And even from our observations so far it is clear that *poetry* as a type cannot appear without metamorphosis. On the one hand, the immense number of real poems represent only variations or metamorphoses of this type. These variations form groups which separate the over-all type of literature into categories and kinds. On the other hand, in each poem a development is realized, which despite all differences may be compared to the growth of a plant, and takes place by means of metamorphoses.

IV. METAMORPHOSIS

In poetry, *metamorphosis* is given with the genius of the language and with the sequence of words and sentences. It has a certain parallel in music and in this respect poetry and music are connected, as against painting and sculpture, which have no such metamorphoses. The sentences themselves, by the sequence of their words, constantly introduce something new that enters into manifold connections with what has already been said. In poetry this connecting is of a special order and strength, for here all the statements contribute toward the creation of a unified form, a form which arises and exists in a reality different from that of words and sentences. Let us here remind the reader of our earlier observation that the sentences proceed from word to word in a single dimension. At any given moment only *one* word is present. The form-giving pattern of meanings which emerges from them presents an

abundance, growing with each sentence, at every point of the sequence of sentences, and is manifest as a growing form.

Now, the "growth" does not just add something "more"or "longer,"
but it changes what has already been said by further fashioning of
the whole. Thus the interplay of parts and forces, which is brought
about by the flow of the language, causes the metamorphoses in
which the poetic form is realized. These metamorphoses come to
light in the rhythm of sounds, concepts, ideas, images, events, and
characters. They belong to the most intimate consummation of life
for *every* literary form, even that of classic repose. In order to avoid
the impression that in the case of such metamorphoses we deal
with involved or possibly contrived thought complexes, an example
will serve as simple illustration.

There may be a suspicion that Goethe's poetical work could, indeed, be fathomed by a morphological approach, but not a realm
of literature that is inspired less by organic feeling for life than
by a desire to create an intellectual structure. Let us, then, choose
the example from the *Roman Octavia* by Duke Anton Ulrich von
Braunschweig, i.e., a work of the courtly high baroque. Following
the pattern of Barclay's *Argenis,* the introduction outlines a background of world history for the period in which the telling makes
the events begin. However, with his broad, portal-like treatment
the author goes considerably beyond Barclay:

"Rome now hovered between fear and hope." With the first word
the main clause gives a mere indication of a spatial and historical
reality, but it is pregnant with meaning. In this very pregnancy,
which, as it were, strains for closer definition and development, the
germinal nature of a poetic matrix can be very clearly seen. It should
be taken into account here that "Rome" at the beginning of an epic
work initially guides what follows in a direction different from that
of an ultimate question concerning, let us say, longitude and latitude,
population or geological conditions. Now, the meaning of "Rome"
immediately creates a directing groove and dynamism; it "hovered
between fear and hope." It is easy to see how the meanings of "fear"
and "hope" have here been linked by means of the verb "hovered"
into a unified meaning of a superimposed order and how this total
meaning invades the meaning of "Rome." The sentence runs from
"Rome" through "now hovered" to "between fear and hope." It
brings out one after the other and at the same time, in the process,
establishes strong, motile relationships. However, in so doing it does

not juggle just any objects at will, but in the semantic sphere brings out a process which may be conceived as analogous to growth, in other words, as metamorphosis.

Now as the sentence continues: "of one day being freed from the yoke which the inhumanity of Nero had imposed on her," the same process of metamorphosis takes place after its fashion in these dependent clauses. In the course of it, the newly added semantic component strikes backward into the keyword "Rome," and develops there—develops from there, too, by virtue of the added clauses, and the anticipatory movement as it obtains in the process of hovering between fear and hope. Again, what is given in the single words —"yoke," "inhumanity," "Nero," "being freed," "imposed upon"— is woven together into a motile image. This image is not only something new in respect to the main clause or something additional which at the words "imposed upon her" would stand alone and in its own right. Rather, "Rome" is very much present with these words. From its vague implications it has now developed some features, just as a fertilized egg slowly and steadily develops its cleavages. This shows us something of the interweaving in the texture of poetic language. We may also see how the semantic structure and the literary appearance of form depart, as it were, from the sequence of words and sentence, from which they emerge, and how they shape themselves in another order of existence as a growing unity. It appears, above all, that literature by virtue of its nature, the type of thing it is, necessarily embodies a process, a becoming. This is quite independent of whether a process is being described or complete immobility is presented. That is to say, the becoming realized in any piece of literature is the becoming of its *form*. Hence all meanings, material and immaterial, mobile or immobile, are nothing but its elementary raw material.

The text, going on with a "because," now begins to make hidden forces discernible. They are operative in the "hovering between fear and hope;" they are especially at work in "Rome," and as the metamorphosis makes them apparent, they powerfully expand the idea of this "Rome:" "because not only the desertion of Vindex in Gaul and the situation of Galba in Spain threatened this tyrant with destruction, but heaven itself by means of dire portents gave indication that it was wearied of further tolerating such extreme wickedness." If we continue to pursue the sequence of the sentence from word to word, we realize that the linear lengthening of the sentence produces first smaller and then larger unities. In several, almost spasmodic expansions they give to the image "Rome" in her hovering between fear and hope a depth and a menacing red-bloodedness, such as was only indicated by way of foreboding in the main clause.

The geographic spread to Gaul and Spain is now followed by a temporal expansion of "Nero" in his genealogy back to Augustus and an exposition of the dire portents. The concept of "Rome" becomes material, part of a process, perceptible in mood, and with that the embryo of the active form grows in an initial phase of the language-borne metamorphosis.

The beginning of the next paragraph, presenting a new metamorphosis, produces in the germinating form an image that, in its gradual development, is to be an especially important contributing force in the creation of the total form. It is the figure of the principal hero, at first emerging only vaguely, one might say "cotyledonlike." "In such a dismal period King Tyridates of Armenia was in Rome, actually in the suburb at the dairy farm of Severus. With Vasaces, his commander-in-chief and confidential adviser, he spent his time there in considerable confusion, for his mind was filled night and day with thoughts of his present situation and his love, causing him to contemplate his strange destiny." We need not repeat the analysis of the formative processes, since they are closely related to the previous ones in their deepening and expanding effects. But it should be remarked that in the next lines, as the general back-and-forth movement of unnamed forces continues, a definite event is clearly taking shape around a few projecting, fixed points: "One morning sweet springtime enticed him out of his room, which since his arrival he had never quitted." This definite happening then branches out by gradual or abrupt growth in all directions and ever more profusely. It is characteristic for the anticipatory and retroactive effects of the metamorphoses that the condition of Tyridates, here outlined, gains more concrete fullness from the story of Claudia in the second volume, which tells its past history; but that it demands a certain concreteness from the start.

Herewith our main concern may have become clear, namely the sense in which we can speak of metamorphoses in literature. Of course, practically everything still remains to be done here for a deeper appreciation in literary research. We are indeed convinced that this area, so far quite overlooked, is of the greatest significance for the development of poetics. For closer investigation must yield series and groups of various kinds of literary metamorphoses which would reveal the foundations of the entire poetic mode of existence. But the first thing is to demonstrate how in literature we do not deal simply and summarily with actualities, but find it, rather, a function of poetic reality to shape general types into perceptible beings, individual entities, through metamorphoses effected by means of discursive language. The sequence of words and sentences is not a mere accumulation of concepts, but in the fusing of meanings accomplishes the development of perceptible unities taking shape in a realm beyond the statements. Each part affects all, and all parts affect each. In this motile interplay of forces the form emerges from one metamorphosis to the next. The form exists, not only at the end of a work, but as early as the completion of the first metamorphosis, just as a plant or an animal represents its true form in every stage of its growth. Each piece of literature must also "decide" in the course of its development upon certain definite realities among those available, and in the end no further possibilities of change or of development exist. In nature death occurs at this point, but in literature we witness instead of disintegration a certain consummation when that stage is reached. (For the reader literature as a language-borne reality is essentially repeatable.) The fact that the end of any work represents a particular degree of decision should be stressed as an important element in morphological poetics.

We already stressed that metamorphosis is not an arbitrary or random change and alteration. It conforms to inner laws and its modifications do not destroy connections but create them. To pursue this lawfulness, this inner consistency, is the chief task of morphological research. Again, we seem to have here a kind of progressive articulation that is analogous to the growth of a plant. Goethe analyzed this progression into a *vertical* and a *spiral tendency*. They are in a polar relation to one another and point to a polarity of the ultimate phenomenon of life, that of male and female. The vertical propensity impels toward lining up, moving directly ahead, forward, and upward, while the spiral propensity is the embodying, digressing, revolving element. In the metamorphosis both act with and within one another. If we imagine them as separated, their operation and relation may be likened to a beanstalk winding about its pole. Something similar may be observed in the development of literary forms. In the play of interpenetrating forces, those that drive forward and urge on may be distinguished from those that expand and distend. In this sense the elements of doing and happening, and sometimes also those of rational order and arrangement, possess something of the vertical tendency. Those of mood, feeling, suffering, contemplation, as well as of circumstances (the setting) have something of the spiral tendency. Thus the first paragraph of the introduction to the historical novel examined above predominantly exemplifies the spiral force. With the beginning of a definite happening, the second paragraph obviously introduces another element, in which the vertical tendency prevails. We may fairly attempt to interpret poetic metamorphosis, too, as an interaction of vertical and spiral tendencies. In so doing we may for simplicity's sake speak of "directive force" and "expansive force." It is obvious that here, too, we have analogies to human life.

The far-reaching analogy between organic and literary form now makes it possible for us to approach the problem of *time* in literature. Reading a given sequence of sentences requires a definite length of time that can be measured by the clock. But this time is by no means identical with the time in which the literary form moves. Here several aspects must be distinguished.

In the drama almost every report by a messenger takes a shorter time than the events described. But it does not only require less time, it also takes place on a time level different from that of the portrayed events. This, in turn, is to be differentiated from the time experience of the author which implicitly prevails in his works, as has been shown by E. Staiger. And in the growth of the form by means of the anticipatory, regressive, and diffusive metamorphoses another "time" is present, in which the one-dimensional sequence no longer holds good at all. This is an aspect of metamorphosis which corroborates what was said above about the timelessness and placelessness of a literary creation. But here we also encounter an analogy with biological time, definitively treated by V. von Weizsäcker in his *Gestalt und Zeit* (*Form and Time*). I can only mention that it deals with the "impossibility" of "undertaking biological time determination by merely applying the gauge of objective time to biological phenomena. This is not a question of accuracy; it is senseless to attempt such measurements. The reason for that, we might say, is that life does not exist in time, but time in life or, more accurately, time is *created* by the existence of life." This view was expressed long ago by Herder, in his essay on Shakespeare: "Have you not, gentle clock-setter of the drama, had times in your life when your hours became moments and your days hours? Or, on the contrary, times when the hours seemed like days, the wakeful nights like years? Have you encountered no situations in life when your spirit dwelt wholly apart from you? Have you never felt, how, in dream, time and place disappeared from your ken? Have you never felt how unessential such things must be, mere shadows in comparison with what action and reaction of the spirit are? Is it not solely in the power of this spirit to create for itself space, measure of time, a world of its own, however and wherever it will? And now consider what worlds you consign to chaos when you confront the poet with your watch, in order that he may teach you to dream by it! In the course of his events, in the successions and concurrences of *his* world, that is where his space and time are." This, too, can point the way for closer investigations of metamorphosis in literary works.

V. SPECIES

The metamorphic progress of individual literary works makes it possible for the general type, *poesis*, to evolve into a concrete, specific form. Our earlier observations have already shown that in the metamorphoses, from which the various works emerge, *typical parallels* and typical differences prevail. This may be clearly seen, for instance, if we watch how in the total course of such metamorphoses the vertical or the spiral tendency, the directive force or the expansive force dominates. Furthermore, there are cases where directive force and expansive force strike a balance. These are the beginnings of groupings which separate the general type of "poesis" into less general types. Here that other kind of metamorphosis appears of which we already have spoken. Contrasted to the general metamorphosis from which all poetic compositions emerge, this is a specific metamorphosis that individuates literary creation as such into several *varieties of creation*. While the former prevails from germ to completion of the work, the latter operate between the various phases of its becoming. In the former the general type grows to be an integral reality, in the latter it unfolds into various types of growth. For example, in the metamorphoses of its growth a plant becomes this specific rose, but the rose, the carnation, or the tulip represents metamorphoses of the prototype "flower," just as beech, linden, and oak are metamorphoses of the prototype "tree." Something similar seems to happen in the realm of literary reality. The fact that poetics distinguishes *species and varieties* in literature certainly has a morphological basis.

But with this we have neither proved nor disproved that the traditional differentiation into a dramatic, epic, or lyric species corresponds throughout to the morphological divergencies of the type *poesis*. It can, of course, be determined that lyric poetry in general shows a preponderance of the expansive force, that the drama favors the directive force while the epic tends toward a balance of the two. But, on the other hand, it also seems as though precisely such a balance is realized in the most perfect creations of all the "species." Pertinent examples in lyric poetry are Hölderlin's "Hymn to the Rhine" (*Rheinhymne*) and Goethe's "Permanence in Change" (*Dauer im Wechsel*); in the drama *Antigone, Bérénice, Hamlet, Faust;* in the epic *Wilhelm Meister's Apprenticeship.*[3]

It remains undecided whether this relation of directive and expansive forces is what produces literary species, even though its grouping effects cannot be doubted. Something similar applies to "time": it appears to revolve in lyric poetry, flow in the epic, rise and rush ahead in the drama. A further consideration would be the kind of reality that is posited. In lyric poetry proper the relation to a "here and now" is obviously irrelevant, while in the drama and the epic the objective and theoretical elements, as they are established or indicated by the verbal and propositional meanings, play a noticeably more independent role.

For a substantial extension of morphological poetics it is essential that we observe without bias the formation of groups, and test their range as well as their potency to create types. The formative law of the language-borne operative and creative unities can and must be our touchstone here. On the one hand, we should search for kindred groups by means of a thorough comparison of the individual metamorphoses, and on the other, investigate the traditional concepts of species to establish what formative laws are common to those works which a given species includes.

[3] The designation of this work as an epic is comparable to Eliot's frequent citing of the Divine Comedy as drama. The *epic effect* (like the dramatic effect in Dante) is not *epic structure*, and the work as an example may be misleading here.—Ed.

The practical utility of the concepts of species—drama, epic, lyric—makes it plausible that they indicate something real in the realm of literature. But so far this real element is generally not accurately determined. On the contrary, it is often defined only with empty notions or discussed in terms of fuzzy impressions. Even if we grant a considerable validity to such groupings, the question still remains whether in the case of the lyric, epic, and drama we deal with species (in something like the botanical sense). It is a question whether by means of these "species" we actually grasp the decisive unfolding of the comprehensive type *poesis*. Certainly what I mentioned elsewhere applies, namely that a given tree is not first this specific beech, secondly a beech in general, and thirdly also a tree. It is the one only insofar as it is the other. In other words, the type does not manifest itself except in a particular kind and in an exemplary, specific, individual reality. But the morphological problem of literary species asks directly *which* typical formative laws of poetic realization characterize the particular variety of a work.

At any rate, there are certain morphological groupings of lesser pretension that are more tangible than the traditional literary species. In lyric poetry, even without reference to any such species, the song and the ode stand out as group unities, created by means of a formative law. In the cases of what we call hymn, elegy, and ballad this becomes much more problematical. Kluckhohn has recently differentiated the various kinds of drama. Here, too, the morphological approach may well be useful. It is evident that such groupings as the "historical novel" are derived from the subject matter and can thus only very indirectly affect the literary form. (Articles in *Helicon* III and IV by Wehrli and v. Wiese have shown what constitutes the unifying element in this connection.) But it is just as obvious that the problem of species can be solved only by a morphological approach. Thus we have no choice but to pursue this problem on the basis of a morphological poetics in quiet, individual work on the material itself, the forms of the work, step by step. For we are, after all, not dealing with a theoretical system, but trying to comprehend the activity of creative nature in the configurations of the poetic realm. Here the question of species must be considered in connection with the type problem, in order to avoid a process of mere classification.

VI. BEAUTY

How morphological poetics should approach the problem of beauty is, in a way, already indicated above. Morphological poetics is not aesthetics, but science of form. It differentiates the image according to formative law, not according to aesthetic appeal. It has nothing to do with any definition of what from one standpoint or another may be accepted as "beautiful" or rejected as "ugly." But it must be greatly concerned with a comprehension of the extent to which an embryo takes shape, pure and unimpaired, in the development of a form. When in the interplay of all "parts," all affecting each and each the others, a consummated unity takes shape, we obviously encounter something that may be called morphological beauty. And in the range of morphological beauty we may distinguish the classical, romantic, naturalistic, and others.

When Goethe looked at seashells and crabs and exclaimed "How true, how existent!" he indicated the manifestation of morphological beauty. And this morphological beauty is a mighty protophenomenon—Johannes Secundus called it "Vis superba formae." What the reader can gain from this depends on his kind of imagination and taste, which ordinarily are to a large degree theoretically determined. This belongs to the utilitarian realm, like the choice of food, not to the science of form. Morphological poetics must strive to avoid having its discernment of form and its laws clouded by tendencies of taste and theories of beauty. For, to restate our conclusion: *Poesis* per se is language-borne form, brought into being for its own sake, by a formative natural force. Poetic form is a reality of language and of nature.

VII. WORK, BEHOLDER, AND AUTHOR

From the basic principles of morphology we can derive certain conclusions regarding the much-debated question of the relation of a poetic work to the author and the contemplator. As a reality of nature, literature is created by a natural force operating within an individual. As a reality of language it is directed especially to the attentive public.

While plants and animals live independently of their chance observers, language images by their very nature address themselves to auditors. It is even part and parcel of a literary form's full reality that it be perceived, completed, observed. In a manuscript or a book, only the letters are actual; their mere existence would not be essentially different from a spot on the paper, a depression in the sand, if the letters were not designed to be read. Unread, they only constitute the *possibility* of a language body;[4] they realize that body only by being read. They do this in co-operation with the reader. And the reader is called upon to become a *beholder* of the semantic structure emerging from the language body, in order that the created form may really emerge. Since it actually *appears* as the result of such co-operation, such fusion, a certain formative activity on the part of the beholder is a prerequisite for its full reality. The paths of this formative activity are to a large extent predetermined by the established language structure, hence we may look upon it as a reproduction. Still, the inescapably reproductive activity has a considerable leeway, and this leeway is essential to poetic form as such. It is not something that would be brought about by the psychological inadequacy of the observer, but it belongs among the morphological basic facts.

Here we have arrived in an area different from that of utility, philosophical evaluation, or choice in accordance with taste. The beholder is no more a univocal, conceptually determinable factor than the work itself. He, too, lives through individual and racial metamorphoses, and the realization of the poetic form always depends on the concurrent state of his own realization. This is shown particularly by what elements in the interplay of unifying forces he finds determinant, *i.e.*, which ones he can experience in the light of his own evolution. All of us have noticed that at various periods in life we have "got out of" one and the same piece of literature very different reactions and interpretations, not in the sense of affirmation or rejection but in how we perceive it. Whether we accept and "realize" the Max—Thekla "parts" in the Wallenstein trilogy as intrinsic or as injected depends to a large degree on the complex of forces on which the individual beholder is drawing. It should be especially noted that those situations in the literary creation which have not been approximated in the beholder's own experience are

[4] This ungainly expression is dictated by the author's equally awkward term, *Sprachleib.*—Ed.

assimilated only dimly and theoretically by him. On the other hand, situations that have deeply affected him in comparable circumstances, he will recreate colorfully and vigorously where they occur in poetry. The line from Corneille's *Cid* "O miracle d'amour! O comble des misères!" ("O miracle of love! O crown of misery!") may seem to one reader a brilliant rhetorical hyperbole, to another reveal the keenest experience of real life. A person with broader and richer potentialities of experience will, as a beholder, develop the structure of meanings to quite other heights and depths than one with insignificant or conventional experience. In this process, the form of the work remains the test of competence or incompetence. But above all the range of the various possible realizations remains a morphological trait of the form per se, and its poetic power always remains to be qualified by the ability of the contemplating reproducer (as we might call him). This is highly significant for the "correct" interpretation of a literary work.

On the other hand, what the reader or beholder does not in any sense produce is the language-body. Naturally, the language reality from the start creates the need to establish meanings and their range. But the propositions which create the potential semantic structure and establish its range are the exclusive work of the author. In this basic sense the *poet* is the creator of language.

The psychology of the creative process and the author's biography cannot be directly elucidated by morphological poetics, but only utilized. Yet the science of form should contribute to the clarification of certain differences which might otherwise easily go unnoticed. How it may do this, appears from the following: The form of a work is a progression of unified metamorphoses. *This* becoming is of a wholly different nature from that of the creative process. Whether the author writes his work from the first sentence to the last or starts with sections in the middle is of no consequence to the development which finds expression in poetic metamorphoses. Delays and accelerations in the writing are on an entirely different plane from those indicated by the semantic structure. Thus the stichomythies of the Greek tragedy follow in rapid succession, no matter whether the poet created them with one stroke or arrived at them through repeated polishing and changing. Similarly any personal circumstances of his writing or dictating enter only indirectly into the form of the work. This holds for everything from his balky pen and husky throat to his vital feeling, when in the successful

development of a character's tragic destruction he experiences the
supreme joy of achievement. Even the conscious intent and conscious theory of the poet are not necessarily congruent with the form
created by him. This is shown by Hebbel's tragedies, which as we
know do not at all conform to his theory of the drama. Similarly,
Spitteler's *Olympic Spring* (*Olympischer Frühling*) deliberately
attacks every kind of worship, and yet is filled with a great religious
longing. But, on the other hand, and despite all this, the most intimate relationship exists between the poet and his work. Only it
is not of such nature that isolated statements in the work can simply
be recast into characteristics of the poet, or biographical facts and
his theoretical opinions be directly identifiable in the work.

Here we encounter poetic talent as a creative natural force. The
language body brought forth by this talent is not in any way intended to convey the adjustments and reactions of a given individual to the happenings of his present, past or future. The function of the language body is rather to create *form*—this is the central
core of literature and consequently emerges no matter what the
point of view. In this form the features of the personal poetic talent
find expression, *i.e.* the features of the personality of the poet with
its experiences and forms of activity, with the directions character-
izing his thinking, feeling, desires, and actions. For the creative
force seems to take possession of the endowed poet's personal talents
and transmutes them into elements of its own. The concentration
of their interplay into images as they encounter the world seems
to be one of the peculiarities of talent. (This is conclusively shown
by various passages in Rothacker's *Schichten der Persönlichkeit*). If
we now repeat our query regarding the nature of the relation between the poet and his work, our discussion so far points in a definite
direction.

This relation is not comparable to that of a glazier and the pane
he cuts, for even in every spoken statement the speaker is not merely
technically involved but also personally. This applies in greater
degree to *poetic* language formulation. On the other hand, it cannot be said that his sentiments are put on paper with his heart's
blood, as Schubarth very clearly puts it in one of his utterances.
Literature, whether it be more or less direct in its expression, is
never the experience itself. We have works whose form directs our
observation to the experience of the author. Others—and this is
obviously true in the case of certain kinds of drama and epic—
necessitate a disregard of their formalistic intent, if we wish to

examine the experience of the poet. But *poesis* is always a language-borne form that exists for its own sake. It is the specific, language-borne appearance of something universal which is portrayed ("manifested") only in the particular, and therefore a symbol in the strictly Goethean sense, like every specific manifestation of life, of nature. This symbolic form is part of the language of nature, as are colors, sounds, and odors, with this difference, that poetic works display more varied facets than the "elementary phenomena of nature." A statement from the introduction to Goethe's *Theory of Colors* is entirely applicable to *poesis:* "Thus Nature speaks to our known, falsely known, and unknown senses; thus she speaks to herself and to us by means of a thousand phenomena."

Inasmuch as the poetic creation emerges from the author's self knowledge and world-knowledge, just as a tree acquires nourishment from the soil and the atmosphere, a poetic work, when analyzed, permits conclusions regarding the experience and the personality of its author. And not only the elements derive from the author, but also the unified form, the *eidos,* is molded into the poetic image by the natural talent incorporated in his personality. This goes far beyond the relation of the tree to its soil.

This kind of a relation may perhaps best be understood, if one conceives it, in a wider sense, physiognomically. The shape of the skull, facial expression, gestures, quality of the voice do not constitute the whole person, but they contribute to his manifestation. Poetry as a language-borne form is neither the author nor his experience. It is an image belonging to an entirely different realm of reality, governed by its own laws, just as mathematical propositions belong to a realm of reality different from that of the mathematician. But the individual work brings into view the natural force incorporated in the author himself. As a photographic or phonographic record fixates a phase of his total physiognomic metamorphosis, removes it from the passage of time and makes it repeatable, so the work lets the author appear physiognomically as the embodiment of a natural force. Literature is not primarily the record of theoretical insights or the expression of emotional processes or the disclosure of material relations and events, but form, as it were, in its own fashion and by its own grace. But in the very form of this kind of existence it gives us a manifestation of the poet, as in a corresponding manner the shape of the skull and articulation of the limbs, facial expressions, voice, or even handwriting are manifestations of an individual.

The basic insight of morphological poetics, that literature is language-borne reality of form, thus does not need to be impaired by the close connection between the author and his work. If we conceive of this as physiognomic in the sense indicated, we can also accept the further observation that the relation between the author and his work is neither a material one, nor one limited to the realm of the intellect. It is, rather, the relation between a creative natural force and its image, between a life and its perceivable manifestation.

But this again is a distinctly morphological relation. It requires thorough investigations. Meanwhile, it becomes obvious from the start that in this process the problems of a systematical division of literary works along historical, ideological, racial, national, and sociological lines must be faced and methods of solution worked out. Even the question of the poet's biography appears in a new light. It is further shown that morphological poetics cannot find its laws in every piece of versified language but only in the works created by an original formative force. After all, a numerically very great majority of works imitates alien laws of form and thus does not manifest original basic laws. To this extent morphological discernment requires a feeling for poetic quality, for otherwise we would be like blind men speaking of colors. In the long run it will be specifically by the aid of morphological poetics that we may hope to characterize the original and the imitated forms.

These questions are of no direct concern to the literary historian, for to him poetic works are nothing but documents, evidences of the historical complex of events, and from this vantage point he actually dissolves the form of the works.—If in the process he ignores the history-shaping force of artistic form, that is a question of historical methodology which cannot be pursued here.—Morphological poetics, which throughout takes into consideration the historical element, captures and comprehends precisely in poetic form something of the "open secret" of nature.[5] By such means it can bridge the gap between natural science and the intellectual disciplines. Within its limits it can disclose the sources of life.

[5] A detailed explanation of the methodological assumptions as well as a selection of the pertinent literature will be found in my publication "Die Gestaltfrage in der Literaturwissenschaft und Goethes Morphologie." *Die Gestalt, Abhandlungen zu einer allgemeinen Morphologie.* Edited by W. Pinder, W. Troll, and L. Wolf, (Number 13), Max Niemeyer, Publisher. Halle a/S, 1944.

A Boston Criticism of Whitman

JOHN BURROUGHS

IN AN ARTICLE on Whitman in the June *Atlantic,* the writer says, among other things, that his poetry is not noble, because it celebrates pride and does not inculcate the virtues of humility, self-denial, etc.,—thus reading the poet by the letter, rather than by the spirit. The charge that Whitman's poetry celebrates pride is fully met by the fact, that it also celebrates and bears along in equal measure the antidote of pride; namely, sympathy. Its sympathy, its love, is as broad and all-inclusive as its pride is erect and positive. Whitman was aware, from the outset of his career, how important this fact is; for he said in the preface to the first edition of his poems, in 1855, that the soul of the great poet "has sympathy as measureless as its pride, and the one balances the other, and neither can stretch too far while it stretches in company with the other. The inmost secrets of art sleep with the twain. The greatest poet has lain close betwixt both, and they are vital in his style and thoughts."

'Leaves of Grass' is of course designedly positive and aggressive, and is meant to arouse and dilate rather than to soothe and lull. If it is nearly all in the major key, it is because it has to do with the major elements of life, of character, of nationality. Are many of the minor keys touched in Homer or Aeschylus or Dante? We look for the minor notes of life,—the pleasures of the domestic and social instincts, the pleasure with flowers, birds, sequestered walks, and special phases of nature,—in the minor poets, the poets of sentiment. In the poetry of power, the poetry that courts and emulates the cosmic laws, that seeks to "convey a sentiment and invitation of the earth," we should not expect these things. Yet in 'Drum Taps,' and in many of the subsequent poems, the strain is often tender, and full of subdued, even sobbing tones.

To complain of the urge, the pressure, the strenuousness of the body of Whitman's work, seems to me very much like complaining of a ship under full sail, or of an express train at the top of its speed. It may not always fall in with one's mood, but the poet is not studying one's mood; he would fashion the mood to suit the verse. The 'Song of Myself' is a tremendous exhibition of power. In it the poet sweeps through the whole orbit of human experience; it shows the genesis of a great personality,—how the man is nourished and riveted and made sure of himself, and how he finally escapes from the material into the spiritual. It is unrestrained in the sense that great action, great power, or the forces and processes of Nature, are unrestrained. Is a man, then, never to let himself out, never to assert himself, never to give full swing to what there is in him, by reason of the beauty of the law of obedience, of self-denial, of self-sacrifice? Here we touch upon ethical considerations, here we touch upon the rule of life. How does this rule apply in art, in literature? Certainly not by checking effort, by thwarting originality, by denying genius. The poet's life may be full of self-renunciation; but he must not deny himself to his reader,—he must not withhold that which defines him and makes him what he is. He may give way to others in life; but he must not give way to others in his book. If he gives us Tennyson or Browning instead of himself, we feel defrauded. "Consciousness of power, entirely self-centered, exults in manifestation." Why should it not? Would we have it deny itself, and refuse the manifestation? Why, then, do we protest against it in Whitman's case? Not because it contravenes some other law, but simply because it is too strong for us. Whitman's page, especially in his earlier work, has that pristine, unconventional quality of things and life in the open air,—an elemental force and *insouciance* that we cannot always stand; we long for the art and bric-a-brac and coziness of indoors.

The law of restraint, of self-forgetfulness, shows itself in the work of the great poet, or any artist, by a certain poise and continence. The work is true to itself, follows its own law, has a certain reserve and indirectness; is never strained or forced, permits no extraneous matter, is equal to itself and to its task. As an artist, Victor Hugo, for instance, practised no self-denial, had no continence or self-restraint, had no respect for the centre of gravity of things at all. Whitman's faults, whatever they are, are not of this nature. He has the phlegm, the reserve power, the inertia, of the Northern races.

He bears the restraint of rhyme and metre in the few cases in which he used them, well, because his was a fluid, flexible, poet's nature; but the larger freedom of his unmeasured yet balanced lines is more in keeping with the spirit and aims of his work.

As a poet, Whitman's course was heroic, and shows the most stern self-denial. He denied himself, for the most part, all the arts of the poets,—the advantages of rhyme, metre, the gloss and language of poetry; and elected to stand or fall upon the naked spirit of his work. All outward and meretricious aids he foreswore, and stands by himself alone. Is that selfishness?

Of narrow, personal, ignoble egotism, Whitman had none at all. His look, his manner, his gait, his life, were not those of an egotist. His self-denial and renunciation were extreme. He claimed nothing, asked nothing, for himself that he would not share with the lowest. He is self-assertive in his poems, because that is one of the *motifs* of his books; yet it is himself typically, himself as Man, and not as a separate and specially privileged person. It is not Goethe's egotism, but the egotism of democracy,—of a man that finds all men divine. One *motif* of Whitman's work is to exalt and glorify man as he is, in and of himself, apart from all special advantages and acquisitions, and to bring the physical or animal part flush with the spiritual and intellectual. A British essayist says of him: "Whitman represents, for the first time since Christianity swept over the world, the re-integration, in a sane and whole-hearted form, of the instincts of the entire man; and therefore he has a significance which we can scarcely overestimate." It is this entire man which Whitman stands for and celebrates. Christianity, or the perverted form of it which has prevailed in the world, has belittled man, has denied and degraded his physical part and made light of the world in which he is placed. Science belittles him; it goes its own way, and finds man but an accident, the ephemera of an hour; democracy belittles him by sinking the one in the many; the individual is nothing, the masses everything. Whitman offsets all this in the most determined and un-compromising manner. The man, the individual, is everything; the whole theory of the universe is directed to one person, namely, to You. All bibles, all literatures, all histories, all institutions, grow out of you as leaves out of the tree. Much might be said upon this point; this thread runs all through the poems.

> "Whoever you are! you are he or she for whom the earth is solid
>   and liquid;
> You are he or she for whom the sun and moon hang in the sky;
> For none more than you are the present and the past,
> For none more than you is immortality!"

It is a very serious mistake to say, as the *Atlantic* critic does, that only in the Lincoln poem, 'Oh Captain! My Captain!' does Whitman lose the thought of himself in the thought of his country. The one ruling thought of his life, and of every line he ever wrote, was the thought of his country. It was more than a thought: it was a passion that enwrapped and filled his whole being, and was the mainspring of his entire work. The old prophets of Israel were no more the will-ing and self-forgetting mouthpiece of the spirit of democracy and his country.

Whitman was the poet of the great cosmic forces as they appeared in Man, in personality, in the state, in races, and in Nature; and the sweeping mass movement of his verse is in keeping with these things. The only restraint suggested and the only restraint required is that of the rifle-bullet that goes to its mark. The corset of rhymed and measured verse no doubt improves and helps bring into shape the muse of many a poet; but why should we insist upon this partic-ular restraint being imposed upon every poetic spirit, and charge those with lawlessness and disobedience who repudiate it?

The law of life of great poetry or great art is, he that would lose his life shall find it, he that gives himself the most freely shall the most freely receive. Whitman merged himself in the thought, in the love of his country, and of his fellows; he identified himself with all types and conditions of men; he literally made himself the brother and equal of all. He thought of himself only as he thought of others in and through himself. In his life he was guilty of no self-seeking; he deliberately put by all that men usually strive for—immediate success and applause, wealth, honors, family, friends—that he might the more fully heed the voice from within. He chose the heroic part in his poetry and in his life. When the supreme hour of trial came to his country, he served her as he was best able to serve her, by ministering to her wounded and dying soldiers out of the abundance of his sympathy and love.

Modern Ballet

ÉMILE VUILLERMOZ

FOR SEVERAL YEARS, the dance has had such success in the
realms of literature, painting, and music, that it has ended up drunk
with triumph. At the present time, it is passing through a crisis of
megalomania. It no longer has the divine nonchalance, the innocent
and lively joy that formerly and traditionally, thanks to painters and
sculptors, glittered on the brow of its appointed Muse. And
Carpeaux's Dionysiac group that decorates the façade of our National Academy of Dance and gives only a rather remote idea of
the choreographic work going on inside the building, has, in any
case, no connection at all with most of the accomplishments of our
present-day Terpsichores.

But let us not be too quick to regret. True, we have the right
to smile at certain priestesses of an ideological and metaphysical
saltation, who seem to have ambitions that are "beyond measure",
in every sense of the word. But in spite of everything, their fervour
and agitation are productive. There is no longer one technique
of the dance; there are a hundred, which is enough to make purists
of the *jetté-battu* despair and at the same time comforts willing
audiences. For there can never be too many plastic forms for expressing the infinite complexity of a musical text, and every dancer
234

who invents a successful new form of bodily expression becomes a benefactor of the twin arts. Apollo will take care of his own.

BESIDES, why should there be only one valid technique of the dance? And who has the right to take an art which calls out for an extensive vocabulary, and limit it to a patented formula?

Obviously everyone must begin with about the same early professional education—and this indispensable muscular preparation is too often ignored by certain naive bacchantes, too quick to replace it by an ardor and a faith which are not always communicable. But when the "trade" is solidly acquired, its prosaic aspects can always be eliminated in a most free and unexpected way by the creative imagination.

One of the great mistakes of choreographic art has always been to adhere too subserviently to a purely aesthetic theory, applying its canons to any apprentice ballerina. The "personal equation" of a woman's body has not been sufficiently taken into account. The gestures and attitudes of a Zambelli, who has the disembodied slimness and agility of a dragon-fly, are laboriously taught to some short and plump young lady, and the results are deplorable. Whereas the same dancer could perhaps have moved us had the choreography been more appropriate to her particular build. According to the demands of her narrow or vigorously moulded hips, her sturdy or spindle-shaped legs, her fragile or strong arms, the curve of her shoulders, her chest, and her back, and by the pedagogical powers of her teacher, whatever they be, a woman should, whether she likes it or not, forsake Tamar Karsavina's ideal for Isadora Duncan's, Anna Pavlova's technique for Loie Fuller's, and become a Jeanne Ronsay, or a Trouhanova, a Napierkowska or a Regina Badet. And, as they say in the law-courts, justice will be done!

A woman's body creates its own technique. We can see it in variety shows, in which entertainers such as Spinelly, Mistinguett, or Dourga, all in very different styles, sometimes attain plastic realizations of remarkable ingenuity and unmistakable grace, because of the perfect and methodical use of their personal resources. We have seen it when certain deserters of the Opéra Comique corps de ballet, in going from one stage to another, gave unexpected proof of hitherto unsuspected technical talents: while vaudeville and operettas had not suddenly endowed them with genius, they did escape from the rigid limits of the classic quadrilles, in which they remained mediocre performers. They freed themselves from the slavery of transcendent formulas that were too difficult for their humble means, and were able to develop, outside of any academicism, the hidden qualities of grace, strength, flexibility, skill, or charm which nature had bestowed upon them.

The young students of our subsidized corps de ballet, who courageously work for their Ph.D.s in choreography, will disdainfully comment: "They have stopped really dancing." But they will be wrong. Those independent girls have simply left the university. They are similar to Ph.D. candidates who launch out into the novel, poetry, or journalism; their achievements will occasionally be mediocre, or they may now and then produce a masterpiece. But it is no more advisable to centralize and unify the teaching of the dance than it would be to limit all of French literature to the works of graduate students.

I should not like this modest reflection to be taken as an encouragement to dilletantism or as a manifestation of ingratitude towards dancers and writers who are well-versed in grammar and syntax. Let us quickly emphasize all that we owe to the "humanities" of the dance.

WE HAVE NOT always been very fair to the classical technique. And it is true that, in France at least, it has been gradually intellectualized to the point of desiccation. The ballet in opera had promoted an imperceptible evolution of the dancer towards the articulated marionette. The geometric stiffness of the "steps" and traditional groupings, along with the conventional costume, transported the ballerina into a mechanical world, far from the human plane. Certain technical feats and certain of the so-called difficult figures are terribly lacking in grace and charm. An exceptionally gifted dancer could perhaps miraculously conceal their poverty, but most interpreters have failed in this difficult task. And performers were so accustomed to disdaining those banal anachronistic gymnastics, perpetuated solely for the pleasure of our old subscribers, that any woman who stamped around the stage to music without wearing the traditional pink slippers and get-up, was hailed by them as a liberator of genius.

It did not take us long to realize that this was rather a hasty judgment. Greek tunics and bare feet were the cause of more than one cruel disillusion. And at precisely the same moment, coming as a curious paradox, dancers such as Fokine, Nijinsky, Karsavina, and Pavlova arrived from the heart of Russia to give us a demonstration of the excellence of pure French tradition in classical choreography. For many of our compatriots, it was a veritable revelation. No one had expected to find such respect for the past in those revolutionaries, and the proximity of the dances of *Prince Igor* and *Le Sacre du Printemps* gave startling significance to the toe-dance of *Les Sylphides*.

It then became apparent that the stereotyped aesthetics of the tights and pink slippers, the short puffed-out skirt of white tulle, the pinched-in waist, severe hair style, and bare arms were not an absurdity. In the Russian sanctuaries of the dance, the virtuosity of Vestris was preserved intact, and the interpretations of Chopin given us here, took their inspiration from the acrobatic manual of the 18th century *haute école*. Of course that superior technique required a systematic emancipation from all the constraints of our humble earthly condition so as to move towards an ideal of agility, rapidity, nimbleness, and super-human balance.

The classical costume makes that liberation easier. It transforms the dancer into an incorporeal, airy, and weightless creature. By neutralizing her femininity, it changes her into a fairy, an elf, a sprite, or a butterfly. It creates the woman-insect with her slender and elastic limbs, gauze wings, and constricted waist; and the woman-flower with frothy petals, and arms as delicate and supple as climbing vines. By the artificial means of the toe-dance, she would seem to free herself from the laws of gravity, giving the impression of floating between the earth and the sky, and just barely touching the ground with the tip of her scornful toe. It causes her entire body to become longer, finer, miraculously slenderer, and delicately balanced, instead of resting on two large platforms in direct contact with solid ground. The huge gauze corolla that blossoms round her hips, hides their indiscrete flowering which affirms, with a pride inappropriate in a dancer, the nobility of her maternal destiny. That quivering white froth slims down the waist, which takes on a waspish fragility, and gives a frail slenderness to the legs and arms, which should not be of flesh but should rather evoke the willowy tremor of an antenna or a stamen. This voluntary transubstantiation must be resolutely accepted and fearlessly accentuated, if need be, in order to spiritualize even more that higher state, that mysticism of pure choreography.

BUT THAT WOULD CALL for an exceptional vocation. The religion of Terpsichore has its minor orders. Young lay sisters should not be forced, on principle, to become Saint Theresas. For adolescents who refuse to become disembodied, there are other ways of serving the dance and music. Those new devotions, which are not schisms, have been multiplying for several years. They are not all of equal fervour but it would be foolish to discourage them. They have the value of demonstrative experiments from which useful lessons can be drawn.

They attract attention to the study of important problems. They help in the progressive transformation of the plastic style required by the evolution of musical language. Classical dance was based on the principle of melodic structure: if it is ever to include modern masterpieces in its repertoire—and it should—it will indeed be forced to modify its rhythmic balance and make its conception of the measure more flexible. Without forsaking anything of its high doctrines, it has the duty of following the new prosody of our composers.

Classical dance has arrived at the same embarrassing moment that poetry went through when the time came to substitute free verse for regular verse. Music written for our corps de ballet has been based, up to this point, on plays of rhymes and symmetrical caesuras. It now must be broken of its habit of alexandrines and taught the fleeting and subtle harmonies of free verse or rhythmic prose. The example of *Daphnis et Chloé* has shown us that this transformation was relatively easy for interpreters in full possession of their techniques. Zambelli, with most elegant independence, managed to sketch out lightly the capricious arabesque of Ravel's melodies on the very stage on which she had been accustomed prudently to trace the figures of stock waltzes, as regular as the "eights" of the man who, during intermissions, sprinkles the stage with water and seems to write out the fundamental laws of the *rond de jambe* and the pigeon-wing.

A lesson such as that should not be wasted. Classical technique can be renewed without necessarily being betrayed. It cannot continue to ignore the evolution of music. It is flexible enough to adapt to all styles and all syntaxes. After having followed the strict rules of prosody, it can perfectly well go on to parsing and analyzing. Dancers such as the music-loving Sakharoffs have shown us how, in pulling apart a melodic phrase as methodically and accurately as a philologist, its most hidden architectural meanings can be brought out and all the facets of a harmonious expression made to sparkle. Choreographers have no right to disregard the future possibilities of such valuable indications.

They must not be slaves of their academic prejudices. In accepting foreign dances, they must show discrimination, but a benevolent curiosity as well. The Ballets Russes have shown us that it was possible to create an excellent academy of western choreography with students and teachers of a profoundly Asiatic aesthetic culture. Our national taste is no more jeopardized by the Oriental and Persian dances, whose voluptuous languor and subtle sensual grace have been popularized in France, than it formerly was by the Turkish masques of the court ballets. We can, on the contrary, draw profitable lessons from them. They will teach us that, side by side with the spiritual dance, a dance exists in which a woman's body imposes its sovereignty and music responds to the flesh instead of imposing its own laws. And this new form of collaboration, also, can produce masterpieces.

Choreographic art of the future will be made up of all those scattered elements. We predict that it will be rich, eloquent, dynamic, and persuasive. It has already rejected the traditional pantomime composed of ready-made formulas. It can make itself understood by means which owe nothing to the other arts. It is becoming complete and profound. And, even were this to sound like odious blasphemy, I am one of those who see in it—after the inevitable failure of lyric drama—the last, most certain, and most universal refuge of the lyricism of tomorrow.

Art and Craftsmanship

ANANDA K. COOMARASWAMY

IN REPLY TO THE ENQUIRY, What is art? an answer may be made as follows: Art is the involuntary dramatisation of subjective experience. In other words, the crystallisation of a state of mind in images (whether visual, auditory or otherwise). This excludes from art the practical activity of mere illustration, which involves only the combination of empirical observation with skill of craftsmanship. Even the setting down on paper of the signs, lines, words, musical notes, etc., that serve to communicate aesthetic experience by the indications of gesture, or audible sounds, is a practical activity [1] to be distinguished from that of creation. However swiftly the record may follow on the heels of the single spiritual activity of intuition-expression, it is always the externalisation of an already completed cycle. The words of a poem, the lines of a drawing, are not expressive: they are the catalytic stimuli to a renewed aesthetic activity, or expression, on the part of the hearer. It is therefore by ellipsis that we call them expressive, as it is by ellipsis that we speak of a physical work of art as beautiful. It is scarcely needful to add that questions of personal taste or interest have nothing to do with aesthetic values, however legitimately they may govern conduct.

[1] In Kinema phraseology, that of "registering."

240

The element of skill enters only into the voluntary practical activity of externalisation, the use of the language of stimulation. We cannot measure qualities of art by measuring degrees of skill. In fact, there are no degrees of art: nor is it possible to speak of a progress or degeneration of art, in individuals or schools, as we can speak of progress or loss in the realm of knowledge, technique and skill. In the words of Blake: "The human mind cannot go beyond the gift of God, the Holy Ghost. To suppose that art can go beyond the finest specimens of art that are now in the world is not knowing what art is; it is being blind to the gifts of the Spirit." Wagner and Raphael are not necessarily superior to Palaestrina and Giotto because of their more elaborate technique or superior facility. We can only ask,—In which have we evidence of most profound vision? which of these artists is the greater vessel? For this is what we really mean when we relinquish our preoccupation with the accidentals of technique and accomplishment, and still observe that at various moments in the history of an individual or of a school there is a varying degree of vision. This is not a variability of art, but of the individual. Two men at the same time, or one man at different times, may go down to the sea, with a bucket or a cup, and bring back a bucketful or a cupful of water: but each brings back the same water, whether the vessels be large or small, of gold or clay. In other words, however broad or narrow, noble or ignoble, the subject of the art, however elegant or crude the language, art is always recognizable as art. All that we can demand of an artist is that he should offer us living water: for this water has a miraculous quality, and even though it be offered in a thimble it will fill a bowl. One can only say that there are greater and lesser artists, as there are greater and lesser lovers: but we can no more speak of progress in art than we could speak of progress in love.

If Mrs. Eddy speaks of the same truth that Jesus speaks of, it is not because of her defective literary education that she fails to touch us, but because of the less intensity or clarity of her experience. The most awkward means are adequate to the communication of authentic experience, and the finest words no compensation for the lack of it. It is for this reason that we are moved by the true Primitives and that the most accomplished art craftsmanship leaves us cold.

It is as hard for the learned artist as for the rich man to enter the Kingdom of Heaven. In saying this, we need not forget that

the gates are as widely opened to the learned and the rich as to
the illiterate and the poor. If anything, too little honour has been
paid to craftsmanship and knowledge in recent times. Skill and
sophistication, learning and wealth, are neither good nor bad in
themselves—that is to say, they can be used or misused. And both
are relative terms. Most great artists have been learned in their
own time and place (Giotto was acclaimed as a realist), and there
is nothing in the coincidence of the external signs of art with the
dimensional aspect of nature, which of itself precludes the possibility of communicating by such signs an authentic spiritual experience. We cannot separate the tares from the wheat by distinguish-
ing a naturalistic from a symbolic language. It is not by an
intellectual or categorical activity that we can judge of the intensity
of any artist's vision. We cannot judge except by our response; and
whether or not we can respond will depend on our own state of
grace.

The Eye Is a Part of the Mind

LEO STEINBERG

WE BEGIN WITH the interrogation of witnesses. Two men are called to defend the reversal of aesthetic values in their time. The first is Giorgio Vasari, the tireless biographer to whose *Lives of the Painters* we owe half the facts and most of the figments current on the artists of the Renaissance. The other, Vasari's junior by four centuries, is André Malraux, whose *Psychology of Art* forms a brilliant brief for the moot values of the modern, neo-mystic taste in art.

Speaking of Masaccio, the great initiator of the naturalist trend in Western art, Vasari states: "The things made before his time may be termed paintings merely, and by comparison his (Masaccio's) creations are real."

And Malraux, hailing Manet as the initiator of the modern trend in art, asks: "What then was painting becoming, now it no longer imitated or transfigured?" And his answer: "Simply—painting."

A startling consonance this, between the "painting merely" of Vasari and the "simply painting" of Malraux. Strange also that the self-same epithet should denote scorn in one man's mouth and high praise in the other's, and yet for both bear the same connotation.

For what exactly did Vasari have in mind? That Masaccio's work,

243

and that which flowed from his influence to make the mainstream of the Renaissance, was a true representation of the external world; whereas the earlier Byzantine mosaics were pictorial patterns whose forms were not determined by reality. Being undetermined by nature, he called them "paintings merely"—just as he might have called scholastic metaphysics "thinking merely," since it too formed a speculative system adrift from the experience of life. Vasari's point was that medieval pictures implied no referent outside themselves. Renaissance painting, on the contrary, was valid because in it every element corresponded with its prototype in nature.

And Malraux? What does *he* mean when he pits the "simply painting" of Manet against the styles of other ages? Why, precisely the same thing. Representational art for him is weighted with extraneous content and transcribed appeal, with reference to things and situations that exist outside the picture frame in general experience. Manet pries art loose from the world. "Modern art," says Malraux, "has liberated painting which is now triumphantly a law unto itself." No longer must a painting borrow its validity from natural analogues. Its meaning—if self-significance can be called meaning —lies wholly within itself. Wherever art is seen with modern eyes —seen, that is to say, as "a certain compelling balance in colors and lines"—there, says Malraux, "a magic casement opens on another world . . . a world incompatible with the world of reality." It was for this incompatibility that Vasari spurned medieval art; it is on this very account that Malraux glorifies contemporary painting.

Thus juxtaposed our authors confess that what is here involved is not a difference in aesthetic judgment, nor even in the definition of art. We are dealing rather with two distinct valuations set upon reality, and the overt gap between the Renaissance and the modern aesthetician is evidence of a rift far more deeply grounded.

We will ask later whether either Malraux or Vasari was justified in seeing "merely painting" anywhere. For the moment we may say that Malraux speaks the mind of his generation when he declares that the representation of external nature has nothing to do with art. "Creating a work of art is so tremendous a business," says Clive Bell, "that it leaves no leisure for catching likenesses." As long ago as 1911, Laurence Binyon wrote with satisfaction: "The theory that art is, above all things, imitative and representative, no longer holds the field with thinking minds." Albert C. Barnes reminds us that only painters "unable to master the means of plastic expression, seek to awaken emotion by portraying objects or situations which have an appeal in themselves. . . . This attraction, though it is all-important in determining popular preference, is plastically and aesthetically irrelevant." And, as Sheldon Cheney insists: "It can hardly be too often repeated that the modernist repudiates the Aristotelian principle 'Art is Imitation.'"

But this position presents a serious quandary, for the first glance at art through the ages shows unmistakably that most of it is dedicated precisely to the imitation of nature, to likeness-catching, to the portrayal of objects and situations—in short, to representation. Now there are three possible formulas by which this contradiction between evidence and creed may be resolved. The first asserts that representation has always been an adventitious element in art—a concession made to populace or church. Modern art, then, differs from historic art not in essence but in degree of purity. This is the view put forth by Roger Fry and Barnes and their respective schools. The second choice is to concede that representation did function essentially in the arts of the past, and that modern art, by eschewing the outgoing reference, constitutes something radically different and new. This is the implication of such continental critics as Ortega y Gasset and Malraux, who endorse the meaning elements in the historic styles, yet claim for modern art exemption from associated values. It is also (aesthetics makes strange bedfellows!) the view of the bourgeois who repudiates all modern art as an unfunny and too long protracted hoax.

The third alternative is to suggest that modern art has not, after all, abandoned the imitation of nature, and that, in its most powerful expressions, representation is still an essential condition, not an expendable freight. It is this third view which this essay will seek to establish. It will try to show that representation is a central aesthetic function in all art; and that the formalist aesthetic, designed to champion the new abstract trend, was largely based on a misunderstanding and an underestimation of the art it set out to defend.

II

We have said that most historic art is vitally concerned with representation. And lest the word is thought to offer too much latitude, we will commit ourselves further to say that about half the great art generated by mankind is dedicated to the accurate transcription of the sensible world.[1] This is as true of the best paleolithic art as of Egyptian at its finest moments. It applies to the entire Hellenic effort down to third-century Rome.[2] It applies equally to the great Western wave that lies between Giotto and the Post-Impressionists. Nor is it any the less true of Chinese painting—so self-conscious that it operated for a thousand years within six explicit canons; of which the third called for "conformity with nature," or "the drawing of forms which answer to natural forms." All of these schools—and there are as many more—strove for the mastery of nature by convincing imitation.

Perhaps it will be said that artists closer to us in time would not have subscribed to this errant quest. Here is a sampling of their depositions: Manet declared (Malraux notwithstanding) that he painted what he saw. Van Gogh's avowed aim was to be "simply honest before nature." Cézanne exclaims: "Look at that cloud! I would like to be able to paint that!" And he says: "We must give the picture of what we see, forgetting everything that has appeared in the past." Even for Matisse "the problem is to maintain the intensity of the canvas whilst getting near to verisimilitude."

Such quotations, given a collector's leisure, could be piled to random height. They are adequately summarized in Constable's dictum which defines the goal of painting as "the pure apprehension of natural fact."

Yet artists and critics, for half a century and more, have been denouncing the representation of nature as a fatal side-stepping of artistic purpose. And whoever has the least pretension to aesthetic culture speaks *de haut en bas* of "that power which is nothing but technical capacity in the imitation of nature." [3] This famous slur, reverberating in the prejudice of almost every modern connoisseur,

---

[1] It would be missing the point to include here only such art as looks convincingly lifelike to us. What matters is the artist's effort and intention. Thus the most summary abstractions in primitive pottery designs often signified to their makers the highest available degree of representational truth. One may delight in the refined stylizations of the "Unicorn" tapestries at the New York Cloisters; but he should remember that both artist and weaver had pushed naturalism to the limit of their knowledge, and as far as the medium allowed.

[2] "The story of Greek art is the story of a step by step discovery of the true nature of appearance by the liberation of vision from its conceptual bonds," wrote Roger Fry.

[3] The words are taken from the great, prophetic art historian Alois Riegl.

has become standard critical jargon. The picturing of overt nature is written off as mere factual reportage, worthy only of the amateur photographer, a mechanical skill, patently uncreative and therefore alien to the essence of art.

The objection to this view is not far to seek. To begin with, "technical capacity in imitation" implies what no one seriously believes: that nature confronts man with a fixed, invariant look. For what else does it mean to speak of "mere skill in copying the model" (the words are Malraux's), but that the model's appearance is an objective fact susceptible of mechanical reproduction? We know better than that. Appearances reach us through the eye, and the eye—whether we speak with the psychologist or the embryologist—is part of the brain and therefore hopelessly involved in mysterious cerebral operations. Thus nature presents every generation (and every person who will use his eyes for more than nodding recognitions) with a unique and unrepeated facet of appearance. And the Ineluctible Modality of the Visible—young Dedalus' hypnotic phrase—is a myth that evaporates between any two works of representation. The encroaching archaism of old photographs is only the latest instance of an endless succession in which every new mode of nature-representation eventually resigns its claim to co-identity with natural appearance. And if appearances are thus unstable in the human eye, their representation in art is not a matter of mechanical reproduction but of progressive revelation.

We can therefore assert with confidence that "technical capacity in the imitation of nature" simply does not exist. What does exist is the skill of reproducing handy graphic symbols for natural appearances, of rendering familiar facts by set professional conventions. We have cited a canon from the beginning phase of Chinese painting; here is another from nearer its dead end:

There are ten ways, say the Chinese academicians, of depicting a mountain: by drawing wrinkles like the slashes of a large axe, or wrinkles like the hair on a cow's hide; by brushstrokes wrinkled like a heap of firewood, or like the veins of lotus leaves. The rest are to be wrinkled like the folds of a belt, or the twists of a rope; or like raindrops, or like convoluted clouds, etc.

With rigorous training the Ming painters could, and did, acquire a dazzling proficiency in drawing the right wrinkles and so suggesting the available, respectable, familiar facts about natural panoramas. They had mastered the skill of applying certain academic tricks for the drawing of mountains—but this is most emphatically not the same as skill in drawing actual mountains. The mechanical, the uncreative element lies not therefore in imitating nature, but in academicism, which is the passionless employment of preformed devices. Representation in art is the fashioning of graphic symbols to act as analogues for certain areas of visual experience. There is a mightly difference between this fashioning of symbols, this transmutation and reduction of experience to symbolic pattern, and the use of symbols ready-made. In works that seem to duplicate a visible aspect of nature we must therefore distinguish between the recitation of a known fact and the discovery thereof, between the dexterous use of tools and their invention.

This distinction must be upheld for all representational art. Seen in this light it becomes quite absurd to charge Victorian academicians with too fastidious an eye for natural forms. Their fault was not, as Roger Fry maintained, "the fervid pursuit of naturalistic appearances," but that they continued to see and represent the facts of nature in terms of a spent convention. The so-called naturalism of the nineteenth-century academicians was worthless because it was impelled by precept and by meritorious example, instead of by pure visual apprehension. These men never imitated nature; they copied earlier imitations and applied those formal principles which, they believed, had made their models so effective. That they sometimes painted from life is, of course, beside the point; for they still saw life in the aspect which their vision was conditioned to expect.[4] Thus the malady of Victorian art (and of some lingering official art today, notably in Soviet Russia) is not naturalism, nor literal representation, but the presumption to create living art out of impulses long dead and mummified; which ailment is not confined to realistic art. For academicism will blight non-objective figurations and abstract designs as readily as illustrative, anecdotal pictures. One has only to walk into an up-to-date New York art school to see how academic are those repetitious canvases that imitate Braque and Picasso down to the planimetric mandolin.

This is not to say that a convention invariably chokes artistic creativity. It does so only when too fully conned and understood, when the uphill drive of aspiration is relaxed and the professors of

[4] Even Sir Joshua Reynolds, in his first Discourse, laments that students "make a drawing rather of what they think the figure ought to be than of what it appears."

the brush can settle down to mass production. An artist searches for true vision, but having found it, leaves in his successors' hands the blueprint of a new academy. Almost anyone with a modicum of talent and sufficient application can possess himself of another man's mode of representation. (Were this not so, the forger's craft would not exist.) But he cannot discover it. He can learn after one lesson in perspective how to give an illusion of depth to a design (an illusion, by the way, based largely on our habit of routine consent). But this lesson shall not arm him with the passion of an early Florentine who first ventures through the picture plane and, like daydreaming Alice, finds a wonderland beyond. The same rules of perspective mean one thing at the Beaux Arts; in Mantegna's studio, in Uccello's workshop, they meant quite another. Space, that had congealed into a solid crust during the Middle Ages, was here dented, pierced and vaporized. Bodies were inserted and, against resisting pressure, as on reluctant hinges, pivoted into depth. There is in Uccello's work a tensity which springs directly from his craving to know how bodies will behave in the *terra incognita* known as the third dimension. And the reports of his discoveries, such as the bold foreshortenings in "The Battle of San Romano," are proclaimed in tense and urgent gestures. And what is true of perspective applies equally to anatomy. The gulf that separates a Pollaiuolo nude from one by Bouguereau is not all a matter of significant design. The one was born of nature's union with an avid sensibility; the other makes a parade of a habitual skill. One says, pointing to the array of anatomic facts—"Here lies the mystery"; the other says—"Here lies no mystery, I know it all."

The modern critic who belittles all representational concerns, because he sees them only as solved problems, underrates their power to inflame the artist's mind and to intensify his vision and his touch. He will fail of appreciation if he cannot appropriate the artist's will to state his concept of reality. Nor need he know how much of anatomic ignorance prevailed in Pollaiuolo's time to judge the measure of the artist's revelation. For Pollaiuolo's effort to articulate each muscular inflection is permanently sealed in the form. Like all works connected with discoveries of representation, his pictures lack the sweet ease of accomplishment. His images are ever aborning, swelling into space and taking life, like frozen fingers tingling as they warm. It is not facts they purvey; it is the thrill and wonder of cognition.

But is this sort of cognition relevant to aesthetic value? To be sure it is. We are told that the artist's design seeks to impose enduring unity and order on the undifferentiated content of experience. To bring his organizing powers into fullest play, the painter must haul his perceptions out of their limbo and annex them to his plan. A Michelangelo, busying himself in anatomic studies, knows that the apparent turbulence of a man's muscles must become in his design as inevitably ordered as was the long, unswerving contour of Masaccio. A score of muscles newly differentiated, a new vocabulary of expressive gesture, a newly seen relation between motion and shape, these become part of that living diversity to which unification is the victorious response. They are the stuff of the aesthetic program. And in bringing novel visual experiences to his art, Michelangelo, so far from abandoning Masaccio's ground, is doing precisely what his forerunner had done. For he is still engaged in the "pure apprehension of natural fact." The Mannerist, on the other hand, he who displays Michelangelo's musculature over again, is not at all repeating Michelangelo, since what he arranges on the canvas lives already in the domesticated state. It had been won for art already.

In realistic art, then, it is the ever-novel influx of visual experience which incites the artist's synthesizing will, summons his energies and so contributes to the generation of aesthetic form. And this perhaps explains why periods of expanding iconography, of deepening observation and growing imitative skill so often coincide with supreme aesthetic achievement. When the limits of the depictable in nature suddenly recede before the searching gaze, when earlier works come to seem inadequately representative of truth, then the artist's power multiplies. Hence the beauty of those Fifth Dynasty reliefs in Egypt, when, almost suddenly, all life comes to be taken for the artist's province; or the unsurpassed grandeur of the Middle Kingdom heads, when the uniqueness of the human face is first perceived. Hence the upsurge of aesthetic force in Sixth and Fifth Century Greece, when new insights into human nature call for embodiment; or in Quattrocento art when the untamed reality of space has to be disciplined and reduced to the coordinate system of the plane canvas or wall.

The Impressionists formed another group of passionate investigators into natural fact. Was it accident that these same men evolved powerful new formal conceptions? Malraux chooses to see no connection between the significance of their forms and their representational pursuits. "That the banks of the Seine might look more 'lifelike' in Sisley's than in Theodore Rousseau's work was beside the mark," he says. Beside the mark, possibly, for the modern doctrinaire, but obviously not so for Sisley.

And Cézanne? Nowadays every schoolboy knows that Cézanne was interested in picture construction. We incline to forget that he was just as concerned with the construction of Mont Sainte-Victoire and the vibration of sunlight; that he studied the subterranean geologic energies which had rolled up the landscape of Provence, and pondered those pervasive unities of nature in which forms are compacted despite their apparent edges. Today's fashionable cant represses Cézanne's deep obsession with reality, "the spectacle that the Pater Omnipotens spreads before our eyes." When he warns his friend Emile Bernard, to "beware of the literary spirit which so often causes painting to deviate from its true path—the concrete study of nature—to lose itself all too long in intangible speculations," he seems to be speaking not so much of the critics he knew, as of those more recent who profess to know him. The truth is that Cézanne's work embodies profound insights into nature. And the inner logic of his form is unthinkable without his ardent apprehension of natural fact.

By what hazard do these moments of whole-hearted nature-imitation synchronize so often with unforgettable art? In the formalistic system of ideas the recurrent coincidence of significant form with deepened observation remains unexplained. To avoid perversity we do better to grant that nature-imitation in art is neither mechanical skill nor irrelevant distraction. The most that can be said in its disfavor is that we of this century happen to have turned our interest elsewhere.

III

Where your treasure is, there (dropping the h) will your art be also. Every picture is to some degree a value judgment, since you cannot represent a thing without proclaiming it to be worthwhile.

Now the arts discussed in the foregoing section pertained to those schools whose purpose was, at least in part, to depict the open sights of nature. One and all they endorsed Constable's plea for the pure apprehension of natural fact.

But natural fact can be purely apprehended only where the human mind has first endowed it with the status of reality. Only then is the act of seeing backed by a passion, being focused on ultimate truth. From Masaccio to Cézanne men prized overt nature as the locus of reality, and to it they directed their capacities of apprehension. But if we invoke a civilization for whom nature was a pale and immaterial reflection of ideal types, we shall expect to find it careless of the outer shapes of things. Its art will strive to incarnate those forms which are the permanent exemplars behind the drift of sensuous appearances. This indeed is the course taken by Christian art after the fall of pagan Rome.

We can now modify Constable's dictum and propose that art seeks the pure apprehension of natural fact wherever natural fact, as registered by the senses, is regarded as meaningful reality. Where it is not so interpreted we shall find some form of anti-humanist distortion, of hieratic stylization or abstraction. But—and this is crucial—such abstraction will continue to apprehend and to express reality. Though it rejects the intimations of mere sense perception, it does not thereby cease to be representational. Only the matter that now calls for representation is drawn from a new order of reality.

Let us list briefly some of the formal features governing Early Christian and Byzantine art. Comparing it to the preceding style of disenchanted Hellenism, we are struck by a rigid frontality in the disposition of figures, by a minimum of variation in gesture, and the replacement of individual likeness by canonic type. We note that movement is arrested, that the natural bulk of things is flattened and all forms are gathered in a single plane; distance is eliminated in favor of ideal space, purple or gold; color becomes pure, unmodulated, and the shadow—that negating spirit who haunts only the art of the West—vanishes in the diffusion of an unremitting light.

These devices sound, as indeed they look, other-worldly. Yet we can say without paradox that their employment proves how deeply involved was the art of Byzantium, and of the Western Dark and Middle Ages, in the effort at truthful representation. This is readily verified by reference to Neo-Platonist aesthetics.

The most valuable source here is Plotinus, whose thought, by way of Dionysius and Augustine, shaped the spirituality of the first Christian millennium. What, asks Plotinus, speaking of the plastic arts, are true distance and true size? And his answer is a philosophic premonition of the Byzantine manner.[5] If we see two men, the one close by, the other far away, the latter will appear ridiculously dwarfed, and the interval between the two will seem absurdly shrunken. A given distance, therefore, is so many measures of falsification. Since deep space is the occasion of delusion, true distance can exist only within the nearest facing plane; true size is the dimension of each form within that plane.

The argument may be extended to true color. If the red of a red object fades in distance, this effaced, degraded color is not "true." The truth must be an even red in the proximate plane. Furthermore, shadows are to be shunned for doing violence to truthful color, for there can be neither truth nor reality where there is not illumination. Thus to Plotinus the proper rendering of a red sphere would be a disk of pure, ungraduated hue. It is the chiaroscurist—a pander to the sense of sight—who mistakes the nature of reality and therefore sins against the light. "We dare not keep ourselves set toward the images of sense," Plotinus says.

Do Byzantine images seem incorporeal? How else should they represent the truly real? "The body is brute," says Plotinus; "the true man is the other, going pure of body." And he proceeds to reprove them who on the evidence of thrust and resistance identify body with real being.

Do Early Christian figures seem monotonously like, immobile and unchanging? We are forewarned by Plotinus that "bodies live in the species, and the individual in the whole class; from them they derive their life and maintenance, for life here is a thing of change, but in that prior realm it is unmoving."

Finally, do the eyes in medieval faces seem excessively prominent? The eye sees the sun, says Plotinus, because it is itself sunlike. Window of the soul, it bespeaks the presence in the body of that radiant emanation which sustains matter in being. Should not the artist therefore state the eye's true nature rather than comparative size? Values having more reality than facts, it is they that determine the ethos and technique of medieval art.

[5] See A. Grabar on *"Plotin et l'Esthétique Médiévale"* in *Cahiers Archéologiques*, Vol. i, 1945.

Clearly, then, the formal conventions of this Christian art came into being in the interest of representational truth; not, to be sure, of direct visual facts, since such facts were metaphysically discredited, but of an ideal, extra-sensory reality.

Obedient to its mystic vision, Christian art proceeded to erect a system of representation by abstraction. Here a certain limited affinity to our own contemporary art suggests itself. There is indeed striking resemblance between the repudiation of naturalism in our time and Plotinus' day. The latter had written that "the arts give no bare reproduction of the thing seen but go back to the ideas from which nature herself derives." Compare this with Paul Klee's: "The modern artist places more value on the powers that do the forming, than on the final forms (of nature) themselves." And even Roger Fry, who had no stomach for mystical speculation, says of Cézanne—who was all modern art to him—that he rendered "not appearances, but the causes of appearance in structure."

As the greatest apostle of the modern aesthetic faith, the case of Roger Fry is a rewarding study. And it is noteworthy that he was unaware of his own implications. He fervently believed that the prime business of art, in fact its sole legitimate concern, was "abstract unity of design." "Painting," he exclaimed, "has thrown representation to the winds; literature should do the same and follow suit!" Yet, gazing at an academic portrait, he passed this elegant quip (quoted in Virginia Woolf's biography): "I cannot," he said, "see the man for the likeness."

This went far deeper than Fry would have granted. He had meant to say that he could not see the essential man beneath the clutter of external traits. But he unwittingly confessed that he did want to see this inner man. While affirming that the valuable image did not manifest itself in mere visibility, he also admitted that the truth which lay concealed behind the model's mask, could and should be represented by some graphic symbol. It will be seen at once that Fry was speaking from a philosophic premise for which his formalistic theorizing left no room. He mistook for an aesthetic doctrine what was actually a shift in philosophic orientation. And he was not calling for the end of representation in art, but for the representation of a different content, to be tapped from a new order of reality.

Fry's sensitive recoil from Victorian academicism—or naturalism, to give it his preferred misnomer—was therefore based on two

objections, neither of which he acknowledged. First, that it substituted standard commonplaces for pure vision, and second, that
it continued to portray an aspect of nature which in the philosophic
conscience of his age had lost reality and meaning. For the inver-
sions of modern psychology and the iconoclasm of contemporary
physics have once again, as in the Middle Ages, subverted our
faith in the reality of palpable appearances. And it is right and
proper for the modern artist who is worthy of his time that he
should turn his back on the apparent, since he holds with Plotinus
that "all perceptible things are but signs and symbols of the imperceptible." Thus the relevance of naturalistic representation to
art depends on no aesthetic doctrines, but on prior metaphysical
commitments. And the argument for and against representation,
which has agitated critics for so long, has rarely been fought at
its proper level.

IV

Has modern art, then, like Byzantium, broken with the sensible
world? Is it true that art, having paid its debt to nature, is now
finally at liberty? Let us consider first those modern works which
still maintain natural forms at some degree of recognizability. To
the formalist their distortions seem sufficiently justified as serving
the higher needs of design. Yet in these works the illustrative element is there, and—no matter how abstracted—takes its point from
its residual resemblance to familiar sights. "The deformation of
natural forms" of which Klee speaks in his journals presupposes in
us a conception of natural forms undeformed. Meyer Schapiro,
speaking of Picasso's "Girl before a Mirror," points out that "Picasso
and other moderns have discovered for art the internality of the
body," that is, the inner image of the body as conjured up by fear
and desire, pleasure and pain. But this inner image is communicable
only as related contrast to the outer. Everyone knows how clumsy
the human foot feels when pursuing a bird. The mammoth foot
in Miro's "Man Throwing a Stone at a Bird" is thus an eloquent
hyperbole, a piece of graphic gigantism. It makes its point not as
largeness—a pure, abstract value—but as enlargement, which implies an external referent. The distance which the form has traveled
in the way of distortion is apprehended by the beholder and be-

comes a vital element of the narrative structure. Familiar nature is not, after all, ignored. It survives as the distanced, but implicit, norm.

This principle of representation by distortion and exaggeration for expressive ends is found, of course, throughout the history of art. It is the common device of all caricatures. No matter how remotely they have ventured into fantasy, it is the stretch and span between norm and distortion that constitutes their wit. The same is true of expressionism and of much so-called abstract art. A term of reference still lies outside the picture frame in human recollection and experience, as it does for the most clinically realistic pictures.

To an eye still immersed in the visual habits of the nineteenth century, the abstract way often seems willful and offensive. To a mind indoctrinated with modern aesthetic theory, it often looks like—"simply painting," the projection of inbred phantasmagoria. Both judgments, we believe, are failures of appreciation, since abstraction *from* nature is still a telling mode of representation, whose hyphen with common reality is stretched but never snapped, except in the most thinly decorative works.

There is another feature in contemporary abstract art which ties it to the world of sense and separates it from all anti-naturalistic styles of the past—its boundless freedom of selection from natural sights. The conceptualism of ancient Egypt or Byzantium had constrained itself to show every form from a preferred angle, convinced that one aspect alone could reveal its essential nature. Thus the Egyptian foot appears persistently in profile, as though the human foot in essence were a profile form, all other postures being accidentals. Domiciled in eternity, the Egyptian or Byzantine foot is not susceptible of change.

Modern abstraction brooks no such restraints. Six centuries of arduous research into the changing nature of appearance are not so easily dismissed. Accordingly, in modern abstract art, a difficult, foreshortened front view of a foot is met head-on, and finds its abstract formulation as readily as the diagrammatic profile. The modern painter, if caught in the orbit of Picasso or Paul Klee, discovers a formative principle not in the foot as such, but in the foot in every possible predicament. He sees not one transcendent, universal formula for man, but a distinct abbreviation for man in every pose, mood, situation. Klee himself finds a symbolic cipher not for

Woman, the Eternal Feminine, but for a certain middle-aged lady coming home loaded with packages.

It is quite true that Klee seeks ever the form-giving principle behind the thing, and strips it, like the mystic, of its superfluity; his representations rest upon his vision of a world whose surface forms conceal an occulted reality. In his own words, he seeks "a distant point at the source of creation, a kind of formula for man, earth, fire, water, air, and all the circling forces." Klee here seems to repeat a commonplace of mysticism. And yet his work, one of the most potent influences behind modern abstraction, is of devastating originality, utterly destructive of the mystic premise that there is one immutable reality available to detached contemplation. For Klee finds his occult reality incarnate in each fleeting, perjured gesture of this world. In his intuition the nature of man is not to be found in any timeless essence, soaring like Egyptian or Byzantine man above vicissitudes. Man, to Paul Klee, is what he does and where he is. Man is a "Juggler in April," an "Old Man Figuring," a "Mocker Mocked," an "Omphalocentric Lecturer." Vainly you scan these works for any single pictographic type; in every sketch the symbol is freshly apprehended and fashioned anew. If this is mysticism it is certainly not of the medieval, contemplative kind. It is a restless, existential mysticism, peculiarly our own.

Or watch Picasso's "Three Musicians" in the Philadelphia version. Despite an apparently remote cubistic formalism we can say with confidence that the three men in the picture are furnished with six hands. But saying this we have already said too much. Having availed ourselves of the non-visual concept of *the human hand,* we have implied that Picasso here deals with a six-fold repetition of a single item. But he does nothing of the kind. He knows, or knew in 1921, that a man's hand may manifest itself as rake, pestle, mallet, cup, cantilever, pincer, vise or broom; as waving banner or as decorative fringe; that it is a nubile and unstable element, contracting easy marriages with other forms to build up into compound entities. In actual vision the hand is an infinity of variegated forms. Its common factor is not any ontological handshape, but a protean energy with only a positional and functional relation to the arm, and to the object handled. Thus, in the "Three Musicians," a fist hugging a fiddle's neck is one sort of efficient force expressed by one decorative shape; four digits flat upon a keyboard are of another sort entirely. Picasso here banishes the *a priori* vision which must ever find conceptual permanence despite visible change. His manual formulae stand not for Being, but for function, operation. Adaptability and change are the sole measure of reality. And it is on behalf of such reality, as well as of design, that his sleights of hand are wrought. To describe the "Three Musicians" as a finely patterned abstraction of invented anatomies is an injustice to the matter of Picasso's revelation.

It follows that the modern abstractionist does not necessarily write off the "accidents" of visual appearance. He welcomes their occurrence, but pictures them as the negotiable shapes assumed by transient energy. And in this adaptability to every optic impulse modern art is more closely linked to its naturalistic ancestry than to the unworldly stylizations of the past. Its affinity with medieval art remains, after all, purely negative. Modern and medieval art agree that reality is not so much revealed as masked by surfaces. But, as at a carnival, the choice of a mask may betray the reveler's characteristic nature, so surfaces bespeak something as to the truth below. And the truths inferred by modern and by medieval artists lie at opposite poles of interpretation.

v

It remains to speak of so-called non-objective art. Here surely all connection with the outer world is cut. The forms that here emerge mean nothing, we are told, but private states of feeling; and, for the rest, they are pure form, a music for the optic nerve. The following passage from Ortega y Gasset ("On Point of View in the Arts," *Partisan Review*, August 1949) may serve as an example of the common view: "Painting," Ortega writes, "completely reversed its function and, instead of putting us within what is outside, endeavored to pour out upon the canvas what is within: ideal invented objects. . . . The [artist's] eyes, instead of absorbing things, are converted into projectors of private flora and fauna. Before, the real world drained off into them; now they are reservoirs of irreality."

This seems to us an open question still. For we are forced to ask: by what faculty of mind or eye does the artist discover and distill the forms of his private irreality? Whence come the plastic symbols of his unconditioned subjectivity? Surely no amount of introspection will yield shapes to put on canvas. And if this is so, from what external quarter proceed those visual stimuli which the artist can identify as apt and corresponding to his inner state?

Obviously, any attempt to answer such a question will be so highly speculative as almost to vindicate in advance the voices of dissent. Yet it seems worth considering the testimony of those artists and critics who have pointed to the impact of science on contemporary art.

The impact operates on several levels and takes various forms. There is, first, a constant stream of suggestion issuing from the laboratories. Wittingly, or through unconscious exposure, the non-objective artist draws much of his iconography from the visual data of the scientist—from magnifications of minute natural textures, from telescopic vistas, submarine scenery and X-ray photographs. Not that he undertakes to render a particular bacterial culture or pattern of refracted light. The shapes of his choice are recruited in good faith for their suggestiveness as shapes, and for their obscure correspondence to his inner state. But it is significant how often the morphology he finds analogous to his own sentient being is such as has revealed itself to human vision scientifically multiplied. It is apparently in these gestating images, shapes antecedent to the visible, that many abstract painters recognize an intenser mode of natural truth. On these uncharted realms of form they must impose aesthetic unity; from them they wrest new decorative principles—such as the "biomorphic" motif in modern ornament and applied design. Nature they imitate no less than did Masaccio. But where the Renaissance had turned to nature's display windows, and to the finished forms of man and beast, the men of our time descend into nature's laboratories.

But the affinity with science probably goes further still. It has been suggested that the very conceptions of twentieth-century science are finding expression in modern abstract art. The scientist's sense of pervasive physical activity in space, his intuition of immaterial functions, his awareness of the constant mutability of forms, of their indefinable location, their mutual interpenetration, their renewal and decay—all these have found a visual echo in contemporary art; Not because painters illustrate scientific concepts, but because an awareness of nature in its latest undisguise seems to be held in common by science and art.

The question is, of course, whether nature as the modern scientist conceives it can be represented at all, except in spectral mathematical equations. Philosophers of science concur in saying it cannot. Even such divergent thinkers as A. N. Whitehead and Bertrand Russell join hands when they declare that the abstractions of contemporary science have irrevocably passed beyond man's visual imagination. "Our understanding of nature has now reached a stage," says J. W. N. Sullivan, "when we cannot picture what we are talking about."

But this utterance of the philosophers contains an unwarranted assumption, to wit, that whereas man's capacity for intellectual abstraction is ever widening, his visual imagination is fixed and circumscribed. Here the philosophers are reckoning without the host, since our visualizing powers are determined for us not by them but by the men who paint. And this our visual imagination, thanks to those in whom it is creative, is also in perpetual growth, moving *pari passu* with the extension of thought.

Thus the art of the last half-century may well be schooling our eyes to live at ease with the new concepts forced upon our credulity by scientific reasoning. What we may be witnessing is the gradual condensation of abstract ideas into images that fall within the range of our sensory imagination.[6] Modern painting inures us to the aspect of a world housing not discrete forms but trajectories and vectors, lines of tension and strain. Form in the sense of solid substance melts away and resolves itself into dynamic process. Instead of bodies powered by muscle, or by gravity, we get energy propagating itself in the void. If, to the scientist, solidity and simple location are illusions born of the grossness of our senses, they are so also to the modern painter. His canvases are fields of force; his shapes the transient aggregates of energies that seem impatient to be on their way. In the imagery of modern art waves of matter have usurped the place of tangible, visible things. And the perpetual form, whether in motion or at rest, is dispossessed by forms of transition.

The representation of the trajectory in art has its own history, like the representation of the visage of Christ. Emerging in certain Rembrandt drawings as a scribbled flourish in the wake of a volatile angel, it comes in the late work of Turner to invade painting itself. And in Brancusi's "Bird in Space" the path of motion at last

---

[6] In his *Art as Experience* John Dewey writes: "Nothing that man has ever reached by the highest flights of thought, or penetrated by any probing insight is inherently such that it may not become the heart and core of sense."

claims the full sculptured dignity of mass. It is senseless to call such a work non-representational, for there is no ignoring here of nature. The trail of a projectile is, after all, as real as the object flung. And though it wants tangibility, it is as surely part of the natural world.

So much then for the dissolution of the solid in contemporary art; the substantial object has been activated into a continuing event. As for space, it is no longer a passive receptacle, wherein solid forms may disport themselves, as once they did in Renaissance and Baroque art. In modern paintings—barring those which are nostalgic throwbacks to the past—space is an organic growth interacting with matter. There is a painting by Matta Echaurren, entitled "Grave Situation," in which long tensile forms stretch through a space generated by their motion—a space which nevertheless seems to compel the curvature of their path.

It takes some effort to concede the heroic creativity of such envisionings. Granted that they do not depict what we normally see. But to call them "simply painting," as though they had no referent outside themselves, is to miss both their meaning and their continuity with the art of the past. If our suggestion is valid, then even non-objective art continues to pursue art's social role in fixating thought in aesthetic form, pinning down the most ethereal conceptions of the age in vitalized designs, and rendering them accessible to the apparatus of sense.

On the Problem of Musical Hearing

HELMUT REINOLD

OUTLINE OF THE SUBJECT

Music is possible and has meaning in our lives because we are able to hear. Whoever surrenders ingenuously to music need not think about that, but for the musicologist hearing is the starting point of all his thinking and research. For without hearing there is no music; and there is no music which does not obey the laws of human hearing.

Musical hearing is therefore not only a musicological problem, but as a human faculty it is first of all a purely anthropological one. Although this shows that musicology and anthropology are related, hearing is nowhere—even in theoretical anthropology—as central a problem as it is in musicology. From this it is evident that the musicologist cannot simply appropriate from other fields of science what he wants to know about hearing. He must look with his own eyes at our human faculty of hearing musically, must include its problems in his own thinking, and in so doing focus his attention on other interrelations, as for instance the medical scientist does. For, after all, the physiological processes in which medicine is interested, the acoustic measurements possible from the physical

262

standpoint, lie on an entirely different level. Regarded with a view to what is humanly essential, they are on a much less central plane than musical hearing, externally and internally, which, according to E. Kurth, "really . . . (deceives) us in a most peculiar manner about external happenings, so that they penetrate our inner being in complete disguise." [1]

But the fact that different planes of hearing are relevant to the various sciences respectively does not mean that musicology should simply push aside the insights into the nature of hearing attained by other disciplines, and go its own way. On the contrary, it is only through the configuration of these cognitions found on various planes, and through the hidden implications behind them, that musicology can achieve the first points of reference for the clarification of its basic problem.

Musical hearing is among the highest achievements of which man is capable, and it takes place simultaneously on various levels of the individual as a whole. It is a psychic process, since man is a being with a soul.[2] It is a social process, since every man is also a fellow creature; and it is a historical process, since every man lives in a historical world.[3]

Such a multi-stratified problem cannot be attacked and solved all at once on the whole front. Rather, in order to be able to break up the total problem of musical hearing into successive subproblems, we have to search for the basic stratum which leads into the total problem, leaves open the transition to other strata, and is neither contradicted nor cancelled by newly added factors. The fundamental stratum in this total problem is the vital process of hearing, for without being a living creature the hearing human being can be neither a spiritual, nor a social, nor a historical creature. Now it is clear that the total phenomenon of musical hearing can also be broken down in a different manner; for hearing as a biological process is a problem of nature, whereas musical hearing as a historical process is a problem of culture.[4] The relation of

---

[1] E. Kurth: *Musikpsychologie.* Bern, 1947, p. 1.

[2] "Soul" is interpreted as the entirety of processes of the human inner life.

[3] In this sense, including also the person who does not perceive historically.

[4] A variation of the pair of concepts that D. Katz introduces (*Sozialpsychologie,* in his *Handbuch der Psychologie,* Basel, 1951, p. 308). Previously, H. Riemann had already counted "musical theory among the natural sciences, inasmuch as art is nature." (Letter to Franz Liszt, cited by W. Gurlitt, *Hugo Riemann,* in "Abhandlungen der Geistes- und Sozialwissenschaften," Klasse der Akademie

natural and cultural factors to one another, however, is of an importance which would far exceed the limits of our inquiry. For the various strata of musical hearing are not stacked one above the other in the sense of an addition, but they mesh, as will be shown, in definite configurations and fuse into a new totality. In so doing, the cultural factors select a limited number from among the innumerable possibilities given by nature [5] and arrange them in a constellation, thereby forming something new. Since the laws inherent in the natural factors are not invalidated in this process, we see those same natural factors at work in the historical-cultural phenomena of musical hearing, although in a new arrangement. But the limit can be shown unequivocally, up to which the hypotheses of musical hearing can be comprehended on the basis of the naturalistic problem alone. It lies exactly where hearing enters into the structure of a given single personality.

A great deal more might be known today about the natural factors of the vital process of hearing, if musicology had occupied itself more fully and more independently with hearing, on the basis of its own purely musical problem.[6] For it has been shown that the peculiarities of the musical element have a high cognitive value for the theory of the senses. At least twice within the past sixty years have musical phenomena had an almost revolutionary effect on the theory of sensations. In 1890 Chr. von Ehrenfels, starting from the nature of the melody, wrote his famous dissertation *Über Gestalt-qualitäten*. Decades later E. Straus, in a book perhaps less noted by the nonspecialist, helped to refute the mechanistic conception of the senses by means of the musical phenomenon of the complete rest, the "problem of the void," as he called it.[7]

der Wissenschaften und der Literatur, Sitz Mainz, Jahrgang 1950, No. 25, p. 13.) But his concept of natural science is different from the one that is employed here. Riemann must have overestimated the influence of the natural factors on the totality of musical hearing when he emphasizes that "we have every reason to imagine that the difference between the kind of hearing prevailing thousands of years ago and today is minimal." (Gurlitt, *op. cit.*, p. 21.) Recently J. Handschin (*Der Toncharakter*, Zürich, 1948, p. 310) differentiated between things "given by nature" and those which are "based on inclination, discretion, and even convention . . ." in the "historical and ethnographical sphere of music."

[5] Culture, in this sense, means "selection." Riemann called this selective function of hearing "logical activity." Cf. Gurlitt, p. 12.

[6] For the scientific background of this development, compare my article "Musik, Wissen und Musikwissenschaft," in *Festschrift für Willi Kahl*, Cologne, 1953 (in type script).

[7] E. Straus, *Vom Sinn der Sinne*. Berlin, 1935, pp. 111 ff.

Since phenomena of musical hearing have served to overthrow mechanistic thinking in the theory of sensation, it would be absurd to attempt a clarification of the natural factors of musical hearing through a mechanistic conception of this vital process. This does not mean that knowledge of the nature of hearing gained by mechanistic thinking should be left unnoticed; but we can no longer limit our problem to the reception of tonal stimuli by the organ of Corti and their transmission to the brain,[8] and thus treat hearing in isolation from the total vital process. There is also an obvious absurdity in any attempt to explain away the real phenomenon of hearing, to prove that in reality no such things as hearing and something heard exist, but that we deal only with stimuli, reflexes, and such, which is in the last analysis what every atomistic-mechanistic school of anthropology does.[9] But if we emphasize the admittedly subjective character of the vital process of hearing, and if we start from this as the real and decisive element, then considerable difficulties of a thematic and methodic nature crop up. The mechanist takes an easy way out when he believes he can answer the question of the smallest unit of hearing with his machinery of stimuli, reflexes, and sensations. But matters become more difficult, if it is admitted that no vital process, including hearing, can be explained in mechanistic terms. Thereby sensory perception, rather than sensory reception, moves to the fore in our inquiry as the focal point of the whole problem. For sense impressions, which are really a pure intellectual construction,[10] and all the conclusions based on them have their origin in a mechanistic-atomistic theory of man.[11]

Thus the problem of perception, with its broad theoretic-anthropological background, seems to be the decisive fundamental fact towards which a musicology must be oriented. Perception becomes the basic premise of all music as far as inquiry and methods are concerned. Especially in an initial attempt, such as the one offered here, methodological clarity is an absolute requirement. The standpoint [12] from which we have to approach our problem depends not only on the topic and the inquirer, but also on the

---

[8] This approach covers a large area of G. Révész' *Musikpsychologie*. Bern, 1946.

[9] *Vide* E. Straus, *op. cit.*, Introduction.

[10] *Vide* M. Scheler, *Die Wissensformen und die Gesellschaft. Erkenntnis und Arbeit*, Leipzig, 1926, pp. 356 f., 339 f.

[11] E. Straus, *op. cit.*, Introduction.

[12] Concerning the problem of a standpoint in musicology, compare my article in the *Festschrift* cited above.

basic facts we discover. A whole series of sciences have yielded results, widely dispersed and discovered under the most varied aspects, that are at our disposal as bases and supports, but they were
largely gained by a scientific approach. This highly heterogeneous
material seems, at first glance, to contain nothing that eases
our problem. There seems to be no connecting path from the laws
of reflex action to a Beethoven symphony. And yet, this symphony
as a cultural phenomenon is tied with a thousand threads to the
vital process of hearing. There is a path from the focal point of
perception to the musical work of art as the fruit of hearing, if we
are not satisfied with demonstrating the well-known "objective"
data of hearing and connecting them in a series. We have to inquire further for the significant connection between these data—
a process which modern natural science itself is adopting more and
more.[13] It is obvious that the epistemological and methodological
problem of the strata [14] has to be scrupulously observed, for in the
context of the whole problem a reflex-Gestalt combination ranks as
something entirely different from the simple reflex. Probably the
most difficult question involved in our inquiry is the psycho-
physical problem. The fact that we cannot discuss it thoroughly
here should not be regarded as an evasion. I hardly need to state
that we are not committed here to a primitive psycho-physical
parallelism. But, on the level from which an approach to our problem is at all possible today, it means a great deal to know that in
the case of specific psychic processes quite specific physical ones
also play a part.

The problem of the nature of musical hearing will here be explained from facts ascertained by the sciences of life, and from the
conceptual connections among those facts. Taking this as a starting point, every further differentiation in the cultural problem of
musical hearing as well as in philosophical considerations is possible. It remains to indicate the procedure of discussion: from a distinction between the acoustic mode and the other sensory modalities
we shall proceed to establishing the hierarchy of the senses; from
there we will go on, via general synesthesia, to higher orders. In

[13] Compare G. von Bergmann, *Das Spiel der Lebensnerven und ihrer Wirkstoffe.*
Potsdam, 1947, pp. 12, 24 f.; also, F. J. J. Buytendijk, *Über das Verstehen der
Lebenserscheinungen.* Habelschwerdt, 1925, pp. 29–30.
[14] *Vide* Scheler, *op. cit.,* p. 362; E. Rothacker, *Probleme der Kulturanthro-
pologie,* Bonn, 1948, p. 165 f.

a discussion of hearing as a play-activity we then reach the boundaries of the naturalistic problem. Only beyond these boundaries, with the integration of hearing in the individual personality, do those cultural factors enter into it that determine its status as musical hearing. In other words, from the concept of the acoustic mode we want to penetrate to the functional process of musical perception. During the development of our subject, the necessity of noting the general as well as the particular [15] in each significant step will considerably influence the progress of our speculations.

I. CONCEPT, STRUCTURE, AND RANK OF AUDITORY PERCEPTION

a) *The concept of auditory perception*

Perception connects our inner being with the externality of our "environment," [16] the "world" [17] in which we live. Even the word "perception" [Wahr-nehmung=true-taking] contains something essential: perception [Wahr-nehmung] is not truth in the absolute sense,[18] but that which is taken as true from the very center of an individual being, *i.e.*, something entirely subjective, yet none the less true. But every perception which in itself is not something finished or implicit, but develops from the relation between a person's internal and external world, does not take place on the level of a single sense. To make possible a complete and multiform picture of the "world," the sensory organization, thanks to which we are able to perceive, is differentiated into various senses, and each of these senses captures one or another aspect of the phenomenon, each having its own mode.

What we notice first in the acoustic mode, which is the crucial one for us, is the "sequence" of auditory impressions. Not that

[15] Goethe, *Maximen und Reflexionen*. Krönersche Taschenausgabe, pp. 150–2. The methodological significance of this point of view was the subject of a recent speech by F. Sander: "Goethe und die Morphologie der Persönlichkeit," Nineteenth Congress of the German Society for Psychology, Cologne, 1953.

[16] Vide J. von Uexküll, *Die Lebenslehre* Zürich-Potsdam, 1930.

[17] Cf. for a critical discussion of the concepts of "environment" and "world," A. Gehlen, *Der Mensch*. Bonn, 1950.

[18] V. von Weizsäcker, "Wahrheit und Wahrnehmung," in *Diesseits und jenseits der Medizin*. Stuttgart, 1949.

sequence were not possible in other sensory modalities, as for instance the visual sense, but there we do not find sequence an essential condition. So we may specify: Hearing starts from a sequence which may well fuse into a sort of simultaneous impression; on the other hand, the primary character of other sensory modes— e.g., vision [19]—is a simultaneous impact, which can then issue in a sequence. From this we derive the basic problem of musical hearing. For if hearing is primarily a sequence, i.e., takes place in time, then it can only be felt as movement, and each movement requires not only time but also space. But if a total image is to result, this primary sequence of hearing presumes, first of all, that we are capable of correlating processes which objectively take place at different times, and that we can even in some measure, perceive them as simultaneous.[20] This explains why the physical components of perceptions, including those of hearing, can contribute but little towards our understanding of them.

For, "while physics proceeds from the expressed perception and analyzes its content, corrects it through accurate measurements, and eliminates the subjective element, an experiment in perception [21] takes the opposite approach, from the objective fact, and observes how the sense organ perceives it. The two methods are, in a way, antipodal."

Once the "constitutional gift of antilogical perception," i.e., the ability to apprehend the non-simultaneous as simultaneous, is established, surprising vistas may open in the realms of art to the trained eye, not of the art historian, but of the anthropologist. Thus the physician V. von Weizsäcker can now give reasons why "art is able to show motion in rigid forms," and set up criteria for the evaluation of a work of art that now, suddenly, become obvious: "The greater the artist the more has he been able to express motion in immobility, just as the great mime expresses the timeless, permanent physiognomy of the soul simply by means of motion." [22] This criterion might well be employed in music, too.

If now we place the acoustic mode in the "hierarchy of the senses," which, as L. Székély points out, reaches from the more object-related to the more subject-related sensory perceptions, the quite special

[19] Not in the case of the sense of vibration.
[20] Instructions for experiments are given by Weizsäcker, op. cit., p. 15.
[21] And therefore, to a certain extent, the theory of perception.
[22] Weizsäcker, op. cit., pp. 15, 25.

and significant position of auditory perception in this scale becomes evident. For at the one end of the scale are "the existence and condition [*Dasein und Sosein*] of material objects, at the other, the fact that we feel this way or that. . . . From this it seems clearly to follow that sensory phenomena are ranged between an objective and an emotive extreme."

Beyond their capacity of "not being experienced as affects of a bodily part," (as is the case with taste and temperature experiences) auditory perceptions can become separated from their object, "move to the forefront of experience, become independent, stand and hold attention by themselves, as for instance in music." Since the polarity within the sensory modalities is "not a matter of either-or, but of more or less" (Hornbostel), sensory impressions of both the object-related and the ego-related poles of the hierarchy may appear in hearing.

Modern sensory physiology maintains that "the entire apparatus of perception is a uniformly functioning system. There is no process, be it ever so elementary or complex, which does not take place within the entire organ." As Székély pointed out, the gestalt theory especially has contributed to this recognition.[23] V. von Weizsäcker has certainly given the gestalt concept itself a new and precise formulation in the theory of perception, for it is "no longer an unknown agent, such as the 'whole' or the 'gestalt'" which shapes perception, but "the apparently quite unlimited cooperation in the nervous system of *all* parts during *every* activity. . . ; a principle of general synaesthesia involving all sensory and partially sensory fields . . . Accordingly, there could really be not senses, but only a sensibility, one sense."[24] But this general synaesthesia requires equalizing and connecting functions among the coöperating senses. It becomes apparent now "that brightness in the various sensory fields is not merely an analogy, but is based on a process which underlies all sensory processes."[25] The B(rightness)-excitation is transferred as one of the intermodal partial processes from one

[23] L. Székély, "Über den Aufbau der Sinnesfunktionen," *Zeitschrift für Psychologie*, Vol. 127.

[24] Weizsäcker, "Einleitung zur Physiologie der Sinne," *Handbuch der normalen und pathologischen Physiologie*, Vol. XI.

[25] Székély, *op. cit.*, p. 263. Handschin, however, (*op. cit.*, pp. 408 ff.) voices criticism regarding the question of brightness, yet does "not want to deny thereby . . . an 'intermodal' field, *i.e.*, a field which bridges the several sensory realms." (p. 410.) He finds "a sort of polarity in the 'intermodal.'"

sensory field to others and influences them. In musical hearing, therefore, one should expect not only coöperation of the entire sensory apparatus, but also the participation of intermodal processes.

If hormonal processes can be established as physical concomitants of the B-excitations,[26] then this points to a connection between metabolism, secretion, and perception that will play a special role in our consideration. Since W. Börnstein, like Székely, advances the "very plausible idea . . . that in the transformation of the excitations (as experiments with tonus have shown) the entire muscular apparatus with its active metabolism takes part," one must assume "that the B-reactions, their concomitant secretory processes, and the tonus processes all occur in intimate physiological and functional connection." For "according to the actual circumstances each sensory process is, to use Börnstein's expression, a 'sensory-motor synergy.'"[27]

Thus an objectively comprehensible, essential process is recognized that proves the theory of auditory perception which Plessner developed philosophically. He claims that the realm of sounds reveals the stratum "in which that kind of understanding and motor response lies, whose interaction makes a musical performance possible through the mediating function of the acoustic mode; this is the stratum of deportment and behavior." From this direction Plessner reaches his formulation: "Being musical is nothing else than being master of one's own transport under the influence of tones."[28] This insight will become fruitful for musicology only when we know the conditions for such transport.

The interrelation between hearing and motor response also sheds new light on the problem of motion in musical hearing. If hearing is the perception of a motion in time, then auditory motion can occur only as it has some sort of space at its disposal. Every motion fills space or traverses space. There are, then various kinds of motion and, as we now discover, also various "forms of spatiality."[29] The

---

[26] Székely, *op. cit.*, p. 259. Straus, *op. cit.*, p. 145 (critical).

[27] Székely, *op. cit.*, pp. 260–1.

[28] H. Plessner, "Zur Anthropologie der Musik," *Jahrbuch für Aesthetik und Kunstwissenschaft*, 1951, p. 120. With the concept of "behavior" the initial point of a musicology here becomes apparent.

[29] E. Straus, "Die Formen des Räumlichen." *Der Nervenarzt*, 1930.

hotly disputed question whether tone (or, rather, music) has a spatial character has engendered a famous scientific confusion: for on the one hand, everyone must recognize that music evokes impressions of space, but on the other hand this led at once to an attempt to reduce those impressions to associations.[30] Thus access to the problem was obstructed, and E. Straus has shown that the cause of the misunderstanding was a false conception of space. For "indeed, tone cannot be localized in a single spatial point. This lack of *local* definitiveness probably was the reason for denying the acoustic realm a basic *spatial* existence, which denial, however, is not at all justified."[31] A. Wellek, while he expressly notes the spatial appearances as "immediate phenomenal characteristics of tone,"[32] believes that they must be traced to connections with the organic sensations.

Besides primary temporality, then, primary spatiality and primary motility must be attributed to audial perception. This characterization may be extended to music: music is sounding motion in temporal space. The tension between the equipollent and complementary elements of time, motion, and space is of the greatest importance for the understanding of music[33] and—as we shall see—for its relation to life and historical experience. It integrates the internal and the external, the listener's subjective feeling and objective awareness, into a unity, wherein the impressions and reactions of all the senses, the whole organism, and—to put it cautiously—its entire psycho-intellectual conditions and correla-

[30] *Cf.* E. Straus, *Vom Sinn der Sinne,* esp. p. 251 ff. Handschin is very critical concerning the question of space. He starts from the tone and considers it "wrong track," if "the pitch is not understood as something concretely sensory . . . but is devitalised into a kind of 'spatial point!'" He inclines more toward those "who 'more cautiously' speak of a "spatial analogy.'" *Cf. Der Toncharakter,* pp. 238, 373, and 406 f. But precisely this concept of analogy seems dangerous; the tone, placed in the acoustic spatial form may very well lead an independent existence. Indeed, we may even consider acoustic space a container, a prerequisite for the life of tone.

[31] E. Straus, *Die Formen des Räumlichen,* p. 636. K. v. Durckheim in his "Untersuchungen zum gelebten Raum," (*Neue psychologische Studien,* VI), goes on from there to the cultural problem.

[32] A. Wellek, "Der Raum in der Musik," *Archiv für die gesamte Psychologie,* Vol. 91, p. 401.

[33] The cultural significance of the tonal system and the determinants of a form are not considered at this stage of our problem.

tions, *i.e.*, the whole hearing individual must needs be involved. Thus the dominant position of hearing in the fundamental nature of man is revealed in basic outline.

b) *The place of auditory perception in the human make-up*

Since all data given so far about the nature of auditory perception stem from natural science, they should be confirmed, now that we come to consider the body's equipment for hearing. First of all we must distinguish clearly between "structure" (anatomy) and "performance" (physiology) of the hearing organism, even though both aspects interpenetrate, indeed, condition each other: the structure as a prerequisite for performance, the performance as activated structure.

The make-up [34] of the human body contains the possibilities and limitations of our hearing. According to J. v. Uexküll,[35] the "centrifugal" organic structure of all living creatures can have meaning only in view of a centripetal function, since form and function are closely interwoven. Hence we must consider the conditions for human hearing on the basis of man's bodily structure as a whole.

But it has been proven experimentally that the "blind formative plans" of the separate parts of an embryo are governed by an "organizer," to speak in the terms of H. Spemann, which possesses "an autonomous, active, formative plan." [36] Such autonomy can be meaningful only if the autonomous formative plans are to produce the form for a later autonomous function. Therefore we shall consider the conditions of human hearing, too, in relation to its special character in the autonomy of the total organization of the human body, for the biological principle of "division of labor" stands, from the beginning, "side by side with the principle of centralization as equivalent but of opposite direction." [37]

If we consider the hearing faculty as a whole we notice connections leading from the organ of hearing to distant parts and many organs of the entire body. All these connections go through the

[34] Uexküll, *op. cit.*, p. 24 f., and elsewhere.
[35] On whose work we base this biological consideration.
[36] Uexküll, *op. cit.*, p. 37 ff.
[37] *Cf.* O. Steche, "Arbeitsteilung bei höheren Organismen," *Handbuch der normalen und pathologischen Physiologie*, Vol. I, Berlin, 1925.

brain,[38] whose most important functions, according to V. v. Weizsäcker, are "first the collecting of sensory impressions into perceptions, and then the directing of the voluntary motions to produce actions." [39] It is significant that the bent towards action, the basic concept of anthropological thinking,[40] is already visible in the structural plan of the human being.

W. v. Bechterew succeeded in proving anatomically the direct connections between the visual and auditory radiations within the total system of the sensory organs—whereby, incidentally, the principle of general synaesthesia is reflected in the structural plan [41]— and besides these sensory connections, anatomy also recognizes motor connections, such as the optic-acoustic reflex path, the paths to the extremities, to the genital area.[42] The fact that, in relation to the brain, many of these paths go in two directions, afferent and efferent, increases considerably the functional potentialities implicit in the structural plan. If we consider further that the structural plan of the human organism is attuned to the relationships between the internal and external world of the individual,[43] hearing assumes a considerably more central position which is reflected in its structural localization, than when we consider it from a purely topographic-anatomical point of view.

[38] For the anatomical interrelations, see the work, unsurpassed even today, of L. Edinger, *Einführung in die Lehre vom Bau und den Verrichtungen des Nervensystems* (Leipzig, 1921), although it shows that it was written at a time when the concept of association was still considered more central than today.

[39] Weizsäcker, "Ueber das Nervensystem," *Diesseits und jenseits der Medizin,* p. 39.

[40] *Cf.* Gehlen; also Rothacker, chapter 1.

[41] Recently discovered pathways between the vegetative centers of the diencephalon and the cortex shed new light on the subject; *cf.* E. Kaila, "Physiologische Grundlagen der Psychologie," Katz, *Handbuch der Psychologie.* (But more recent and perhaps more scientific observations by S. Poliak do not bear out Bechterew's findings.—Ed.)

[42] Rauber-Kopsch, *Lehrbuch und Atlas der Anatomie des Menschen,* Vol. iii (Leipzig, 1943), pp. 189, 475 ff.; also H. Rein, *Physiologie des Menschen* (Berlin, 1943), p. 356. Since H. Husmann ("Der Aufbau der Gehörswahrnehmungen," AfMw, 1953) presented us for our purposes with a résumé of the specialized findings of anatomy and physiology, I shall refer to this work in all specific questions.

[43] Uexküll, "Definition des Lebens und des Organismus," *Handbuch der normalen und pathologischen Physiologie,* Berlin 1925, Vol. i, p. 9 f.; also K. Jaspers, *Allgemeine Psychopathologie,* Heidelberg 1946.

If we look at the formal organization of the auditory sphere as an autonomous whole, the strict separation of the individual autonomies within the sphere of hearing becomes immediately evident. Here, as between and within all receptors, it is visible even on an anatomical level. The receptor organ of hearing, like those of the other senses, is quite unequivocally isolated; and also like every sensory organ it has its own nerve tracts which can be clearly differentiated well into the brain. Such a structural arrangement is meaningful only in view of a later function which takes place in the forebrain strictly autonomously and without interference from other sensory stimuli. All the more noteworthy is the fact that in the *organon statoacusticum* two functions are joined, as the medical term indicates. In this purely anatomical, neat separation of the receptors from each other there must be some special significance for later functioning. Still another factor deserves mention: for the observer of the structural plan the unlimited possibilities of combination within the brain, by which the principle of general synaesthesia is prepared and expressed in the structural plan itself, are all the more impressively evinced for the observer by the sharp separation of the autonomous receptor-effector systems.

c) *Hearing as the most central and important sense in the general synaesthetic complex*

The structural plan presents no essential obscurities in regard to the receptors and their conductors to the brain, which are designed to transmit the sensory stimuli Uexküll calls code-signals (*Merkzeichen.*) [43a] But from the anatomical point of view, and especially from the "biological" one introduced by H. Braus, the connections prepared within the brain by the structural plan are more difficult to fathom, and have yet to be discussed in relation to the functions of the "ordinal signals" (*Ordnungszeichen*), from which the localization problem has developed. But this was precisely the question that led to insights which may be decisive for musicology. As shown by the anatomical findings of Börnstein's research on "The Progressive Order of Functions in the Sphere of Hearing," [44] a localization of the auditory function in specific areas of the cortex

---

[43a] Tinbergen (*A Study of Instinct,* Oxford 1951) translates this word as "sign-stimuli," a term that would probably not be acceptable to Reinold.—Ed.

[44] The research was based on brain injuries.

is out of the question.[45] Ustvedt, in his broad studies starting from brain pathology, also comes to the conclusion that "research was led astray . . . by the theory of localization." [46] And yet, the office of the ordinal signals—local, directional, and temporal—which decode the incoming impressions and make orderly perception possible, must be preformed in the structural plan. E. H. Weber, in the middle of the nineteenth century, already viewed the spatial sense as a "general sense"; K. Vierordt extended this concept of a general sense further to the sense of time.[47] The question of ordinal signals and general sense is ripe for anatomical discussion with respect to the organ of hearing, because, according to E. v. Cyon, the structural and functional mechanism of the ordinal signals is to be found in the labyrinth of the ear, the "organ of the mathematical sense for space and time." Starting from Flourens' research, Cyon bases his theory on extensive experiments,—a theory which J. v. Uexküll recently acknowledged, in a very prominent context, as a "brilliant idea." [48]

The first interesting and telling result was "that the nerve centers of the semicircular canals must participate decisively in the formation of the spatial concepts," [49] and furthermore that "the organ of temporal sense is also located in the labyrinth"; and finally, that "by virtue of the directional perception of the semicircular canals, the spatial and temporal qualities of the auditory sense are of much greater importance than those of touch or sight; to these perceptions we owe our power to imagine, or rather to conceive, the infinity of the universe; direction is by its very nature indivisible and unlimited. Thanks to perception of tone and sound, inasfar as they give us a knowledge of numbers,[50] we have an idea of the

[45] W. Börnstein, *Der Aufbau der Funktionen in der Hörsphäre,* Berlin 1930, p. 123.

[46] H. J. Ustvedt, "Ueber die Untersuchung der musikalischen Funktionen bei Patienten mit Gehirnleiden, besonders bei Patienten mit Aphasie," *Acta medica Scandinavica,* Vol. 93, supplement 86, Helsingfors 1937, p. 660. The same volume (pp. 7–60) contains a historical survey of research in localization. Also, from the psychological point of view: J. C. Flügel, *Probleme und Ergebnisse der Psychologie* (Stuttgart 1951), pp. 34–39, and elsewhere.

[47] E. v. Cyon, *Das Ohrlabyrinth als Organ der mathematischen Sinne für Raum und Zeit,* Berlin 1908, pp. 392–3.

[48] Uexküll, *Definition des Lebens und des Organismus,* p. 3.

[49] Cyon, *op. cit.,* p. 161.

[50] Handschin recently pointed out these highly important connections: "The basic correspondence between the tonally comprehensible and the numerically

infinity of time, for the nature of number is such that it can be developed infinitely." From this it can be concluded that "the musical sense and the mathematical sense are functions of the same organ." [51]

Cyon succeeded therefore in giving to Weber's and Vierordt's concept of the general senses a "firm, physiological basis." [52] From there he reached the final conclusion, particularly relevant to our problem, "that the ear is the most important of all our sensory organs." [53]

The significance of this conclusion for musicology and realms beyond musicology becomes evident when we remember what D. Vierordt said about a hundred years ago:

"If a positive answer to the much-discussed question about the origin of temporal perception should ever become possible to science, it would lead to nothing less than the knowledge of the nature and essence of the soul and its interrelation with nervous and muscular activity; [54] for to understand the gradual emergence of the temporal perceptions and cognitions implies that the psyche, from its very first stirrings, constructs genetically" [55]—an approach which should be of the greatest epistemic value in the treatment of music as an art of time.

That such a decisive discovery as the establishment of hearing as man's highest and most essential sense has not been taken up or duly acknowledged either by anatomy, or by sensory physiology, or by psychology, or finally by psychology of music—to say nothing of general musicology—can surprise only one who is not familiar

comprehensible . . . , this correspondence between numerical reality and psychical reality, which appears on a different plane, between the objective and the subjective, appears to us like a miracle." (*Der Toncharakter*, p. 112.) [Note: whereby the special position of the acoustic mode in the scale of the senses becomes further evident, comp. above, p. 269.] Also, W. Wiora, "Der tonale Logos," *Die Musikforschung*, iv, p. 13, remarks: "A fundamental principle of music confronts us here: an unconscious translation from numerical relations to specific sensory qualities is part of its nature (in short, qualification of proportions)."

[51] Cyon, *op. cit.*, pp. 420, 423.

[52] We have thus reached the borderline between the principles of the structural plan and those of the functional plan.

[53] Cyon, *op. cit.*, p. 425.

[54] The connections between the motor-sensory synergy and the "*Gestalt*-sphere" are here envisaged, almost a century before their conceptual establishment.

[55] Cyon, *op. cit.*, pp. 413–14.

with the mechanistic-naturalistic tendencies of scientific development in the nineteenth century. Otologists themselves have but recently begun—as for instance Güttich [56]—to emphasize the crucial position of hearing; and it is noteworthy that this has elicited special praise for Güttich's work.[57] In the era of "separative thinking" [58] in science during the nineteenth century and until far into our times, especially in physiological questions, "description really held the place of honor." [59] But when biology, and with it anatomy and physiology, turned to the study of form and the living whole, as for instance in Uexküll's theory of life and of the organism, Cyon's work was reinstated in its proper scientific place. Cyon's conclusion that the ear is the most important of all sensory organs is furthermore affirmed by research in part conducted from an entirely different approach. It was especially by M. Schneider's work that the central significance of the ear in the world-image of aboriginal cultures has been brought to notice, and that musicology was reminded of the important position that hearing, as the only sense which can beget understanding, occupies in Chinese philosophy.[59a]

II. AUDITORY PERCEPTION AS A VITAL FUNCTION

a) *Its place in the functional system of man*

The potentialities of the action-pattern of the organism derive from the structural pattern.[60] Action in the biological sense presupposes an impulse and a goal, and lies, as it were, between the two.[61] Energy is therefore needed which, when released, provides the impulse, and a quality which directs it towards an autonomously

[56] A. Güttich, *Kurzgefasstes Lehrbuch der Erkrankungen des Ohres.* . . . Stuttgart 1948, p. 1.

[57] Theissing, *Zentralblatt f. Hals-, Nasen- und Ohrenheilkunde,* Vol. 41, (1951), p. 337.

[58] *Vide* Sedlmayr, *Verlust der Mitte.*

[59] Buytendijk, *op. cit.,* p. 14.

[59a] In what sense Chinese culture can be called "aboriginal" is not altogether clear.—Ed.

[60] *Cf.* Uexküll, *Die Lebenslehre.*

[61] The physical concept of action lies on an entirely different plane and does not concern us here.

attainable goal. This requirement is met by a principle that is known in physiology to govern the activities of muscle and sensory cells, the principle of "specific energy," [62] which clearly indicates, once more, the ineluctable need of an "environment" for every act of the organism.

Like Uexküll, we now distinguish within each sense two autonomous factors that condition and complement each other: the primary receptor organ that receives the stimuli and the secondary organ which further processes them.[63] But the fact that all nerve conductors have double tracts and become exceedingly complicated, especially in the brain, raises the problem of conducting the stimuli surely and reliably from receptor to effector organ. Nature solves this task by the principle of inherent tonus in every ganglion cell. Since this has its effect on the neighboring cells, too, it creates "within the individual ganglion cells, . . . a tonus differential which depends on the [absolute] intensity and is decisive for the direction in which the stimulus is conducted within the network of nerves." By this tonus principle the threshold of the autonomous cells may be either raised or lowered, and thus by "artfully placing the limens in accord . . . the entire nervous system becomes a uniformly functioning whole.[64]

This highly differentiated system, however, with its thousands of possible permutations is for the time being nothing but an instrument of potential action. If a concrete performance is to result, a higher directive must control it.

Sensory physiology, therefore, begins by collating all the uniformities of reflex combinations in which place, manner and form of the stimulus [65] collaborate and where, thanks to our motile imagination (*Bewegungsphantasie*),[66] further enriched by extraneous sensory symbols, "perception and motion" from all departments of sense fuse into unitary "realms of gestalt" (*Gestaltkreise*).[67] But if the imaginal context of an isolated perception is drawn into the greater context of a goal-directed action, then a new principle, rooted in the highest centers of the total organism, goes into effect.

[62] *Cf.* Uexküll, *op. cit.*, p. 69.
[63] *Ibid.*, pp. 77, 81.
[64] *Ibid.*, pp. 77, 81.
[65] *Cf.* Weizsäcker, "Reflexgesetze," *Handbuch der normalen und pathologischen Physiologie*, Vol. x, pp. 37–43.
[66] *Vide*, Gehlen.
[67] *Cf.* Weizsäcker, *Der Gestaltkreis*. Leipzig, 1940.

In this connection Uexküll introduced a new concept, which for him, with his eye on the animal world, opened a way to the understanding of instinctive action, but for us, dealing as we do with human beings, must assume a wider and at the same time more neutral meaning. Uexküll speaks of "impulse melodies." [68] These resolve the goal of the action pattern "into a series of impulses that are just as meaningfully connected as the tones of a melody." [69]

If we now turn from the general principles of the action pattern to the internal arrangements of the specialized hearing apparatus, *i.e.*, the organ of perception and action, we see the sensory stimuli acting upon the cortex as "code signals" (*Merkzeichen*) to build up a "code-world" (*Merkwelt*).[70] In regarding the auditory process from our biological angle, we find that our attention shifts from the objective, physicalistic measurement of the stimuli received by the ear to the act of noting (*Merkung*), that activity which the excitation of the peripheral organ elicits, via the sensory nerve, from the decoding organ.

If the code world is to serve man in his totality, it must have content and order. The code signals therefore fall into two main groups: the material signals (*Inhaltszeichen*), which are subdivided into various "related spheres" of the particular sensory qualities, and the ordinal signals, among which we distinguish three kinds: signals of place, direction, and instant.[71] Now the two main tasks that Weizsäcker assigns to sensory psychology as a biological discipline become apparent: first, "to correlate the stimulus-excitation process with the content of our perception" [72]—the "correlation problem"—and secondly, "since at any point. . . . the individual qualities of all spheres may meet without disturbing each other," [73] "to classify and determine the contents of our perception; whether it be done by using an anatomical, physiological, psychological, phenomenological, or any other point of view which suits the purpose," [74]—the "classification problem." Posed in this manner, the issue can be attacked at just that decisive point where the trans-

[68] Their relationship to "conations" in McDougall's sense should be pointed out.

[69] Uexküll, *Die Lebenslehre*, p. 83.

[70] *Ibid.*, p. 89.

[71] *Idem.*

[72] Weizsäcker, *Introduction* . . . , p. 57.

[73] Uexküll, *Die Lebenslehre*, p. 90.

[74] Weizsäcker, *op. cit.*, pp. 57–8.

formation of the acoustic vibrations begins, which leads to that complete disguise in which, as E. Kurth remarked, they enter our consciousness. This "contradiction between being and appearance," which becomes evident when we oppose external, objective measurements to internal, subjective sensory perception, must be considered "not an incongruity, but a condition of life," [75] as Weizsäcker points out. If we first try to examine the limits of the auditory realm from the subject's point of view, we find that the so-called threshold values, seen from inside, have quite another character than when they are viewed from outside. This reduces to absurdity the concept of an absolute threshold, for it becomes evident "that for the determination of such thresholds not only the properties of the stimuli (intensity, extensiveness, duration) are of importance, but also the condition in which the person happens to be." [76] The stimulus, therefore, is correlative with the excitability [77] of the subject, of the individual. Let us further keep in mind "that a state of complete nothingness cannot definitely be established, but rather that even in the absence of external stimuli an 'internal' stimulus, perhaps a continuous state of excitation which corresponds to metabolism in quiescence, is always present. The transition to a noticeable external stimulus would then constitute a differential threshold; an absolute threshold would, accordingly, be nothing but the differential threshold during the transition from internal to external stimuli." [78]

With Hering, Freud, Pikler, *et al.* we can thus see in each stimulus a disturbance that breaks through the stimulus protection, and each process of perception becomes an "overcoming of an additional excitation." [79] Again we find the interaction between the internal and external that Weizsäcker summed up in the bold dictum: "the 'world' is a living organism." [80]

The problem of brightness leads deeper into the amazing differentiation of these relations. Börnstein was able to show "the regular dependence of exactly corresponding tonus shifts in the musculature

[75] Weizsäcker, *Ueber das Nervensystem*, p. 45.

[76] Weizsäcker, *Einleitung* . . . , p. 14.

[77] *Vide* Ph. Broemser, "Erregbarkeit, Reiz- und Erregungsleitung," *Handbuch der normalen und pathologischen Physiologie*, Vol. I, Berlin, 1925.

[78] Weizsäcker, *Einleitung* . . . , p. 14.

[79] Székély, *op. cit.*, p. 260.

[80] Weizsäcker, *Ueber das Nervensystem*, p. 46.

on acoustic stimuli, and to ascribe the direction of the shift in tonicity to brightness and darkness reactions, respectively. On the basis of this observation and others made in pathological cases, Goldstein assumes 'that the physiological functional link between the visual and the motor apparatus forms only part of a much more extensive relation which at least connects all sensory apparatuses with the motor apparatus.'" [81]

From all this it is plain that to describe the field of hearing, with its constantly changing field of action—and the other sensory areas as well—by giving the usual data of frequency range and dynamic scope, is not telling us much. Optimum hearing, the range of the field of hearing, its close-meshed texture, and the width of the threshold for volume, have been thoroughly invesigated experimentally, and the results are easily accessible. Depending on the method used in measuring, the investigators have attributed to the sense of hearing either the highest acuity, or a sharpness equal to that of sight. Although opinions on this question still differ today, it should be manifest that hearing has the finest temporal threshold of all the senses.[82] Other data also support the thesis that the organ of hearing, as we have seen, is not only the most important, but also the most finely differentiated of all sensory organs.[83]

It remains to consider the special conditions of the auditory function in music. The structure of the auditory realm shows, both in structure and effect, a decline of efficiency towards its extreme limits; which is readily explained by the purely biological meaning of the senses.[84] For man, the tonal range of speech is biologically the most important part of the whole field of audition; therefore the functional limitation has an entirely positive reason, because it excludes possible peripheral interference. While almost all ani-

---

[81] Székely, p. 260.

[82] Cyon, p. 409. Handschin (p. 392) points out the remarkable fact that "we can speak of precise perceptual measurements only in the acoustic, not the optic field."

[83] I am aware of the problem incurred by comparing various sensory functions; *cf.* M. Gildemeister, "Hörschwellen und Hörgrenzen," *Handbuch der normalen und pathologischen Physiologie*, Vol. XI, where M. Wien's investigations, too, are examined and confirmed. But Güttich, p. 18, attributes a much more differentiated functional capacity to the ear than to the eye.

[84] It is, of course, nonsense to designate our ability to hear tones as a "luxury," as E. Jentsch does in *Musik und Nerven*. Wiesbaden, 1904, vol. I, p. 7. *Cf.* by way of contrast Cyon, pp. 417–18.

mals are incapable of producing pure tones or musical sounds, because the "sound stimuli that absolutely dominate the 'acoustic
world'—in animate as well as in inanimate nature—are noises" [85]
man, endowed with speech, finds it necessary to differentiate tonal
pitches and qualities. The special conditions at the periphery of the
audible range, however, open the way to Köhler's studies of pitch.
Börnstein has summed up the main results, to the effect that "perception of pitch is dependent on certain conditions—of the given
stimuli and the receiving individual—which are narrower than those
for hearing in general." [86] If pitches cannot be distinguished, there
are still various degrees of brightness amongst the "acoustic factors
of perception." The degrees of brightness are relevant to our question in three respects: as elements in general synesthesia, for the
production of a sensory-motor synergy, and for the differentiation
of musical hearing from human hearing in general.

b) *The participation of three general factors*
in the hearing process

Every biological function is partly determined by three general
factors. First, it entails an expenditure of forces that have to be replaced. Furthermore, as we shall see, biological activity has a constitutive character in the whole course of life, at least up to a certain goal-point. Finally, each act of a living subject takes place in
an environment which has effective forces of its own and can therefore influence the act.

The equalization and reconstruction of the used-up energies is
attributed to the "mechanizers of the function." [87] For us the question of fatigue [88] is of special importance; not so much its physiological genesis as its function in the total functional pattern. Fatigue
means first of all a warning signal, indicating that the forces re-

[85] Börnstein, p. 18 f.; but this deals also with the world of sound for song birds.
[86] Börnstein, p. 37.
[87] Uexküll, *Die Lebenslehre*, pp. 63–4.
[88] Titles from the literature of fatigue: *Arbeit und Ermüdung*, Berlin, 1927;
Bornemann, ed., *Ermüdung: ihre Erscheinungsformen und Verhütung*, Lüneburg,
1953; A. Dürig, "Die Theorie der Ermüdung," in Atzler, *Körper und Arbeit*,
Handbuch der Arbeitsphysiologie, Leipzig, 1927; M. Offner, *Die geistige Ermüdung*, Berlin, 1928; P. Plaut, *Handwörterbuch der medizinischen Psychologie*,
p. 131 f.

quired for a complete performance are not available. But since the nature of fatigue "is not only of a physiological nature, but has its psychological origins as well," [89] a conceptual distinction has to be made between physiological fatigue and psychological weariness,[90] even though this separation can not yet be carried out experimentally. Hence a sensory stimulus, for instance an auditory impression, may fail for two reasons to produce a perfect excitation: [91] it may encounter a nervous system which, through fatigue, is limited in its capacity to react, or one which by reason of weariness is not ready for full reaction—two basically different situations. It is significant that "complicated and little practiced activities, more dependent on volition and requiring more attention," [92] tire soonest, whereas practiced activities, and especially the so-called automatisms, resist fatigue longest. But since the notion prevails "that fatigue is first of all fatigue of the central nervous system," [93] it is relevant that physical labor, too, leads to fatigue of the higher and highest functions; a fact which will open far-reaching vistas in the field of musical hearing to a later sociology of music.[94] The great resistance of the peripheral nerves to fatigue [95] confirms their extraordinary biological importance, but it does not change the graduated fatigability of the central organs. If it appears "that the finesse and exactitude of a motor performance is diminished if any part of the mechanism fails because of fatigue" [96] —so-called combination disturbances—this corroborates still further the highly differentiated play of tonus in the sensory-motor synergy, and the "unity of perception and motion" in the "imaginal realm" (*Gestaltkreis*) which is of such great importance to the problem of musical hearing.

It remains to be mentioned that the law: the more vital the func-

[89] Plaut, p. 131.

[90] *Cf.* H. Betke, "Arbeit und Ermüdung, Ermüdungsausgleich, Erholung," *Arbeit und Ermüdung*, Berlin, 1927, pp. 29–30.

[91] *Cf.* Griesbach, *Arbeit und Ermüdung*, pp. 86–7.

[92] Offner, p. 6.

[93] E. Sachsenberg, "Ergebnisse wissenschaftlicher Forschung auf dem Gebiet der Ermüdung . . . ," *Arbeit und Ermüdung*, p. 61.

[94] I discussed these relationships with reference to the situation in German musical life during the nineteen-twenties (unpublished).

[95] *Cf.* Offner, p. 128.

[96] G. Atzler, "Physiologie der Ermüdung," *Arbeit und Ermüdung*, p. 6.

tion, the lower the fatigability, is, under certain conditions, count-
ered by an equalizing process, because after fatigue has taken
place the "intoxication" of fatigue can delay its effects for a while
and veil its existence.[97]

At Uexküll's "critical point" between the formative and the active
periods,[98] the organism is only the *potential* of a function; its function as a true life process begins only when it enters into a vital
relationship with its environment. At the end of its essentially extra-
environmental formation period the organism must therefore seek
contact, step by step, with its environment to be able to realize its
possibilities. This establishment of contact between the organism
and the environment is largely the task of the senses that participate decisively in the construction of a so-called "historical basis
for reaction" [99] of the organism. "The nervous system, endowed
with a historical basis for reaction has . . . a currently determined
structure, but can change it step by step according to external influences." [100]

It deserves notice that the earliest reactions of an infant are to
auditory stimuli—a further proof of the central position of hearing in the organism—and the "kicking" in response to the auditory
stimuli points once more to the close connection between perception
and motion. Bases of reaction, however, have meaning only where the
possibility of learning is provided. But there is no learning without
practice. So the principle of practice completes the providential
plan that is given in the organism. Practice makes the establishment
of the contact with the environment quicker and more differentiated,
because the reaction periods become shorter. Thereby the energy
for action is more economically utilized. It is true that practice also
fixates the reactions, so the "mobile, undirected, youthful, often
playful element" [101] in the reaction is lost. Finally, the principle
of practice is able to compensate to a certain extent for that of
fatigue; it can even circumvent fatigue because it makes actions

[97] *Cf.* Offner, pp. 6–7. Marginally the investigations should be mentioned here
that were made, especially around the turn of the century, of the connections
between hearing and the cardiac and respiratory activities. Bibliography by
Jentsch, Vol. II, pp. 18 ff.

[98] Uexküll, *Die Lebenslehre,* pp. 59 ff., 10 ff.

[99] *Idem.*

[100] Uexküll, *Definition* . . . , p. 14.

[101] Buytendijk, *Wesen und Sinn des Spiels,* Berlin, 1934, p. 22. Here the problem of play enters our investigation.

possible "with a lesser expenditure of energy, often by increasing exclusion of the central nervous system." [102]

Since the organism becomes fully active in all its psychological and physiological capacities only when its contact with the environment is established, and it has become, in some sense, so conjoined with its environment that they are like one living thing together, we have to shift our point of view in further pursuit of our question; we can no longer center our ideas round the physical organism, but must base them on the bi-polar interplay between subject and environment.

For man, as a cultural being, the problem of "injustment" (*Einpassung*), as Uexküll calls these processes,[103] acquires wider meaning. But since the principles of action which nature has evolved for man have an effect which transcends the biological, it seems from the human point of view almost as if the very purpose of our biological endowments were to make these super-biological effects possible.[104] And here we come to a point that borders on the problem of musical hearing. In this direction, we can pursue the nature of that faculty further only if we consider concrete historical situations historically as well as psychologically and socially. But at this stage of the naturalistic problem another question, important in relation to musical hearing, has to be made explicit. Its premises, however, already touch on cultural problems: the question of the abnormal [105] fields of hearing. As in so many cases, pathology here gives us an insight into systems that would otherwise remain obscure, but which are of great importance on the cultural level of musical hearing.

Defects in hearing appear when the organ of hearing itself or organs that participate decisively in the function of hearing are overloaded, or exposed to loads which they were never meant to carry. Aside from brain diseases, such as tumors, inflammations, degenerations and vascular processes [106] of various origins, occupa-

[102] Ebbinghaus, cited by B. Kern, *Wirkungsformen der Uebung*, Münster, 1930, p. 45.

[103] *Cf.* Uexküll, "Die Einpassung," *Handbuch der normalen und pathologischen Physiologie*, Vol. I.

[104] *Cf.* J. Ortega y Gasset, *Betrachtungen über die Technik*, Stuttgart, 1949, especially pp. 58 ff.

[105] For the concept of the "normal" *vide* Jaspers, *Allgemeine Psychopathologie*, pp. 236 f.

[106] These we cannot consider further here.

tional damage is the most frequent.[107] Particularly damage by noise
and by chemical poisons points towards certain social structures
operative in those whose hearing is impaired; and these same structures necessarily engender others that have significance for otological
aspects of musicality.[108] But we know "nothing so far . . . about
the true extent of occupational damage to hearing" [109]—to say nothing about the defects of hearing in general—for many who have
hearing defects are not aware of them; and, what is of equal importance, the measurements of hearing defects that are put on
record are made from an occupational and not a musical standpoint.[110]

If we ask what is the influence of impaired hearing on the auditory
field, we must differentiate between central hearing defects and
peripheral ones, although their effects often overlap. Damage to
the peripheral organs lead first of all to a narrowing of the boundaries of the acoustic field, and only secondarily to a reduction of
the range for distinctions between loud and soft; for central hearing damage, Börnstein's "law of concentric narrowing" holds true.
This says: "When a part of the acoustic cortex is damaged . . .
the remainder takes over the function of the whole, but with reduced effectiveness, according to a certain principle. The . . . biologically most important tonal range . . . is least affected." [111]
The essential fact about the consequences of all aural injuries is

[107] For occupational damage see: Beck and Holtzmann, "Lärmarbeit und Ohr,"
Arbeit und Gesundheit, 10, Berlin, 1929; O. Glogau, "Die Schädigungen des
Gehörs und der Atmung in amerikanischen Fabrikbetrieben," *Das österreichische
Sanitätswesen,* 29, 1917; O. Mauthner, "Gehörorgan und Beruf," *Würzburger
Abhandlungen,* Vol. xiv, 1914; M. Nadoleczny; "Gehörorgan und Berufswahl,"
Veröffentlichungen des deutschen Vereins für Volkshygiene, 2, 1904; A. Peyser,
"Ueber Berufskrankheiten des Gehörorgans in Sozialhygiene und Sozialversiche-
rung," *vide* title Glogau; O. Voss, "Berufs- (Gewerbe-) Krankheiten des Ge-
hörorgans," *vide* title Glogau. Psychological supplement: G. Anton, "Zur Psy-
chologie der Schwerhörigen," *Zeitschrift für Psychologie,* Vol. 127.

[108] For these relations the documents of social and health insurances ought to
be interesting to a certain extent. In another place I discussed the historical
significance of these facts in our modern technological world and their effects
on the musical development of recent times, considered from the social point
of view.

[109] Peyser, p. 90. I am not aware of more recent investigations of the problem
which may be assumed not to have changed very much.

[110] How far the methods of modern audiometry might be of use here does not
enter into this context.

[111] Börnstein, p. 120.

that the "lowering of the upper limit plays a relatively small role compared to the general impairment of hearing." [112] For with the narrowing of the field of hearing a retrenchment of the highest functions of the sphere of hearing takes place. Börnstein calls them "acoustic image functions," or "superior functions"; they constitute the typically human propensity for hearing and understanding language (another proof of the pre-eminence of hearing is the incomparably graver psychological effect of deafness than, for instance, of blindness [113]) and for hearing intonation and music, while the "noise functions," being "basic acoustic functions," are retained longest.[114] From all this we see clearly the "tendency towards preservation of the biologically most important organic system,[115] and Weizsäker's principle that "we are physiologically incapable of becoming fragments." [116]

III. THE LISTENER'S ENCOUNTER WITH
MUSIC IN THE GAME OF AUDITION

a) *On the evolution of the world of musical hearing*

Having outlined the purely biological premises of hearing, we now turn, at the periphery of the naturalistic problem, to the evolution of the world of musical hearing as a life problem. In order to be able to place hearing in a relation to music in general, we must first of all project the auditory function into time-space, since any form of music can be realized and received only as temporal passage. A psychical time-space, of course.[117] Now the cardinal function of musical hearing is to perceive forms in a mental time-space. But how is this possible, if these gestalt qualities are not previously known in any way to the perceiving subject? Here we touch upon the famous struggle between the nativists and the empiricists, to which our anthropological point of view gives a new and, if we we may say so, more fruitful turn. Köhler has convincingly proven

---

[112] Beck-Holtzmann, p. 15.

[113] *Cf.* G. Anton.

[114] *Cf.* Börnstein, p. 109.

[115] *Idem.*, p. 120.

[116] Cited after Börnstein, p. 109.

[117] The problem of "psychical time," which should be of great importance in musicology, cannot be discussed here.

that the "gestalt problem in perception . . . does not permit an empirical reduction." [118] Scheler pointed out the dependence of the "space-time gestalten" of all sensory qualities on physical constitution.[119] In this way the nativist-empiricist problem shifts from the generally barren either-or issue to that of interdependence.

Thus it would have to be ascertained how far the efficacy of the "preëstablished gestalten" [120] extends. This means drawing the boundary between native constitution and psycho-socially conditioned development. Now, Scheler has pointed out that "preëstablished experience of gestalt exerts an influence, and indeed a very powerful one, on later gestalt experience." According to Scheler, "Gestalt experience, like the experience of existential form in general . . . tends to become 'functionalized', and then determines in considerable measure what further gestalt experience will be possible. . . . This 'experience' does not explain gestalt perception in general, but can only refer the more complicated gestalt perceptions back to simple laws of image formation—and, in fact, to laws which are common *ab initio* to the physical and psychological realm, *i.e.*, are of a genuinely ontological nature." [121] From this Scheler concludes, first of all, that gestalt experience cannot be explained by "adaptation." [122] But it further appears that perception is "a dissociation process, not an association process" [123] which occurs when "preëstablished gestalten" are aroused by environmental stimuli. Or, as Jaensch characterized the developing refinement of perception: "The elements, insofar as they are ascertainable at all in the intended sense, result far more from the disintegration of a concrete totality, than contrariwise, in that a totality should arise from a combination of original elements." [124] The more refined the reaction to current environmental stimuli becomes, by virtue of the potential dissociations, the greater will be the danger that the perception of gestalt will dissolve. At a certain stage of the contact between the inner and the outer world the principle of "inhibition" becomes operative, to the effect that impressions

[118] Quoted by Scheler in *Erkenntnis und Arbeit*, p. 378.

[119] *Ibid.*, pp. 372–78–9; for the concept of "space-time images": Uexküll, *Die Lebenslehre.*

[120] *Idem.*

[121] Scheler, *op. cit.*, p. 378.

[122] To be carefully distinguished from "adjustment" as Uexküll uses it.

[123] Scheler, *op. cit.*, p. 412.

[124] Quoted by Scheler, p. 413.

no longer need to be flashed directly to the motor system, but may be transformed into kinetic imagery.[125] While the infant still reacts to every tonal stimulus with movement of the whole body, an older child reacts in a more differentiated and inhibited manner, and the adult for the most part only with "inner," invisible and outwardly inhibited movement.

In debating the principles of gestalt experience, however, our problem is complicated by a supervening factor, which is, to put it quite neutrally, an unidentified, driving force in a psychical and vital process. As soon as we admit that man himself participates in the shaping of perception, and perception, as Scheler points out, holds a crucial place in the theory of cognition,[126] we have to inquire for the central and directing forces of perception. The concept of "drive" has many facets, and is looked upon with prejudice in many quarters. Let us rather speak with Scheler quite generally of a stress in all animate being, to express only the dynamic principle that we have encountered several times before in the discussion of such concepts as dissociation, inhibition, and autonomous shaping of stimuli. Although I cannot enter into the polemics over the fine shades of meaning given to the terms instinct and drive, it should be pointed out that in the most divergent lines of psychology and the biological sciences there is general agreement that only a dynamic psychology and biology can do justice to the dynamic forces of life.[127]

By giving direction to our human drives the spiritual and active pattern of an individual personality develops between the poles of preëstablished constitution and gestalt experience, dissociation and inhibition.[128] In these variable, unfolding tendencies and attitudes the field of audition, too, is involved. But here we reach the borderline between the naturalistic and the cultural problems implicit in musical hearing, for above the naturalistic level we no longer deal with a field of hearing, but only with the world of hear-

[125] In regard to "inhibition," special emphasis on ethnological aspects, Scheler, pp. 435 ff.; *cf.* also Gehlen, likewise in regard to motile imagination.

[126] *Cf.* the proof in *Erkenntnis und Arbeit.*

[127] The various orientations of psychoanalysis and gestalt-psychology, as well as the "hormic" psychology of McDougall proceed from the dynamic principle. *Cf.* Buytendijk, *Ueber das Verstehen der Lebenserscheinungen,* pp. 20 ff., 30. The author emphasizes the importance of "biological foundations" in psychological and sociological fields, too.

[128] *Cf.* McDougall, *Aufbaukräfte der Seele,* Stuttgart, 1947. [*Energies of Men.*]

ing of the individual, who makes his selections from the naturally given conditions and possibilities of the auditory field, and thereby creates something new: the world of musical hearing of a historically situated human being.

b) *Introduction of the play concept into our study*

Between the poles of preëstablished constitution, gestalt experience, dissociation, and inhibition directed by the forces of human impulse, lies the play realm [128a] of musical perception: the highest form of organization in the field of hearing, and its crowning achievement. I am using the term play realm consciously, for the problem that now emerges, from the purely biological view of musical perception as a progressive event, *i.e.*, as a process, is that of play. For it will presently appear that musical hearing is a play between acoustic stimuli and the entire scope of gestalt experience derived from the perceptual and motor world of the perceiving individual. Again we are confronted with general synesthesia and the laws of gestalt—but this time on the highest organizational level of hearing, namely that of musical perception.

The defining characteristic of play, from the bio-physiological point of view, is its peculiar quality of motion. Buytendijk has given us a comprehensive study of the relations between play and motion. Starting with the assumption that play "comes out of life itself," he holds that "it behooves the biologist, even more than the psychologist, to interpret this wonderful process." [129] Therefore Buytendijk starts with the vital conditions of play, much as I did with those of musical hearing, and he finds its most essential condition to be motion. Since the problem of motion has already been recognized as one of the main factors in the structure of musical hearing, important points of contact may be expected to exist between hearing and play. Buytendijk started with "juvenile" motion, *i.e.*, the stage in which all possibilities of motion are still open; in the "undirectedness" of such motility and in the "drive towards motion" he recognized two main characteristics of youthfulness, which, by the way, is not necessarily restricted to a particular age.[130] It is "obvious

[128a] Reinold's word is *das Spielfeld;* but since the literal translation "play-field" means what in German is called *das Sportfeld,* "play realm" seemed the best choice.—Ed.

[129] Buytendijk, *Wesen und Sinn des Spiels,* pp. 11, 24, 62.

[130] *Idem.*

that all games are carried out through motions, and that therefore these are not only means, but essential parts of the play activity." [131] In order to be "playful" [132] the motions have to be light and also largely incalculable,[133] which is possible only within the realm of time–space. We now encounter the principle of inhibition in a different connection, for every fixation of motion is play-inhibiting.[134] Even in the play of children a "functional change" takes place through "fixating processes," and "one of these changes is represented by the transition from play to sport." [135] One more thing: in play, too, inhibition has the effect of turning real bodily motion into "virtual motion." [136] Herewith we have reached the point of contact between play and perception. As Buytendijk notes—and after our discussion this is indeed obvious—the "various senses . . . are not of equal value for purposes of play, and they have, moreover, different functions in the dynamism of bodily motion. Sound perception not only elicits motion (real and virtual), but also creates, in this unity of perception and motion,[137] a dynamic time image which likewise has no tendency toward closure.[138] And in line with Plessner's "unity of the senses," Buytendijk arrived at "the assumption of a conformity between musical experience and vital dynamism which is . . . most clearly demonstrated in playing music." [139] But in play each motion assumes a peculiar character, that becomes visible in the relation between music and dance. E. Straus distinguished between motion "through space" and dance motion "in space." [140] Motion through space presupposes primary

---

[131] *Idem.*

[132] On "The Concept of Play and Expressions for it in Language," see J. Huizinga, *Homo ludens* (Cologne, n.d.), pp. 45–74, and Buytendijk, *Spiel*, pp. 18–21.

[133] This makes for a peculiar connection in the play of musical hearing with the "fore-hearable." *Cf.* Plessner, *Zur Anthropologie . . .* , pp. 117–8.

[134] This fact will prove of great socio-psychological importance in the cultural problem of musical hearing.

[135] Buytendijk, *Spiel*, p. 48. Here, too, certain broad outlines of the cultural problem show up.

[136] *Cf.* Buytendijk, *Spiel*, p. 62, for virtual motion, which, next to the principle of "tension," furnishes (perhaps unconsciously) the basis for Kurth's psychology of music; though it is treated here from a different point of view.

[137] Buytendijk, before the formulation of Weizsäcker's concept of the "sphere of the image," here introduced this concept practically into his analysis.

[138] Buytendijk, *Spiel*, pp. 60, 130.

[139] *Idem.*

[140] Straus, *Formen des Räumlichen*, p. 647.

directedness towards a goal, *i.e.* precisely that which robs play of
its characteristic. Motion in space, however, creates the sphere of
play and also that of musical hearing. Straus also made a further
point, namely: that every experience involves two basic kinds of perception: the pathetic and the gnostic, being seized, and seizing.[140a]
In the play realm of musical hearing, however, gnosis is possible
only through pathos; this, perhaps, is the highest form of being
seized, for we can be seized without arriving through it at gnosis,
at conceiving.[141]

c) *Musical hearing as a game of audition*

If we now conclude our reflections on the conditions of musical
hearing as a play of and with sonorous motion in a time-space, by
considering the play realm of this play and its process as something
natural, and not yet determined by the traits of a cultural situation, we shift our methodological position. So far, our basic image
was that of man, from which we derived all the premises of musicality; but now we turn our attention to the play between the hearing individual and music; [142] for "playing means . . . not only that
someone plays with something, but also, that something plays with
the player," [143] which is a mutual affair.

Two questions arise. First, what music demands of its human
partner, and secondly, what man expects of music in this game.

Because the play between music and the hearer has a spatio-
temporal form, we can—by analogy [144]—treat it as four-dimensional;
and we shall construct the four-dimensional space-time of this
auditory play step by step.

If we consider musical hearing a game of and with sonorous
motion, then both partners in this game must first of all demand
mobility of one another, and—as will be shown—approximately

[140a] In German, *Ergriffenwerden* and *Ergreifen;* the latter is surreptitiously
changed to *Begreifen,* "conceiving."—Ed.

[141] *Op. cit.,* p. 639 ff. Only from this premise is the old argument, whether
music appeals to the emotion or to the intellect, possible. The narrowness of
an either-or in this question becomes obvious. One is more often inclined to
consider music as an emotional art, because the emotional connections are
more apparent than the cognitive ones. Here a second important relation is
already hinted at, namely that of music to theology. *Cf.* E. Schlink, *Zum
theologischen Problem der Musik,* Tübingen, 1945.

[142] This refers also to creative "inward" listening.

[143] Buytendijk, *Spiel,* p. ·117.

[144] *Cf.* A. Wellek, *Der Raum in der Musik,* p. 114.

the same degree of mobility. The listening partner must participate in the process of musical motion, and he must be able to adjust himself to it in leading the game. Since, for the auditory partner, this depends on specific physio-psychological conditions, a true hearing-game can come off only between music and a listener of approximately the same experience in motion [145] and the same will for motion. Each musical work has its own field of motion with a certain spatial expanse which contains innumerable possibilities of motion and which is at the same time a field of tensions, with ultimate limits of tonal as well as dynamic gradations. Within the listener's auditory realm, only a certain field is actually available to him. But to what extent is it available, in any given individual case, for actual processes of motion? That depends on his motor constitution, his vital and dynamic experience. Here, too, the ultimate limits have to be distinguished from the tension pattern within the field.[146]

Let us add to the three dimensions of the play realm the fourth one, namely the duration of the game, for the play realm as a field of motion can be realized only as a space-time interval. It must be surveyable by the partner, and surveyed by the player. This problem of form in the game, which is the real issue here, exists for both partners: for the music as well as for the auditor. Though we may ignore the form-and-content problem (despite any new facet it might show) with regard to music, we cannot but meet it when we turn our attention to the listener. The peculiarity of our perception, which I remarked at the outset, namely that phenomena which are actually not simultaneous can be integrated into lines of motion or even can symbolize states, is presupposed by any game between man and music, too. Tracing dynamic patterns in a space-time field, patterns which, in music or anything else, move toward an uncertain destination (which is truly playful,) [147] requires a psychological and purely physical tension that exceeds the duration of the auditory game. Psychologically it is linked with the "enthusiasm" with which the listener approaches the game, gives himself up to it, aspires to it and sustains it. This "aspiration" is deeply grounded in the texture of the soul and in the "attitudes" of the audio-partners, and sets off a whole "activity sequence" which

[145] This gives access to the theoretical comprehension of interpretation.

[146] Starting-point for a sociological discussion.

[147] For the problem of "uncertainty" in music, *cf.* Plessner, *Zur Anthropologie der Musik*, pp. 117 f.

we, like McDougall, may call "conations" or "conative unit." [148]
From the physical point of view the tension of the listening partner
depends primarily on his physical condition, and most directly his
momentary condition. Fatigue, above all, may act as a play-in-
hibitor because it excludes the higher intellectual functions or slows
them down and, as we have seen, robs the interplay between perception and internal motility of its brilliance as well as of its precision. There is, indeed, also a form of fatigue that leads to play.
This is "not exhaustion, but satiation, tension, or weakness of motive.
Then playing really affords recreation, renewed readiness for heightened tonus and work." [149] In considering the differentiated conditions for the listening-game it soon becomes evident that a great,
though often unconscious art is demanded of the auditor. The ideal
listening-game comes off only rarely, but we must search for the
characteristics of this ideal kind of play, and a study of its un-
successful forms may pave the way for us.

The playing range and the duration of the game are staked out
for both partners, but in any game both partners have to be familiar
—if only intuitively—with the rules; for a true game requires not
only the element of uncertainty, but also of formally determined
limitation.[150] The full [151] possibilities within the limited space-time
of the game give rise to its own form-and-content problem. If an
audio-player finds his partner in the game to be a piece of music
in which he cannot participate or which his own dynamic constitution or experience does not let him follow through its play
of motion and tension, then the music will take its course part of
the time outside the perceptual world of the listener who had been
asked to join the game. In the extreme case, therefore, an auditor
might be confronted by a play activity which would *have to* remain
incomprehensible to him, for purely psychological and physiological
reasons. If the listener is honest, he will say such music is "boring";
so there can be music which is vastly superior to the listener in
every respect, and which need not be boring at all for other listeners.[152]

[148] *Cf.* McDougall, *Energies of Men.*
[149] *Vide* Buytendijk, *Spiel,* pp. 156, 119, and elsewhere.
[150] *Idem.*
[151] Buytendijk, *Spiel,* p. 26, for the meaning of Guardini's concept of "fullness" in relation to the nature of play.
[152] If other rational grounds are often claimed in such a case, that claim usually
lies in a different plane, *i.e.,* that of prejudice.

Another factor of true play leads us to a second possibility of its miscarriage: the sphere of the mysterious, removed from everyday life, in which true play takes place.[153] The position of music is singular precisely in this point; for of all sensory qualities the medium of tone is most powerfully ringed with the magic of the mysterious, the remote. Despite its deep connectedness with actuality, it produces that uncertain element and the possibility of playing with the listening partner (quite contrary to the way of the *word*, for instance, with which it is only conceptually related [154]), by virtue of our motile and vital experience, which gives to music a cognitive character, howbeit a pathic one.

Just as the encounter of a listening partner and a piece of music which far exceeds his range of play leads to an unsatisfactory and boring game, the opposite complication may arise when the auditor meets a muscial piece of so limited a range that the game loses its air of unpredictability and, above all, its mystery. Again an unsatisfactory listening-game is the result; it, too, may be boring, but in a different sense: if the music is too devoid of the ambiguity, surprise and mystery of aural play, if the proposed game is too patent, too easily surveyed, and lacks the motility and tension he desires, then the game breaks up on the superiority, or at least on the sense of superiority, of the auditor, to whom the game seems "banal." As often happens, the psychology of language confirms our reasoning: in French "banal" means "everyday, trite"; it designates just that which makes the atmosphere of play impossible; for play leads us away from all that is commonplace, trite, and therefore ever repeated and fixed, into a new world of the indefinite and mysterious, removed from the everyday world.

An ideal listening-game can therefore occur only if the music and its auditor are two opponents whose realms of play coincide in some way. For it is an absolute condition for the success of a mature, perfect game that two equivalent players should oppose each other. And there is one further essential factor: the atmosphere in which the game takes place. Real play can only develop in leisure; [155] of

[153] *Vide* Buytendijk, *Spiel*, pp. 129 ff.

[154] Transitions are to be found in lyric poetry.

[155] *Cf.* J. Pieper, *Muse und Kult*, München, 1946. The concept of true play relates music with theology. E. Schlink, *Zum theologischen Problem der Musik*, pp. 9, 16, and elsewhere, sums up the "elements of order and freedom" in the "concept of play." Music means "a peculiar attempt at world-transcendance in playful acceptance of law." (pp. 17–18.) K. Barth, *Die*

course, the suggestive power of music may be so great that it induces leisure in the hearer—and this is perhaps the highest tribute one can pay to the role of music in our lives.

OUTLOOK ON THE CULTURAL AND EPIS- TEMOLOGICAL PROBLEMS INVOLVED IN MUSICAL HEARING

We have followed the naturalistic problem of musical hearing from its source in the acoustic sensory mode to its development as a game, and thereby reached the point beyond which musical hearing becomes a cultural problem. Since the conditions and laws of hearing that derive from the nature of man were not treated here in isolation, as an objective, topographical, scientific issue, but were conceived as a vital humanistic foundation on which a theory of musical hearing, and indeed of musicality itself, could be erected, the validity of the laws and principles here established transcends that lowest level and extends to the entire sphere of musicological thinking. I have repeatedly indicated, in a musicological context, how certain cultural phenomena can be explained only by an interrelation of natural and cultural factors. The socio-musicological categories that present themselves from such an anthropological point of view will, however, have bearings on music history, too, and call many of its principles and methods in question.[156]

If controversies over these questions are inevitable in the historical realm of musicology, a wider sphere of problems is made accessible by our new biological foundation of musical hearing which is still virgin soil, at least for musicology. I am thinking of certain epistemological problems of hearing, which musicologists will not be able to sidestep forever. These scholars will not be able to take issue with such new ideas as for instance those of Plessner [157]

protestantiche Theologie im 19. Jahrhundert (Zürich, 1947), utilizes the concept of play especially for the music of the eighteenth century (cf. pp. 49, 51–2, et al.); "How devotedly did people in this age make music, and—what is perhaps . . . even more characteristic—with what devotion were they able to listen." (pp. 49–50.) This proves what we aimed to show, namely that our discussions give access to the historical situation, to the cultural problem of musical hearing.

[156] Cf. H. Reinold, Zur Bedeutung musiksoziologischen Denkens für die Musikgeschichte, Festgabe Fellerer, Köln, 1952 (typewritten).

[157] Plessner, Einheit der Sinne, Bonn, 1923.

and Straus, until they themselves will take cognizance of the nature of hearing and treat it from their own point of view; for the conditions and principles of musical hearing which I have adduced are decisive factors in shaping the philosophical and epistemological problems in which it figures. Questions such as the distinction of perception from cognition and feeling, the differences between a verbal and a musical medium, or between music as experience and music as occurrence, now become decidable. These are epistemological questions that have had great historical influence, but, as aforesaid, are always partly determined by the scientific conception of musical hearing. This fact has two great implications: in the first place, that the purely speculative separation between natural and philosophical sciences, which has no empirical justification at all and has proved fatal to more than just musicology, can be overcome. We may, then, take the whole subject of musical hearing, its organic as well as its cultural conditions, as one unified problem again. In the second place, that the end of this investigation is not only a starting point for an organic transition to other levels of thought, but also opens new perspectives to further scholarship.

The Image in the Rock

JOHN B. FLANNAGAN

OFTEN THERE IS an occult attraction in the very shape of a rock as sheer abstract form. It fascinates with a queer atavistic nostalgia, as either a remote memory or a stirring impulse from the depth of the unconscious.

That's the simple sculptural intention. As design, the eventual carving involuntarily evolves from the eternal nature of the stone itself, an abstract linear and cubical fantasy out of the fluctuating sequence of consciousness, expressing a vague general memory of many creatures, of human and animal life in its various forms.

It partakes of the deep pantheistic urge of kinship with all living things and fundamental unity of all life, a unity so complete it can see a figure of dignity even in the form of a goat. Many of the humbler life forms are often more useful as design than the narcissistic human figure, because humanly, we project ourselves into all art works using the human figure, identifying ourselves with the beauty, grace, or strength of the image as intense wish fulfillment; and any variant, even when necessitated by design, shocks as maimed, and produces some psychological pain. With an animal form, on the contrary, any liberty taken with the familiar forms is felt as amusing—strange cruelty.

298

To that instrument of the subconscious, the hand of a sculptor, there exists an image within every rock. The creative act of realization merely frees it.

The stone cutter, worker of metal, painter, those who think and feel by hand, are timeless, haunted by all the old dreams. The artist remembers, or else is fated by cosmic destiny to serve as the instrument for realizing in visible form the profound subterranean urges of the human spirit in the whole dynamic life process—birth, growth, decay, death.

The stone carving of an alligator called *Dragon Motif* was simply chiseled with primary interest in the abstract circular design. Yet in so doing fascinated by something of the wonder and terror that must have made the fearsome monster fantasy—an old dream. Vitalized by that perfect design pattern, the circle, fitting symbol of eternity, the movement is both peripheral and centrifugal. Restless, it moves ever onward, finally to turn back into itself, an endless movement.

With such abstract purpose, instead of classic poise, there is more of the dynamic tension that is movement, even accentuated by devices that are restless such as a deliberate lack of obvious balance in design and the use of repetition to heighten the occult activity with velocity, as in the psyche of our time—speed without pauses or accents.

Even in our time, however, we yet know the great longing and hope of the ever recurrent and still surviving dream, the wishful rebirth fantasy, *Jonah and the Whale—Rebirth Motif*. It's eerie to learn that the fish is the very ancient symbol of the female principle.

In the austere elimination of the accidental for ordered simplification, there is a quality of the abstract and lifeless, but lifeless only contra spurious lifelikeness. Instead of which a purely sculptural attempt by the most simple unambiguous demonstration of tactile relations, the greatest possible preservation of cubic compactness, carved to exclude all chance evasive spatial aspects to approximate the abstract cubical elemental forms and even to preserve the identity of the original rock so that it hardly seems carved, rather to have endured so always—inevitable.

The artistic representation of the organic and living now takes on an abstract lifeless order and becomes, instead of the likeness of what is conditioned, the symbol of what is unconditioned and invariable, as though seeking the timeless, changeless finality of death. Sculpture like this is as inevitable.

All as part of the profound social purpose of art—communication. We communicate something of the record of the human spirit.

Problems of a Song-Writer

MARIO CASTELNUOVO-TEDESCO

I HAVE WRITTEN a great many songs in my life; I have published more than one-hundred and fifty (not to mention all that have remained in my desk) and I have composed them in all the languages I know—Italian, French, English, German, Spanish, Latin. My ambition—even more than that, a profound urge within me—has always been to unite my music to poetic texts that arouse my interest and emotion, to interpret them and at the same time to set them forth in lyric expression, to stamp them with the authentic and therefore undetachable seal of melody, to give utterance to the music that is latent within them, and, in doing so, to discover their real source in the emotions that brought them into being. In short, it is the "need for song" that has spurred me on, a need quite natural and altogether familiar to Italians. But, at least during the 19th century, my countrymen satisfied this need predominantly through theatre music (in which the quality of the words—which were often only a pretext—counted little); whereas my preferred territory has been the more intimate one of vocal chamber music, and my aim that of approaching the purest and highest poetic expressions, not only in Italian, but in foreign languages as well. That is why I have set to music not only Saint Francis of Assisi, Dante,

301

Petrarca, Redi, and Leopardi, but also Vergil and Horace in Latin; in French, the poets of the Pléiade, de Musset, Proust, Gide, and Valéry; in Spanish, the popular poets of the Romancero; in German, Heine; and finally, in English, Shakespeare, Milton, Walter Scott, Shelley, Byron, Wordsworth, Keats, Elizabeth Browning, and Walt Whitman. It is because of this long experience and devotion that I think I am able to speak of song with some fundamental knowledge and that I propose to study in this short essay the different problems to which this form of composition gives rise—not expecting to exhaust the field, which is entirely too vast, but only hoping that my remarks will stimulate someone else to further investigation.

The "need for song"—most authorities claim, and I believe so too—was probably the cause of the first musical manifestation of primordial man, a manifestation that was doubtless one of his first in any art. He was impelled to express (in song as well as in words) elemental feelings (such as joy and grief), appeals to the supernatural, calls to battle—resulting in songs of love, religion, celebration, war; songs that were first transmitted by oral tradition and were then, in more civilized times, made permanent in writing. And it is also in the more civilized periods that the association of poetry and music began to take on a more definitely artistic form. This association soon produced different, specialized *genres;* it divided into several "branches" (often far removed from one another, at least in appearance)—epic, religious, convivial, lyric, dramatic—, according to the aspirations or needs of the human community. It is the lyric expression that chiefly interests us for present purposes, a type that answers a rather "subjective" and "individual" urge (whereas the other *genres* respond rather to "collective" needs). And lyric song itself developed into two, often widely divergent branches: on the one hand, the folk-song, that rich and elemental harvest planted by instinctive and anonymous artists; on the other hand, a more refined and cultivated *genre* resulting from a more conscious amalgamation of poetry and music, a type that served (especially in the Middle Ages, the Renaissance, and up to the 18th century) as the intellectual and aristocratic art of the court. But it must be added that, as in the folk-song, there are often traits of a very individual character, vigorous and powerful; great artists of all periods (including the moderns) in their happiest expressions have succeeded in assimilating the simple and healthy spirit of the folk-song into their own richer and more personal language. In any case, I believe we may say that, in all periods in which there is an abundance of lyrics set to music, there is a flowering of lyric poetry, and that the proportions of the two correspond in a more or less steady ratio. The parallel would make a most interesting subject of study, and, as far as I know, although partial investigations may have been made, a complete one is still lacking. I do not think of making the attempt myself (especially in this paper), but I point it out to historians and musicologists "of good will", and I can not refrain from suggesting several chapters that might prove particularly attractive: without going back to the Greeks (of whose music we unfortunately know too little), the art of the troubadours, the influence of Arcadian poetry on the Italian *aria da camera,* the relations of Romantic poetry to the German *Lied,* and those of symbolist and impressionist poetry to the songs of the French moderns (Fauré, Debussy, Ravel). In these last two relationships (easier to study because the documents are more recent), the evidence is striking. I do not believe that the flowering of the *Lied* would have been so vigorous and abundant if the poets had not provided it with such seeds, offering to musicians (and in forms particularly appropriate to music) hundreds of poems likely to inspire and move them. One may say that musicians sometimes preferred mediocre texts to great poetic works and that their talent nevertheless allowed them to give us remarkable pages, sometimes masterpieces; but I answer that without Goethe we would not have had such "miracles" as *Der Erlkönig* or *Gretchen am Spinnrade,* and without Heine we would not have had the *Dichterliebe,* the most perfect of love cycles. And with the French, the influence of Baudelaire, Verlaine, Mallarmé, and Maeterlinck on modern musicians is evident (as is that of impressionist painting), even in their style in general, as is shown by those of their musical works that are not associated with a text.

NOW THAT WE HAVE ARRIVED —necessarily at too rapid a pace—at modern times, let us pause to consider the problems that confront present-day composers in writing songs. I deal here with the song in its most simple and elementary form, which is that for a voice accompanied by a single instrument (nowadays the piano). Obviously, the song with orchestra offers other possibilities and makes other demands on the composer—such as greater variety and vaster dimensions.

First of all there is the choice of the poem. I know it is not easily made. I have already said that composers of *Lieder* found a wide choice among the works of their contemporaries, the Romantic poets, who felt in the same "vein", who had the same sensitivity; as one may say also of the French musicians at the end of the century, who discovered kindred spirits in the "twilight" poets. But to go back to the same texts that they treated would be useless or at least dangerous: one would have difficulty in interpreting them—I do not say better, but even as well as did the celebrated musicians who have already done so in what might be called "definitive" fashion; the re-setting, at best, would be but an echo of the same experience. We are still too near the older musicians to try an essentially different interpretation, and the individual expression that should be present is therefore precluded. I cite only one exception to the poets of the recent past whose works are, at least for the present, insusceptible of fresh interpretations; that exception is Heine, whose melancholy and sentimental side the Romantic musicians so often and so happily expressed, but whose ironic and mordant side they completely neglected. For us as modern composers (perhaps more skeptic, but also more ready for subtle and varied nuances) he still offers possibilities; and I myself have set to music, which a Romantic musician would undoubtedly have considered "sacrilegious", two poems of his, *Am Teetisch* and *Der wunderbare Traum*. Perhaps we have little opportunity of successfully setting contemporary poetry, which often (it may be the fault of the times) offers few attractions to a composer's fancy: it is sometimes an arid poetry, a collection of verses and rhythms interesting as an intellectual game, but frequently too esoteric to arouse a sympathetic chord in another artist's heart. I have spoken of "verse": to make verses is not necessarily to make poetry, especially musical poetry. Frequently, artistic prose, having a rhythm that is wisely and harmoniously disposed, gives a stronger suggestion to the musician than does a mediocre poem (and it presents no greater technical problems). I cite, for example, the *Chansons de Bilitis* (on prose texts by Pierre Louys), in which Debussy gave us most exquisite examples of his sensitivity—not to mention entire operas, such as *Pelléas et Mélisande* and *Boris*

Godounov—two indisputable masterpieces—, in which Debussy and Musorgsky set the prose of Maeterlinck and Pushkin. (I myself have been more deeply inspired by the *Fragments* of Marcel Proust in prose than by many a fine piece of contemporary writing in verse.)

"But", one will ask, "what are the qualities of a poem requisite to its suitability for musical setting? What is the ideal poem?" Naturally, it is difficult to say. The answer depends especially upon the sensitivity of the composer, and also upon the *genre* he prefers: he may have a stronger leaning towards dramatic or lyric, gay or sentimental poetry. Just the same, I believe there are some necessary conditions common to all-first, one that goes to the essence: the poem must have an "expressive core"; it should express a "state of soul", whatever the musician's preferences may cause the nature of that state to be; it should, in any case, be capable of awakening a "resonance" in the composer's soul; it should express the "core" in a perfect, simple and direct, clear, and harmonious form, rich, but without too many words. A certain "margin" should be left for the music: from this point of view, an intimate and restrained poem is preferable to a too sonorous and decorative one. (I cite a typical case: the great Italian poet, Gabriele d'Annunzio, who, with his vast wealth of words, seems to have amused himself by creating a sort of overwhelming and flamboyant verbal music, is a real difficulty to the composer. That is why, I think, attempts to set his poetry have succeeded so rarely, with one notable exception: the admirable *I Pastori* of Pizzetti.)

There are also other conditions, those of dimensions, of form. The poem should not be too long (unless the song is for voice and orchestra, a type which, as I have said, offers other possibilities); nor, on the other hand, should it be too short (unless there are to be several songs in a cycle). From this point of view also, the Romantic poets offered ideal texts to their musicians—texts not only expressive, varied, and harmonious, but of reasonable length. Great Italian poetry, however, presents many difficulties in this respect. One cannot set "The Divine Comedy" to music, and, among the smaller forms, the sonnet (a prime favorite of Italian poets) is most unadaptable to music—first, because of the content, which is often too philosophic and intellectual; next, because of its almost too strict a form; and finally, because of the difficulty of balancing quatrains and tercets into different musical periods. The less strict forms of the *canzone* and the *ballata* are generally preferable, or poems that are entirely free.

I HAVE SAID that contemporary poetry does not frequently offer inducements to composers; but we have a great heritage from past centuries in the literatures of all countries and all languages. And when I speak of foreign languages, I have in mind original texts, not translations. Translations of poetry are almost always "betrayals". (*Traduttore, traditore.*) Even if there is not a betrayal of the contents, there is a betrayal of rhythm or of form, and these are poetic elements too precious and essential to be neglected.

This leads us to another problem: the often discussed one of the "musicality" of the different languages. That quality doubtless differs in degree from one tongue to another; but each language has its own special expressive possibilities (at least according to the fairly wide experience that I have had), and they are worth the trouble of trying out.

If one asks me what the most musical language is, naturally I answer, "Italian!" First, because it is my own language; then, because it is universally recognized as the most agreeable and easy language to sing. Broad, expressive, sonorous, it lends itself admirably to song, and one can easily understand why Italy is considered the fatherland and even the source of *bel canto*. But my admiration and preference for my native language do not prevent me from recognizing the qualities of other languages also. French, doubtless less suitable for impassioned outbursts (and consequently for song), is nevertheless subtler and lends itself to more exquisite nuances. Spanish has certain characteristics similar to those of Italian, except for a hardness sometimes more severe (and also, in compensation, a softness sometimes more languorous). I shall not say much of Latin, the mother of all these languages, except to note that it is generally regarded as a language especially fitting for sacred purposes, as the language of prayer. One is apt to forget its rich secular literature. I recall that, in my first years of study in Florence, the Director of the Conservatory was scandalized because I composed choruses on the Eclogues of Vergil instead of choosing to write motets. I have never tried Greek (distant memory of my early studies!) and in Hebrew I have composed only one chorus. German is an admirably rich language, quite in a class by itself by virtue of the forcefulness of its declamation, which permits vocal leaps that would be quite inexplicable in other languages (and also explains why Wagner is untranslatable).

I have left English for the last, not because I consider it less musical, but, on the contrary, because I am surprised that its musicality is so often doubted. I must confess that I too approached it with certain misgivings, so unfavorably had I been conditioned. My first encounter with English was by way of Shakespeare. Dissatisfied with an Italian translation of "Twelfth Night", from which I was setting several songs to music, I wanted to know the original text, and I was overjoyed and surprised to discover its language to be not only of a perfect beauty, but also of astonishing "musicality". I could not rest until I had set to music all the songs I could find in the tragedies and comedies, and I was miserable when I had exhausted the supply. In Shakespeare I found my ideal, the human richness, the greatest psychological profundity, united with the most supple and varied poetry. I have often been asked whether, in setting Shakespeare to music, I had been preoccupied with historical considerations—that is to say, with composing music in the Elizabethan manner. The answer is "No", because Shakespeare has seemed to me the most alive and most modern, the most eternal and universal of all poets (more so even than Dante), and I feel him to be a "contemporary". After Shakespeare came Shelley, and then the others I have mentioned, up to the American Walt Whitman, that great fraternal soul. Certainly, the English of Shakespeare and Shelley was not that of the man in the street; their poetic language is of supreme musicality, and I believe that one can discover in the great English lyrics treasures similar to those the German Romantics offered to the composers of *Lieder*.

To be sure, English does present some remarkable difficulties to the songwriter. One, for example, is its great number of monosyllabic words, which it is difficult to distribute over a melody in an expressive fashion and, at the same time, with correct accentuation. But, on the other hand, it is perhaps just this—its very lack of "sonorous substance"—that lends English its charm, and makes it one of the most "spiritual" and transparent languages I know.

I HAVE ALREADY MENTIONED "song", "melody", "accent"; and I shall now reconsider them briefly together with some other problems and difficulties that confront the composer.

What is "song"? It is difficult to define. Fundamentally, it is a "gift of God", a deliverance of the human soul. And I have often said that, if I were to envy some great musician of the past, it would not be Bach for his fugues, or Beethoven for his symphonies, or Wagner for his music-dramas, but perhaps Schubert for some of the simplest of his *Lieder*, such as *Du bist die Ruh* or *Litanei*, miraculous flowers of the spirit, as consoling as a friendly smile or a gentle tear.

But if one refuses to be satisfied with a transcendent explanation, it will be possible to arrive at a more positive and satisfactory one by way of defining "accent". Accent is the expressive quality that results when one throws into relief, while creating a melody, certain syllables in a word, words in a phrase, and phrases in a sentence. This aspect of rhythm, this expressive relief, this correct prosody, is not all there is to a song; musical declamation (which sometimes can be very efficacious) is not yet song itself. Song, while incorporating it, must go beyond it—must be a synthesis, a sublimation. The placing of accent is a mechanical process, and every conscientious musician can accomplish it; a complete song, on the other hand, is a product of artistic creation, and its fashioning is reserved for artists of talent, for the fortunate few who are gifted with both sentiment and fantasy.

Another problem is that of having a knowledge of the singing voice, but it is a secondary problem that can be solved intuitively. Every musician who truly "feels" song writes well for the voice; those who write poorly for it are those who regard mastering its special requirements as a mechanical process. In any case, we must, in this connection, take into account the diverse natures of the various languages. As already pointed out, Italian possesses a greater sonorous expression; French and English (I believe) admit of a more limited emotional range; while German permits vocal leaps that would be absurd in other languages.

And now we come to the last problem, the practical problem— how actually to write a song. That is quite personal. And heaven forbid that I should try to promulgate cut-and-dried theories. Each system is good, provided it gives satisfactory results. It has often happened to me—and, I am sure, to my colleagues also—that the question is asked (especially on the part of women): "How do you compose your music?" or "How do you set a poem to music?" or even "How are you inspired?" Questions so difficult to answer!

However, one can say something. For example, to the second of these questions, I am likely to reply that, when I find a poem that particularly interests me or arouses my emotion, I commit it to memory and, at the same time, naturally, I analyze its form, its character, its distribution of phrases, its possibilities for contrast, etc. After some time, when the poem has entered my blood, so to speak (this may take anywhere from a day to several months), I sing it quite naturally: the music is born. For me to love a poem is to *know* it, it is to sing it! So much for the vocal part. But in a song there is also the instrumental part, commonly called the "accompaniment", as though to impute to it a secondary character, even though it is by no means the least important portion of a song nor necessarily the easiest one to evolve. To produce it properly is a matter of finding the right atmosphere, the "background", the environment that surrounds and develops the vocal line. It is also a question of expressing through the instrument what the voice alone cannot express. Finally, it is a question of creating something that will combine with the vocal line to form a quite inseparable and complete unity. This something exists in the poetry too. One need only strike upon it. Just as the voice part is born of the poem, so is the accompaniment given rise by it also (through the medium of the composer's intuition as well as through analysis): it is latent in the poetry. I have already said that every poem-for-music must have, above all, an "expressive core"—which may be formed of one or several fundamental elements—, a core that provides the key to the poem itself. It is this key, it is these elements, that one must discover and to which one must give utterance through almost "symbolic" musical means. I have said that song is a synthesis; accompaniment itself is a synthesis too (even if it grows partly out of analysis, which seems contradictory). What will these "symbolic" means be? They must be several and of rather different natures. But I believe I may state that the simplest will be the surest and most efficacious. I myself began, in my first songs, with accompaniments rather complicated in harmony and rhythm. Afterwards I always tried to simplify, rather, I must say, through instinct than through reason. I tried to express my thoughts by the simplest and most natural means, even if, to some, these might seem less "interesting". These different "symbols" (and the greatest composers of *Lieder* have supplied us with examples) may consist of a melodic element, a thematic cell (which is sometimes in the voice part too), a rhythm (which may likewise stem from the voice part, or may, on the contrary, be entirely opposed to it), an instrumental figuration (we have hundreds of celebrated examples; as for me, a simple *arpeggio* sufficed for my Shakespeare song, "Arise", a chromatic scale for my setting of André Gide's *Ballade des biens immeubles*) or, finally, some harmonic element—a series of chords or even a single chord. (I note, as something of a curiosity, that, when I added to my Shakespeare Songs two derived from "Hamlet"—"Ophelia" and "The Clown in the Churchyard"—I constructed them both on this chord:

and that, when I later began an Overture to "Hamlet", it was on this same chord that the initial theme was built, quite naturally; which would signify that this chord is singularly "Hamletesque" or, at least, that it is associated in my subconscious mind with the idea of "Hamlet"— I leave it to the psychoanalysts.)

THIS DISCOURSE has been a great deal longer than I had intended. I must bring it to a close.

I began by saying that song was the first musical manifestation of man. I believe that it will also be the last. As long as humanity remains, it will sing. And I should like to imagine that its "farewell to life" will also be a song. In the meanwhile let our song be of life.

And let me express a hope: that English-speaking people (Americans especially) find in their admirable poetry—which has given so much joy to me, an Italian—a rich source of inspiration for their song literature, towards the furthering of happiness and fraternity among men, as their great poet Whitman would have wished.

The Histrionic Experience

PETER RICHARD ROHDEN

THE AVERSION TO analyzing artistic problems goes back to the Romantic Movement. The Romanticists established the conception of the divinely endowed artist into whose workshop no human eye is able to penetrate. The element of truth in this idea is that the source of artistic creation lies in the unconscious. But this may be said of any creative achievement, metaphysical systems as well as the deeds of heroes and the dogmas of religion. Nevertheless, it has not occurred to any philosopher to monopolize philosophy for himself, and the supreme power of religion rests on the claim that every soul has to grapple with the secret of faith.

Hero, sage, and saint, therefore, are types which, by stages, merge into general human nature; they are the highest magnifications of potentialities that are latent in every human being. Why then, should the artist be regarded as unique? Does not historical experience show that long generations in the history of mankind never heard of the artist as a special type?

This does not mean that we favor dilettantism or adolescent lyricism. But does the admission that the majority of people have at some time made verses detract one bit from Goethe's greatness? In analyzing the dramatic art, moreover, language supplies us with an important hint: we often say of a fellowman that he "puts on an act," and thereby admit that we are dealing with an impulse which goes far beyond the limits of the theatre.

Now, the fact that the average human being in his daily life may take an attitude that resembles the art of the actor proves that the delight in transformation is rooted in human nature. This entitles us to the question of why we perform dramas or look at them at all.

What is it that distinguishes a person in a play from a "real" person? It seems to be the fact that the former stands before our eyes as a fully developed totality. We see our fellowmen only in a fragmentary fashion, and the faculty of self-knowledge usually is so much impaired by vanity and desire that it amounts to nothing. What we call "dramatic illusion," therefore, is the paradoxical phenomenon that we know better what is going on in the mind of a Hamlet than what stirs our own minds. For Shakespeare, the poet-actor, shows not only the act but also its motives, and in such a comprehensive way as we never see them combined in real life.

This establishment of a rational connection between character and fate transcends reality, even if it does not—as in Schiller—assume the specific form of "idealization," the heightening towards the moral-normative. The "greatness" of an Oedipus or a Macbeth does not depend on the fact that they are better men than we, but on the integration of their actions and sufferings with a super-individual order of existence that lends them significance. The amoral deities of some religions go to prove that the longing of man may be directed towards a sheer increase in strength, just so it gives life some meaning that transcends the contingencies of mere empirical existence.

What, then, happens within the soul of the actor when he plays Hamlet? Some maintain that the performer only acts "as if" he were Hamlet; others, that he is "really" Hamlet. Both attempts at interpretation are inadequate. To "be" Hamlet, or even only to act as if one were Hamlet, presupposes that a Hamlet "reality" exists outside the histrionic creation. One can "imitate" only a given reality. However, the congruence of character and fate which Shakespeare established in his *Hamlet* exists only within the tragedy. Each representation of Hamlet is therefore a creation, not a reproduction. Even the poet participates only indirectly in the creative process on the stage. *Ad libitum* comedy shows to what a high degree the actor can emancipate himself from the dramatist. And it is but by a misconceived idealism, rooted in today's preponderance of the literary play, that an actor considers himself the "servant" of the poet. Certainly, anyone endowed with theatrical imagination can derive an approximate picture of the action by reading a Shakespearean drama, just as a musician can hear the melody and the rhythm when reading an orchestral score. But reading cannot replace actual presentation. If the poet really could transmit everything to the actor, then not only would anyone be able to play Hamlet, but there would also be only one correct Hamlet interpretation, whereas in fact each great performer plays Hamlet differently.

What the dramatist delivers is the words and ideograms of a psychic existence. It is left to the actor to integrate these words through speech melody, speech rhythm, and gesture into a unit which only then gives the full reality of "Hamlet." Whoever designates the histrionic art as reproductive, because it is tied to the "text," must logically deny the poet his creativity because *he* merely manipulates the language of his native land. But a stanza from *Iphigenie* is something different from the sum of its words subjected to a metric scheme; the same magic atmosphere that separates the work of the poet from the everyday concept elevates the actor's vitally intoned and embodied word-gesture above the poetic "verse-ideogram."

But how does this histrionic magic come about? Through an interaction between a surrender to the emotional current and a conscious drive towards form. Thomas Mann has pointed out to us in *Tonio Kröger* and in *Königliche Hoheit* that a sincere sentimental overflow is not sufficient to create a work of art. The disconcerted astonishment of the young prince, when for the first time he grasps the concept of artistic self-discipline, is one of the most delightful passages in the novel. The same holds true for the actor. If an actress playing Iphigenia were to permit herself to be so overcome by her emotion that she actually broke down in uncontrollable sobbing, she would force the director to break off the performance by quickly lowering the curtain. To "become absorbed" in the role without retaining a supervisory control over its performance would be the surest means of destroying the dramatic "illusion."

For this illusion is based on the very fact that the performer knows all about the character from the beginning; this makes it possible for him slowly to intensify his power, to reserve it for an apparently quite uncontrollable outburst, and then allow it grad-

ually to ebb away again. Feeling and expression of feeling are, to
be sure, sometimes connected, but they are subject to different laws.
Even in daily life we notice that the expression of genuine emotions
may at times assume forms of bad taste. Anyone used to self-
observation has noted that a statement is the more convincing the
more consciously its formulation is controlled.

The histrionic art, therefore, is not based on some sort of "repres-
sion": so that Wegener would have developed into a blue-bearded
despot and Elisabeth Bergner into an ecstatic saint if only our
present civilization admitted of such characters. The potentialities
of those characters are transferred by the actor not into the reality
of actual life, but to the stage. Between the several realms of reality
there is only one bridge, that of analogy. A religious philosopher
who speaks, for instance, of the wrath of God, is guilty of an an-
thropomorphism. He transfers a human characteristic to the deity,
whereas he is really dealing with a simile. A like relation exists between real and artistically formulated emotion. The portrayer of
Othello is not jealous, but "jealous"—insofar as we mean to express
the ideogrammatic character of the affect by the quotation marks.

Even though, accordingly, we reject both the attempted definitions of the histrionic experience as, respectively, a "so-being" and a
"so-acting," yet there lies in them a core of truth which language
indicates in the ambiguity of the word "stage-play." [1] For the
"stage," the spectacle, is not only for the audience, but also means
the inner vision (*Innenschau*) by which the actor gains access to
his role. And according to the interrelation of "stage" and "play,"
i.e. surrender to the stage-reality and control of this surrender, in
the individual artist, two actor types may be distinguished. In the
case of one, the "comedian," the primary factor is the joy in playing,
the pleasure found in the change of character with its trappings of
masks, costumes, and mummery. This type is very little ego-con-
nected, but is the more ego-dependent. Since each part is for him
only an opportunity to satisfy his urge for play and metamorphosis,
his accomplishment is to a large degree independent of the poetic
value of the play. An actress of this type is recognized by her preference for male parts, just as the comedian in general prefers character portrayals that are alien, if not opposite, to his role in private

---

[1] The German word is "*Schauspiel*," here broken with a hyphen, *Schauspiel*. The translation had to be adapted to the nearest equivalent, "stage-play,"
where "stage" has to take the place of *Schau*, "spectacle" ("show").—Ed.

life. The best example is the melancholy of the clown, where psychical artistry is combined with physical acrobatics.

If this type is equated with man at large, it constitutes the ultimate refinement of the social phenomenon which we call "acting." He who acts aims at a kind of self-presentation which places his ego in the most favorable light. Hence he is not concerned with interpretation but with impression. Still, one must beware of judging the comedian only by the worst of his kind. Not only Possart but also Matkowsky was one of them. In postwar Germany this type is on the decline, just as generally speaking the most brilliant representatives belong to the Romance cultures. In the French drama, from Corneille to Rostand, there are parts which can be played only by comedians. Just consider the manner in which a Cid delivers his emotions front stage, or how a Cyrano de Bergerac plays catch-ball with his feelings.

Hence it is no accident that we have to designate a Frenchwoman, Sarah Bernhardt, as the most brilliant representative of this type. To the melancholy German and—as has been proved by guest performances of the Russians—to the Slavs, this type is alien. The German wants introspection rather than play and prefers the character actor in whom the surrender to the part outweighs the joy of metamorphosis. This type of actor, which since the time of Kainz and Eleonora Duse has found its most important representatives in Moissi, Werner Krauss, Klöpfer, George and Elisabeth Bergner, is the counterpart of the comedian. His psychological receptivity enables him to submerge himself to a much greater extent in the personality to be represented. He who personally knows actors of this sort must have noticed that they often carry the expression, and especially the look, of a character that they portrayed for hours after the performance. For the pain and the pleasure of a character whom they impersonate become real to them in a much more profound way than to a comedian, because they represent him empathically.

Thus representation becomes almost substitution, which in the case of the intensified excitability of the character actor can go so far as to produce a sympathetic emotional reaction from the sufferings of a part he is playing. Those who enjoy medical terminology may well speak of hysteria. In the case of such a neurotic actor we are dealing with a manic type in whom the borders between normality and derangement are often fluid. Even if the well-known story of the actor who plays Napoleon and then suddenly imagines he *is* Napoleon, is probably too crass ever to have occurred, even the slightest sign of depression during the withdrawal from a role into private life proves the danger of this kind of "ecstasy."

But precisely on the basis of this immediate link with the part can the lesser versatility of the ecstatic performer be explained. The number of roles that "suit" him are naturally limited. For he cannot artificially establish the experiential contact; above all, he cannot cover a mistake or a sudden disruption by his artistic skill. Floodlights and the smell of backdrops, the purple robe and the scepter have no magic power over him who derives his art from his psyche and not from the props. Therefore each part is for him an experiment which necessitates a revision of his artistic resources. But whenever his stream of experience is permitted to flow unhampered the gain in depth compensates for the loss in breadth. Then there arise images of such compelling power as the Wallenstein of a Werner Krauss or the Saint Joan of an Elisabeth Bergner, where each intonation, each gesture has its immovable place; in short, creations of "such stuff as dreams are made on," and yet of such a consuming inner truth that they leave all reality behind, burst asunder the frame of the merely theatrical, and knock at the gates of cosmic existence.

Sketch for a Psychology of the Moving Pictures

ANDRÉ MALRAUX

HAD IT BEFALLEN Giotto, or even Clouet, to travel round the world, all the paintings they set eyes on would have seemed of a more or less familiar order. Nor would they have had much trouble in establishing communication with Chinese or Persian fellow-artists. For all approached their task of *representing* the thing seen, in the same way, and dealt with the same set of problems.

Had Rubens or Delacroix made the same journey, all the paintings they set eyes on would have struck them as archaic; similarly their own works would have bewildered the non-European painters. For their methods of representation differed from those of the Asiatics. Chinese and Persian artists were ignorant of, or disdained, depth, perspective, lighting and expression. Europe had come to differ from the rest of the world in its idea of the function of painting. And, after the close of the baroque period, there was this fundamental cleavage between Western and all other arts, past and present: that the former devoted its researches to a three-dimensional world.

There were several reasons for this, which I shall deal with elsewhere.[1] Christianity had imported into a world that had known little else than representation of a more or less subtly symbolical nature,

[1] In my *Psychology of Art.*

317

something hitherto unknown, which I would call "dramatic representation." Buddhism has scenes, but no drama; pre-Columbian American art, dramatic figures but no scenes. Even the decline of Christianity, far from weakening this occidental sense of the dramatic actually strengthened it, and at the same time heightened another sense, of which the sense of drama is only one of several manifestations—the sense of Otherness, that desire for volume and figures in bold relief which is peculiar to the West, and links up with its political conquest of the world. Europe replaces flat tone by relief, chronicles by history, tragedy by drama, saga by the novel, wisdom by psychology, contemplation by action—and, as a result, the gods by Man.

The criteria of present-day taste can only be misleading in this connexion; for a great deal of the best modern painting is, like the oriental, in two dimensions. The problem is not of an aesthetic order, but strikes deeper. It derives from culture itself, the relations between man and the outside world. At one pole of human expression are the mime, the actor and narrator in the *No* play, declaiming through their masks, Chinese and Japanese dancers; and, at the opposite extreme, a language tantamount to shorthand, the mysterious whisperings of a dark night, a face whose fugitive expression fills a twenty-foot screen . . .

The visitor to one of our national galleries, who has no feeling for painting as an art, gets an impression of a series of efforts (not unlike those of certain sciences) to *re-present* natural objects. To him a Rubens seems truer-to-life, and thus more convincing, than a Giotto; a Botticelli than a Cimabue; for he regards art as a means of reproducing the universe according to the data furnished by his senses. From the XIIIth Century up to the time of the baroque masters, there was steady progress in the technique of exact resemblance. And European painting during that period was at once this "mirror held up to nature" and an effort to represent persons and things (especially fictional scenes) under the most evocative and engaging guise. It is the confusion between what we should call to-day the art of painting and the technique of representation, that leads the Sunday afternoon visitor to our galleries to say approvingly of such and such a figure (always a post-Renaissance work) that it seems almost to be "talking to you." It was the same confusion that led the Florentine populace to applaud Giotto's figures as being "truer than life;" and the enthusiasm of the Tuscans for the "new" Madonnas was not perhaps so very different from that which would ensue to-day were television suddenly to enter every home.[2]

But at the close of the baroque period came an event unprecedented in the annals of painting. Ceasing to search for new methods of representation, the painter turned away towards what art has come to mean for us to-day: a specialty of artists. Never again was a picture to draw enthusiastic crowds to view it. Line and colour were to become more and more the revelation of an inward vision. And while the secret flower of modern painting blossomed forth, the votaries of representation took to a frantic headlong quest of movement.

It was no "artistic" discovery that was to enable movement to be come by. What, with its gesturings like those of drowning men, baroque art was straining after was not a modification of the picture itself, but a picture-*sequence*. It is not surprising that an art so obsessed with theatrical effect, and made up of gestures and emotions, should end up in the cinema.

II

When photography came into its own in the middle of the nineteenth century, western painting formally made over two of its former spheres of action: the depiction of emotions and the "story". It became once more an art of pure form and was again, in certain instances, restricted to two dimensions.

For the purposes of an Identity Card the photograph is wholly adequate. But for representing life, photography (which within thirty years has evolved from a phase of primitive immobility to a more or less extravagant baroque) is inevitably coming up once more against all the old problems of the painter. And where the latter halted, it too had to halt. With the added handicap that it had no scope for fiction; it could record a dancer's leap, it could not show the Crusaders entering Jerusalem. And from the "likenesses" of the Saints to the most absurd historical fantasies, men's craving for pictures has always been directed quite as much to what they have not seen as towards what they know.

Thus the attempt, which had been carried on four centuries

[2] Written in 1940.—Ed.

through, to capture movement was held up at the same point in photography as in painting; and the cinema, through enabling the photography of movement, merely substituted moving gesticulation for unmoving. If the great drive towards representation which came to a standstill in baroque art was to continue, somehow the camera had to achieve independence as regards the scene portrayed. The problem was not one of rendering the movements of a person within a picture, but of conveying tempo, the sequence of successive moments. It was not to be solved mechanically by tinkering with the camera, but artistically, by the invention of "cutting."

So long as the cinema served merely for the portrayal of figures in motion it was no more (and no less) an art than plain photography. Within a defined space, generally a real or imagined theatre stage, actors performed a play or comic scene, which the camera merely recorded. The birth of the cinema as a means of expression (not of reproduction) dates from the abolition of that defined space; from the time when the cutter thought of dividing his continuity into "planes" (close-up, intermediate, remote, etc.) and of shooting not a play but a succession of dramatic moments; when the director took to bringing forward the camera (and thus enlarging, when necessary, the figures on the screen) and moving it back; and, above all, to replacing the theatre set by an open field of vision, corresponding to the area of the screen, into which the player enters, from which he goes out, and which the director *chooses* instead of having it imposed on him. The means of reproduction in the cinema is the moving photograph, but its means of expression is a sequence of *planes*.

The tale goes that Griffith, when directing one of his early films, was so much impressed by the beauty of an actress in a certain scene that he had the camera brought nearer and a re-take made, which he incorporated in the final version of the picture. Thus the close-up was invented. The story illustrates the manner in which one of the great pioneers of filmcraft applied his genius to the problems of the moving picture, aiming less to influence the actor (by making him play, for instance, in a different way) than to modify the relation between him and the spectator (by increasing the volume of his face). It illustrates, too, a fact we are aware of but tend to overlook: that decades after the humblest photographer had formed the habit of photographing his clients full figure, half length or face only, as desired, the cinema took what was for it a bold, decisive forward step when it began registering half-length figures. For till then "planes" were an unknown quantity; the camera and field being static, the act of taking two figures half-length would have involved shooting the whole scene in the same manner.

Thus it was, by the adoption of variable planes, by this new freedom given director and cameraman in their dealings with the objective, that the cinema was endowed with possibilities of *expression*, that it was born as an *art*. Thereafter it was able to select the "shot" and co-ordinate significant "shots"; by selectivity to make up for its silence.

III

The talking picture was to modify the *data* of the problem. Not, as some have thought, by perfecting the silent picture. The talking picture was no more a bringing to perfection of its silent predecessor than was the elevator of the skyscraper. Modern cinema was not born of the possibility of making us hear what the characters of the silent film were saying, but of the joint possibilities of expression due to sound and picture acting in concert. So long as the talking picture is merely phonographic, it is as unsatisfactory as was the silent picture when it was mere photography. It rises to the rank of an art when the director understands that the forerunner of sound-cinema is not the gramophone record but the radio sketch.

When a group of artists presented on the radio the Trial of Joan of Arc, and the Session of Thermidor 9, their first task in each case was to compose an original work, the verbal structure of which was conditioned by the method of reproduction to be applied to it. There was no question of asking actors to read out passages from the *Moniteur;* they had to begin by selecting certain phases of the famous Session from the detailed report in the Gazette, and make a *montage* of them. For the record of the Session which has come down to us is, like all such *verbatim* reports, far too long to bear audition.

We are inclined to suppose that this selection leaves, in fact, no option; that there were certain outstanding moments in that eventful night when Robespierre fell, which every art alike is bound to utilize. Indeed at first sight one might conclude that in every complex of events, in every life, certain elements are of a nature to provide the raw material of art; the rest being so much lumber, amorphous and inert. This view is due to a confusion between the suggestive, significant, vitally "artistic" element and the historically memorable factor or remark. True, there are highlights in every chaos, but they are not necessarily the same highlights for every art. When Robespierre's voice is failing, the crucial fact for the radio may be that failing voice; for the cinema it may be, for instance, the gestures of a sentry intent at that moment on bundling some children out of the room, or fumbling for his tinder-box.

In the twentieth century we have for the first time arts that are inseparable from mechanical methods of expression; not only capable of being reproduced, but intended for mass-reproduction. Already the finest drawings can be adequately reproduced; before the century is out the same will probably be true of paintings. But neither drawings nor paintings were *made* to be reproduced; the artist had nothing of that sort in mind. Whereas what is enacted on a studio set by living actors is *per se* doomed to transience; it has less intrinsic value than a used engraving plate. It was *made* to be photographed, and for that end alone, just as a radio play is made to be recorded and then broadcast.

But the expressive range of recorded sounds, somewhat limited in the case of radio and gramophone records, becomes immense when the picture adds its visual counterpoint. The cinema in relief will be, when it comes, a technical advance; but the sound film stands to the silent as painting does to drawing.

At first it was so little recognized that sound was opening up a new field of expression that the talking film tended to bring the cinema back to where it had started, the moving picture at its crudest. Just as the first films were photographic records of stage effects and no more, so the early "talkies" aimed no higher than to be phonograph records of stage-plays. The dialogue was ready to hand, the footage suitable—and the result deplorable!

IV

The theatre in countries such as Russia, Germany and the United States, where it had kept its full vitality, had for twenty years been tending towards cinema. Great stage-managers were straining every effort to force a stage-play to become something more than a series of conversations. A play is—people talking; the aim of such men as Meyerhold was to *suggest* a world encompassing the dialogue. The talking film made it possible to add a complete setting to the dialogue, a real street or a fantastic background, the shadow of Nosferatu as well as sky and sea.

The life of the theatre is bound up with the expression of emotions, and the fact that its scope is limited to words and gestures made it seem, when faced with the competition of the talking picture, almost as handicapped as was the silent film.

A small head in an enormous auditorium, such is the stage actor; a film actor is an enormous head in a small auditorium. All to the advantage of the latter; for moments that the theatre could never render save by silence could, even on the silent screen, be implemented by the play of emotion writ large on a face.

Moreover, the size of the figures on the screen enables the actor to dispense with the gesticulation and other symbolic byplay needed by stage-acting if it is to take effect. Beside a good silent film it was the stage-play that had the air of being a dumb-show performance. Despite the microphone (indeed because of it) the hurried or breathless delivery of the cinema is truer to life than that of the best actor, if he is playing in a large theatre-hall.

The chief problem for the author of a talking film is to decide *when* his characters should speak. On the stage, remember, there is someone talking all the time . . . except during the intervals. The *entr'acte* is one of the great standbys of the dramatist. Things take place while the curtain is down, and he can convey them by allusions. To bridge these time-gaps the novel has the blank page between the parts; the theatre, the interval; the cinema, next to nothing.

A film director will retort that he has the division into sequences, each sequence ending on a fade-out, which suggests the lapse of time. That is so, but only relatively so; it suggests a lapse of time in which nothing occurs. (With some exceptions, special cases such as *The Blue Angel*, which call for individual analysis.) Unlike the time-gap of the interval during which all sorts of things may happen, that of the fade-out permits of scarcely any allusion to what has filled it, if that involves a change affecting any of the characters. The only methods of suggesting a long, eventful lapse of time in the film are bound to be symbolic devices (e.g. clocks, calendars with the dates fluttering past). On the other hand, while the stage-play can never move back in time, from a man's middle age to his youth, for instance, the film can manage this, though none too easily.

Roughly, the sequence is the equivalent of the chapter. The cinema has not those ampler divisions expressed by the parts of a book and the acts of a play. True, the silent film had parts; they are suppressed in talking films, and this is where the cutter comes up against one of his knottiest problems; for the "talkie" allows no gaps, continuity is the essence of its technique.

Because it has become narrative, its true rival is not the play but the novel.

v

The film can tell a story; there lies its power. So can the novel, and when sound films came in, the silent films had borrowed greatly from the novel.

A great novelist is a "producer" of sorts and we can analyse his methods from that angle; whether his aim be to tell a story, to depict or dissect characters, or to explore the meaning of life; whether his talent runs to copiousness as with Proust, or tends to crystallization as in Hemingway's case, he is bound to narrate—in other words, to epitomize, to stage-manage, to "present". What I mean by the "production" of a novel is the instinctive or deliberate selection by the author of the moments he sets store on and the methods used to make them salient.

With most writers the hall-mark of "production" is the transition from narrative to dialogue. Dialogue in the novel serves three purposes.

Firstly, that of exposition. This was the technique prevalent in England at the close of the nineteenth century; the method of Henry James and Conrad. It tends to obviate the absurd convention of the novelist's omniscience, but replaces it by another still more palpable convention. The cinema uses that sort of dialogue as sparingly as possible; likewise the modern novel.

Secondly, to bring out character. Stendhal aimed at bringing out Julien Sorel's character far more by his acts than by his way of speaking; but in the twentieth century what I may call "tone of voice" came to rank high in the novelist's technique. It became a method of expressing personality, indeed a vital element of character. Proust hardly seems to see his characters, but he has a blind man's adroitness in making them speak; one feels that many scenes from his books would, if well read, be more effective on the radio, where the actor is invisible, than in the theatre. But the cinema, like the theatre, attaches less importance to dialogue; for the acting should suffice to bring a character to life.

Lastly, there is the *essential* dialogue, that of the dramatic "scene." This calls for no further development. It is what every great artist makes of it: suggestive, terse, impassioned; whether it emerges in sudden, splendid isolation (as in Dostoievsky) or is linked up with the scheme of things (as in Tolstoy). For all great writers it is the supreme method of energizing narrative, gripping the reader; it enables them to conjure up scenes before his eyes, adding the third dimension.

The cinema has recently discovered this sort of dialogue, and owes much of its present vigour to it. In the most modern pictures the director switches over into dialogue after long passages of silent film, exactly as a novelist breaks into dialogue after long stretches of narrative.

The novelist has another weapon to his armoury; he can imbue a critical moment in his character's career with the prevailing atmosphere, the climate of the outside world. Conrad uses this device all but systematically, and Tolstoy owes to it one of the finest romantic scenes in literature, the wounding of Prince Andrew at Austerlitz. The Russian cinema used it ably in its great period; but it is dropping out of use as box-office receipts mount up.

The novel seems, however, to retain one notable advantage over the cinema: it can delve into the inner consciousness of a character. Nevertheless, the modern novelist seems less and less disposed to analyse his characters in their hours of crisis; and, moreover, such a dramatic psychology as Shakespeare's and, to a great extent, that of Dostoievsky, in which the secrets of the heart are conveyed by acts or veiled avowals, can be no less artistically effective, no less revealing, than complete analysis. And, finally, the element of mystery in every character left partly unexplained, if it be conveyed as, thanks to the marvellous expressiveness of the human face it can be, on the screen, may well serve to give a work of art that curious *timbre*, as of a lonely voice seeking an explanation of life's riddle, which endows certain memorable reveries (Tolstoy's magnificent short novels, for example) with their compelling majesty.

VI

These pages are a series of reflexions on a method of expression; they have no necessary connexion with the industry which aspires to set the whole world dreaming of a *milieu* whose atmosphere seems to a French mind approximately that of our Paris Boulevards at the close of the Second Empire. From the puerile beginnings of the silent film to its apogee, the cinema seemed to have made vast strides; what has it achieved since then? It has perfected lighting and technique, but it has made no outstanding discoveries in the field of art.

By "art" I mean here the expression of significant relations between human beings, or between minds and things. Some of the best silent films, Germanic and Scandinavian, realized these possibilities. The American cinema of 1940, followed by that of other countries, is concerned above all—naturally enough from a commercial point of view—with enhancing its entertainment value. It is a form not of literature but of journalism. And yet, as journalism, it is constrained to have recourse to an element from which art cannot be permanently banned: the element of the Myth. For a full decade the cinema has been dallying with the Myth.

Symptomatic of this game of hide-and-seek that has been going on is the relation between scenarios and film-stars, especially the female stars. A screen star is not by any manner of means an actress who goes in for film work. She is a person capable of a modicum of dramatic competence, whose face expresses, symbolizes, incarnates, a collective instinct. Marlene Dietrich is not an actress as Sarah Bernhardt was an actress; she is a myth, like Phryne. The Greeks gave their instincts vague biographies; thus do modern men who invent for theirs successive life-stories, as the myth-makers invented, one after the other, the labours of Hercules.

So true is this that the film artists themselves are vaguely conscious of the myths they incarnate, and insist on scenarios that bear them out. Thanks to close-ups the public knows them as it never knew its stage idols. And the artlife of the film-star takes a different course from that of the stage idol; a great actress is a woman who can incarnate a large number of different rôles; the star, a woman who can give rise to a large number of scenarios built to her measure.

The dumb-show performances of an earlier age grafted countless adventures on to certain characters of the Italian *commedia*. And cinema-goers know well that, however much a scenario-writer attempts to create original characters, the actor always imposes his own personality on them. In former days there was a "Pierrot" series: "Pierrot Takes to Stealing," "Pierrot on the Gallows," "Pierrot Drunk," and "Pierrot in Love." So now we have Greta Garbo the Queen, Greta the Courtesan; Marlene the Spy, Marlene the Harlot; Stroheim at Gibraltar, Stroheim at Belgrade, Stroheim at the Front; Gabin in the Foreign Legion, Gabin as a Pimp. And so forth. But the perfect example is Charlie Chaplin. I saw in Persia a film that has no existence, called *Charlie's Life*. Persian picture-shows are given in the open; on the walls surrounding the enclosure sat black cats watching. The Armenian exhibitors had made a *montage* of all the Charlie "shorts" and done the job with skill. The film ran to a considerable footage and the result was breath-taking. It was the myth pure and unadulterated; it had a huge success.

What the actor thus demonstrates holds good probably for the scenario as well. *The Ring of the Nibelungs* is a famous myth; René Clair's international success, *The Million*, a rejuvenation of the Cinderella fairy-tale; there is an element of myth in *Potemkin*, in *The Mother*, in *Caligari*, in *The Blue Angel*, in the great Swedish pictures, in all Chaplin's films. Amongst other modern myths, Justice (in its individual or collective forms) and Sex are far from having outlived their appeal.

The cinema is addressed to the masses; and, for good or evil, they love the myth. A fact that war brings home to us; the parlour strategist is a far less common figure in wartime than the myth-monger who assures us "on good authority" that the enemy chop children's hands off. The lies of journalism and sensational magazine articles batten on the myth.

The myth begins with Sexton Blake, but it ends with Christ. The masses are far from invariably preferring what is best for them; still, on occasion, they are drawn to it. How much did the crowds who listened to St. Bernard's preaching understand? But what they did understand, at the moment when that unaccustomed voice struck deep into the secret places of their hearts, was well worth understanding . . .

Also, we must never forget—the cinema is an industry.

Music and Myth in Their
Mutual Relation[1]

MAX KRAUSSOLD

MUSICAL-DRAMATIC LITERATURE constitutes a special kind on the stage and does not compete with the modern drama, which requires discerning and supplementary reflection. The portrayal of real life with its psychological and social problems, its milieu and other details, its "individual causality" (Othello, Macbeth), should be left to the drama. Likewise, the great mass of historical material, objectively presented in accordance with its period features and cultural characteristics, belongs to the drama. Operatic, or musical-dramatic work on the other hand requires a special kind of thought and subject matter. What it demands is not some "great" theme, say of heroic nature or the like, not simply "grandeur" of plot, loftiness of situations in general. Nor can the "great idea," of which so much is said in connection with the musical drama, be exhaustively treated in a gratifying, single theme, such as the redemption motif. The vital nerve center of the musical-dramatic work is *embodiment, representation of the unreal*, comprehensible portrayal of higher and especially inner experience. The work of the musical-dramatic poet is to embody this experience in a

[1] Abridged by the author from a longer essay on "The Realm of Musical-Dramatic Thought and its Originality."

form which makes its extraordinary and transcendent character directly and sensuously apparent. This proposition is a necessary supplement to the preceding one. Only with that addition do we find a firm foothold for the understanding and the creation of the peculiar world of opera and its proper subject matter.

An image created in this sense will not resist fusion with the world of melody. In every other kind of dramatic plot the addition of music is superfluous or even detrimental, because certain contradictions will emerge. But in opera a power of illusion should emanate from the stage, and should simultaneously inspire in the audience an imaginative capacity attainable only via another, mood-shaping art. Music is the mediator between the stage action and the imagination of the listener. Music transfigures the imperfect stage representation into an ideal, stirs the human soul to its utmost depth, inspires ecstatic devotion. Wagner magnificently defined the state produced in us by the deep influence of music as "the willing anticipation or the anticipatory will of the listener." The enraptured spectator comprehends not only with his eyes and his intellect but also with a higher unconscious sense. To maintain intuition at this exalted level requires more than an occasional accompaniment for separate parts of the play. The whole work must be pervaded by music, filled and transformed by tonal magic, elevated to a realm of feeling to which the dramatic presentation aspires, but which it cannot attain by its own unaided efforts. The impression is achieved by the unusual effect of singing instead of speaking the lines. But music remains—and this seems to me the most important point—a free art. Music need not "express" anything definite, anything conceptual; it is not merely the servant of poetic thought. True enough, in art forms that centuries of work have developed and perfected, it is closely wedded to the text, and "causes the inmost emotional tone to sound" (Pfitzner). Outwardly as well, music follows the stage action in detail even to the point of sound-painting. (After all, the composer, too, receives his creative inspiration from the poetic material.)

But the magic worked by music, the emotional receptivity it engenders, stem from its very own emotional sphere, from harmony and *melos*. They rest on the musical sense evaluating the composition, and are fundamentally independent of the plot, heretical though this statement may sound. An unmusical person cannot grasp the nature of music. To him it is only a "pleasant noise," an emotional sound-effect, a nerve stimulus. Friedrich Theodor Vischer, an excellent scholar and writer, was not a musical person. Once he claimed that the Nibelungen cycle was especially suitable for a great opera because it offered so much opportunity for music in connection with festive scenes, with pomp and pageantry. This remark on tonal functions bespeaks the mechanistic conception of music and its effects. But music is a great realm filled with creative miracles, a world by itself. Great thinkers and poets have applied the skill of their words to do justice to the mysterious origins and nature of music. (We are thinking of Schopenhauer, Nietzsche, Jakob Burckhardt, *et al.*) E.T.A. Hoffman calls music the mysterious language of a faraway realm of spirits. This statement contains a certain fanciful extravagance which characterizes the other extreme in the appraisal of music (superficial appraisal or underestimation). The romanticists were often much inclined to interpret music in too metaphysical a way, and to look upon the musical drama as the "consummation of their transcendental longing" (Ehrenhaus).

Music is another world, but a world of its own. It is not *the* world of faith, not "the supernatural world," not that of infinity or of eternal love as such. But it harbors the embodiment of such a world, that of higher and inner experience, and gives to the "symbol," in the noblest sense of the word, a directly affective super-reality, intensifies it to the point of credibility. In its commitment to a world of ideas and motifs which can attain artistic success only in conjunction with music, music-drama receives not only its logical justification, but also a mission. The opera as a whole is no longer an "impossible" work of art.

In this connection it is interesting to note how often the older librettos, poetically quite insignificant, which really owed their entire worth to the music, still contained a fortunate "musical-dramatic" idea and thereby yielded gratifying results. Let us choose for illustration a couple of the older masterworks very dear to our hearts. Among Mozart's immortal creations the "Magic Flute" and "Don Juan" provide the librettos that claim special attention in this connection.

The "Magic Flute" exhibits the simplest imaginable relationship with a musical-dramatic set of ideas. Certainly Schikaneder's libretto, unbalanced and badly patched together from two different drafts, is hopeless and irreparable as a literary product. Years ago the meritorious Munich critic Theodor Göring tried to restore the reputation of the author, and recently Hermann v. Waltershausen in his sagacious *Studien zur musikalischen Stillehre* made an honest attempt to do the same. But our artistic conscience will always resist any recognition of Schikaneder. Still, unintended by him, the subject matter and plot of the "Magic Flute," this hodgepodge of Oriental myths, Free Masonry, and remnants of ancient wisdom, contains an excellent musical-dramatic core that transcends the level of fairy opera popular in his day.

The successful translation of simple, sublime ideas of a supersensuous sort into images, embodiments, and characters endows the libretto with a higher qualification. This direct representational power extends even to the details. The central figures in the action are Tamino and Pamina. Neither one is a sharply delineated personality, nor are they common human types. Instead they are ideal figures, i.e., born out of and created for the idea. For clarification it might be added that Tamino is the embodied masculine spirit of the leader who consciously strives for a loftier existence beyond the limits of matter; Pamina is the feeling female who gains insight into his higher world only through her instincts of steadfast love and loyalty. But all of this remains secondary to the general impression.

A droll, impulsive and animalistic couple, Papageno and Papagena, supply the counterpart. Above the human beings is a kind of middle realm, that of the Queen of Night with her retinue and other followers, which in part miscarries and is poorly introduced ("oriented"). The three ladies and especially the three boys with their quite muddled relation to the plot must be charged to Schikaneder.

Then above this imperfect supernatural element are Sarastro and his priests, sages and keepers of the holy of holies and the ultimate mystery, an upper realm of the ethereal world oriented toward the light. The trials of the novices in the "Magic Flute" are of a sensory nature (ordeals by fire and water). Resplendently the temple gates open in the finale as they are at last admitted, a shining symbol of progress into enlightment, redemption, and salvation after a difficult life journey.

On every side beautiful, noble, but by no means profound basic ideas, comprehensible without any reflection. Symbols, ceremonies, and spiritual values do not need to play any great role, and the supernatural relationships do not merit any solemn exposition. Perception and perceptibility are everything. In this simple, natural, and yet often brilliant obviousness, whose intended suprareal sig-

nificance is retained to the point of loftiness by the music of a
Mozart, lies the vitality and tolerability of the text to the "Magic
Flute."

As we know, no less a person than Goethe was stimulated by
the subject matter and added a second part to the "Magic Flute,"
trying to give the whole a deeper meaning. But his fine and poetic
little play would scarcely have been so suitable for being set to
music as Schikaneder's awkward, but simple and clear patchwork.
Goethe created many new interrelations, introduced many reflections, but it is all expounded in the poetic treatment. The symbols
of the original piece need no longer be emotionally accepted, for
they have been given their exact and definite meaning. This second
part calls for histrionic declamation, and where such is specifically
required music is given a false position. Consider this passage:
"Pamina with her attendants. The small chest is brought. Because
of a portent she wishes to dedicate it to the sun, and the chest is
placed on the altar. Prayer, earthquake. The altar sinks and the
chest with it. Pamina's despair. The scene is so arranged that the
actress with the aid of the music can express a significant series of
emotions." This is amateurish melodrama and has nothing to do
with musical-dramatic essence. The mysterious night of the earlier,
sentimental plot has given way to poetic daylight. Contrived and
ambiguous connections excite intellectual attention, incite reflection and philosophical contemplation.

At this point a singular counterpart to the "Magic Flute" of more
recent date may also be mentioned: "The Woman Without a
Shadow" by Hugo v. Hofmannsthal (Richard Strauss). The composer himself described it as a kind of "Magic Flute" in a modern
version; whether the poet had any such intent in view may be left
undetermined. A comparison of the musical compositions is, of
course, out of the question, for here we are only interested in the
text as a peculiar literary genre. The vague, oriental-fantastic fairy
world in itself with its abundance of mythical beings and indistinct minor characters offers a certain resemblance to the "Magic
Flute." But above all the central idea and its treatment are the same
—a mystical ordeal of two married couples struggling toward a
divinely blessed, harmonious existence and heavenly glory. But
while the poetic formulation in the "Magic Flute" is awkward and
often overly naive, the "Woman Without a Shadow" appears capricious, artful, overrefined. As often happens, we here encounter an

example of how a literary work of no intrinsic worth may be lifted into the sphere of musical-dramatic emotions, while a more pretentious and actually superior work of poetic art is unable to attain its purpose. The "Magic Flute" is symbolic, the "Woman Without a Shadow" symbolistic, as we understand it. That is to say, [in the latter] the interrelations between the sensuous and the nonsensuous are comprehensible only by means of contemplation, not by direct observation. For example, the prolonged comparison between the woman without a shadow and the woman without children is symbolistic. So is the obtrusive enigma of the Unborn, who prove to have the last word in the piece. The "Woman Without a Shadow" serves up a fancy fare instead of simple human truth. In fact, it reveals a modern tendenciousness in its keyed-up eroticism, while professing to be a fairy play.

The musical-dramatic suitability of "Don Giovanni" is not so easily sensed as that of the "Magic Flute." Here, too, the libretto by da Ponte (from another version by Bertati) despite its beautiful Italian, is a feeble accomplishment crammed with wretched details and all kinds of nonessentials. The subject matter is old and has often been given dramatic treatment both before and since "Don Giovanni," as in "El Burlador de Sevilla," formerly attributed by error to Tirso da Molina. And yet, from this insignificant version by da Ponte a basic musical-dramatic core emerges, pure and unclouded, which makes the libretto appear as an especially lucky stroke. At first the plot gives the impression of being a moralizing little story for simple souls, in which homebred virtue prevails and heaven itself condescends most instructively to make an example of the villain. But again, as in the case of the "Magic Flute," closer inspection shows us, with sensuous immediacy, a splendid contrast —as required by the musical-dramatic universe of ideas—between the real and the unreal (here mundane and celestial), the struggle of two worlds, most intimately portrayed. Don Juan is the embodiment of one of these worlds. He is no "type," for only later did he become the prototype for a certain breed and its characteristics. Nor is he a psychologically well defined character, and least of all only a "dissoluto punito" or a "young, very frivolous cavalier." Rather he is the personification of the irrepressible, earth-engendered vital force, the sensual drive in fairest form, cruel as Nature, his mother and mistress, and therefore really superhuman in conception. Such a being knows no surfeit, no longing for something else, no fear, no inhibitions—and no repentance. (All these would be psychological reactions, permissible only in the description of some sybarite.) The very lack of any repentance whatever, even in the face of death, which is considered necessary in most plays, is an especially gratifying feature in the libretto of "Don Giovanni."

The feeble efforts of Octavio, Donna Anna, and Elvira are doomed to fail when encountering Don Juan, for only supernatural powers are able to put a stop to his activities. Providence itself strikes him down, disguised as a victim of Don Juan's crimes who for a few hours is given life and ghostly power. (The theme of the avenging statue is very old.[2] Sweetly diluted and distorted to the point of inanity, it turns up in Hérold's opera "Zampa," proving that a great theme should not be dragged through all kinds of formulations and murdered time and again.)

The end of Don Giovanni—as the most various critics have remarked—should always be the destruction of the hero, never the musically charming but superfluous and dwindling finale. Don Juan's struggle with the Commandant is more sublime, even if we disregard the splendid music, than in Grabbe's powerful drama "Don Juan and Faust." There the marble statue merely pronounces the sentence, and Satan as executor and executioner of the divine justice first strangles Faust, then carries off Don Juan to hell, in order to weld together the souls of the two miscreants. In Grabbe's work the brooding, reflective element comes strongly to the fore. Don Juan has become the conscious sensualist who meditates on his own insatiability. But at the same time he displays brilliant versatility in his wishes and longings, as indicated by his motto and last words on earth: "King and fame, my country and love!" Faust on the other hand represents the arrogance of the spirit. The vast work by Grabbe is a drama of the intellect and not quite producible on the stage. But as a musical drama, too, it would be wholly unsuitable, because the flow of ideas is too abstract and complicated. Furthermore, the grandiose language absorbs too much of the mood of the whole and would not permit the added unfolding of another liberal art.

As the Don Juan material excited the poetic imagination before Mozart, so it has done again in the nineteenth century [3], and has been

[2] Cf. Hans Heckel: *Das Don Juan-Problem in der neueren Dichtung.* Stuttgart, 1915.

[3] Hans Heckel, *op. cit.*

changed and recreated in every possible way. Especially since
the character of Don Juan was established once and for all as
Mozart had created it, the problem was destined to tempt the
dramatists to strive for a denouement within a natural framework.
Instead of the simple miracle form, which, without the music,
was bound to appear as a clumsy supernatural intervention, they
found a consequential development, such as perhaps a self-in-
duced ruination, lying near at hand. In this process the hero, instead of being the embodiment of an idea, became a typical libertine
or a psychologically analyzed individual who shapes his own fate.
This injection into the play of cause and effect I consider a dramatic treatment of the basic idea, just because the development
of the events is based and rooted in the characters. When, for example, a Spanish poet lets Don Juan Tenorio enter a monastery in
the end, this rests on the observation that worldlings and unbelievers
gladly seek refuge in the arms of the church after a stormy life.

From the numerous treatments of the Don Juan material, which
we have no reason to catalogue here, we shall choose and briefly
consider only two examples. They allow us to draw the clear distinction between the musical-dramatic and the (purely) dramatic
on the basis of the explanations given so far. Nicolaus Lenau's
"Don Juan" is by no means a finished play ("a dramatic poem"),
but only a loose, fragmentary series of scenes in dialogue. But the
story of the hero is completely carried out in the dramatic sense.
At first Lenau's Don Juan is animated by a glowing desire for love:

> The magic circle, undefined and spacious,
> Of divers women beautiful and gracious,
> I fain would plunder in a storm of bliss,
> And breathe my life out in the last one's kiss.

(In Lenau's work, too, the interminable meditation on his own
nature engaged in by Don Juan appears labored and is often annoy-
ing.) But every intoxication is followed by a sobering-up, every
limitless debauchery by exhaustion. Don Juan's fiery mood is soon
submerged in jadedness and boredom:

> I am indeed by my own strength betrayed,
> The fire of my blood has been allayed,
> My manhood as with mildew overlaid.

Quite typical and correctly interpreted by the poet is the longing
that breaks forth time and again, a desire to be able to savor life

once more, but differently from the first time, the wish to be young and pure again. It is also a fine inspiration of Lenau's that his death-coveting hero, turning from life in disgust, does not wish to die by his own hand:

> An alien deathblow must my body strike,
> Illness or violence, anything you like. . .
> To punch my own nose is no sport for me,
> Nor would I ape the ways of destiny,
> With my own hand the fatal blow accord;
> But let me die by an opponent's sword!

Then the play is brought to an odd conclusion. The avenging agent of a higher world appears, but it is not the Commandant himself, whom Don Juan has invited, as he did in the opera. Instead, the son of the murdered victim, Don Pedro, enters Don Juan's house as a presumptuous avenger. He is accompanied by a crowd of women, at one time or another seduced by Don Juan, and their children, in order to pronounce sentence on the villainous ruler in the realm of love. Faced with this absurd and almost ludicrous scene, Don Juan is seized by a bizarre mood. Derisive and sarcastic, he conquers the vain young fop with flashing blade before all the witnesses from his past. But then, determined to seize the opportunity and end in beauty, he suddenly drops his sword and receives the fatal blow.

> A mortal foe's my captive in this strife,
> But this is boring, too, as is the whole of life.
>
> (He throws away the sword;
Don Pedro runs him through.)

This clever evasion of suicide is one of the high points in Lenau's ever spirited and linguistically elegant work.

On the other hand, suicide as last resort brutally asserts its rights in Otto Anthes' play "Don Juan's Last Adventure." Originally intended as a spoken play, it was later set to music by Paul Graener. Here the driving force for Don Juan is his first genuine love, a young girl full of the finest joy of life and nobility of mind. The tricks of the still irresistible charmer, who considers himself no longer worthy of such great happiness, are perhaps not to be taken too seriously, and indeed they miscarry. The appearance of her fiancé breaks the spell. She wants to go away with him, and it is far from Don Juan's thoughts to detain her in the whirl of pleasures.

He recognizes the worthlessness of a wasted life and after the parting from her kills himself. Despite the wound he remains standing as long as he is still able to catch a glimpse of her. This is really an interpretation of the Don Juan character which descends to an undifferentiated sentimentality and has nothing in common anymore with the immortal prototype. The music appears dispensable, almost superfluous, since the listener needs no mood of surrender that elevates him above reality.

And thus in view of all this, despite predecessors and successors, despite many failings of its own, the old Don Juan text remains the only possible musical-dramatic form for the idea and its content. Precisely the miraculous element and the imposed supernatural solution of Mozart's work are made comprehensible to the spectator not only (according to Wagner) "as being in conformity with the nature of things," but also as a higher experience in direct imagistic form.

THIS INSIGHT into the nature and the possibilities of a musical-dramatic world of ideas has given us the right point of view for clarifying one of the most important questions pertaining to the modern opera, the *relation between music and myth.*

Do mysterious threads really run from one to the other? Does some contact exist, perhaps from the earliest beginning, between the mythical world and music? Wagner called myth the vital principle, the root of all (musical-) dramatic art. (Friedrich Nietzsche expressed a similar opinion in his period of enthusiasm for Wagner.) Also leaning on Wagner, Hermann v. Waltershausen [4] has very recently taken up this idea and treated it independently. In the first part he says: "While the escape into unreality by itself constitutes the best condition for the unfolding of musical expression, it is myth that most completely reveals the quintessence of music, because the myth itself is idea and precisely through its rendition in melody becomes the ultimate and highest abstraction from the phenomenal world." I cannot declare myself in complete agreement with this statement, and still less with the following: "For music is the expression of the ideas of life and of their conflict-creating ramifications and contrasts."

But music, being affective, is completely alien to these same "conflict-creating ramifications" of life, and by the same token does

[4] *Studien zur musikalischen Stillehre,* Munich, 1920.

not lend itself to an amalgamation with the real drama and its problems. Myth is to me not an abstraction from the phenomenal world, but a primordial poetic formulation of the impressions which the mysterious ways of nature and world events inspire in the unsophisticated individual, in accordance with the known and familiar images of his own environment.

The connection between myth and music, or rather between myth and musical drama is not an idealistic-mystical connection. It rests essentially on the facts we have expounded so far. There is a certain similarity between the myth-maker and the poet who works in the musical-dramatic spirit, due to the form in which they create. Both seek a revelation of inner experience as well as unrealistic experience in comprehensible form and in plastic portrayal. Wagner, in a very readable chapter [5], has given a notable explanation and analysis of the longing of the mythic mentality for the concrete and the tangible. Let us quote just a brief passage: "Every formative impulse of the people is directed in the myth toward the sensory expression of the most far-reaching connection of the most varied phenomena in most concentrated form. As this concept, formed at first only by the imagination, gains in clarity, it adapts itself entirely to human characteristics, despite the fact that its content is superhuman and supernatural . . ."

The musical-dramatic poet, instinctively or quite consciously, can invoke and exploit the world of mythical as well as rather more legendary forms for the realization of his idea. He seeks a happy, effective, emotionally appealing materialization of the supernatural, the super-real. For this purpose he can draw on already existing creations and characters of an older mythology as a continuous heritage of human nature and imagination, as pre-formed products whose meaning persists in the memory of later generations and remains self-evident. He can use them, even when his own intent and their basic sense no longer coincide. The wealth of mythical images handed down from ancient times is a fund of material for the operatic poet, and here an additional point of contact, rich in relationships, between myth and opera comes into view. But at that

[5] *Oper und Drama* II: "Das Schauspiel und das Wesen der dramatischen Dichtkunst." [This passage, in the standard translation by Wm. Ashton Ellis, may be found in *Richard Wagner's Prose Works* (London, 1893), Vol. II, p. 154; but Ellis' rendering is so far from readable that the present translator offers his own instead.—Ed.]

point, myth is no longer the dominant element nor, as it were, an intrinsic part of the poetic challenge, but only a sphere of creativity. The musical-dramatic poet may also attempt to conjure up a new, but similar world on the basis of earlier myths and concepts, as James Grun undertook in his *Rose vom Liebesgarten* (Rose from the Garden of Love). He may do all this, but he is not "mythically confined," and free, artistic invention is open to him. Perhaps Wagner inwardly felt this when he wrote his famous passage: "If we now wish to describe exactly the work of the poet according to his highest imaginable ability, we must call it the myth that has been justified from the angle of clearest human consciousness, corresponds to the viewpoint of ever-present life, and has found in the drama its most comprehensible portrayal." [6]

From this we can gather something very much like what we have tried to set forth. Only it seems to me that the word "myth" in this generous interpretation of poetic intuition is not quite in order. For "myth" means, after all, primarily "word," then "tradition," hence in the sense of that which has been thought and formed in the distant past. To the Greeks the concept was really nothing more than tribal narrative, in which historical facts and legends were *ab initio* commingled. Consequently, just as we have rejected the word "(abstract) symbol" for purposes of our problem, we should also try to avoid the use of "myth" in too broad a sense. The myth, ever newly invented, simply is for the opera the direct sensory portrayal of the unrealistic, transcending and relinquishing both the representation of types and of psychological differentiation.

Waltershausen, too, was unable to free himself from the idea of a mysterious injection of the "mythical" into music (a kind of *unio mystica*). In his introduction to the "Magic Flute," which despite its brevity contains much that is pertinent and significant, he says: "All operas which are not based on the dualistic, Faustian, social, or erotic myth are sterile. Don Juan is Meleager, the conflict of the superman with the social order; 'Figaro' is an opera of revolution; the social struggle and the picaresque tale, respectively. The 'Abduction from the Serail' is Oberon or King Rother, the old myth of the kidnapped bride. The 'Magic Flute,' finally, is dualism itself in its purest form." These intrinsically profound observations rest on too far-fetched comparisons. In "Don Juan" the

[6] Cf. *op. cit.,* II, p. 220.

musical-dramatic nucleus is certainly not the pale reflection of a
Meleager myth, which should not come to the mind of even an
erudite listener, but the marvelously obvious clash between the
force of nature in its highest power and a higher world, embodied
in Don Juan and the Commandant. The musical-dramatic mood of
the "Magic Flute" is not derived simply from the magic formula
"mythical-dualistic," but as we have seen above, lies in the happy,
natural translation of nonsensuous ideas into simple, effective
images. The "Marriage of Figaro" is the most magnificent comic
opera, made immortal by Mozart's divine music. But not a trace
of myth is contained in Beaumarchais' flirtatious and frivolous
rococo story, no matter how you turn it. The "Abduction" is no
bride-snatching myth, but one of those harem stories that were
so popular in the eighteenth century and later, with the magnani-
mous Unbeliever as the central character. Bride abduction is, it
seems to me, no myth at all, but only an incident frequently recurring in ancient legends. As Wagner has well said, an immeasur-
able wealth of revered occurrences and actions crowd the myth;
there we witness natural phenomena, such as night and day, or
the rising and setting of the sun, condensed by the imagination into
acting personalities. For instance, slaying the dragon (the light
destroys the dragon of darkness) and the awakening of the virgin
(the sun awakens the sleeping earth) belong to the store of such
profound cult conceptions. But the case of the kidnapped bride
is simply a matter of obvious fact, which springs from an ever-
recurring set of circumstances in the life of virile and bellicose
societies. Moreover, if such an incident, which also occurs in myth,
is transferred to any given setting, perhaps even a modern and
civilized one, it can no longer be looked upon as "mythical." Naturally, a text composed with this assumption in mind is not therefore worse than another, but the musical-dramatic element must,
after all, have some firmer foundation.

If we were to subject ourselves to the labor of gleaning a "mythical" significance from all the opera librettos, in order to test their
musical utility, this would be a thoroughly abortive undertaking.
The word "myth" has been so generalized that it has become on
the whole a quite vague and tenuous concept, by means of which
all kinds of platitudes and aphorisms can be covered. In the end
we could perhaps even ferret out a "mythical" shadow of an idea
in "Cosi Fan Tutte," about which Waltershausen neatly stated that

it was incapable of survival because it lacks the myth. (The eroticism in this piece is devoid of any ethical basis.) For instance, the the eternal infidelity of woman, prompted by whim, curiosity, desire for a new experience, and hankering for a change—this is an old story, no less familiar to all peoples than the high song of Penelope's faithfulness or that of the Germanic Gudrun. "Cosi Fan Tutte" as well as "Figaro" are merely comic operas. If "Figaro", in which we cannot find a mythical trace either, is much more durable than "Cosi Fan Tutte," this can be credited to both the much livelier music and the superior, more clever libretto without any ethical side references.

Waltershausen also recognizes as possibly productive for the writing of an opera an independent "national myth," in addition to those mentioned, such as appears, for instance, in Barbarossa, "the idea of the calumniated German mind." But the chosen illustration actually confirms our conception, for the Barbarossa of the Kyffhäuser mountain and Emperor Friedrich of Untersberg have, after all, already become symbolic figures. They have little in common with the historical personalities, no matter whether the reference is to Frederick Barbarossa I or to Frederick II. Such a national myth could, to be sure, acquire musical-dramatic force at the hands of a poet, because it will always harbor a dominant embodiment, independent of strict historical reality.

Modern Architecture:

Toward a Redefinition of Style

VINCENT J. SCULLY, JR.

IN AN ESSAY of this length it will be less valuable, I think, to begin by attacking the admittedly ambiguous concept of style than to accept the word in broadest terms as meaning a body of work exhibiting family resemblances. In dealing with the modern world it is especially necessary to do this, since we need an eye for resemblances to guide us as we seek an elusive image which is essentially of ourselves. All of us who engage in this search owe a debt to work which has gone before, especially to Hitchcock's pioneering researches: embodied in his *Modern Architecture* of 1928 and in his and Johnson's *International Style* of 1932. Yet by far the most influential book which has dealt with this problem has been Giedion's *Space, Time, and Architecture*, published in 1941 and now in its third enlarged edition. Giedion's view of nineteenth- and twentieth-century architectural development has been especially influential among architects, who—through an iconoclasm they have imbibed from some of their pedagogical masters—have otherwise tended to be suspicious of historical investigation in any form. Their approval of *Space, Time, and Architecture* would seem to have arisen from the fact that it gave them what they wanted: a strong technological determinism, a sense of their lonely, rational

342

heroism in the face of an unintegrated world. But it gave them more: myths and martyrs, and a new past all their own. It presented them with an historical mirror, so adjusted as to reflect only their own images in its glass. What they did not want was to be told that they were working in a style. That is, they wished to be recognized but not identified, and for this there were many reasons, some superficial and some profound. *Space, Time, and Architecture* brilliantly avoided the difficulty of identification by producing instead a formula, that is, "Space-Time." This cabalistic conjunction (or collision) had both the qualities necessary for an acceptable architectural slogan: at once a spurious relation to science and a certain incomprehensibility except in terms of faith. Like all the best slogans it could mean anything because, even as one shouted it, one might entertain the comfortable suspicion that it need not, in fact, mean anything at all. It is, on the other hand, a phrase which one can all too easily avoid using when seeking definition. For example, the events of the years around 1910, which do in fact culminate a long development, may be described in simpler and more generally applicable words, such as fragmentation and continuity: fragmentation of objects into their components and the redirection of these elements into a continuous movement in space.

Yet *Space, Time, and Architecture* has had considerable effect upon us all, and conclusions as influential as those presented by it cannot be challenged without alternative conclusions being offered at some length. Therefore I feel compelled to attempt what perhaps should not be attempted at this restricted historical distance: that is, not only to isolate if possible the primary characteristics of the architecture of our era but also to name it. I should like to call it what Wright calls his own work but with, I hope, a more historically based and objective use of the term: The Architecture of Democracy. Out of modern mass democracy's program this architecture has grown, and the character of that democracy it demonstrates. I see it as having developed in two great phases, with a third phase just beginning. The first may be called the phase of fragmentation, the second the phase of continuity, and the third the opening phase of a new humanism. (And this last word also I would hope to define in precise architectural terms.) The development between phases is chronological but overlapping, and none of the phases, not even the first, has wholly ended. Under them all, and usually in tension with them, has run a counter instinct toward what I think we must call "classic" or, more correctly, "classicizing" values, and this instinct is probably stronger at present than it was a generation ago.

Giedion's early researches into the Romantic Classicism of the later eighteenth century had convinced him that the effects of this period were largely negative so far as the development of contemporary architecture was concerned. Thus he tended to look back beyond it to his own view of the baroque for historical precedent, and to see later creative architecture as developing despite the events of those revolutionary years. Yet if we seek an image of ourselves it is precisely at the beginning of the age of industrialism and mass democracy that we first find it, in terms of fragmentation, mass scale, and a new, unfocussed continuity. In Piranesi's prophetic *Carceri* etchings of 1745, the baroque harmonies of subordination, scale, climax, and release are fragmented and exploded into a vast new world of violence. The orbits of movement come into collision, and the objectives of the new journey are as yet unknown. Man is small in a challenging but crushing ambient which seems to work according to its own laws and from which the elements, such as columns, to which the individual had been accustomed to orient himself, have been removed. Through this new world the engineers, released by nineteenth-century positivism and materialism from the burden of humanist tradition, have moved freely. The Galerie des Machines of 1889 creates the new scaleless ambient in steel, to serve a typical program of mass industrialism: the housing of vast batteries of machines, symbolized by Henry Adams' Dynamo. In Max Berg's reinforced concrete Centennial Hall of 1913 at Breslau, the world of Piranesi is housing mass man, almost as Piranesi himself had imagined it. Vast scale, the smallness of the individual, and violent continuity are its themes. In the Livestock Judging Pavilion at Raleigh, in an advanced structure of continuous parabolic arches from which a canopy in tension is slung, men and animals are small together in a disoriented universe of flight and movement—one which creaks and groans as the structure moves like the rigging of the *Pequod*, wind-driven on a quest one cannot name. Here that vision which Focillon recognized in Piranesi is realized: of ". . . une architecture à la fois impossible et réelle."

Returning to the later eighteenth century, we find a further fragmentation of the baroque synthesis of freedom and order in terms of two movements: one an impatient revolutionary search for harsh, pure, geometric order alone and the other for an apparently total freedom from geometry. Each of these movements continues in a sense to the present day. The first, which may loosely be called Romantic-Classicism, can be seen alike in the projects of Ledoux and in the earlier work of Le Corbusier. This relationship is ignored by Giedion but was pointed out by the late Emil Kaufmann in his book of 1933, *Von Ledoux bis Le Corbusier*. The other movement, exactly contemporary, may loosely be called Romantic-Naturalism, and its asymmetry and nostalgic naturalism in siting and materials are demonstrated alike by Marie Antoinette's *Hameau* of 1783 and by much present suburban architecture, especially on the West Coast of the United States. Critics such as Bruno Zevi have held the later phases of this movement to be of overriding interest and importance.

Yet to accept "classicism," so-called, and "romanticism," so-called, as polarities which are typologically irreconcilable, as the nineteenth century tended to do, is to accept as a natural state that fragmentation of human experience of the whole which the nineteenth century for a time created. To believe that variety and change (the "picturesque" of the nineteenth century) should be necessarily antithetical to order and clarity, is not only to see the past in fragments, as a part of nineteenth century thought did, but probably also to encourage that desire for restricted identifications—such as national ones—which has been a counter irritant in, though hardly a solution for, modern mass society.

When the dubious polarities are brought into resolution toward the close of the nineteenth century they are resolved in terms of an even more insistent nineteenth-century belief: that in the dynamism of morphological continuity. Scientifically oriented, such confidence embodies—as Egbert has pointed out—a kind of Darwinian optimism in the emergence of species and types through the process of development itself. In America, characteristically the most typical offspring of the new age, Sullivan—himself enthusiastic about "morphology"—produces out of the materials of mass industry the types for the new, mass metropolis: vertical continuity for the freestanding tower, ideally to be set in a square or a park; horizontal continuity for a space-bounding building, to define a street or a square. Thus in the Guaranty Building, in a plastically plated system, the vertical supports are stressed and

visually doubled; in the Carson-Pirie-Scott store they are withdrawn behind the surface (except at the corner) and especially
masked by ornament on the lower floors so as not to interrupt
the horizontal continuity of the window bands and of the volume
of the building above. Sullivan's ornament carries continuity out
into more fluid forms, and in Europe during the same period—in
Art Nouveau and its related movements—such fluidity is intensified.
In Horta and Gaudi the images evoked are those of the forces that
move through nature, as seen especially in water, plant life, and
lava flow. One feels oneself in a Bergsonian world of flux and becoming, in an endless continuity which recalls, at the end of the
scientifically confident nineteenth century, the intuitions of the
first scientists of all in western civilization: of those Ionian philosophers who themselves embraced the concept of continuity and
who, in Thales, saw water as its essential element. Once more,
with Heracleitos, we "cannot step twice into the same river, because fresh waters are continually flowing in upon . . ." us.

During the early twentieth century, however, we encounter in
Europe a reaction against these images of continuity on grounds
both technological and classicizing. In Perret, in 1905, the union
of a kind of Cartesian rigor of thought with a technological determinism like that of Viollet-le-Duc produces in reinforced concrete
a closed and visually discontinuous rectangular skeleton which
is in the tradition of French classicizing design. Similarly, in the
work of Behrens and Gropius in Germany, the determining factors
are a rigid technological *sachlichkeit* and an aesthetic preference—
justified by Gropius on moral grounds—for the clear, sharp-edged
forms of German neo-classic design. In a sense Romantic-Classicism
and a new Romanticism of the Machine coalesce here. Both represent—despite Gropius' glazed corners—a reaction against continuity in favor of a machined permanence of classicizing.

In America, however, the compulsion toward continuity was
strong. In a development out of the nineteenth century resort houses
by the sea or in the suburb, Wright develops, by 1902, his cross-
axial plan and his interwoven building fabric of continuous roof
planes and defining screens. He attacks the concept of the skeleton
frame, and says, "Have no posts, no columns," again, ". . . In my
work the idea of plasticity may now be seen as the element of continuity," and again, "Classic architecture was all fixation . . . now
. . . let walls, ceilings, floors become seen as component parts of

each other, their surfaces flowing into each others." He goes on, "Here . . . principle . . . entered into buildings as the new aesthetic, continuity," and he acclaims ". . . the new reality that is *space* instead of matter." He calls this new reality of continuous space "The Architecture of Democracy," and hails Whitman as its prophet. The analogy here is in fact profound. D. H. Lawrence, for example, has made us aware of the deep compulsion toward movement—toward "getting away"—which has played so large a part in American symbolism. In Cooper, Dana, Melville, and Mark Twain the symbols evoked are those of the seas or the river. In Whitman they focus upon the "Open Road," along which—in terms of a democratic mass compulsion which would have been understood by De Tocqueville—*everyone* must travel and for which there is no goal but forward. The cities of men are to be left behind, as Jefferson would have had them left, and the infinitely extending axes of movement cross like country roads in a boundless prairie. In the low ceilings—". . . I broadened the mass out . . . to bring it down into spaciousness," wrote Wright—there is compulsion forward and flow like Mark Twain's river carrying us along. The compulsion is to get away: away from the traditions of western civilization, farther west to Japan and the Orient, if possible, as Tselos and others have pointed out.

There is no need to dwell here upon Wright's direct influence through the Wasmuth publications in 1910 and 1911, upon Gropius and other Europeans in the 'teens, since this has already been indicated elsewhere. But one should point out that in a Mondrian of 1915, touched by this spirit, there rises a deep bloom like the sea which then resolves itself into crossing currents like those of the Wright plan. This profound impulse toward continuity is then "classically" stabilized by Mondrian in clear rectangles sliding and moving around an armature of interwoven lines: which it is just possible may owe something to drawings and stripping details by Wright, reproduced by Wasmuth. These lines Mondrian himself writes of as being "continuous" beyond the painting frame. Mondrian's synthesis then forms the basis for a compromise in design in the work of Gropius and the Bauhaus. The continuous armature— which would be the building frame—is discarded, but the planes are used as thin sheets which enclose or define spatial volumes. Continuity in the form of a sliding relationship between elements is brought into a kind of union with the fragmentation of building mass and with picturesque composition, and the separate functions are enclosed in those same sharply defined boxes which are at once machined and neo-classic. This amalgamation or synthesis becomes the "International Style" as isolated for us by Hitchcock and Johnson and as influential upon the work of many architects ever since.

However, it was another pupil and collaborator of Behrens—and the most romantic-classic of all the German architects of the twenties—who still most fully developed in Europe the examples toward continuity which had been offered by Wright and De Stijl. In Mies van der Rohe's project of 1925 a cubical massing is stretched in plan by the continuous directional lines of Mondrian. The discipline is that of crossed spatial axes which recall Wright's cross axis plans of many years before. Now, however, the movement is less compulsive and even more flowing, loosened and syncopated like a dance pattern and certainly owing much to the researches into continuity and its interruptions which had been carried on by such De Stijl artists as Van Doesburg.

By 1929 Mies has found a way to bring opposites into harmony. His Barcelona Pavilion is a masterpiece of the "International Style" precisely because it brings together as a harmony—and in a clearly separated structural and screening system—the American compulsion toward that Open Road which allows of no conclusion and the deeply seated European instinct for defined permanence and enclosure. Present, too, in the gleamingly polished surfaces, is the European Romanticism of the Machine. In a way the Barcelona Pavilion represents a new system of freedom and order but within a rather restricted emotional range, and, unlike the baroque synthesis, without a single focus or a fixed conclusion. Nor is it a plastic and pictorial system like that of the baroque, but a skeletal, planar, and "constructivist" one.

For a period during the thirties this international synthesis of the nomadic and the permanent was apparently sympathetic to Wright, at least in compositional if not structural (or polemical) terms. A comparison between the Barcelona Pavilion and a Wright house of ten years later should make this fact clear; and the adjustments expressed here have also continued to direct the work of many architects.

But Wright, unlike Mies but like Picasso, is mighty; and he thinks like him in terms of compelling force. The monumental stability which both Wright and Picasso achieve in the later thirties out of the most violent oppositions and movements make both *Falling Water* and the *Guernica* "classics," as it were, of the continuous phase in modern form.

Yet Wright is driven by his compulsion toward movement. Only the complete continuities of the circle can answer his need, and his poetic imagery remains close to the great nineteenth-century symbols of the road, the sea, and the river. The human observer is pulled inexorably into a current. This sweeps him under water into a cave which opens up into a pool. He is compelled to undergo the rite, as of immersion and purification. The building solids, whether structural or screening, are treated even more than before as purely space defining elements: they enclose it like a shell or they grow in it. Truly space, not matter, is the "reality" here. This fact raises certain questions concerning the position of man. As he is compelled into the ultimate continuities where all is done for him, against what does he judge himself? Where does he define his stand? How, on the one hand, can he be released from compulsion in order to know himself; how, on the other, can he be challenged not in terms of changing ambients but in unmistakably human terms?

Wright's answer is that of a westering pioneer, that one need not ask the question but go on. He will not provide humanity with references to itself in building mass. When, in the 'teens and twenties he had sought a monumental weight to answer human needs for ceremony more deeply than his suburban tradition had been able to, it was to the compact, hill- or mound-evoking masses of Mayan architecture that he had turned (as in the Barnsdall House of 1920). Again: it is outside of classic humanism. Similarly, at Taliesin West, it is the Mexican dance platform which has been compacted here; above is spread its opposite in the tent of the nomad. All the forms have reference to those of nature, not of man, and the building fabric as a whole, however massive or interwoven, is still expressed not as a sculptural body but as a flexible and opening sheath which defines a channel of continuous space. Along this dry river the viewer is compelled—through a building which is pure ambient—to carry out that journey which culminates the myth. He must move forward, beyond the places of men, until he comes at last to the pure emptiness of the desert and the beckoning hills beyond.

Since 1937, however, when Mies van der Rohe came to the United States, a movement has been growing in this country itself to reject such compulsive continuity and its concomitant asymmetry and to create instead a more fixed and symmetrical kind of design. Mies' early classicism thus serves him well at the Illinois Institute of Technology, where he lets what continuity there is expand naturally from a symmetrically conceived central space. In this way his cubical buildings are in modular harmony with the rectangular spaces created by them, and he is released from the compulsion—as the Harvard Graduate Center is not—of forcing closed blocks to define a continuous and fluid space which is out of harmony with them and which properly belongs to another mode of buildings.

Mies thus rejects the old International Style compromise and insists, with a new compulsion, upon the skeleton cage of the steel frame. This is the classicizing "fixation" against which Wright had inveighed. It is also the lines rather than (or as well as) the planes of Mondrian. It involves a classicizing sense of types, where the vertical and horizontal solutions of Sullivan are further clarified and frozen. Mies' recent design, in its modularity and urbanity, has often been compared with that of the Renaissance. Certainly, in contrast to Wright's Broadacre City and its images of the Open Road, Mies now offers the images of the Renaissance townscape and the permanent order of the urban piazza. But Mies' forms in steel frame are thinner, less sculptural, than those of Renaissance buildings, and they have also the sharply willed linearity which seems typical in all ages of classicizing or neo-classic work.

In the buildings of those distinguished architects like Philip Johnson and Eero Saarinen who have acknowledged their debt to Mies, such classicizing or, in their case, more markedly Romantic-Classic quality is intensified. For example, the release from a compulsion to make space flow asymmetrically and the acceptance of fixed discipline and order often give rise in their work to a rather Palladian *partie* of closed corners and central openings. It also produces the separate forms of vaults and domes once more,—where men are no longer directed along flowing routes but are left alone in a clear and single volume—and the buildings themselves are seen as sharp and abstractly scaled entities which recall those of Boullée and Ledoux. At the same time, while architects humanely react against the narrow expediency of much contemporary building, still their buildings would not yet seem to be fully humanist ones. Saarinen's Auditorium at M.I.T. and Johnson's Synagogue at Portchester are certainly the result of a humanist search for clear, permanent, and man-centered forms, but—though bright in color and luminously conceived—they are still curiously lunar and remote. Eloquent but detached, the buildings of these architects sometimes seem to embody, perhaps most appropriately at the necessarily machine-like General Motors Technical Center, a certain quality of modern mass anonymity—at its best releasing, at its worst inadequately cognizant of the vital pressures and tensions which make human life. Their thinness and weightlessness also arise from another fact, however, which is that, in their design, space is still the "reality" over matter, and the solids are either simply a frame or a thinly stretched membrane which encloses a volume. Thus the buildings are not bodies but containers, and there is good reason to believe that Johnson and Saarinen are aware of the limitation. Certainly Saarinen's Chapel at M.I.T. would seem to be seeking more "physical" values.

This brings us to a central problem. It has been accepted by most critics of recent times that space is in fact the "reality" of a building. Indeed, our generation has talked of little else. Yet, whether or not we accept Kashnitz-Weinberg's conclusions in his book *Die Mittelmeerischen Grundlagen der Antiken Kunst,* we still find that there is imbedded in the mind of western man the memory of two opposing architectural traditions. One tradition, which becomes Italic, is indeed concerned with the dominance of interior space and with what Wright has termed the "great Peace" of such space, since it is associated with the protection and hope of rebirth offered by the female deities of the earth and—in the neolithic period, as in Malta—may indeed be a constructed hollow cave, in the shape of the goddess herself. One is reminded of Wright's obsessive business with the water glass. Le Corbusier, attempting like most modern men to reconstruct a usable past for himself, has studied such architecture in its Roman phase, as at Hadrian's Villa, where Hadrian himself would seem to have been evoking the images of this tradition (which brings to mind, for example, the modern cult of the house). Le Corbusier, like Hadrian, understood perfectly what this was all about. "Un trou de mystère," he writes, and we are shown his cave-sanctuary project for Mary Magdalen, commissioned by the possessed Trouin at Sainte-Baume. But there is in antiquity, according to Kaschnitz, and obviously, another tradition, having to do not with the female engulfment of interior space but with a sculptural, challenging evocation of the gods of the outside and of the sky. Thus the megaron cella is surrounded by the peripteral colonnade. This produces an architecture which is upright and which supports weight, and which has at once a purely sculptural scale and a curious analogy, felt empathetically, to the standing bodies of men. Le Corbusier writes in 1923 of the Parthenon columns: "nothing . . . left but these closely knit and violent elements, sounding clear and tragic like brazen trumpets." He speaks of the space as swinging clear from them to the horizon verge. And we should remember that Le Corbusier's comments were published in a book entitled *Towards a New Architecture* (*Vers une Architecture*).

The problem of the volume as interior and having essentially no exterior—unless one allows the space to be the whole "reality," as Wright would do—has concerned all architectural ages which have cared for the image of man. The Romans masked the volume with the column until a dwindling of classical tradition made it seem no longer so necessary to do so. The Gothic architect, on the other hand, organized his vaults so that the whole system became an integument like the column system itself, though on rather dematerialized and scholastic terms. The Renaissance engaged the columns in the wall or built up its window details as aggressive solids.

Le Corbusier grapples with this problem from the very beginning of his design. His Citrohan houses of 1922 are pure megaron volumes, with an open end and closed sides, though with an interior space which, one should point out, seeks the tumultuous and challenging qualities of cubism rather than the flow of Wright and De Stijl or the "great Peace" of feminine protection. On the exterior Le Corbusier finally supports his volume upon his columns, but both are thin and tight in the manner of the twenties, and the space is still the "reality," with the solids affecting us only as poles or membranes. By 1930, in his Swiss pavilion, Le Corbusier has gone a step further. Two opposites are joined. Some of the pilotis have the muscular mass of weight supporting elements, but the box of rooms above is still pure skin around a space.

By 1946, however, in the *Unité d'Habitation* at Marseilles—in a housing program which attempts to answer one of the typical challenges of mass democracy—Le Corbusier has arrived at a more integrated system. The mighty pilotis support a framework in which the megaron-like apartments are set. Each of these has its pronaos or porch integrated with a brise-soleil which makes it impossible for the eye to read the building as merely a skin around a volume. Similarly, use-scale elements, which also cause us to see a building as simply a hollow, are suppressed. On the other hand, the *Unité* cannot be read as a solid, like an early Mayan building, nor as a frame, like a Japanese one. Instead its solids appear to be in an almost one to one relationship with its voids. Since, therefore, the building in fact seems to have only that space which is integral to the articulated system of its mass it can no longer be seen as an ambient or a box or a hill but only as a sculptural body: a quality which has been noted by many critics. Since, however, we empathetically experience upright bodies in terms of our own, the building becomes a humanist one. I define architectural humanism here in the terms used by Geoffrey Scott in his book *The Architecture of Humanism*, of 1914. Of the humanist architecture of antiquity and the Renaissance, Scott wrote, "The centre of that architecture was the human body; its method to transcribe in stone the body's favorable states; and the moods of the spirit took visible shape along its borders, power and laughter, strength and terror and calm." Such humanism, as it has meaning in the present, does not yearn weakly toward an Edwardian sediment of worn-out details, as a small and rather mauve group of critics now does. Instead it seizes and challenges the present, makes especially the alternately cyclopean and airborne world of the engineers comprehensible in human terms, and seeks its fellowship in the deepest patterns of the human past.

Scott then went on as follows: "Ancient architecture excels in its perfect definition; Renaissance architecture in the width and courage of its choice." In these terms it would appear that the *Unité d'Habitation*—in the modern material of reinforced concrete—is more like Hellenic architecture even than it is like that of the Renaissance to which it bears certain resemblances. It would seem to have passed beyond choice toward a new definition of space and body and to have brought the modern age, finally, to the frontiers of a new humanism. As the impatient nineteenth century discovered the joys of spatial continuity, the beleaguered twentieth seeks a new image of man.

Now, as at Chandigarh, the human being returns to the landscape; he no longer dissolves into it as he may do in the lonely dream of Wright. Nor is he an intruder there who simply interrupts

the land—as a classicizing cube might do—instead, as in the Greek
temple, his architecture is one which, through its purely sculptural
scale and its implied perspectives, can at once leave the major landscape elements alone to be themselves and can at the same time
bring the whole visible landscape into human focus. It deals now
with a double reverence, both for the beloved earth and man.

But it does more than this. Like Classic Greek architecture itself
it stretches us with the challenge it presents in terms of our capacity
to grasp the whole of things afresh, and the images it evokes are
multiple. Like the Parthenon to the Virgin Athena—whose attributes are alike of mind and force, of female sympathy and male
power, and which was, of course, during the middle ages a church
to the Virgin, first as Sophia, then as Theotokos, "God-Bearing"—like
the Parthenon, Notre Dame du Haut at Ronchamp is active, but
instead of rising tensely upward toward its center, as the Parthenon
does, it splits out of the Euclidean envelope in a weight-shifting
lunge to the southeast corner. Its architect tells us that the form, as
a "vessel" on a "high place," is intended to respond to a "psycho-
physiologie de la sensation . . . ," which is Scott's "empathy," and
to ". . . une acoustique paysagiste, prenant les quatre horizons à
témoin . . ." Indeed the outside pulpit is like the clapper in the
great bell. But Ronchamp is other things as well. Its hooded chapels
(the hidden one behind the lectern, blood-red) are apsidal megara
which recall in plan and elevation not only Le Corbusier's drawings
of the Serapeion in Hadrian's Villa but also certain neolithic earth
sanctuaries in Sardinia which are related in shape to the Serapeion.
Rising and turning from its chapels, the main body of the church,
instead of bulging with its contained volume—which would cause
it to be seen simply as a shell—instead presses in both walls and
catenary slab upon its interior space until, within, one is conscious of
enclosure in a positive body, and, outside, the whole becomes one
pier which thrusts upward as a material force. Cave and column—
in the words of the Litany, ". . . Spiritual Vessel . . . Tower of
David . . . House of Gold . . . Tower of Ivory . . ."—become
one.

Thus we cannot look at Ronchamp without considering the
capacity of architecture to function as a sculptural "presence," as a
Greek temple does. Perhaps alone of modern buildings Le Corbusier's church deserves the Acropolis, and, in the mind of its

architect, indeed swings upward from it into splendid sound, itself a "brazen trumpet," an acoustic bell.

It is clear that architecture has come to a challenging moment. The "problem of monumentality," which is the problem of commitment both to the absolutes of completeness and to the present, now solves itself. Now the image of the river—along which we float like Huck and Jim, fugitives and spectators in a dreamlike time—is arrested by the image of the demanding presence on the high place: in the fixed temenos, rising from the caverns of the earth, but turning toward the open sky. It may not be fortuitous that we are also driven here away from Henry Adams' symbol of the Dynamo toward his counter symbols of the Virgin and St. Michael, where the Archangel, too, "loved the heights." We are informed, at any rate, that our fate in the present remains more wholly human than we had recently been led to believe and that the world as we can know it is made up not only of nature, nor of machines, nor the search for an illusory security, but of the blazing ardour of searching men. It may be that in the face of total challenge the values of humanist civilization, as yet not dead, call to us, and we take our stand.

Yet a further point, and an obvious one, should be made: Ronchamp is not the Parthenon which, though blazing, is cool and, though intellectually clear-eyed, retains a pure tribal reverence. Ronchamp is both more primitive and more detached, like modern humanity. Its hooded towers are at once primitive fetishes and anthropological demonstrations. It is aware of the primitive shout of triumph and the shriek of fear and, at the same time, of the fortress which is no fortress, the roof that breaks apart, the precarious balance of forces over the threatened door. Ronchamp is thus not the clear, poised union of physical and metaphysical experience which the Parthenon is. Instead Ronchamp rises up desperately in violent challenge like a burst of engines. Yet its essential choice is that of Camus who, like Le Corbusier, fixes finally upon Hellenic values as a means of bringing to a close that destruction of the present created by "L'Homme Revolté." The image for both these artists is of man born again to a sense of his tragic dignity, "a shaft which is inflexible and free."

In the end the historian himself can probably seek definition of style only in this way. Slogans, tags, and formulas of development are useful, but in the end they cannot define modern architecture or any art as it exists but only as it becomes. Thus at their worst, when dealing with the present, they may at once undervalue it, limit it, even destroy awareness of it, in their will for change. True definition, for any period, can only come when the nature and especially the objectives of the self—with its hope, its memory, and its consciousness of the present—are truly identified and humanly defined. Out of such definition arises that sense of identity which is style.

Index

The Library of Congress has cataloged this book as follows:

Langer, Susanne Katherina (Knauth) 1895–   *ed.*
  Reflections on art; a source book of writings by artists, critics, and philosophers. Baltimore, Johns Hopkins Press [1958]

  364 p. illus. 24 cm.

  1. Art—Philosophy. 2. Aesthetics—Addresses, essays, lectures.
3. Music—Philosophy and aesthetics.   I. Title.

N79.L2   701.17   58–59767 ‡

Library of Congress

ABIGAIL E. WEEKS MEMORIAL LIBRARY